The Continuing Evolution
of Family Law

The Continuing Evolution of Family Law

Nigel Lowe

Gillian Douglas
Cardiff Law School

Family Law

Published by Family Law
a publishing imprint of
Jordan Publishing Limited
21 St Thomas Street
Bristol BS1 6JS

Whilst the publishers and the author have taken every care in preparing the material included in this work, any statements made as to the legal or other implications of particular transactions are made in good faith purely for general guidance and cannot be regarded as a substitute for professional advice. Consequently, no liability can be accepted for loss or expense incurred as a result of relying in particular circumstances on statements made in this work.

© Jordan Publishing Limited 2009

All rights reserved. No part of this publication may be reproduced, stored in a retrieval system, or transmitted in any way or by any means, including photocopying or recording, without the written permission of the copyright holder, application for which should be addressed to the publisher.

Crown Copyright material is reproduced with kind permission of the Controller of Her Majesty's Stationery Office.

British Library Cataloguing-in-Publication Data

A catalogue record for this book is available from the British Library.

ISBN 978 1 84661 169 8

Typeset by Letterpart Ltd, Reigate, Surrey

Printed in Great Britain by CPI Antony Rowe, Chippenham and Eastbourne

FOREWORD

I was fortunate enough to attend the 'Looking Back – Looking Forward' conference organised and hosted at Cardiff University during the academic year 2007–2008 by Professors Gillian Douglas and Nigel Lowe. It was a wide-ranging and fascinating conference, with speakers from the highest echelons of research, academia and practice in the field of family law.

Following the success of the conference, the two Professors are to be congratulated for bringing together the speakers' papers in this comprehensive publication, *The Continuing Evolution of Family Law*. Taken together, the papers explore a range of historic and thematic perspectives in the development of family law, both to explain how we have reached our present child focused system and to provide an informed basis for consideration of the future of family justice.

Each of the chapters is free-standing and will be enjoyed as an authoritative and in-depth consideration of a particular strand in the fabric of family law. The Editors' introduction skilfully brings these strands together, pointing the reader to the major influences in the evolution of the socio-legal system in which family lawyers now practise.

I welcome this publication and join with the Editors in their hope that it will promote a general understanding and appreciation of their subject. It will surely fulfil their intention to provide a reference point in 50 years' time for those concerned to examine a further half century of the law's response to social change.

Sir Mark Potter

President of the Family Division
March 2009

PREFACE

The catalyst for this volume of essays was the 150th anniversary of the enactment of the Matrimonial Causes Act 1857 and the 50th anniversary of the publication of one of the first books avowedly about 'family law', *A Century of Family Law* edited by R M Graveson and R Crane and published in 1957. These two milestones in family law and family law scholarship provided an opportunity to bring together in two one-day conferences at Cardiff University, during the academic year 2007/08, leading scholars and members of the judiciary to take stock of the current position, to reflect on developments and to indulge in some speculation about how the law might develop in the future. We were fortunate indeed to attract to Cardiff many of the leading luminaries of the family law world in England and Wales, as our list of contributors to this work demonstrates. In the first of the conferences the speakers were asked to reflect upon past developments, while in the second the speakers were asked to 'look forward'.

Although each speaker was allocated a broad topic, it was a matter for their individual choice what particular aspect(s) would be discussed and over what period. In this latter regard, some of the reflective papers looked back over 150 years, but others concentrated upon the last half-century. Correspondingly, those looking forward sometimes concentrated on the more immediate future, while others attempted to look further ahead. In the result, the papers provide the collective thoughts of experienced academics and practitioners on a variety of issues from a variety of perspectives. In addition to those papers the opening chapter, written by the organisers, identifies and discusses some general overall themes touched upon by the invited speakers, and others that were not covered by them.

We hope that the book will promote a general understanding and appreciation of the continuing evolution of family law and, if it is not too immodest a hope, to provide a work that will stand the test of time such that, like *A Century of Family Law*, it will be used as a reference point in any review in 50 years' time. In any event, the book should be of interest to both those studying and practising Family Law.

We would like to express our gratitude to a number of people, not least the President of the Family Division, Sir Mark Potter, for writing the

Foreword; to Sharon Witherspoon, Deputy Director of the Nuffield Foundation (which institution has played no small part in promoting research into family issues) for chairing the March conference; to Jordans and Greg Woodgate in particular, both for helping to sponsor the conferences and for publishing this book; to Dawn Morgan, Julia McCarthy and Steve Dyer, all of Cardiff Law School, who provided invaluable help in the administration of the conferences, and to the Law School Research Committee, for providing funds to help support the conferences.

Gillian Douglas

Nigel Lowe

Cardiff Law School
St Dwynwen's Day, 25 January 2009

CONTENTS

Foreword	v
Preface	vii
List of Contributors	xv
Table of Cases	xvii
Table of Statutes	xxv
Table of Statutory Instruments	xxix

Chapter 1
The Continuing Evolution of Family Law — 1
Modernity and family law — 1
  Law in context — 2
  International influences — 3
The changing demographic picture — 3
  Adult relationships — 3
    Marriage — 3
      Age at marriage — 4
      Remarriage — 4
      Civil weddings — 4
    Cohabitation — 5
    Divorce — 6
    Having children — 8
      Births outside marriage — 8
      Lone parenthood — 8
      Stepfamilies — 8
    The elderly — 9
    Diversity of the population — 9
      Same-sex partnerships — 9
      Ethnic minorities — 10
A process of evolution — 10
  The cultural legacy of religion — 12
  State intervention in the family — 15
  The gender and class dimensions in family law — 20
Adapting family law to social change — 24
  The neglect of the elderly — 24
  The re-discovery of domestic violence — 26
  The transformation of adoption — 29
    The changing nature of adoption law and practice — 29
    The rise and fall of private law adoptions — 30

The rise and rise of public law adoptions	31
Broadening the concept of adoption	33
Other changes made by the 2002 Act	34
What of the future?	36
Conclusion	37

Chapter 2
The Troublemakers: Cranks, Psychiatrists and other Mischievous Nuisances – their Role in Reform of English Family Law in the Nineteenth and Twentieth Centuries — 39

Introduction	39
Priorities for reform: divorce or property?	40
Edith Summerskill: married women's property	41
The defeat of Dr Summerskill and the 'Women of England'	42
Why did divorce come first?	45
Do 'rights' matter? The case of the guardianship legislation	47
Caring for deprived, neglected and abused children	49
Transforming ideas into laws	51
Leo Abse: the most effective law reformer in twentieth-century Britain?	52
Conclusion	55

Chapter 3
Looking Back on the Overlooked: Cohabitants and the Law 1857–2007 — 57

Introduction	57
The extent and nature of cohabitation	59
Attitudes to cohabitation	62
The legal treatment of cohabitants	66
Conclusion	83

Chapter 4
Removing Children from their Families – Law and Policy before the Children Act 1989 — 85

Introduction	85
The statutory framework	87
Care proceedings: the grounds	87
Care proceedings: practice and procedures	90
Reception into care	94
Assumption of parental rights: the grounds	95
Assumption of parental rights: policy and procedures	97
Access to children in care	99
The prerogative jurisdiction of the High Court	101
When wardship was available to local authorities	101
The unavailability of wardship to parents and others interested in a child	102
Sarah's story	106
Conclusion	109

Chapter 5
Cultural Change and the Family Justice System — 111
Introduction — 111
Ground clearing — 112
    The family justice system — 112
    The problem of defining 'cultural change' — 114
The roots of the system — 115
    Rapid cultural and economic social change increase public anxiety and lead to authoritarian measures of social control — 115
    Periods of relative social stability facilitate the development of community based support services — 116
    From priests to psychiatrists – the translation of 'spiritual wellbeing' into modern child welfare and mental health thinking — 117
Emergence and convergence of the family justice system in late modernity — 118
    Post-war conceptual advances in the behavioural and social sciences concerning the family — 119
The development of family-focused social policy and social work — 122
    The growth of university social work training — 122
    Post-war child care policy and practice — 122
    The Seebohm Committee and reorganisation of local authority social services — 124
    The post-war development of the probation service's civil work — 125
    Unified local family courts – a feasible reality or mirage? — 126
    The influence of socio-legal 'consumer' studies of the family jurisdictions — 128
Family justice in the postmodern age – fragmentation, reversion and decay? — 129
    Postmodernity and the family — 129
    Children, critical life transitions and the family justice system — 131
    The surveillance and support dilemma — 133
    Enforcement in the family courts – blurring the distinction between the criminal and civil jurisdictions — 136
    Official encouragement to make greater use of the magistrates' family proceedings court — 137
    The emergent nature of the government's strategy for family justice — 138
    Implementation of the Carter Review of Legal Aid — 139
    New Labour's stealthily emergent policy for family justice — 141
    Some continuing positive support measures of family justice — 142
Conclusion — 144

Chapter 6
Fifty Years of Family Law: an Opinionated Review — 147
1957 and all that — 147

Family law as a discrete entity	153
Family law's image of the family	153
Family law and social control	155
Marriage and its discourses	155
Family law's neglect of family issues	157
Contrasts with 1957	158
Conclusion – and so to 2057	170

Chapter 7
Law, Family and Community — 173

Individualism	173
Communities and power	174
The role of rights	174
Care and power	175
Silencing the voice	176
Hearing the voice	177
Community legal and advice services	177
Solicitors and barristers	180
Children	181
Mediation	182
Communities, law and responsibility	184

Chapter 8
The Future of Marriage — 187

Introduction	187
What is the legal institution of marriage for? The individuals or the state?	187
The rise of marriage as an equal partnership	189
The flight from marriage: is equality to blame?	192
Threats to the equal partnership	198
Does marriage have a future?	201

Chapter 9
The Future for Ancillary Relief — 203

Introduction	203
Matrimonial regimes	204
Some European features of ancillary relief today	207
European initiatives	214
The first question	216
The second question	216
The conflicts problem	216
The future for ancillary relief	218

Chapter 10
Caring for our Future Generations — 221

Introduction	221
Twenty-first century families	221
Family life under the Children Act 1989	224

Who is family?	225
Reform of the Children Act 1989	227
Critique of the provisions relating to parental responsibility	232
Private ordering	235
Governing the family in the twenty-first century	239
Advising and supporting families	241
Conclusion	242

Chapter 11
The Future of Welfare Law for Children — 245

Introduction	245
The political context	246
The legal history	246
The current political context	247
The undermining process	248
Legal aid	250
Court services	252
Court fees	253
The Public Law Outline	253
Conclusions – the future	256

Chapter 12
Where in the World is International Family Law Going Next? — 261

Introduction	261
The developing internationalisation of English family law	262
Where is internationalisation heading?	271
The continuing impact of human rights	272
The continuing impact of the Hague Conference	274
The 1996 Hague Convention on the Protection of Children	274
The 1993 Hague Intercountry Adoption Convention and the 1980 Hague Abduction Convention	276
The 2007 Hague Maintenance Convention and the 2000 Hague Convention on the Protection of Adults and possible future developments	278
The continuing impact of the Council of Europe	280
The continuing impact of the EU	282
The overall impact of these continuing developments	283
Bringing national laws closer together	284
Can or should family laws be harmonised?	285
The harmonisation debate	287
The work of the CEFL	289

Index — 293

LIST OF CONTRIBUTORS

Gillian Douglas
Professor of Law, Cardiff University

Nigel Lowe
Professor of Law, Cardiff University

Stephen Cretney
Emeritus Fellow of All Souls College, Oxford

Rebecca Probert
Associate Professor, University of Warwick

Mary Hayes
Emeritus Professor, University of Sheffield

Mervyn Murch
Emeritus Professor, Cardiff University

Michael Freeman
Professor of English Law, University College London

John Eekelaar
Emeritus Fellow, Pembroke College Oxford

Brenda Hale
Lord of Appeal in Ordinary

Elizabeth Cooke
Professor of Law, University of Reading; Law Commissioner for England and Wales

Judith Masson
Professor of Socio-legal Studies, University of Bristol

Richard White
Tribunal Judge of the First-tier Tribunal of the Health, Education and Social Care Chamber (Special Educational Needs)

TABLE OF CASES

References are to page numbers.

A (A Child) (Joint Residence: Parental Responsibility), Re [2008] EWCA Civ 867, [2008] 2 FLR 1593, [2008] 3 FCR 107, CA	223
A v Liverpool City Council [1982] AC 363, [1981] 2 WLR 948, [1981] 2 All ER 385, HL	99, 102, 104, 106
A, Re (1993) 16 Fam LR 715	156
AB (An Infant), Re [1954] 2 QB 385, [1954] 3 WLR 1, [1954] 2 All ER 287, DC	103
Agar-Ellis (No 2), Re; *sub nom* Agar-Ellis v Lascelles (No 2) (1883) LR 24 Ch D 317, CA	163
Alex, Re [2004] Fam 297, CA	156
Alhaji Mohamed v Knott; *sub nom* M v Knott; Mohamed v Knott [1969] 1 QB 1, [1968] 2 WLR 1446, [1968] 2 All ER 563, DC	89
Anderson v Berkley [1902] 1 Ch 936, Ch D	67
Andrews v Andrews [1940] P 184, PDAD	73
Andrews v Andrews and Sullivan [1958] P 217, [1958] 2 WLR 942, [1958] 2 All ER 305, PDAD	153
Apted v Apted [1930] P 246, PDAD	73
Attorney-General ex rel Tilley v Wandsworth LBC [1981] 1 WLR 854, [1981] 1 All ER 1162, (1981) 11 Fam Law 119, CA	94
Ayerst v Jenkins (1873) LR 16 Eq 275, Lord Chancellor	68
B (A Child) (Child Support: Reduction of Contact), Re [2006] EWCA Civ 1574, [2007] 1 FLR 1949, [2007] Fam Law 114, CA	234
B (Minors) (Residence Order), Re; *sub nom* B (A Minor) (Residence Order: ex parte), Re [1992] Fam 162, [1992] 3 WLR 113, [1992] 2 FLR 1, CA	162
B Borough Council v S [2006] EWHC 2584 (Fam), [2007] 1 FLR 1600, [2007] 1 FCR 574, Fam Div	157
B v United Kingdom [2000] 1 FLR 1, [2000] 1 FCR 289, [2000] Fam Law 88, ECHR	266
Bainbridge v Bainbridge [1934] P 66, PDAD	73
Baindail v Baindail [1946] P 122, CA	156, 284
Balfour v Balfour [1919] 2 KB 571, CA	150
Barnardo v Ford; *sub nom* R v Barnardo; Gossage's Case, Re [1892] AC 326, HL	16
Barnardo v McHugh; *sub nom* R v Barnardo; Jones's Case [1891] AC 388, HL	16
Barnett v Barnett [1957] P 78, [1957] 2 WLR 272, [1957] 1 All ER 388, PDAD	152
Baylis v Baylis (1865–69) LR 1 P & D 395, Divorce Ct	70
Beaumont v Reeve (1846) 8 QB 483, 115 ER 958	68
Bellinger v Bellinger [2003] UKHL 21, [2003] 2 AC 467, [2003] 2 WLR 1174, HL	262
Benyon v Nettlefold (1850) 3 M & G 94, 42 ER 196	68
Best v Best [1956] P 76, PDAD	160
Binney v Binney [1936] P 178, PDAD	73
Blackwell v Blackwell [1943] 2 All ER 579, CA	42
Blades v Free (1829) 9 B & C 168, 109 ER 63	67
Boreham v Boreham (1865–69) LR 1 P & D 77, Divorce Ct	71
Boyes, Re; *sub nom* Boyes v Carritt (1884) LR 26 Ch D 531, Ch D	68
Bradley v Bradley [1956] P 326, [1956] 2 WLR 654, [1956] 1 All ER 543, PDAD	160
Brown, Re (1910) 26 TLR 257	67
Buckmaster v Buckmaster (1865–69) LR 1 P & D 713, Divorce Ct	69
Bull v Bull [1968] P 618, [1965] 3 WLR 1048, [1965] 1 All ER 1057, PDAD	73

Burdon v Burdon [1901] P 52, PDAD	72
Burns v Burns [1984] Ch 317, [1984] 2 WLR 582, [1984] 1 All ER 244, CA	80
Button v Button [1968] 1 WLR 457, [1968] 1 All ER 1064, (1968) 19 P & CR 257, CA	153
C (A Child), Re (C-435/06); *sub nom* C, Appellant (C-435/06) [2008] Fam 27, [2008] 3 WLR 419, [2008] ILPr 1, ECJ	269
C (A Minor) (1981) 2 FLR 62	93
C (A Minor) (Adoption Order: Conditions), Re; *sub nom* C (A Minor) (Adoption: Contact with Sibling), Re [1989] AC 1, [1988] 2 WLR 474, [1988] 1 All ER 705, HL	33
C (A Minor) (Wardship: Surrogacy) Re [1985] FLR 846	102
C (A Minor), Re (1981) 2 FLR 62	101
Cade v Cade [1957] 1 WLR 569, [1957] 1 All ER 609, (1957) 121 JP 200, DC	151
Carega Properties SA (Formerly Joram Developments) v Sharratt [1979] 1 WLR 928, (1980) 39 P & CR 76, (1979) 252 EG 163, HL	79
Carroll (An Infant), Re [1931] 1 KB 317, CA	13
Chalmers (otherwise Gunning) v Chalmers [1964] P 61, [1963] 3 WLR 634, [1963] 3 All ER 266, CA	73
Charman v Charman [2007] EWCA Civ 503, [2007] 1 FLR 1246, [2007] 2 FCR 217, CA	45, 161, 198, 203, 207, 208, 209, 218, 271
Clark v Clark; Perrens and Cumins (1865) *Times*, March 16	69, 71
Commission of the European Communities v Council of the European Communities (22/70); *sub nom* European Road Transport Agreement, Re (22/70) [1971] ECR 263, [1971] CMLR 335, ECJ	270
Cooke v Head (No 1) [1972] 1 WLR 518, [1972] 2 All ER 38, (1972) 116 SJ 298, CA	79, 153
Corbett v Corbett (otherwise Ashley) (No 1) [1971] P 83, [1970] 2 WLR 1306, [1970] 2 All ER 33, PDAD	159
Cowan v Cowan [2001] EWCA Civ 679, [2002] Fam 97, [2001] 3 WLR 684, CA	195
Crawford v Crawford [1956] P 195, [1955] 3 WLR 855, [1955] 3 All ER 592, DC	151
Crosby (A Minor) v Northumberland CC (1982) 12 Fam Law 92, DC	101
Crossley v Crossley [2007] EWCA Civ 1491, [2008] 1 FLR 1467, [2008] 1 FCR 323, CA	199, 209, 211, 212
D (A Child) (Intractable Contact Dispute: Publicity), Re; *sub nom* F v M (Contact Orders) [2004] EWHC 727 (Fam), [2004] 1 FLR 1226, [2004] 3 FCR 234, Fam Div	142
D (A Minor) (Justices' Decision: Review), Re [1977] Fam 158, [1977] 2 WLR 1006, [1977] 3 All ER 481, Fam Div	93, 102
D (A Minor), Re; *sub nom* D (A Minor) v Berkshire CC; D (A Minor), Re (Baby: Care Proceedings) [1987] AC 317, [1986] 3 WLR 1080, [1987] 1 All ER 20, HL	89
D v XCC (No 1) [1985] FLR 275	105
D v XCC (No 2) [1985] FLR 279	105
Dagg v Dagg (1882) LR 7 PD 17, PDAD	70
Dart v Dart [1996] 2 FLR 286, [1997] 1 FCR 21, [1996] Fam Law 607, CA	190, 191
Davis v Johnson [1979] AC 264, [1978] 2 WLR 553, [1978] 1 All ER 1132, HL	79
Del Vecchio v Del Vecchio, 143 So 2d 17 (Fla 1962)	213
Dickinson v Dickinson (1889) 62 LT 330	69
DM (A Minor) (Wardship: Jurisdiction), [1986] 2 FLR 122, [1986] Fam Law 296, CA	105
Drew v Drew (1888) LR 13 PD 97, PDAD	69
Dyson Holdings Ltd v Fox [1976] QB 503, [1975] 3 WLR 744, [1975] 3 All ER 1030, CA	79
E (Minors) (Wardship: Jurisdiction), Re [1983] 1 WLR 541, [1984] 1 All ER 21, (1983) 147 JP 321, CA	90
Earl Russell, Re [1901] AC 446, HL	46
Essex CC v TLR and KBR (Minors) (1978) 9 Fam Law 15, DC	94
Evans v Evans and Bird (1865) 1 P & D 36	69

Eves v Eves [1975] 1 WLR 1338, [1975] 3 All ER 768, (1975) 119 SJ 394, CA   79

F (A Child) (Indirect Contact), Re [2006] EWCA Civ 1426, [2007] 1 FLR 1015,
  [2006] 3 FCR 553, CA   234
F v Suffolk CC (1981) 2 FLR 208, 79 LGR 554, (1981) 125 SJ 307   89
Farrant v Farrant [1957] P 188, [1957] 2 WLR 134, [1957] 1 All ER 204, PDAD   152
Forbes v Forbes (Cruelty) [1956] P 16, [1955] 1 WLR 531, [1955] 2 All ER 311,
  PDAD   151

G (Children) (Residence: Same Sex Partner), Re; *sub nom* CG v CW [2006] UKHL
  43, [2006] 1 WLR 2305, [2006] 4 All ER 241, HL   195, 223
Garcia v Garcia (1888) LR 13 PD 216, PDAD   69
Garland (Deceased), Re; *sub nom* Garland v Morris [2007] EWHC 2 (Ch), [2007] 2
  FLR 528, [2007] WTLR 797, Ch D   154
Gatehouse v Gatehouse (1865–69) LR 1 P & D 331, Divorce Ct   69
Gault, Re 387 US 1 (1967), US Sup Ct   169
Gillick v West Norfolk and Wisbech AHA [1986] AC 112, [1985] 3 WLR 830,
  [1985] 3 All ER 402, HL   148, 152, 156, 167, 169, 170
Gollins v Gollins [1964] AC 644, [1963] 3 WLR 176, [1963] 2 All ER 966, HL   147
Goodwin v United Kingdom (28957/95) [2002] IRLR 664, [2002] 2 FLR 487,
  ECHR   262
Greenwich LBC v S [2007] EWHC 820 (Fam), [2007] 2 FLR 154, [2007] 2 FCR
  141, Fam Div   277

H (Minors), Re [1987] 2 FLR 12, [1987] Fam Law 196   87
Hammond, Re; *sub nom* Burniston v White [1911] 2 Ch 342, Ch D   67
Hampson v Hampson [1914] P 104, PDAD   72
Heathcoat v Heathcoat (1865) *Times*, March 6   69
Helby v Rafferty [1979] 1 WLR 13, [1978] 3 All ER 1016, (1979) 37 P & CR 376,
  CA   79
Herod v Herod [1939] P 11, PDAD   74
Hertfordshire CC v Dolling (1982) 3 FLR 423   102
Hewer v Bryant [1970] 1 QB 357, [1969] 3 WLR 425, [1969] 3 All ER 578, CA   169
Heyes v Heyes (1888) LR 13 PD 11, PDAD   70
Hindley v Hindley [1957] 1 WLR 898, [1957] 2 All ER 653, (1957) 101 SJ 593,
  PDAD   160
Hines v Hines [1918] P 364, PDAD   72
Hyde v Hyde, *sub nom* Hyde v Hyde and Woodmansee (1865–69) LR 1 P & D 130,
  [1861–73] All ER Rep 175, Divorce Ct   13
Hyman v Hyman [1929] AC 601, (1929) FLR Rep 342, [1929] All ER Rep 245,
  HL   160, 188

I v United Kingdom (25680/94) [2002] 2 FLR 518, [2002] 2 FCR 613, (2003) 36
  EHRR 53, ECHR   262
Izard v Izard (1889) LR 14 PD 45, PDAD   69

J (A Minor) (Adoption Order: Conditions), Re [1973] Fam 106, [1973] 2 WLR 782,
  [1973] 2 All ER 410, Fam Div   33
J (A Minor) (Prohibited Steps Order: Circumcision), Re, *sub nom* J (A Minor)
  (Specific Issue Orders: Muslim Upbringing and Circumcision) Re; J (Specific
  Issue Orders: Child's Religious Upbringing and Circumcision), Re [2000] 1
  FLR 571, [2000] 1 FCR 307, (2000) 52 BMLR 82, CA   14
J v C; *sub nom* C (An Infant), Re [1970] AC 668, [1969] 2 WLR 540, [1969] 1 All
  ER 788, HL   19
Jennings (Deceased), Re; *sub nom* Harlow v National Westminster Bank Plc [1994]
  Ch 286, [1994] 3 WLR 67, [1994] 1 FLR 536, CA   154
Jennings v Jennings (1865) LR 1 P & D 35   69
Johnson v Ball (1851) 5 De & G Sm 85, 64 ER 1029   68

K (A Child) (Secure Accommodation Order: Right to Liberty), Re; *sub nom* W BC
  v DK; W BC v AK [2001] Fam 377, [2001] 2 WLR 1141, [2001] 2 All ER 719,
  CA   266
K v Devon CC [1987] Fam Law 348, DC   99
Keenan v Handley (1864) 10 LT 800, (1864) 2 De G J & S 282, 46 ER 384   68
Kochanski v Kochanska [1958] P 147, [1957] 3 WLR 619, [1957] 3 All ER 142,
  PDAD   159

L (A Child) (Care: Threshold Criteria), Re [2007] 1 FLR 2050, [2007] Fam Law
  297, Fam Div   88
L (A Child) (Contact: Domestic Violence), Re; M (A Child) (Contact: Domestic
  Violence), Re; V (A Child) (Contact: Domestic Violence), Re; H (Children)
  (Contact: Domestic Violence), Re [2001] Fam 260, [2001] 2 WLR 339, [2000] 2
  FLR 334, CA   234, 266
L (AC) (An Infant), Re [1971] 3 All ER 743, 136 JPN 551, Ch D   99, 105
Lambert v Lambert; *sub nom* L v L (Financial Provision: Contributions) [2002]
  EWCA Civ 1685, [2003] Fam 103, [2003] 2 WLR 631, CA   45, 207
Lee v Lee (1984) 12 HLR 114, [1984] Fam Law 243, (1983) 80 LSG 2678, CA   80
Lempriere v Lempriere (1865–69) LR 1 P & D 569, Divorce Ct   70
Lepine v Bean (1870) LR 10 Eq 160, Ct of Chancery   67
Lewisham LBC v Lewisham Juvenile Court Justices [1980] AC 273, [1979] 2 WLR
  513, [1979] 2 All ER 297, HL   97
LH (A Minor), Re (1986) 150 JP 417, [1986] 2 FLR 306, [1986] Fam Law 271, Fam
  Div   102
Lowe v Lowe [1952] P 376, [1952] 2 All ER 671, [1952] 2 TLR 505, PDAD   73
Lowe, Re (1892) 61 LJ Ch 415   67
Lynch, Re; *sub nom* Lynch v Lynch [1943] 1 All ER 168, Ch D   67

M (A Minor) (Access Application), Re; *sub nom* M (A Minor) (Child in Care:
  Access: Appeal), Re (1988) 152 JP 629, [1988] 1 FLR 35, [1988] FCR 450,
  CA   102
M (A Minor) (Child's Upbringing), Re [1996] 2 FLR 441, [1996] 2 FCR 473, CA   168
M (An Infant), Re [1961] Ch 328, [1961] 2 WLR 350, [1961] 1 All ER 788, CA   103, 104, 109
M (Children) (Contact: Long Term Best Interests), Re; *sub nom* M (Children)
  (Intractable Contact Dispute: Court's Positive Duty), Re [2005] EWCA Civ
  1090, [2006] 1 FLR 627, [2005] Fam Law 938, CA   222
M v Berkshire CC [1985] FLR 257   100
M v M (Breaches of Orders: Committal) [2005] EWCA Civ 1722, [2006] 1 FLR
  1154, [2006] Fam Law 259, CA   137
M v M (Child: Access) [1973] 2 All ER 81, DC   169
M v Westminster City Council [1985] FLR 325, [1985] Fam Law 93, Fam Div   89
M v Wigan MBC (1980) 1 FLR 45   96
Mabon v Mabon [2005] EWCA Civ 634, [2005] Fam 366, [2005] 2 FLR 1011, CA   182, 281
MacLennan v MacLennan, 1958 SC 105, 1958 SLT 12, OH   148
MacLeod v MacLeod [2008] UKPC 64, [2008] WLR (D) 402, PC (IoM)   199, 212
Mesher v Mesher [1980] 1 All ER 126 (Note), CA   219
Miller v Miller; *sub nom* M v M (Short Marriage: Clean Break); McFarlane v
  McFarlane [2006] UKHL 24, [2006] 2 AC 618, [2006] 2 WLR 1283, HL   2, 45, 158, 161, 162, 191, 193, 194, 198, 199, 203, 207, 208
Moore v Moore [1892] P 382, PDAD   72
Moore v Moore [2007] EWCA Civ 361, [2007] ILPr 36, [2007] 2 FLR 339, CA   217
Morgan v Morgan (1865–69) LR 1 P & D 644, Divorce Ct   71
Munro v De Chemant (1815) 4 Camp 215   67

National Provincial Bank Ltd v Ainsworth; *sub nom* National Provincial Bank Ltd
  v Hastings Car Mart Ltd [1965] AC 1175, [1965] 3 WLR 1, [1965] 2 All ER
  472, HL   40, 43
Nokes v Nokes [1957] P 213, [1957] 3 WLR 90, [1957] 2 All ER 535, CA   152
Nott v Nott (1865–69) LR 1 P & D 251, Divorce Ct   69

Nottinghamshire CC v Q (1982) 3 FLR 305, [1982] 2 WLR 954, [1982] 2 All ER
 641, DC 90

O (A Child) (Contact: Withdrawal of Application), Re; *sub nom* O (A Child)
 (Termination of Contact), Re [2003] EWHC 3031 (Fam), [2004] 1 FLR 1258,
 [2004] 1 FCR 687, Fam Div 142, 222
O and J (Children) (Blood Tests: Constraint), Re; *sub nom* O and J (Children)
 (Paternity: Blood Tests), Re; J (A Child) (Blood Tests), Re [2000] Fam 139,
 [2000] 2 WLR 1284, [2000] 2 All ER 29, Fam Div 262
O v United Kingdom (A/120); *sub nom* C v United Kingdom (9276/81) (1988) 10
 EHRR 82, ECHR 19
O v United Kingdom; H v United Kingdom (1987) Series A, No 120, ECHR 262
O'D v O'D; *sub nom* O'Donnell v O'Donnell [1976] Fam 83, [1975] 3 WLR 308,
 [1975] 2 All ER 993, CA 191
O'D v South Glamorgan CC; *sub nom* O'Dare Ai v South Glamorgan County, 78
 LGR 522, (1980) 10 Fam Law 215, DC 96, 101
Orford v Orford (1921) 58 DLR 251 148
Ousey v Ousey; Ousey v Atkinson (1872–75) LR 3 P & D 223, [1874–80] All ER
 Rep 635, Ct of Probate 69

P (A Child), Re; *sub nom* B v X County Council; P (A Child) (Placement Orders:
 Parental Consent), Re [2008] EWCA Civ 535, [2008] 2 FLR 625, [2008] 2 FCR
 185, CA 33, 35
P (Surrogacy: Residence), Re [2007] EWCA Civ 1053, [2008] 1 FLR 198, [2008]
 Fam Law 21, CA 223
Page v Page (1981) 2 FLR 198, CA 191
Parker v Rolls (1854) 14 CB 691, 139 ER 284 68
Parra v Parra (Divorce: Financial Provision: Clean Break) [2002] EWCA Civ 1886,
 [2003] 1 FLR 942, [2003] 1 FCR 97, CA 209
Parrott v Parkin (The Up Yaws) [2007] EWHC 210 (Admlty), [2007] 1 Lloyd's Rep
 719, [2007] 2 FLR 444, [2007] 3 FCR 515, QBD 147
Pascoe v Turner [1979] 1 WLR 431, [1979] 2 All ER 945, (1978) 9 Fam Law 82,
 CA 79
Pigott v Pigott [1958] P 1, [1957] 3 WLR 781, [1967] 3 All ER 432, CA 160
Plaskett's Estate, Re (1861) 4 LT 544 68
Practice Direction (Fam Div: Children Act 1989: Applications by Children: Leave)
 [1993] 1 WLR 313, [1993] 1 All ER 820, [1993] 1 FLR 668, Fam Div 181
Prescott (otherwise Fellowes) v Fellowes [1958] P 260, [1958] 3 WLR 288, [1958] 3
 All ER 55, CA 160
Price v Price, 62 TLR 645, [1947] WN 10, 176 LT 10 73
Proceedings Brought by Rinau (C-195/08 PPU) [2008] All ER (EC) 1145, [2008]
 ILPr 51, [2008] 2 FLR 1495, ECJ 269

R (A Minor) (Discharge of Care Order: Wardship), Re; *sub nom* R (A Minor)
 (Care Proceedings: Wardship) [1987] 2 FLR 400, [1988] Fam Law 61, (1988)
 152 JPN 366, CA 102
R (A Minor) (Wardship: Consent to Treatment), Re [1992] Fam 11, [1991] 3 WLR
 592, [1992] 1 FLR 190, CA 169
R (on the application of A) v East Sussex CC (No 2) [2003] EWHC 167 (Admin),
 (2003) 6 CCL Rep 194, QBD 273
R (on the application of Axon) v Secretary of State for Health [2006] EWHC 37
 (Admin), [2006] QB 539, [2006] 2 WLR 1130, QBD 169
R (on the application of Begum) v Denbigh High School Governors; *sub nom* R
 (on the application of SB) v Denbigh High School Governors [2006] UKHL
 15, [2007] 1 AC 100, [2006] 2 WLR 719, HL 14
R (on the application of Law Society) v Legal Services Commission; Dexter
 Montague & Partners (A Firm) v Legal Services Commission [2007] EWCA
 Civ 1264, [2008] QB 737, [2008] 2 WLR 803, CA 251
R (on the application of M) v Birmingham City Council [2008] EWHC 1863
 (Admin), QBD 232

R (on the application of Playfoot) v Millais School Governing Body [2007] EWHC 1698 (Admin), [2007] 3 FCR 754, [2007] HRLR 34, QBD	14
R (on the application of the Howard League for Penal Reform) v Secretary of State for the Home Department (No 2) [2002] EWHC 2497 (Admin), [2003] 1 FLR 484, (2003) 6 CCL Rep 47, QBD	273
R (on the application of Watkins-Singh) v Aberdare Girls' High School Governors [2008] EWHC 1865 (Admin), [2008] 3 FCR 203, [2008] ELR 561, QBD	14
R (on the application of Williamson) v Secretary of State for Education and Employment *sub nom* Williamson v Secretary of State for Education and Employment [2005] UKHL 15, [2005] 2 AC 246, [2005] 2 WLR 590, HL	14
R (on the application of X) v Headteachers and Governors of Y School [2007] EWHC 298 (Admin), [2008] 1 All ER 249, [2007] HRLR 20, QBD	14
R v Avon CC [1985] FLR 252	93
R v Bolton MBC, ex p B, 84 LGR 78, [1985] Fam Law 193, (1985) 82 LSG 1086, QBD	100
R v Gravesham Juvenile Court, ex p B (1983) 4 FLR 312, (1982) 12 Fam Law 207, QBD	91
R v Milton Keynes Justices, ex p R [1979] 1 WLR 1062, (1979) 123 SJ 321, DC	91
R v Plymouth Juvenile Court, ex p F (1987) 151 JP 355, [1987] 1 FLR 169, [1987] Fam Law 18, Fam Div	92
R v R (Rape: Marital Exemption); *sub nom* R v R (A Husband) [1992] 1 AC 599, [1991] 3 WLR 767, [1991] 4 All ER 481, HL	151
R v Secretary of State for the Home Department, ex p Venables; R v Secretary of State for the Home Department, ex p Thompson [1998] AC 407, [1997] 3 WLR 23, [1997] 3 All ER 97, HL	152
R v United Kingdom (10496/83); *sub nom* A v United Kingdom (10496/83) (1988) 19 EHRR 74, ECHR	100
R v United Kingdom (A/136-E) [1988] 2 FLR 445, (1991) 13 EHRR 457, ECHR	19, 262
Rebecca Miles (Deceased), In the Goods of (1890) 62 LT 607	68
Richards v Richards [1984] AC 174, [1983] 3 WLR 173, [1983] 2 All ER 807, HL	27
RM and LM (Minors) (Wardship: Jurisdiction), Re [1986] 2 FLR 205, [1986] Fam Law 297	105
Roddy (A Child) (Identification: Restriction on Publication), Re; *sub nom* Torbay BC v News Group Newspapers [2003] EWHC 2927 (Fam), [2004] EMLR 8, [2004] 2 FLR 949, Fam Div	169
Royal Bank of Scotland Plc v Etridge (No 2); Kenyon-Brown v Desmond Banks & Co (Undue Influence) (No 2); Bank of Scotland v Bennett; UCB Home Loans Corp Ltd v Moore; National Westminster Bank Plc v Gill; Midland Bank Plc v Wallace; Barclays Bank Plc v Harris; Barclays Bank Plc v Coleman [2001] UKHL 44, [2002] 2 AC 773, [2001] 3 WLR 1021, HL	212
Rukat v Rukat [1975] Fam 63, [1975] 2 WLR 201, [1975] 1 All ER 343, CA	159
Russell v Russell [1956] P 283, [1956] 2 WLR 544, [1956] 1 All ER 466, CA	160
Ryan v Sam (1848) 12 QB 460, 116 ER 940	67
S (A Minor) (Care Order: Education), Re; *sub nom* DJMS (A Minor), Re; S (A Minor) v Bedfordshire CC [1978] QB 120, [1977] 3 WLR 575, [1977] 3 All ER 582, CA	90
S (A Minor) (Care: Wardship), Re [1987] 1 FLR 479, [1987] Fam Law 159 (1987) 151 JPN 396, CA	105
S (Children) (Care Order: Implementation of Care Plan), Re; *sub nom* W and B (Children) (Care Plan), Re; W (Children) (Care Plan), Re; W (Children) (Care Order: Adequacy of Care Plan), Re [2002] UKHL 10, [2002] 2 AC 291, [2002] 1 FLR 815, HL	255, 266
S (Children) (Specific Issue Order: Religion: Circumcision), Re [2004] EWHC 1282 (Fam), [2005] 1 FLR 236, [2004] Fam Law 869, Fam Div	14
S (Children) (Unco-operative Mothers), Re; *sub nom* S (Children) (Unco-operative Mother), Re [2004] EWCA Civ 597, [2004] 2 FLR 710, [2004] Fam Law 637, CA	222

S v S, Legal Personal Representatives of S (otherwise C) [1956] P 1, [1955] 2 WLR
  246, [1954] 3 All ER 736, Assizes   147
S, Re [1981] Fam Law 175   105, 108
SA (Vulnerable Adult with Capacity: Marriage), Re; *sub nom* A Local Authority v
  MA [2005] EWHC 2942 (Fam), [2006] 1 FLR 867, [2007] 2 FCR 563, Fam
  Div   159
Salford City Council v C (1982) 3 FLR 153   88
Scott v Scott [1978] 1 WLR 723, [1978] 3 All ER 65, (1977) 8 Fam Law 109, CA   191
Scott v United Kingdom (34745/97) [2000] 1 FLR 958, [2000] 2 FCR 560, 2000
  Fam LR 102, ECHR   36
Shaw v DPP; *sub nom* R v Shaw (Frederick Charles) [1962] AC 220, [1961] 2 WLR
  897, [1961] 2 All ER 446, HL   147
Sheffield (Kristina) v United Kingdom (22985/93); Horsham v United Kingdom
  (23390/94) [1998] 2 FLR 928, [1998] 3 FCR 141, (1999) 27 EHRR 163,
  ECHR   159
Short v Short; Short v Bolwell (1872–75) LR 3 P & D 193, Ct of Probate   71
SK (An Adult) (Forced Marriage: Appropriate Relief), Re; *sub nom* SK (Proposed
  Plaintiff), Re [2004] EWHC 3202 (Fam), [2006] 1 WLR 81, [2005] 3 All ER
  421, Fam Div   159
Smalley, Re; *sub nom* Smalley v Scotton [1929] 2 Ch 112, CA   67
Smith v Roche (1859) 6 CB (NS) 223, 141 ER 440   68
Smith v Smith; *sub nom* Smith v Secretary of State for Work and Pensions [2006]
  UKHL 35, [2006] 1 WLR 2024, [2006] 3 All ER 907, HL   263
Sorrell v Sorrell [2005] EWHC 1717 (Fam), [2006] 1 FLR 497, [2006] 1 FCR 75,
  Fam Div   161
South Glamorgan CC v W and B [1993] 1 FLR 574, [1993] 1 FCR 626, [1993] Fam
  Law 398   169
Stack v Dowden; *sub nom* Dowden v Stack [2007] UKHL 17, [2007] 2 AC 432,
  [2007] 2 WLR 831, HL   199
Starbuck v Starbuck (1889) 61 LT 876   70
Sterne v Sterne [1957] P 168, [1957] 2 WLR 544, [1957] 1 All ER 792, CA   160
Sundelind Lopez v Lopez Lizazo (C-68/07); *sub nom* Sunderlind Lopez v Lopez
  Lizazo (C-68/07); Lopez v Lizazo (C-68/07) [2008] Fam 21, [2008] 3 WLR 338,
  [2008] ILPr 4, ECJ   269
SW v United Kingdom (A/355-B); *sub nom* SW v United Kingdom (20166/92); CR
  v United Kingdom [1996] 1 FLR 434, (1996) 21 EHRR 363, [1996] Fam Law
  275, ECHR   151
Symons v Symons [1897] P 167, PDAD   72

T (AJJ) (An Infant), Re [1970] Ch 688, [1970] 3 WLR 315, [1970] 2 All ER 865,
  CA   103, 104
Taczanowska (otherwise Roth) v Taczanowski; *sub nom* Holdowanski v
  Holdowanska (otherwise Bialoszewska) and Price [1957] P 301, [1957] 3 WLR
  141, [1957] 2 All ER 563, CA   152, 159
Tanner v Tanner (No 1) [1975] 1 WLR 1346, [1975] 3 All ER 776, (1975) 5 Fam
  Law 193, CA   79
Taylor (formerly Kraupl) v National Assistance Board; *sub nom* Kraup v National
  Assistance Board [1957] P 101, [1957] 2 WLR 189, [1957] 1 All ER 183,
  CA   160
Thomas v Thomas (1860) 2 Sw & Tr 113, 164 ER 935   69
Thompson v Thompson [1957] P 19, [1957] 2 WLR 138, [1957] 1 All ER 161, CA   151
Tinker v Des Moines School District 393 US 503 (1969)   169
TP v United Kingdom (28945/95) [2001] 2 FLR 549, [2001] 2 FCR 289, (2002) 34
  EHRR 2, ECHR   20
Trippas v Trippas [1973] Fam 134, [1973] 2 WLR 585, [1973] 2 All ER 1, CA   191

V v V (Ancillary Relief: Power to Order Child Maintenance) [2001] 2 FLR 799,
  [2001] Fam Law 649, Fam Div   23
V v V (Children) (Contact: Implacable Hostility) [2004] EWHC 1215 (Fam), [2004]
  2 FLR 851, [2004] Fam Law 712, Fam Div   142
Vallance, Re; Vallance v Blagden (1884) LR 26 Ch D 353, Ch D   68

W (A Minor) (Medical Treatment: Court's Jurisdiction), Re; *sub nom* J (A Minor)
(Consent to Medical Treatment), Re [1993] Fam 64, [1992] 3 WLR 758, [1992]
4 All ER 627, CA   169
W (A Minor) (Wardship: Jurisdiction), Re; *sub nom* W v Hertfordshire CC [1985]
AC 791, [1985] 2 WLR 892, [1985] 2 All ER 301, HL   86, 105, 106, 107, 109
W (Children) (Leave to remove), Re [2008] EWCA Civ 538, [2008] 2 FLR 1170,
[2008] 2 FCR 420, CA   281
W (Minors) (Wardship: Jurisdiction), Re; *sub nom* AW and EW (Minors)
(Wardship: Jurisdiction), Re [1980] Fam 60, [1979] 3 WLR 252, [1979] 3 All
ER 154, CA   99, 104, 109
W v Nottinghamshire CC [1982] Fam 53, [1981] 3 WLR 959, [1982] 1 All ER 1,
CA   96
W v United Kingdom; B v United Kingdom (1987) Series A, No 121, ECHR   262
Wachtel v Wachtel (No 2) [1973] Fam 72, [1973] 2 WLR 366, [1973] 1 All ER 829,
CA   153, 190
Waller v Waller [1956] P 300, [1956] 2 WLR 1071, [1956] 2 All ER 234, CA   160
Waters v Waters [1956] P 344, [1956] 2 WLR 661, [1956] 1 All ER 432, DC   151
Watson v Threlkeld (1798) 2 Esp 637, 5 RR 760   67
Weldon v De Bathe (1884–85) LR 14 QBD 339, CA   40
Westminster City Council v IC; sub nom KC v City of Westminster Social and
Community Services Department [2008] EWCA Civ 198, [2009] 2 WLR 185,
[2008] 2 FLR 267, CA   284
Wheatley v Waltham Forest LBC [1980] AC 311, [1979] 2 WLR 543, [1979] 2 All
ER 289, Fam Div   95
White (Pamela) v White (Martin) [2001] 1 AC 596, [2000] 3 WLR 1571, [2001] 1 All
ER 1, HL   45, 191, 194, 197, 198, 203, 207, 208, 217, 219
White v White [1952] P 395, [1952] 2 TLR 534, PDAD   73
White v White [2001] 1 AC 596, [2000] 3 WLR 1571, [2000] 2 FLR 981, HL   158, 161,
                                                                                                  162
Whitworth v Whitworth [1893] P 85, PDAD   71
Wilby, Re; *sub nom* In the Estate of Wilby [1956] P 174, [1956] 2 WLR 262, [1956] 1
All ER 27, PDAD   152
Wilkinson v Kitzinger; *sub nom* X v Y (Overseas Same-Sex Relationship) [2006]
EWHC 2022 (Fam), [2007] 1 FLR 295, [2007] 1 FCR 183, Fam Div   271
Williams v Williams (Insanity as Defence to Cruelty) [1964] AC 698, [1963] 3 WLR
215, [1963] 2 All ER 994, HL   147
Wilson v Wilson [1920] P 20, PDAD   73
Wootton Isaacson, Re; Sanders v Smiles (1904) 21 TLR 89   68
Wroth v Tyler [1974] Ch 30, [1973] 2 WLR 405, [1973] 1 All ER 897, Ch D   43

Y (Minors) (Wardship: Access Challenge), Re [1988] 1 FLR 299   100
Yousef v Netherlands (33711/96) [2003] 1 FLR 210, [2002] 3 FCR 577, (2003) 36
EHRR 20, ECHR   20

TABLE OF STATUTES

References are to page numbers.

Abortion Act 1967	31, 147
Access to Justice Act 1999	180, 183
Administration of Justice Act 1970	126
Administration of Justice Act 1982	80
Adoption Act 1976	
s 14(3)	31
s 51A	33
s 56(4)–(7)	34
s 57A	34
Adoption (Intercountry Aspects) Act 1999	36
Adoption and Children Act 2002	30, 32, 53, 96, 227, 230, 280
s 1(2)	34
s 1(4)(c)	35
s 2(6)	34
ss 18–29	35
s 49(1)	32
s 51(2)	233
s 52(1)(b)	35
s 80	33
s 111	193, 238
s 112	35
s 114	167
s 115	167
s 120	133
s 121(2)	255
s 144(4)	32
Adoption and Children (Scotland) Act 2007	
s 32	281
Adoption of Children Act 1926	29, 35, 167
Anti-social Behaviour Act 2003	239
Child Abduction and Custody Act 1985	264
Child Care Act 1980	101, 221
s 1	94
s 2	94, 96
s 2(3)	95, 97
s 3	95
s 3(1)(a)	95
s 3(1)(b)–(c)	95
s 3(1)(b)(i)	95
s 3(1)(d)	96
s 3(6)	98
s 5(4)	99
ss 12A–12G	100
Child Care Act 1980—*continued*	
s 12B(4)	100
s 13(2)	97
s 18	97
Child Maintenance and Other Payments Act 2008	237
s 15	23, 229, 237
Child Support Act 1990	
s 6	229
s 46	229
Child Support Act 1991	19
s 6	23, 237
s 46	237
Child Support, Pensions and Social Security Act 2000	
s 82	262
Children Act 1908	221
Children Act 1948	50, 51, 94, 103, 119, 221
s 2	95
Children Act 1949	29
Children Act 1975	31, 53, 221
s 10(3)	31
s 26	33, 223
s 32	34
s 64	91
Children Act 1989	19, 22, 34, 35, 53, 81, 85, 87, 94, 96, 99, 101, 106, 109, 123, 125, 129, 132, 133, 152, 164, 221, 222, 224, 225, 227, 231, 232, 233, 235, 242, 243, 245, 246, 247, 249, 259, 263, 275
Pt III	167
s 1	14, 258
s 1(1), (3)	231
s 1(3)	14
s 1(5)	236
s 2(9)	235
s 4	133, 193, 235
s 4(1)(a)	21
s 4(1A)	227, 228
s 4A	35, 226, 227
s 4A(1)	8
s 5(3)	233
s 5(4)	233
s 8	133, 181, 231, 272
s 9(3)(b)	225
s 9(3)(c)	231
s 10	181

Children Act 1989—continued	
s 10(2)(b)	231
s 10(5)	227
s 10(5)(b)	231
s 10(5A)	227, 231
s 10(5B)	225, 227, 231
ss 11A–11P	136
s 14A	96
ss 14A–14G	227, 230
s 14A(7), (8), (11)	231
s 14C(1)(b)	36
s 14C(5)	230
s 14D(1), (3), (5)	230
s 14D(3)	36
s 14D(5)	36
s 16A	134
s 20	255
s 22C(5)	222
s 22C(6)(a)	222
s 22C(7)(a)	222
s 31	90, 250
s 31(10)	88
s 31A	255
s 34	262
s 38(6)	169
s 43	254
s 43(8)	169
s 44(7)	169
s 66(1)(a)(iii)	225
s 79A(3)(a)	225
s 105(1)	225
Sch 3, para 4(4)(a)	169
Sch 3, para 5(5)(b)	169
Sch 15	31
Children Act 2004	167, 221
Pt 1	263
s 18	256
s 58	166
Children (Scotland) Act 1995	
s 1(1)	234
s 1(1)(c)	234
s 2(1)	234
Children and Adoption Act 2006	134, 136, 167, 232, 241
Pt 1	136
Children and Young Persons Act 1932	221
Children and Young Persons Act 1933	221
Sch 1	87
Children and Young Persons Act 1963	221
s 1	123, 167
Children and Young Persons Act 1969	87, 91, 96, 101, 104, 221
s 1(2)	88
s 1(2)(a)	90, 94, 102
s 1(2)(a)–(c)	88
s 1(2)(e)	90
s 32A	92
s 32A(1)	91
s 70(1)	90

Children and Young Persons Act 2008	227, 256
s 1	256
s 8	222
s 36	225, 231, 272
Children's Commissioner for Wales Act 2001	263
Children's Homes Regulations 2001, SI 2001/3967	
reg 17(5)(a)	165
Civil Jurisdiction and Judgments Act 1982	267
Civil Partnership Act 2004	9, 55, 82, 271
Clandestine Marriages Act 1753	13
Commissioner for Children and Young People (Scotland) Act 2003	263
Consumer Credit Act 1974,	
s 184(5)	79
Crime and Disorder Act 1998	
s 1	239
s 34	168
Criminal Justice Act 1991	164
Criminal Justice and Courts Services Act 2000	125
Criminal Justice and Public Order Act 1994	
s 142	151
Custody of Children Act 1891	16
Custody of Infant Act 1839	12
Deceased Brother's Widow's Marriage Act 1921	74
Disability Discrimination Act 1995	170
Divorce (Religious Marriages) Act 2002	15
Divorce and Matrimonial Causes Act 1857	59, 69
s 30	69
s 31	70
Divorce Reform Act 1969	4, 7, 12, 43, 53, 69
s 2(1)	46
Domestic Proceedings and Magistrates' Courts Act 1978	22, 27, 79
Domestic Violence and Matrimonial Proceedings Act 1976	26, 79
s 1(2)	79
Domestic Violence, Crime and Victims Act 2004	28
s 1	28
s 10	28
s 12(5)	28
Sch 10	
para 38(2)	28
Equal Pay Act 1970	150, 161

Table of Statutes

European Communities Act 1972	274	Inheritance (Provision for Family and Dependants) Act 1975	78, 211
Family Allowances and National Insurance Act 1961		s 1(2)	206
s 4	76		
Family Law Act 1986	285	Law Reform (Miscellaneous Provisions) Act 1970	54
Family Law Act 1996	118, 155	Law Reform (Succession) Act 1995	81
Pt II	17	Legal Aid Act 1974	
Pt IV	27, 82	s 28(6A)	93
s 42A	28	Local Authority Social Services Act 1970	122, 124
s 47(1)	28	s 7(1)	100
s 62(3)	157		
Family Law (Scotland) Act 1985			
s 9	207		
s 21	154	Marriage Act 1753	15, 58, 150
Family Law Reform Act 1969	196, 262	Marriage Act 1836	2, 13
		Marriage Act 1949	
s 1	85	s 1	156
s 8(1)	156	Marriage Act 1994	4, 149, 156
s 21(3)(b)	262	Marriage (Enabling) Act 1960	74
Family Law Reform Act 1987	81	Marriage (Prohibited Degrees of Relationship) Act 1986	156
s 1	20, 154, 193		
Fatal Accidents Act 1976	79	Married Women's Property Act 1882	206
Sch 1			
para 2(2)	80	Married Women's Property Act 1964	42
		Matrimonial Causes Act 1857	1, 6, 12, 13, 187
Gender Recognition Act 2004	156, 157, 159, 262		
Government of Wales Act 2006		s 6	118
Sch 5, Field 15	285	Matrimonial Causes Act 1878	12, 26
Guardianship Act 1973	49, 192	s 4	26
Guardianship of Infants Act 1925	20, 48	Matrimonial Causes Act 1923	7
		Matrimonial Causes Act 1937	46
Health and Social Services and Social Security Adjudications Act 1983	103	Matrimonial Causes Act 1973	44, 212, 214, 219
		s 5	159
Sch 1	100	s 10A	201
Housing Act 1980	80	s 25	25, 191, 198
Housing Act 1988		s 25(2)(a)	219
s 39	80	s 25(2)(f)	158
Sch 4		s 41	18, 128
para 2	80	s 47	284
Human Fertilisation and Embryology Act 1990	53, 223	s 52(1)	154
		Matrimonial Homes Act 1967	27, 40, 43, 190
s 28	223		
s 31	223	Matrimonial Homes Act 1983	27
Human Fertilisation and Embryology Act 2008	223, 226, 275	Matrimonial Homes and Property Act 1981	43
		Matrimonial Proceedings and Property Act 1970	44, 47, 53, 160, 203
s 35	223		
s 36	223	Mental Capacity Act 2005	279
s 40	223	Ministry of Social Security Act 1966	
s 42	223, 275		
s 43	223, 275	s 4(2)	77
s 46	223	Sch 2	
Sch 6, para 26	275	para 3(1)	77
Sch 6, para 27	275		
Human Rights Act 1998	19, 149, 265, 272	National Assistance Act 1948	76
		National Insurance Act 1946	
s 2	266	s 17(2)	76

National Insurance (Industrial
  Injuries) Act 1946
  s 88(3) ... 76
National Service Act 1941 ... 75

Offences Against the Person Act
  1861
  s 57 ... 147
  s 58 ... 147

Pensions Act 1995
  s 166 ... 161
Pneumoconiosis etc (Workers'
  Compensation) Act 1979
  s 3(1)(c) ... 79
Police and Criminal Evidence Act
  1984
  Sch 1A
    para 14A ... 28
Prevention of Cruelty to, and
  Protection of, Children Act
  1889 ... 163
Private International Law
  (Miscellaneous Provisions)
  Act 1995
  s 5 ... 156
Property (Relationships) Act 1976
  s 11 ... 207
Protection from Harassment Act
  1997 ... 28
  s 1 ... 28
  s 4 ... 28
  s 5 ... 28
  s 5A ... 28

Punishment of Incest Act 1908 ... 164

Recognition of Divorces and Legal
  Separations Act 1971 ... 284
Registration Act 1836 ... 2
Royal Marriages Act 1772 ... 150

School Standards and Framework
  Act 1998
  s 131 ... 149, 165
Serious Organised Crime and
  Police Act 2005
  s 110 ... 28
Sexual Offences Act 2003
  s 25 ... 164
  s 26 ... 164
Social Security (Miscellaneous
  Provisions) Act 1977
  s 14(7) ... 78
Social Security Contributions and
  Benefits Act 1992
  s 130B ... 239

Welfare Reform Act 2007
  s 31 ... 239
Welfare Reform and Pensions Act
  1999 ... 81, 161
Widows', Orphans' and Old Age
  Contributory Pensions Act
  1925
  s 21(1) ... 76

TABLE OF STATUTORY INSTRUMENTS

References are to page numbers.

Adoption Agencies Regulations
2005, SI 2005/389
  reg 16   223
  Sch 1   223
Adoption (Northern Ireland) Order
1987, SI 1987/2203
  art 14   32
Adoption Support Services
Regulations 2005,
SI 2005/691   34

Child Tax Credit Regulations 2002,
SI 2002/2007
  reg 2   226
  reg 3   226
Commissioner for Children and
Young People (Northern
Ireland) Order 2003,
SI 2003/439   263

Day Care and Child Minding
(National Standards)
(England) Regulations 2003,
SI 2003/1996
  reg 5   165

Family Proceedings Rules 1991,
SI 1991/1247
  r 4.11A   135
  r 9.5   131, 137, 143, 182
Flexible Working (Eligibility,
Complaints and Remedies)
(Amendment) (No 2)
Regulations 2007,
SI 2007/2286   226
Flexible Working (Eligibility,
Complaints and Remedies)
(Amendment) Regulations
2006, SI 2006/3314   226
Flexible Working (Eligibility,
Complaints and Remedies)
(Amendment) Regulations
2007, SI 2007/1184   226

Flexible Working (Eligibility,
Complaints and Remedies)
Regulations 2002,
SI 2002/3236
  reg 3   226
Fostering Services Regulations
2002, SI 2002/57
  reg 28(5)(b)   165
  reg 38   225
Fostering Services (Wales)
Regulations 2003, SI 2003/237
  reg 38   225

Human Fertilisation and
Embryology Authority
(Disclosure of Donor
Information) Regulations
2004, SI 2004/1511   223

Magistrates' Courts (Children and
Young Persons) Rules 1970,
SI 1970/1792
  r 17(1)   91
  r 18   91
Magistrates' Courts (Children and
Young Persons) Rules 1988,
SI 1988/913   105
Magistrates' Courts Fees Order
2008, SI 2008/1052   253
Maternity and Parental Leave etc
Regulations 1999,
SI 1999/3312
  reg 13(2)   226
Matrimonial Causes Rules 1957,
SI 1957/619   152

National Assistance
(Determination of Need)
Regulations 1948, SI 1948
  reg 3   76

Paternity and Adoption Leave
Regulations 2002,
SI 2002/2788
  reg 4(2)   226
  reg 6(2)   226

CHAPTER 1

THE CONTINUING EVOLUTION OF FAMILY LAW

Gillian Douglas and Nigel Lowe

In this introductory chapter, we set the scene for the contributions that follow and draw out some key themes which underpin and emerge from our contributors' discussions of the past, current and likely future developments in family life, family policy and family law.

MODERNITY AND FAMILY LAW

As we explain in the Preface, the original motivation for this collection was to mark the 150th anniversary of the passage of the Matrimonial Causes Act 1857 and the 50th anniversary of the publication of *A Century of Family Law*.[1] The year of publication of the book, however, marks two even more important events – the 200th anniversary of Darwin's birth and the 150th anniversary of the publication of *On the Origin of Species*. A N Wilson, in *The Victorians*,[2] identifies the Matrimonial Causes Act 1857 as the point at which men and women became defined by the law, not just as property-owning, but as sexual, beings. He links this to the emphasis, in Darwin's theory of natural selection and evolution, on successful procreation as the means through which natural selection operates. We take the same starting point for the discussion in this book of what we regard as the era of 'modern' family law, and use the idea of evolution as a metaphor for understanding the changes that have happened to family life and family law since that time. Just as Darwin's theory eventually (in this country at least) displaced religious dogma in providing an explanation for the diversity of species, and contributed to the Enlightenment separation of religion from law and morality, so too did the state become the predominant arbiter of family status and regulator of family behaviour, taking over from the ecclesiastical courts and facilitated by the bureaucratisation of government. And, in the same way that Darwinian thinking emphasises the ability to adapt to change as the key to survival, so we suggest that the changes made to family law over the years reflect the extent to which it has had to adapt to the changing cultural, political and social context in which it is set in order to continue to have relevance and effectiveness in regulating and supporting family life. Indeed, the starting point to

---

[1] R Graveson and F Crane (eds) *A Century of Family Law* (Sweet & Maxwell, 1957).
[2] A N Wilson *The Victorians* (Hutchinson, 2002), p 234.

understanding these changes is the way in which *thinking* about family law has itself changed in the period under review.

Law in context

As Michael Freeman emphasises in this volume,[3] one of the most striking differences to be observed in reading the contributions in this collection as compared with those in *Graveson and Crane*[4] is the extent to which the law was seen at that time as—

> 'firmly rooted within a positivistic and legalistic framework. Family "law" was a discrete entity, not part of a social continuum ... The law was seen apart from the values it embodied, and helped to structure and restructure.'

Compare the position now, when empirical data and the insights of non-legal disciplines are used as a means of understanding how and why the law has developed in the ways it has, the impact it has had on family life – and vice versa – and how it might evolve in the future. The socio-legal approach, including especially the collection of empirical information, has come to be relied on to a major extent not only by legal scholars and policy-makers, but also by practitioners and the judiciary. Thus, not only do policy-makers use sociological and psychological findings to shape their proposals,[5] but research into how laws operate, and how the family justice system operates, plays an increasingly important role in influencing opinions and decision-making,[6] and the law is no longer seen as contained within a vacuum, preserved in some way from the contamination of the world outside the court-room and the law report.

This approach was facilitated by the bureaucratisation of family life, which could be said to have begun with the enactment of the Marriage Act 1836 and the Registration Act 1836, which enabled the collection of reliable figures for the number of births, marriages and deaths in England and Wales. Such data gave governments a greater understanding of the population as it grew rapidly during the industrial revolution, and helped them to put in place the measures to ensure order and the efficient exploitation of capital and labour during that time. It also began the statistical and sociological exploration of family behaviour which has

---

[3] 'Fifty years of family law: an opinionated review', Chapter 6 below.
[4] Above, n 1.
[5] See Cabinet Office and Department for Children, Schools and Families *Families in Britain: an evidence paper* (DCSF, 2008), which sets out 'a foundation for taking forward a discourse on how best to promote the family in the 21st century' (p 110).
[6] See, for example, Baroness Hale's reminder, in 'The future of marriage', Chapter 8 below, that the House of Lords had reference to the work of S Arthur et al *Settling Up: making financial arrangements after divorce or separation* (National Centre for Social Research, 2002) in reaching their decision in *Miller v Miller; McFarlane v McFarlane* [2006] UKHL 24, [2006] 2 AC 618.

become a key tool for our understanding of family life, and for the justification for change in family law, in more recent times.

International influences

An equally important sea-change since the 1950s has been the increasing influence of international norms,[7] and comparative law approaches, on shaping family law reforms. There was a narrow, some would say parochial, way in which the law is addressed in *A Century of Family Law*, with its emphasis on English (indeed, conservative middle England) ways of doing things, and its reference to 'the English race'.[8] The international dimension was limited to a consideration of conflicts of laws issues.[9] A striking difference, then, is how this approach has now given way to an openness to ideas and developments from elsewhere. This trend, which perhaps began with the establishment in 1965 of the Law Commission, with its willingness to look at other jurisdictions to learn how things might be done in other ways, has been both strengthened and speeded up by the growing importance of both European law, and human rights law within English domestic law.

THE CHANGING DEMOGRAPHIC PICTURE[10]

Our starting point for understanding these trends is to examine the major social and demographic shifts which have contributed significantly to changes in attitudes and behaviour and which have in turn forced those making family law to adapt it to its continually changing context.

Adult relationships

Marriage

The introduction of reliable civil statistics enables us to trace the trends in the key milestones in family life from 1838, the first full year of civil registration, onwards. In that year, there were 118,000 marriages in England and Wales. The annual numbers of marriages rose steadily until the 1970s, reaching a peak of 480,285 marriages in 1972. But since then, there has been a steady decline, so that in 2006 the number had fallen to 236,980 – the lowest number since 1895 – and by 2011 the married population is expected to be below 50 per cent of the total for the first time ever recorded. This is not a trend limited to this jurisdiction. There

---

[7] See generally, N V Lowe 'Where in the world is international family law going next?', Chapter 12 below.
[8] See Graveson and Crane, op cit, n 1 above, at the Foreword, p xvi.
[9] Ibid, ch 15; A Bland 'The Family and the Conflict of Laws'.
[10] The data cited in this section can mainly be found via http://www.statistics.gov.uk/ through sources such as the Office for National Statistics' series, *Population Trends* and *Social Trends*. Other sources are cited below.

has been a general decline in marriage rates across most of Europe, as well as in other parts of the developed world. The marriage rate in the United Kingdom in 2000 was in fact around the EU average at 5.1 marriages per 1,000 people, with Denmark having the highest rate at 6.6 per 1,000, and Sweden the lowest at 4 per 1,000.[11] In England and Wales in 2007 the marriage rate for those of marriageable age (aged 16 or over) was 21.6 per 1,000 unmarried men and 19.7 per 1,000 unmarried women, the lowest marriage rate ever recorded.

Age at marriage

There has also been an increase in the age at which people now enter into marriage. In 1970, the mean age for men marrying for the first time was 24.43 – the lowest ever recorded. This reflected a steady reduction in the age of first marriage since 1918, when the mean age was 28.14. It did not reach a figure close to this until 1992, when it rose to 28.18.[12] By 2006 it had risen to 31.8 – the highest ever recorded. For women, the figures are comparable, the average age for first marriage reaching 29.7 in 2006, from a lowest point of 22.38, also in 1970.[13]

Remarriage

Not only has marriage experienced a decline, but the number of marriages in England and Wales that were the *first* for both partners has gradually fallen from 1940, when 91 per cent of all marriages were the first for both partners. By 2007, there were 143,440 first marriages, accounting for only 62 per cent of the total. Remarriages rose by about a third between 1971 and 1972 following the introduction of the Divorce Reform Act 1969, which liberalised divorce in England and Wales and by 2007 they accounted for 38 per cent of all marriages, some 88,010.

Civil weddings

A further indication of the decline in the importance attached to religious adherence is provided by the fact that since 1992, there have been more civil marriage ceremonies in England and Wales than religious ceremonies. In 2006 civil ceremonies accounted for two-thirds of all ceremonies, with 55 per cent of these, one-third of all weddings, being performed in approved premises (up from a mere five per cent in 1996, soon after the Marriage Act 1994 permitted such ceremonies).

---

[11] Suggesting that even where countries *appear* to share many aspects of their culture, such as the Nordic states, there is room for significant variation in attitude and behaviour; see D Bradley *Family Law and Political Culture: Institutional Perspectives on Scandinavian Law* (Sweet & Maxwell, 1996).
[12] *Marriage and divorce statistics*, Historical series FM2, Vol 16 (ONS, 2006), Table 3.5a.
[13] Ibid, Table 3.5b.

Cohabitation[14]

As is well known, part of the reason for the decline in marriage has been the growth in cohabitation. Rebecca Probert shows in her chapter[15] how limited the extent of cohabitation was until relatively recently and how significant the increase in its prevalence has therefore been over the past 20 years or so. This increase is a phenomenon apparent across Europe and North America as well as in this country. European countries can be divided into three groupings, according to its incidence: the Nordic countries, where it is very common; the Benelux countries, France, Great Britain, Ireland (very recently) Germany and Austria where it is increasingly common; and Southern European countries where rates are lower. The United States would fall into the 'intermediate' category as well.

In this country, reliable data on the incidence of cohabitation are available from 1986 onwards. In that year, 11 per cent of unmarried men aged under 60 and 13 per cent of unmarried women aged under 60 were cohabiting in Great Britain. These proportions had doubled by 2006, to 24 per cent for men and 25 per cent for women, with higher rates for divorced men, of whom about one-third were cohabiting, whilst 15 per cent of single men and women did so. The peak age for cohabitation for both men and women is in their mid to late 20s, but the age of the cohabiting population is projected to rise. Government projections suggest that whilst in 2003 21 per cent of male and 18 per cent of female cohabitants were aged over 45, by 2031 these proportions will increase to 41 per cent for males and 36 per cent for females.

Cohabitation is no longer a minority experience, but has become the norm for a significant proportion of the population, with two primary significant groupings – the young, never married, and the older, previously married.[16] However, cohabitation is not a uniform relationship – researchers have identified a variety of types of cohabitation which reflect the differing motivations for entering into it. These include pre-marital cohabitation, which may be a 'trial marriage' in which the parties are testing out the durability of their relationship with a view to marrying eventually, or a partnership entered into before the couple are ready to 'commit', and taking the place of what would formerly have been a 'boyfriend/girlfriend' relationship. There are also increasing numbers of

---

[14] For data and sources, see G Douglas et al *A Failure of Trust: Resolving Property Disputes on Cohabitation Breakdown* (Cardiff University/University of Bristol, 2007), ch 2.
[15] 'Looking back on the overlooked: cohabitants and the law 1857–2007', Chapter 3 below.
[16] In many respects, England and Wales are now at the stage the Scandinavian countries had reached at the end of the 1970s, when an important conference of the International Society of Family Law was held on the subject in Sweden, resulting in a seminal collection of essays: J Eekelaar and S Katz (eds) *Marriage and Cohabitation in Contemporary Societies: Areas of Legal, Social and Ethical Change* (Butterworths, 1980). See further, Baroness Hale, Chapter 8 below.

couples who cohabit as an alternative to marriage, although evidence suggests that this is not always due to a positive choice to do so, or a positive rejection of marriage, but may often reflect ambivalence or uncertainty on the part of one or both partners as to the desirability or viability of a 'permanent' relationship with the other.[17]

The demographic evidence certainly shows that the duration of cohabitation is increasing, although it is difficult to calculate this authoritatively. Surveys asking respondents how long their cohabiting relationship has lasted can only indicate its duration up to the time of interview, and not, of course, how much longer it will last. Nonetheless, Haskey[18] reported that the median duration of cohabitation increased between 1986 and 1998, for single men from just under 2 years to just over 3 years, and for single women from roughly 18 months to over 3 years. Divorced men and women's cohabiting relationships lasted about one-third longer. Barlow and James[19] found rather longer durations, with an average of six and a half years and the median exceeding 4 years. They contrast these figures with the median duration of marriages ending in divorce, at 10.7 years in 2003.

Moreover, an increasing number of cohabiting couples are having children within that relationship (rather than marrying when the child is born). The percentage of British families with dependent children has remained stable since the 1980s, at around 60 per cent, but the proportion of these which were formed by cohabiting partners grew from one in 30 in 1986 to one in 12 by 1998 (although it appears that cohabiting couples have fewer children than married couples). Such data suggest that cohabitation is assuming a greater significance in people's life cycles, although it may be premature to assert that it should be regarded as functionally equivalent to marriage.

Divorce

By contrast with the rise in cohabitation, the past decade has seen a halt to the otherwise more or less inexorable increase in divorce witnessed since the original introduction of judicial divorce in the Victorian era. As well as social changes prompting shifts in divorcing behaviour, it is also possible to trace clear linkages in the numbers of divorces (as distinct from marriage breakdowns and separations) in England and Wales with the ease of divorce, and hence to changes in divorce laws. In the first year of the operation of the Matrimonial Causes Act 1857, 24 decrees absolute were granted. Thereafter, numbers rose gradually until the aftermath of

---

[17] See in particular, Douglas et al, op cit and C Smart and P Stevens *Cohabitation Breakdown* (Joseph Rowntree Foundation, 2000).

[18] J Haskey 'Cohabitation in Great Britain: past, present and future trends – and attitudes' (2001) 103 *Population Trends* (Spring) 4.

[19] A Barlow and G James 'Regulating Marriage and Cohabitation in 21st Century Britain' (2004) 67 MLR 143 at 154.

the First World War, which saw an increase from a few hundreds per annum into the two to three thousands. The next change occurred in 1924, following the equalisation of the ground for divorce for both men and women by the Matrimonial Causes Act 1923. From that point on, apart from during the Second World War (reflecting the inevitable strains and temptations of being separated by the exigencies of wartime and military service), more divorces were granted to women than to men. The war caused another jump in numbers, with a 'freak' year in 1947 when the total reached 60,254. Thereafter, with a reversion to 'normality', the numbers declined until a low point in 1958 of 22,654. But after that year, they rose by a few thousand each year until the Divorce Reform Act 1969 came fully into effect, producing a new peak in 1972 of 119,025. As the remaining stigma attached to divorce fell away, the numbers continued to rise, until the highest point was reached in 1993, when 165,018 decrees absolute were granted. Since then, as the age of marriage has increased, and the rate of cohabitation has grown, numbers have turned down, with 2007 recording the lowest number of divorces, at 128,393, since 1976.[20]

This produced a divorce *rate* per 1,000 married people of 11.9, compared with a high of 13.5 in 1991 and a recent low of only 2.1 in 1961. European comparisons may be made, although the rate is measured per 1,000 population (not per married persons only). By this measure, in 2000/2001, countries in northern and western Europe typically had the highest divorce rates, while the Irish Republic and countries in southern Europe had the lowest, reflecting religious and cultural as well as legal and social differences. The EU average was 1.9 per 1,000 people, with a range from Belgium, which, perhaps surprisingly, had the highest divorce rate at 2.9 divorces per 1,000, to Italy and the Irish Republic, which had the lowest rates, at 0.7 per 1,000 people. The rate in the United Kingdom by this measure was 2.6 per 1,000.

It is well known that certain factors make marriages more prone to end in divorce, including getting married at a younger age. This is reflected in the divorce rates – men and women aged 25 to 29 had the highest divorce rates in 2007, at 26.6 divorces per 1,000 married men and 26.9 divorces per 1,000 married women. However, with the general trend towards marrying later, the average age at divorce was much higher, at 43.7 for men, and 41.2 for women. Other factors associated with divorce are pre-marital births, pre-marital cohabitation and a spouse who has previously been married. As we saw above, the latter two are strong trends in recent years, so one would expect the divorce rate to rise. However, it is likely that those couples who would, formerly, have entered into marriage but whose relationships might have been fragile, are now cohabiting

---

[20] ONS *Marriage and divorce statistics* (Historical series FM2 No 16) 'Divorces: 1858–2003, number of couples divorcing, by party petitioning/granted decree' (2006).

instead, and contributing to a higher rate of relationship breakdown amongst cohabitants[21] than amongst spouses.

Having children

Births outside marriage

Not only has marriage become less central to the formation and sustaining of adult intimate relationships, but the next stage in family formation – having children – has seen a similar displacement of wedlock as the sine qua non for 'starting a family'. The rate of births outside marriage has seen a similar significant increase since the 1960s. In 2006, 43.7 per cent of all births in the UK occurred outside marriage, compared with 25.2 per cent in 1988. This increase reflects the rise in cohabitation rather than a rise in 'fatherless' families. Around four-fifths of such births are jointly registered, of which around 60 per cent are registered by parents living at the same address.[22]

Lone parenthood

The rise in divorce and the potential fragility of cohabiting relationships also mean that more children are likely to spend part of their childhoods living with only one parent. The proportion of children living with one parent has more than trebled over the past 35 years, to nearly one-quarter (23 per cent) in 2007. Over this period the proportion of children living with their fathers has remained constant, at around 2 per cent, whereas the proportion living with their mothers has risen from 6 to 21 per cent.

Stepfamilies

Again, a consequence of the growth in divorce and the breakdown of relationships has been an increase in the number of stepfamilies. In 2001, around 0.7 million – 10 per cent – of all families with dependent children in the UK were stepfamilies. Around 57 per cent of these were married couple stepfamilies, and 42 per cent were cohabiting couple stepfamilies.[23] Another way of looking at these statistics is to note that 'step' families are more common amongst cohabitants – 38 per cent of all cohabiting couple families with dependent children were stepfamilies, compared with only 8 per cent of married couple families with dependent children. By contrast, married couple stepfamilies were more likely than cohabiting couple stepfamilies to have natural children in the family as well as stepchildren: 57 per cent compared with 35 per cent.

---

[21] J Ermisch and M Francesconi 'Marriage And Cohabitation' in R Berthoud and J Gershuny *Seven years in the lives of British families* (Policy Press, 2001).
[22] ONS *Birth statistics: Review of the Registrar General on births and patterns of family building in England and Wales, 2006* Series FM1, No 35 (2007).
[23] Of course, in law, only couples who are married to each other are generally recognised as 'step' parents: see, for example, Children Act 1989, s 4A(1) (acquisition of parental responsibility by agreement or court order).

Since children tend to stay with their mother after parental separation, the majority (84 per cent) of stepfamilies in Great Britain in 2006 consisted of the natural mother and her new partner, compared with 10 per cent of families with a natural father and stepmother. Whilst the proportion of children living with their natural mother and a stepfather remained fairly stable (between 83 and 88 per cent), the proportion of children staying with their natural father doubled, from 6 per cent to 12 per cent during the 1990s, although this proportion decreased to 10 per cent in 2006.

The elderly

As Freeman points out,[24] one of the most important demographic trends in terms of implications for the future of family law and policy is the growth in the proportion of the population that is elderly. The UK's population is ageing, with the proportion of the population who are children aged under 16 declining from a quarter in 1971, to a fifth today. The number of people aged 65 and over is expected to exceed the number aged under 16 by 2021. This poses major problems in terms of economic viability and social stability and such problems are common throughout Europe, with several states in the EU already having a greater proportion of the population aged above 65 than under 16.[25]

The problems are exacerbated by the fact that women outnumber men in the population, but are poorer and have worse pensions because of the years they devote to home-making and child-rearing and the structural inequalities in the world of work. In 2006, there were one and a half million more women then men aged 65 or over, and although men's life expectancy is improving at a faster rate than women's, older women will still outnumber men by more than a million in 2026. Two-thirds of women aged over 75 are widowed, compared with one-third of men.

Diversity of the population

Same-sex partnerships

Perhaps the most striking difference in the demographic picture from that which underpinned *Graveson and Crane* is the diversity of the UK's population in terms of ethnicity and differing family forms. The growth in, and the diversity of, cohabiting couples in the past 20 years have already been noted, but it would surely have been unimaginable in the 1950s (or even the 1980s) to envisage the introduction, in all but name, of same-sex marriage through the creation of civil partnerships by the Civil Partnership Act 2004, which came into force in December 2005.[26] In that

---

[24] In Chapter 6 below.
[25] Italy, Germany, Greece, Bulgaria, Portugal, Latvia, Estonia, Spain and Slovenia: ONS *Social Trends 2008*, p 3.
[26] S M Cretney *Same Sex Relationships: From Odious Crime to Gay Marriage* (Oxford University Press, 2006).

month alone, nearly 2,000 couples registered their partnership, and by the end of 2007, 26,787 had been recorded. However, numbers fell back after the initial surge of couples who had been waiting to obtain legal recognition, and during 2007 some 8,728 were registered. Male couples formed a slight majority (between 50 and 60 per cent) of those registered.[27] The question of how far the financial and other consequences of the dissolution of such partnerships should be dealt with in the same way as on divorce now falls to the judiciary to resolve.

Ethnic minorities

Finally, it is important too to note the growth in the proportion of minority ethnic groups which may have different attitudes and norms of conduct in respect of family life to those of the white majority. In 2008, ethnic minority communities constituted 8 per cent of the population in Great Britain; 45 per cent of these were of South Asian origin and 22 per cent African or African-Caribbean. The different communities have distinctive family models: whilst 92 per cent of children living in Indian families, 81 per cent in Pakistani/Bangladeshi and 79 per cent in white families, were living in families headed by a couple, just under 50 per cent of black families were headed by a lone parent. Mixed, Black Caribbean and White families with dependent children had the largest proportions of cohabiting couple families, 12 per cent each. Cohabitation was less common among Asian, Chinese and other ethnic group families (each below 4 per cent).

A PROCESS OF EVOLUTION

It is hardly surprising that, with all these major changes, politicians have become more cautious – or more aware of the complexity – in making general assertions about desirable family forms. There is, for example, a significant difference in tone in the Labour Government's most recent paper[28] on families compared to their first discussion paper published in 1998. Then, their approach was criticised for preferring marriage over other family forms.[29] For example, they proclaimed:

> 'This Government believes that marriage provides a strong foundation for stable relationships. This does not mean trying to make people marry, or criticising or penalizing people who choose not to ... But we do share the belief of the majority of people that marriage provides the most reliable framework for raising children.'[30]

---

[27] Apart from in Scotland, where the proportions were reversed.
[28] Cabinet Office and Department for Children, Schools and Families *Families in Britain: an evidence paper* (DCSF, 2008), p 110.
[29] See eg R Probert 'Cohabitation in Twentieth Century England and Wales: Law and Policy' (2004) 26(1) *Law and Policy* 13 at 26.
[30] Home Office *Supporting Families* (1998), para 4.3.

By 2008, in *Families in Britain: an evidence paper*, they were adopting a more Darwinian approach:

> 'The family has also shown itself able to endure, shape and adapt to changes in social and economic circumstances, and it continues to do so today. So we see an increasing range of family structures, to the extent that there is arguably no longer a one size fits all family in Britain today. But this is diversity and not decline. Warm, loving and stable relationships matter more for our happiness and wellbeing than the legal form of a relationship. And while marriage will remain of central importance, the reality in many people's everyday lives is that more and more families experience a range of family forms throughout their life time. There is no single family form that guarantees happiness or success. All types of family can, in the right circumstances, look after their family members, help them get on in life and, for their children, have high hopes and the wherewithal to put them on the path to success.'

In many ways, then, the family law world that we now inhabit can be seen to have changed out of all recognition even from the relatively recent standpoint of the 1950s. The ideas that same-sex couples (who would certainly not have been so described at that time) could obtain the same legal rights as spouses, or that serious consideration would be given to putting cohabiting partners (who again would have been described in rather more pejorative terms) on a similar par as married ones,[31] would have been inconceivable. Moreover, the possibility that having children outside wedlock would no longer carry a stigma, and that unmarried fathers would have the same parental rights as other parents would have been equally unthinkable.[32]

Yet, in some respects, the law has shown remarkable continuity during the era under examination – the law on obtaining a divorce, for example, would still look very familiar to a Victorian matrimonial practitioner. Whilst the approach to children in need of protection from neglect or abuse might now seem much more 'interventionist' than would have been acceptable at that time, the scholars contributing to *A Century of Family Law* 50 years ago would have recognised aspects of the processes we now use, such as emergency protection orders, and even the requirement to satisfy the threshold criteria – although it is noteworthy that they themselves devoted no chapter to the topic in their own volume. Victorian scholars would also have appreciated the ways, sometimes somewhat haphazard, in which legal reforms have come about in the past century (which Stephen Cretney discusses in this volume),[33] having lived through or benefited from the efforts of nineteenth century reforming

---

[31] Law Commission *Cohabitation: The Financial Consequences of Relationship Breakdown* (Law Com No 307). See further, Probert, Chapter 3 below.
[32] For further consideration of the differences between then and now, see Freeman, Chapter 6 below.
[33] SM Cretney 'The troublemakers: cranks, psychiatrists and other mischievous nuisances – their role in reform of English family law in the nineteenth and twentieth centuries', Chapter 2 below.

'troublemakers' such as Lady Caroline Norton[34] and Frances Power Cobbe.[35] The Faculty of Laws at King's College London would no doubt have regarded themselves as entirely comfortable with the concept of gender equality which now permeates all of family law thinking, even if they included no female contributor in their own volume. And they would also have understood the importance of procedure to the experience of those engaging with what was not then called the family justice system, having been well acquainted with the work of A P Herbert in holding up to ridicule the process of obtaining a 'Brighton divorce' in the 1930s.[36]

How, then, have the demographic and social changes outlined above impacted upon the continuing development of family law, and what challenges might the law have to face in the future? We identify three different strands – cultural, political and social.

The cultural legacy of religion

As noted at the outset, the 1857 Act marks a moment when the source and arbiter of family law and values began to shift decisively away from the Anglican church to the state. However, it would be wrong to assume that secularism held sway from that point onward. Indeed, it is clear that legal attitudes, as demonstrated through both statute and case law, have remained heavily influenced by Christian values. As Hamilton put it, 'Christian ideals and morals infused the common law and later legislation on marriage'.[37] From the 1857 Act, down until the major reform of divorce law in 1969, Christianity, especially Anglicanism, remained a powerful force in influencing the approach taken to family issues. With the general liberalisation of social and moral attitudes during the latter part of the twentieth century, particularly the 1960s and subsequently, it is true that the law then shifted towards a more overtly secular stance, and from the 60s onwards, especially, the established Church had less influence on the direction and content of law reform (which is not to say that it had none, as the continuing peculiarities of modern-day marriage preliminaries and formalities demonstrate). But the development of family law remained in the hands of a *culturally* Christian legislature and a judiciary applying a culturally Christian jurisprudence.

---

[34] Whose campaign for separated mothers resulted in the enactment of the Custody of Infants Act 1839 (known as 'Talfourd's Act'), which empowered the Court of Chancery to give the mother custody of her children until the age of 7, and access to them until the age of majority, provided she had not committed adultery. See A Chedzoy *A Scandalous Woman* (Allison and Busby, 1992).

[35] Who brought 'wife beating' to the attention of the Victorian public, resulting in the Matrimonial Causes Act 1878, which enabled magistrates to make separation and maintenance orders in favour of wives whose husbands had been convicted of aggravated assault on them. See L Williamson *Power and Protect: Frances Power Cobbe and Victorian Society* (Rivers Oram Press, 2001).

[36] A P Herbert *Holy Deadlock* (Methuen, 1934).

[37] C Hamilton *Family, Law and Religion* (Sweet & Maxwell, 1995), p 79.

Thus, even today, in our multi-cultural society, the conception of marriage in English law remains fundamentally that which was set out at the beginning of our 'modern' era by Lord Penzance in *Hyde v Hyde* – a case concerning the (non-)recognition of a Mormon, polygamous, marriage – where he held that:

> 'marriage, as understood in Christendom, may ... be defined as the voluntary union for life of one man and one woman to the exclusion of all others ... it is obvious that the matrimonial law of this country is adapted to the Christian marriage.'[38]

The reference to 'Christendom' was not mere surplusage. The judge was concerned throughout his judgment to emphasise the difference between the Christian concept of marriage which applied within the jurisdiction, and other forms of 'marriage' (if such they might be called) which might obtain elsewhere. The English legal model of marriage, therefore, was unequivocally a Christian model of marriage.

Commentators have noted that, even at the time this dictum was delivered, it was inaccurate, since the possibility of judicial divorce had been made a reality through the enactment of the 1857 Act and the case was itself a suit for divorce.[39] Moreover, entry into marriage through rites other than the Anglican form had been recognised, in the case of Quakers and Jews, since the Clandestine Marriages Act 1753, and for other religions (and none) since the Marriage Act 1836. Nonetheless, it survives as a useful and concise, though incomplete, definition of marriage as it is still basically understood in this jurisdiction, pending a successful challenge under the European Convention on Human Rights.[40] Polygamous marriages, whilst they may be recognised if validly contracted abroad, cannot be celebrated in this jurisdiction, and registered same-sex partnerships are not yet legally regarded as 'marriages', even if popular culture has embraced them as such.[41]

It might be argued that the minutiae of marriage law are bound to carry traces of their canonical origins, but the influence of English Christian culture goes far beyond arcane technicalities. The same influence can be seen in modern-day approaches to disputes between parents over the care and upbringing of their children. At the start of our era, it was enshrined in the common law (but derived from Christian precepts)[42] that the father of a legitimate child had full parental rights, through the concept of guardianship, until the child reached the age of majority at 21, and the

---

[38] (1866) LR 1 P & D 130 at 133 and 135.
[39] See N V Lowe and G Douglas *Bromley's Family Law* (Oxford UP, 10th edn, 2007), p 41.
[40] See below.
[41] From the celebration by the celebrity press of the 'wedding' of Sir Elton John to the story line of the 'marriage' of two gay characters in the longest-running radio soap opera in the world, the BBC's 'The Archers'.
[42] See, for example, Slesser LJ in *Re Carroll* [1931] 1 KB 317, CA at 354.

mother had no rights at all.[43] As is well known, challenges were increasingly made to this absolutist position and mothers eventually gained equal rights over their children.[44] However, the dilemma of how to decide disputes between two equally positioned parents was resolved by asserting the paramountcy of the child's welfare as the determining criterion.[45] In establishing what will be in a child's best interests, the courts have regard to a checklist of relevant factors,[46] to any evidence put forward by the parties and to any recommendations made by a Cafcass officer, and will then exercise their discretion. In so doing, they cannot avoid being influenced by their own mindsets and the prevailing cultural ethos. Thus, in a number of cases concerning religious circumcision,[47] for example, the courts have preferred to take the view that it should be left to the child to decide when he is old enough whether to undergo the ritual procedure, rather than to give effect to the deep significance which circumcision carries for Muslims and Jews as a sign of a child's belonging to a faith community right from his birth. This is not, it is submitted, because of an adherence to a children's rights approach, but because of a view of religion – emanating from Christian beliefs – as something that must be positively embraced through conscious acceptance, rather than something that is an inherent part of a child's identity based on his or her family background.

Yet such cases[48] are becoming more common, reflecting the growth in 'faith' as a perceived issue of public policy, as well as a matter of private identity. As minority ethnic groups which are particularly associated with certain faiths, such as Islam and Sikhism, continue to grow, they will become more influential in setting the public agenda and will be able to rely on their right to freedom of religion enshrined in Art 9 of the European Convention on Human Rights, and equivalent rights and

---

[43] In the case of a child born outside marriage, neither parent initially had any rights over the child, which was classed as a *filius nullius*. However, through amendments to the Poor Law, the mother came to be regarded as exercising parental rights – though this was more to ensure that the liability to care for and support the child was met than to bestow positive rights on women.

[44] See further below.

[45] Now codified in s 1 of the Children Act 1989. See N V Lowe 'The House of Lords and the Welfare Principle' in C Bridge (ed) *Family Law Towards the Millennium – Essays for P M Bromley* (Butterworths, 1997).

[46] Children Act 1989, s 1(3).

[47] See eg *Re J (Specific Issue Orders: Muslim Upbringing and Circumcision)* [2000] 1 FLR 571, CA; *Re S (Specific Issue Order: Religion: Circumcision)* [2004] EWHC 1282 (Fam), [2005] 1 FLR 236.

[48] And many others, particularly concerning the manifestation of religious beliefs: see, for example, *R (Williamson) v Secretary of State for Education and Employment* [2005] UKHL 15, [2005] 2 AC 246; *R (Begum) v Headteacher and Governors of Denbigh High School* [2006] UKHL 15, [2007] 1 AC 100; *R (on the application of X) v The Headteacher of Y School* [2007] EWHC 298 (Admin), [2008] 1 All ER 249; *R (Playfoot) v Governing Body of Millais School* [2007] HRLR 34; *R (Watkins-Singh) v Governing Body of Aberdare Girls' High School* [2008] EWHC 1865 (Admin), [2008] ELR 561. For discussion of such cases, see E Sutherland 'A Veiled Threat to Children's Rights? Religious Dress in Schools and the Rights of Young People' (2008) *Juridical Review* 143.

obligations contained in EU and domestic law.[49] They may seek recognition in the civil law of their particular values and codes of behaviour. There is, of course, a very long-standing precedent for such recognition. Lord Hardwicke's Act of 1753 preserved the rights – and rites – to marry of Jews and Quakers, and modern marriage formalities are a complex collection of rules which permit adherents of these and many other religions to marry according to their own 'usages', provided that they conform to some basic requirements. A more modern example is the Divorce (Religious Marriages) Act 2002. This allows a court to order that a decree of divorce is not to be made absolute until (in effect) a religious divorce has been obtained from the Jewish courts (the Beth Din). This is intended to enable Jewish women, who cannot be granted a religious divorce without their husband's co-operation, to remain married under the civil law until the husband has complied with the religious procedures. The provision could be extended to other 'prescribed' religions, if required.

This utilisation of the civil law coming to the 'aid' of religious communities reflects a new sensitivity to the concerns of religious minorities and shows that, far from an onward, inevitable march towards a purely secular approach to family matters, which one might have predicted at the end of the 1960s, for example, we have instead experienced the resurgence of religious belief as a justification for particular positions and privileges. As the controversy which was prompted by the thoughts of the Archbishop of Canterbury[50] on these matters showed in 2008, it will not be a straightforward matter to reconcile the often competing religious, cultural and political values which underpin family life, but we can surely expect religion to assume a greater significance in the shaping of family law in the future.

State intervention in the family

Alongside the influence of religion on legal attitudes to the family, another key aspect has been the liberal view drawn from political philosophy of the family as belonging to the private sphere and beyond the scope of government investigation and intervention. This attitude was linked to the notion of patriarchy and the husband/father's position as head of the family and household. Society and the state could rely on the male head to keep order within the family and to represent it to the outside world and need not delve further. Thus, until the flowering of the child-saving movement that saw the establishment of charities such as the NSPCC and Dr Barnardo's,[51] the common law remained firmly attached

---

[49] Especially the right under the Equality Act 2006, Pt 2 not to be discriminated against in the provision of goods and services.
[50] 'Civil and Religious Law in England: a Religious Perspective' (Royal Courts of Justice, 7 February 2008).
[51] Such organisations were themselves heavily influenced by evangelical Christianity and saw 'child saving' as the saving of souls: Benjamin Waugh, the founder of the NSPCC,

to the concept of the primacy of parental rights and, until amending legislation was passed in 1891, Barnardo, in particular, lost a number of legal actions where parents who had placed children in his homes then claimed them back.[52] Yet it should not be forgotten that *social* control over family behaviour, and pressure to conform with prevailing values, always played a part in the regulation of family life, and close ties between extended family groups, a less individualistic approach to identity and a strong enforcement of a sense of shame and stigma no doubt served to open up many families to outside scrutiny, even if it was not the scrutiny of the coercive organs of the state. And, as John Eekelaar notes in his chapter,[53] the 'community', be it a family, peer group or ethnic minority, can continue to exert control over individuals within the group, to their disadvantage and jeopardy.

With the growth in recognition of the separate interests – and eventually rights – of other family members, the reliance on the patriarchal head became unsustainable. Older views, which approved or tolerated male violence over women, for example, were no longer acceptable as feminism came to influence attitudes and values. Now, a new dilemma had to be resolved. How could the family unit which forms the 'basic building-block' of society be supported whilst at the same time paying due attention to the needs and vulnerability of those within that unit? What was to be done if the head of the family could not be relied upon to safeguard and promote their wellbeing?

The answer, for the late-Victorians, and for those who later built the welfare state in the 1940s, lay in the realm of public action, at least so far as working-class families were concerned. Whilst the Victorians might rely on charitable initiatives, backed up by legal recognition of their value,[54] twentieth-century governments (even that of Margaret Thatcher) regarded the beneficial power of the state as the key to social improvement, with much of that power delivered through the activities of the courts. The development of a distinct 'family justice system' and the creation of (in all but name) distinct 'family courts' took a long time and arguably still has to be completed, but as Mervyn Murch's chapter[55] shows, the use of the courts to handle family problems became embedded in the social system. Court processes, backed up by welfare services such

---

was a Congregationalist minister; Thomas Barnardo, whose father was Jewish, converted to the Plymouth Brethren in his teens. For a full history, see I Pinchbeck and M Hewitt *Children in English Society* (Routledge and Kegan Paul: Vol 1, 1969; Vol 2, 1973).

[52] *Barnardo v McHugh* [1891] AC 388, HL; *Barnardo v Ford* [1892] AC 326, HL. Legislation putting the onus on the parent to show that he or she was fit to resume care of a child entrusted to another person was enacted in the Custody of Children Act 1891.

[53] 'Law, family and community', Chapter 7 below.

[54] Such as the authorisation of the activities of officers of the NSPCC, or the involvement of 'court missionaries' in the work of the magistrates' courts: see J Doughty 'From court missionaries to conflict resolution: a century of family court welfare' [2008] CFLQ 131.

[55] 'Cultural change and the family justice system', Chapter 5 below.

as those now delivered by Cafcass and local authorities, became an important aspect of the welfare state.

But in a 'free' and liberal society, 'private' life cannot be opened up willy-nilly to the agents of the state, however benign. Murch shows how two basic contradictory social values have been in play in the system's approach to the family; on the one hand, social control over 'deviant' families, and on the other, support to families and children caught up in the complexities of litigation. As Judith Masson demonstrates,[56] modern family law continues to wrestle with the need to strike an appropriate balance between these. Over the period under scrutiny, this has been struck in different places, as can be demonstrated by a consideration of private and public child law (which terms themselves reveal the attempt to preserve a dichotomy between the use of the courts as a voluntarily invoked *service* to aid family members to resolve disputes between themselves, and as a coercive mechanism applied against those family members who do not appear properly to conform to the prevailing social norms concerning the upbringing of children).

Take, for example, the law's approach to the potential risks to children of parental separation and divorce. It is well known that these are statistically associated with an increased likelihood of psychological harm, lower educational attainment, greater social risk-taking (drinking, drug-use), poorer employment prospects, higher rates of relationship breakdown in adulthood, etc.[57] The causal relationship is difficult to identify, and much recent research has emphasised parental conflict and stress, rather than relationship break-up per se, as the contributing factors. But, there is little support for the view that marriages can or should be held together 'for the sake of the children';[58] divorce is readily available and of course, increasing numbers of couples with children are not married to each other in the first place. How, then, can the risks to children be reduced? Since the 1950s, and building upon a recommendation first made by Denning J (as he then was) when reviewing the law in the context of the increase in the overall numbers of divorces after the Second World War,[59] there has been a 'welfare check' incorporated into the divorce process so that the courts may satisfy themselves as to the future well-being of the children of married couples at least. The nature of this check, however, has changed. At a time when divorce was seen as a growing social problem, yet one which was still *out of the ordinary* in the 1950s and 1960s, the 'need' for particular scrutiny of the arrangements that couples made for their children was regarded as justified, even if it

---

[56] 'Caring for our future generations', Chapter 10 below.
[57] B Rodgers and J Pryor *Divorce and separation: the outcomes for children* (Joseph Rowntree Foundation, 1998).
[58] Notwithstanding the last-ditch attempt to reinstate such a view during the passage of the (now abandoned) Family Law Act 1996, Pt II, on which see H Rees *Divorcing Responsibly* (Hart, 2003).
[59] Denning J *Report of the Committee on Procedure in Matrimonial Causes* Cmd 7024 (1947).

meant that middle-class or even aristocratic families would be subject to such a check. As divorce became commonplace, however, socio-legal research uncovered the fact that the 'check' was usually a waste of time for both judges and parents, providing little or no means of actually evaluating the merits of the arrangements and doing little more than reassuring some mothers that they were indeed doing the best they could in the circumstances.[60] By the time the Law Commission undertook its fundamental reform of child law in the 1980s, it could conclude that it was no longer necessary for courts positively to be satisfied as to the arrangements made for the children. But – given the growing body of research emphasising the possible risks to children – some attention still had to (seem to) be paid to the welfare of those individual children whose parents were divorcing regardless of the children's own objective interests. So a new provision was put in place, abolishing the need to see the judge to discuss the arrangements, and enabling the courts to approve the divorce unless positively *dissatisfied* with those arrangements, the details of which were to be gleaned from completion of a pro forma rather than a face-to-face interview with the parent/s. In this way, the assumption that most parents could be *trusted* to do what is best for their children could be applied, whilst providing a back-stop – in theory at least – should suspicions be roused that this was not so, in which case, it would be *legitimate* for the state to 'intervene' – or, at least, try to find out more.[61]

In the past few years, a debate has been generated over whether the family courts should be open to full public and media scrutiny as a means of ensuring fairness in decision-making, even in the 'private law' sphere of disputes between parents.[62] Those advocating such openness include both supporters of fathers' rights who argue that the courts tend to favour mothers,[63] and those concerned that care proceedings are weighted in favour of local authorities seeking to remove children from their families. It is in the 'public child law' domain that state intervention is of course most overt and potentially most coercive. Yet, as is well known, at the same time as campaigns are waged for tighter control over the exercise of their powers by social workers and the courts, an equally insistent and persuasive lobby can be generated when a case emerges which appears to show a lack of scrutiny and urgency in protecting children at risk. Every decade since the 1940s has had its share of scandals, with the same lessons being identified every time – better communication between agencies, better co-ordination of action, and greater attention paid to the child

---

[60] G Davis, A Macleod and M Murch 'Undefended Divorce: Should s 41 of the Matrimonial Causes Act 1973 be Repealed?' (1983) 46 MLR 121.

[61] For consideration of the nature of this process as being equally ineffective as that which it replaced, see G Douglas et al 'Safeguarding children's welfare in non-contentious divorce: towards a new conception of the divorce process' (2000) 63 MLR 177.

[62] Ministry of Justice *Confidence and Confidentiality: Openness in family courts – a new approach* CP 10/07 (2007); *Family Justice in View* CP(R) 10/07 (2008).

[63] An argument comprehensively demolished by empirical research undertaken by J Hunt and A Macleod *Outcomes of applications to court for contact orders after parental separation or divorce* (Ministry of Justice, 2008), discussed further below.

rather than the adults. While the current system may be criticised for its lack of adequate scrutiny of local authority actions, Mary Hayes's chapter[64] reminds us of how little control was exerted over local authorities in the system which preceded the Children Act 1989, a system which, in several key features, was eventually found wanting by the European Court of Human Rights.[65] Yet Richard White's chapter[66] warns of the risks both of reverting to that unaccountable system and to leaving children unprotected due to financial cut-backs and a reluctance to face up to the responsibilities that the state owes to its most vulnerable citizens.

The eventual incorporation of the European Convention on Human Rights into English law obviated the need to go to Strasbourg to remedy the law's shortcomings, but more importantly served to require a 'human rights' approach to be brought into the discourse and thinking surrounding family law. The evolution of family law thus took a new direction. The commentators of 1957 might have traced a linear shift in family law (at least in terms of statutory provisions) towards equality between men and women, fathers and mothers. They could then have demonstrated a move towards 'the child's welfare' as the tie-breaker where parents enjoyed equal rights and equal standing. Of course, neither the shift towards equality, nor the acceptance of the child's welfare as 'paramount' had reached anything like full fruition by 1957. It could be argued that it took until the Children Act 1989 abolished the common law concept of the father's guardianship for mothers to achieve true equality with fathers of children born inside marriage, and until the landmark decision of the House of Lords in *J v C*[67] for the welfare principle to become truly paramount. Commentators in the early 1990s could have noted a further fundamental change in the law, away from a focus on parental rights towards parental responsibility, in relation to both the care – under the Children Act – and the maintenance – under the Child Support Act 1991 – of children. Indeed, as Masson argues,[68] recent proposals concerning the mandatory registration of the father's name on a child's birth certificate also reflect an emphasis on making parents take responsibility for their children.

But the enactment of the Human Rights Act 1998 meant that rights suddenly assumed a renewed importance. It is no longer possible to dismiss an argument based on 'parental rights' as outmoded thinking. Now, a new balance must be struck between the right to respect for family

---

[64] M Hayes 'Removing children from their families – law and policy before the Children Act 1989', Chapter 4 below.
[65] See eg *R v United Kingdom* [1988] 2 FLR 445 (parental rights resolutions); *O v United Kingdom* (1987) 10 EHRR 82 (lack of means of challenging decisions denying contact).
[66] 'The future of welfare law for children', Chapter 11.
[67] [1970] AC 668; see N V Lowe 'The House of Lords and the Welfare Principle' in C Bridge (ed) *Family Law Towards the Millennium – Essays for P M Bromley* (Butterworths, 1997).
[68] See Chapter 10 below.

life of each family member.[69] The welfare of the child will still trump the rights of parents when weighing their competing interests,[70] but proportionality is the new tie-breaker where the dispute is between the family and the state.[71] Whether this is as nebulous and indeterminate a concept as the welfare principle is arguable. Whilst 'welfare' has the benefit of being capable of being tied to factual circumstances (eg is it objectively in the child's best interests to be removed from a long-term foster placement to be placed with strangers of a similar ethnic group with a view to adoption?), proportionality is a legal concept with a growing jurisprudential base drawn not just from family law but across the field of human rights law and it can therefore be tested more rigorously against both domestic and Strasbourg interpretations of its scope. It seems a safe prediction that it will be at the forefront of attention in both judicial and statutory law-making in relation to the family in the years to come.

The gender and class dimensions in family law

Finally, the evolution of family law has been pervasively influenced by gender and class issues. We have already noted the gradual equalisation of the position of mothers and fathers within the married family, with perhaps the most fundamental change coming in the Guardianship of Infants Act 1925, which, as part of the general political emancipation of women at the time, provided that, in any proceedings before a court, neither the father nor the mother should be regarded as having a claim superior to the other in respect of the custody or upbringing of a child.[72] Gender equality developments in family law in the past fifty years have moved from a focus on wives to the position of women in general, and more recently to the position of men as family members too. For example, the decline in the stigma attached to having children outside marriage no doubt benefited unmarried mothers and their children first of all, and the law caught up eventually by abolishing the disadvantages attached to 'illegitimacy' and removing the term from the legal lexicon.[73] But with the growth in cohabitation and the general social recognition in the past decade of fathers as carers of (or at least about)[74] their children, the position of unmarried fathers has also been transformed, so that they now automatically acquire parental responsibility (increasingly seen as a

---

[69] J Herring 'The Human Rights Act and the welfare principle in family law – conflicting or complementary?' [1999] CFLQ 233; J Fortin 'The HRA's impact on litigation involving children and their families' [1999] CFLQ 237.
[70] See eg *Yousef v Netherlands* [2003] 1 FLR 210, ECHR.
[71] *TP and KM v United Kingdom* [2001] 2 FLR 549, ECHR.
[72] See S M Cretney '"What will the Women Want Next?" The Struggle for Power within the Family, 1925–1975' (1996) 112 LQR 110.
[73] Family Law Reform Act 1987, s 1.
[74] See C Smart 'The Legal and Moral Ordering of Child Custody' (1991) *Journal of Law and Society* 485.

valued *status* by the courts)[75] if they are named on their child's birth certificate[76] (and even if they are not living with the mother).

The importance now attached in social policy to men's role as fathers, and father figures, has been a key influence on the development of recent family law. The impact has been most obvious in relation to attitudes to post-separation parenting. The law has moved far away from the 1970s thesis of Goldstein, Freud and Solnit[77] as to the importance for the child of continuity of care with one psychological parent, who should be in control of that child's relationships with others, including an absent parent. The legal approach to resolving residence and contact disputes is to preserve and promote whenever possible an on-going relationship with the (now to be called, apparently less pejoratively) 'non-resident' parent. As Hunt and Macleod[78] have shown, nearly four-fifths of non-resident parents who seek contact through the courts obtain it either by order or agreement, and where no contact is achieved, this is usually because the application is withdrawn or the case is abandoned. If there is no 'presumption' of contact enshrined in the law, there is certainly a powerful 'assumption'[79] that contact is (a) in the child's interests, and (b) to be ordered unless there are strong counter-indications.

So calls for 'equality' have become associated, in this context at least, with seeking equality for men, as much as for women, and if the rhetoric is not matched by the outcome, this reflects the general structure of society, with women continuing to assume the primary responsibility for the day to day care of children, rather than any 'maternal preference' on the part of the judiciary.

The picture is more complicated in relation to the other dimension of relationship breakdown – the division of property. Baroness Hale[80] traces the moves to equality within marriage since the time of *Graveson and Crane*, but notes how society and the economy are still structured along gendered lines, making it much more likely that women will remain at home to care for young children and thus jeopardise their long-term financial security. She also notes the reluctance on the part of some judges and members of the legal profession, echoing the view of Lord Evershed in his Foreword to *A Century of Family Law*, to accept that marriage can

---

[75] See Masson, in Chapter 10 below.
[76] Children Act 1989, s 4(1)(a).
[77] J Goldstein, A Freud and A Solnit *Beyond the Best Interests of the Child* (Burnett Books, 1973). But see further below for consideration of how the thesis continues to have influence in the sphere of adoption practice.
[78] J Hunt and A Macleod *Outcomes of applications to court for contact orders after parental separation or divorce* (Ministry of Justice, 2008).
[79] See S Gilmore 'Disputing contact: challenging some assumptions' [2008] CFLQ 285, who shows that there is no convincing evidence to justify such a strong inclination by the courts.
[80] 'The future of marriage', Chapter 8 below, referring to Lord Evershed in Graveson and Crane, n 1 above, at p xi.

truly be an equal partnership, at least in terms of its economic consequences.[81] Here, it could be argued that law-makers have a harder time in identifying how best to adapt the law to social change. For whilst the status quo in relation to living arrangements for children is generally maintained after parental separation, and thus the law is in line with prevailing social norms, the attempt to produce a 'fair' outcome in relation to property division can be scuppered by both economic circumstances and gendered attitudes flowing from these. Is it *fair* for a wife who has stayed at home raising the children to receive the same half-share in the wealth accumulated during the marriage as the wife who both took the primary care-giving role *and* was an equal partner in the family business? Is it *fair* to require a marriage to have lasted a certain (although the actual duration required will vary from the opinion of one judge to the next) length of time before an equal share will have been 'earned' by the financially weaker spouse? But how is private law to remedy the underlying inequalities in the social and economic structure, and why should the onus fall on an individual husband to make good such inequalities? No satisfactory conclusions have yet been produced to answer these questions, even if the principle of equal shares must, in our view, be maintained as the *right* one for the law to espouse.

The prevailing economic structure reinforces the continuing class-based nature of family law. Until the advent of legal aid in the 1940s, relatively few (though still a reasonable number of) working-class spouses could afford to divorce. The old 'police courts' were the main venues in which the marriages of the working-classes were held up to scrutiny by the courts.[82] These may have now gone, but the three systems of family law identified by the Finer Committee on One-Parent Families[83] in the 1970s continue to function, albeit in slightly altered configuration. Finer identified the divorce courts, the magistrates' courts and the social security system as providing three distinct avenues of recourse for separated parents. It is fair to say that the middle and upper classes generally had nothing to do with the latter two. In the 1980s, despite the re-vamping of the magistrates' jurisdiction by the Domestic Proceedings and Magistrates' Courts Act 1978, the use of the lowest tier continued to decline. Murch and his colleagues[84] found that legal advisers preferred using the county courts, both for maintenance and domestic violence cases. When the Children Act 1989 was implemented, the only proceedings that *had* to be initiated in the magistrates' courts were proceedings under Part IV – child protection proceedings – again, primarily used in relation to families in the lowest social groups. The trend

---

[81] See also G Douglas 'Fairness and equality: the English courts' struggles with property division on divorce' in T Helms and J Zeppernick (eds) *Lebendiges Familienrecht: Festschrift für Rainer Frank* (Verlag für Standesamtswesen, 2008), p 101.

[82] See S M Cretney *Family Law in the Twentieth Century: A History* (Oxford UP, 2003) chs 8 and 11.

[83] Sir M Finer *Report of the Committee on One-Parent Families* Cmnd 5629 (1974).

[84] M Murch et al *The Overlapping Jurisdiction of Magistrates' and County Courts* (University of Bristol, 1987).

to using the county courts for 'private law' continued, especially as most separated couples choose sooner rather than later to divorce, and can therefore reduce their overall costs by taking one set of proceedings in one court rather than two. And the third system – the social security system – became separated off further by the introduction of the Child Support scheme.[85] The Child Support Act 1991[86] required parents with care, who were in receipt of certain types of social security benefits, to co-operate with the Child Support Agency in its attempts to recover the cost of those benefits from the absent parent. So the poorest parents who were dependent upon benefits were forced to use the system, whilst those who were financially better-off could remain in the court system and reach 'agreements'[87] over their children's finances. The requirement to co-operate has now been removed,[88] and a new emphasis put upon the primacy of encouraging private ordering between the parents, although it is hard to see how economically weaker parents are likely to be able to ensure that the amounts their former partners agree to pay bear much resemblance to the levels at which they *could* afford to support their children.[89] It seems that the Thatcher government's creation of the Child Support Agency was a clear affirmation of her belief in the superiority of the coercive power of the state, at least so far as extracting money from lower-class 'deadbeat dads' was concerned. Paradoxically, it is a Labour government which will have done more to bring about the 'privatisation' of the child maintenance obligation than the Conservatives ever did. Indeed, it is likely that the revised child support system, run by the Child Maintenance and Enforcement Commission (C-MEC) will be focused even more upon the 'underclass' segment of the deprived than the old system was.

Meanwhile, as Baroness Hale and Elizabeth Cooke explain in their contributions,[90] the development of ancillary relief law has become ever more concerned with the lifestyles of the rich and famous and ever more remote from the circumstances of the average divorcee. If one of the concerns of the original socio-legal scholars was to develop an understanding of the way family law operated by exploring the 'law in action' rather than relying on the 'law in the books', the need for a reality check has become increasingly urgent in trying to evaluate how the law of

---

[85] For a full history and critique, see N Wikeley *Child Support: Law and Policy* (Hart Publishing, 2006).

[86] Section 6. A parent with care could be exempt from the requirement if she could show 'good cause' for wishing not to comply (such as fear of violence from the other parent if he were pursued for payment) but otherwise was subject to a benefit reduction amounting (after the penalty was stiffened in 1996) to 40 per cent of the income support adult personal allowance.

[87] Such agreements being valid even where the court itself actually fixed quantum, provided that the parents agreed in advance to a nominal order, with the court then being asked to vary it: see *V v V (Child Maintenance)* [2001] 2 FLR 799.

[88] Child Maintenance and Other Payments Act 2008, s 15.

[89] See N Wikeley 'Child Support: The Brave New World' [2008] Fam Law 1024.

[90] See Baroness Hale 'The future of marriage', Chapter 8 below; E Cooke 'The future for ancillary relief', Chapter 9 below.

financial provision on divorce actually 'works' in the 'ordinary' case. Hitchings[91] conducted a small qualitative study of solicitors which seeks to explore this question, but did so by seeking their responses in relation to two scenarios rather than examining their actual case-loads. Thus, whilst their *approach* to the average or low-income divorce could be discerned (an emphasis on practical matters and satisfying needs, but with some attention paid to the case law through a consideration of equality and whether a *Mesher* order would be appropriate), it was not possible to determine how far in practice equal shares are, or are not, a common outcome. As the Law Commission has decided not to heed the calls by the Court of Appeal to conduct a review of the law, there is time, as Cooke notes in her chapter, to carry out much more extensive research to gain a better picture of what is actually happening on the ground, and whilst she is no doubt right to conclude that 'Prediction is impossible' as far as determining how the law will develop in the coming years, it is a safe bet that sooner or later, a fundamental re-evaluation will have to take place.

ADAPTING FAMILY LAW TO SOCIAL CHANGE

In this final section we consider three discrete topics that are not discussed in detail in the following chapters but which provide further examples of how family law adapts to social needs. They also illustrate the developing interplay between private and public law and civil and criminal law.

The neglect of the elderly

One topic falling outside the speakers' remit is that concerning the elderly, which in turn reflects the fact that few, if any, family law courses include the issue either. Yet the demographic trends referred to earlier in this chapter clearly point to the care of the elderly being of increasing concern in the coming decades.

One reason that caring for the elderly is not generally perceived as a family issue is that ultimate responsibility for doing so lies on the state. That could, however, be transformed if it became accepted that children should have a legal responsibility to maintain their elderly and needy parents. This indeed *is* the position in Singapore under their Maintenance of Parents Act.[92] Section 3(1) of that Act provides:

> 'Any person domiciled and resident in Singapore who is of or above 60 years of age and who is unable to maintain himself adequately may apply for an order that one or more of his children may pay him a monthly allowance or any other periodical payment or a lump sum for his maintenance'.

---

[91] E Hitchings 'Everyday Cases in the Post-*White* Era' [2008] Fam Law 873.
[92] Children are also liable to maintain their parents under Spanish law: see Art 143.2 of the Spanish Civil Code.

Applications are made to the Tribunal for the Maintenance of Parents, which can make a maintenance order if it considers it 'just and equitable' to do so, given that the child is able to provide maintenance and the applicant parent is unable 'in spite of efforts on his part' to do so.[93] When ordering such maintenance the Tribunal must have regard[94] to all the circumstances, including matters similar to those to which an English court must have regard when making orders for ancillary relief pursuant to s 25 of the Matrimonial Causes Act 1973, such as the applicant's financial needs and resources (though taking into account 'the manner in which the applicant has spent his savings or dissipated his financial resources'), any physical or mental disability of the applicant and financial resources and expenses of the respondent etc.

Whether a similar liability would ever be imposed upon children under English law can be debated, but it is of interest that the Council of Europe's 'White Paper' *On Principles Concerning the Establishment and Legal Consequences of Parentage*[95] makes specific allowance for the possibility by Principle 26(2), which provides:

> 'National Law may provide for the obligation of children to maintain their parents in need'.

Comments accompanying this proposal[96] simply state that:

> 'it would be up to national law to determine whether as a legal consequence of parentage a child should pay maintenance to parents. Where such a duty exists it would be for the State concerned to fix the conditions (eg whether such a duty can be enforced against a minor child, when the parents shall be considered "in need", etc)'.

The Singapore legislation makes no reference to the age of the child, relying instead upon the ability to pay, but it does address an issue not adverted to by the Council of Europe, namely, the parent who is undeserving by reason of their treatment of the child. Section 5(3) of the Maintenance of Parents Act provides:

> 'If the Tribunal is satisfied upon due proof that the applicant abandoned, abused or neglected the respondent, it may dismiss the application or may reduce the quantum of maintenance ordered by such amount as may be just.'

Developing this point further, one could imagine, were such an obligation to be imposed, for calls to be made to make provision enabling children to 'divorce' their parents, so that no future liability could arise.

---

[93] See s 5(1).
[94] Section 5(2).
[95] CJ-FA (2001) 16 Rev.
[96] Ibid, para 77.

Before leaving this topic it is worth referring to an article by Zenz, in which she argues for the application of family law doctrines, particularly child law principles, to the protection of the elderly.[97] There does indeed seem a clear analogy between the need to protect and safeguard vulnerable children and the equally vulnerable elderly. Whether family lawyers will turn their attention to the elderly over the next half-century is a fascinating question. One area where they might is with regard to inter-generational domestic violence.

The re-discovery of domestic violence

Although violence in the home is a phenomenon long recognised by legal commentators,[98] public awareness of the problem and legislative response to it had, until the 1970s, been fleeting. Parliament responded through the Matrimonial Causes Act 1878 to a public campaign drawing attention to the brutal treatment of many working-class women,[99] by empowering a criminal court before which a man had been convicted of aggravated assault against his wife to make, inter alia, separation and maintenance orders. But it was to be another century before public awareness was again drawn to this issue.[100] Not surprisingly, therefore, the issue was not touched upon in *A Century of Family Law*, nor incidentally in the major family law textbooks until after the enactment of the Domestic Violence and Matrimonial Proceedings Act 1976.[101]

The major catalyst for the 're-discovery' of domestic violence was the work of Erin Pizzey who, in the early 1970s, set up a women's aid refuge in Chiswick and whose book, *Scream Quietly or the Neighbours will Hear*[102] attracted widespread publicity. This quickly led to the setting up of a Select Committee of the House of Commons, which was highly critical of the limited protection offered by the law.[103] In turn, this led to the passing of the Domestic Violence and Matrimonial Proceedings Act 1976 which, redressing the accepted limitations of both the criminal and civil law, introduced two new civil law remedies, namely a non-molestation order and an ouster order.

---

[97] 'Old Age and Family Law' [2003] Fam Law 340.
[98] See, for example, the references in Bacon's *Abridgment* in 1736 to Tit Baron and Feme (B) and by Blackstone's *Commentaries* 455 in 1766 as to the common law power of husbands to beat and confine their wives.
[99] See Frances Power Cobbe *Wife Torture in England* (1878).
[100] See s 4, under which custody of any children of the marriage under the age of 10 would be vested in the wife.
[101] The first treatment of the physical protection of a spouse as a discrete topic in Bromley's *Family Law* was in the 6th edition (1981) and in Cretney's *Principles of Family Law* in the 3rd edition (1979).
[102] (Penguin, 1974). Note also M Borkowski, M Murch and V Walker *Marital Violence* (Tavistock, 1983) and, for a review of the law's response to domestic violence between 1974 and 1996, see S M Cretney *Family Law in the Twentieth Century, A History* (Oxford UP, 2003).
[103] See the *Report of the Select Committee on Violence in Marriage* HC 553 (1974–75) and on *Violence in the Family* HC 329 (1976–77).

These two new remedies were intended to provide speedy redress to victims of violence by giving personal protection against further violence and by securing, at least for the immediate future, occupancy of the family home. They had the advantage of avoiding the need to take substantive civil law proceedings such as divorce to obtain injunctive relief, and providing a better remedy than that afforded by the criminal law. The perceived shortcomings of the criminal law included the reluctance of the police to become involved in a 'domestic' incident in any event, the lack of protection afforded to a victim pending any trial, the focus upon the accused rather than the victim and the general leniency of sentences where proceedings were pursued.

The 1976 Act only provided remedies in the county court, but soon after, magistrates' powers were expanded to provide similar but not identical remedies[104] to make 'personal protection orders' and 'exclusion orders' under the Domestic Proceedings and Magistrates' Courts Act 1978. The law was further complicated by the existence both of a third statutory regime, under what became the Matrimonial Homes Act 1983,[105] which was solely concerned with occupation of the matrimonial home, but which permitted applications by spouses for ouster orders in the High Court and county court, and of the High Court's inherent powers to grant injunctive relief.

It was the existence of what had become a legal 'hotchpotch'[106] that led to further reviews of the law and policy, inter alia by the Law Commission.[107] This review led, eventually,[108] to the enactment of Part IV of the Family Law Act 1996, which harmonised (albeit in a relatively complicated way) all the courts' powers, but which basically maintained what had become the two standard civil law remedies of non-molestation orders and of what became known as 'occupation orders'.

While the civil law had developed in the way just described, the criminal law had not remained static. At the operational level, following the issue of a Home Office Circular in 1990,[109] many police forces established Domestic Violence Units to provide a specialist service offering liaison between police and victims, advice to investigating officers, training in how to handle domestic violence incidents and co-operation with other

---

[104] Orders could only be made upon proof of physical violence being inflicted by a spouse.
[105] A consolidation of the Matrimonial Homes Act 1967.
[106] As famously described by Lord Scarman in *Richards v Richards* [1984] AC 174 and who first called for the law to be reviewed.
[107] See *Report on Domestic Violence and Occupation of the Family Home* Law Com No 207 (1992). Note also the reviews of services and policies, inter alia by Victim Support *Domestic Violence: Report of a National Inter-Agency Working Party* (1992) and the Home Affairs Committee *Third Report on Domestic Violence* HC 245 (1993).
[108] An earlier attempt through the Family Homes and Domestic Violence Bill had to be aborted because of opposition by a number of Conservative MPs based on (ill-founded) fears that its provisions would undermine marriage by offering protection to *unmarried* couples. In fact such protection had long been offered by the 1976 Act.
[109] Home Office Circular 60/1990.

agencies in tackling the problem. A further development, following the issue of a revised Circular in 2000,[110] was the creation of a presumption of arrest, inasmuch as officers became required to produce written justification of any decision not to arrest a person suspected of domestic violence. This development was underpinned by an amendment to the Police and Criminal Evidence Act 1984 making common assault an arrestable offence.[111]

A more substantive development came with the enactment of the Protection from Harassment Act 1997, which was intended to criminalise what was popularly referred to as 'stalking'. However, the unintended by-product of this legislation was to provide new remedies for domestic violence. The Act created two offences[112] (of harassment and putting a person in fear of violence), introduced a power to make restraining orders to prevent the commission of further offences,[113] and created a new civil action in the form of what may be termed a statutory tort of harassment, under which an action for damages may be brought in respect of actual or apprehended harassment contrary to s 1 of the 1997 Act.[114]

The 1997 Act, because of its unexpected application to domestic violence, proved more popular than expected, with nearly 6,000 prosecutions in the first year of its operation, as against the 200 predicted. It also marked a shift towards the criminal law as the perceived better means of dealing with domestic violence. That shift became more pronounced under the Domestic Violence, Crime and Victims Act 2004 which, inter alia, made a breach of a non-molestation order a criminal offence.[115] This change was accompanied by the removal of the court's power to add a power of arrest to a non-molestation order[116] upon the basis of the government's declared intention[117] that the application of criminal sanctions should be the preferred option. The early indicators, however, are that these latter changes have not proved successful and have in fact caused a serious and worrying reduction in applications seeking protection.[118]

---

[110] Home Office Circular 19/2000.
[111] Police and Criminal Evidence Act 1984, Sch 1A, para 14A, inserted by the Domestic Violence, Crime and Victims Act 2004, s 10. In fact the distinction in general between arrestable and non-arrestable offences was subsequently abolished by the Serious Organised Crime and Police Act 2005, s 110.
[112] Sections 2 and 4.
[113] Sections 5 and 5A (inserted by the Domestic Violence, Crime and Victims Act 2004, s 12(5).
[114] Section 3.
[115] Family Law Act 1996, s 42A (inserted by s 1 of the 2004 Act).
[116] Section 47(1) of the Family Law Act 1996 was repealed by Domestic Violence, Crime and Victims Act 2004, Sch 10, para 38(2).
[117] See the comments by H H Judge J Platt 'The Domestic Violence, Crime and Victims Act 2004 Part 1 – Is it Working?' [2008] Fam Law 642.
[118] See inter alia M Hester, N Westmarland, J Pearce and E Williamson *Early Evaluation of the Domestic Violence, Crime and Victims Act 2004* (MOJ Research Series 14/08) and Platt, op cit.

No doubt the alleged shortcomings of the 2004 Act will stimulate further debate as to 'whether the civil or the criminal law route is more effective in achieving the common goal which is to get the domestic abuse to stop'.[119] But, as another commentary has pointed out:[120]

> 'there is no easy way forward. The much greater focus in recent policy making on the criminal justice route as the response to domestic violence may admirably reflect an increased awareness of the criminal nature of such behaviour and a determination to leave behind patriarchal value judgments about its seriousness. On the other hand, there is a danger that the views of the victim can be lost in a willingness to react "toughly" and to ignore her long-term needs.'

Given the experience of the past quarter of a century one wonders whether definitive answers to these dilemmas will be found during the next 50 years.

The transformation of adoption

Although adoption is not discussed in any of the subsequent chapters, it was the subject of a contribution by T E James to *A Century of Family Law* in a chapter entitled 'The Illegitimate and Deprived Child: Legitimation and Adoption'.[121] Coupling adoption with illegitimacy and concentrating on the status aspects of adoption reflected the general thinking of the time, which continued at least until the 1970s. As Freeman says in his contribution to this book, the only issues relating to children that were discussed when he was a student in the mid-1960s were 'legitimacy (or rather illegitimacy) and adoption'. That was also the recollection of one of the present authors when taught at the end of that decade.

The changing nature of adoption law and practice

At the time James was writing, adoption had had a short history, being introduced only 30 years earlier by the Adoption of Children Act 1926. But it had already undergone one fundamental change. Although from the outset adoption meant the irrevocable transfer of parentage, at any rate for the lifetime of the parties, under the 1926 Act it had no effect upon succession.[122] That latter position was altered by the Adoption of Children Act 1949. As has been observed,[123] that change ended any argument (based on the idea that adoption merely suspended the parent-child relationship for the parents' life) that adoption was a special

---

[119] Platt, ibid at 643.
[120] N Lowe and G Douglas *Bromley's Family Law* (Oxford UP, 10th edn, 2007), pp 260–261.
[121] See Graveson and Crane, n 1 above, ch 3, pp 45–55.
[122] See s 5(1) and (2) respectively.
[123] By N Lowe 'English Adoption Law: Past, Present and Future' in S N Katz, J Eekelaar and M Maclean (eds) *Cross Currents* (Oxford UP, 2000), p 313.

form of guardianship.[124] However, important though that change was, in the 50 or so years since 1957, adoption law and practice has undergone such further fundamental changes that in many ways it has become barely recognisable from the earlier model. As one commentary (written before the Adoption and Children Act 2002) put it,[125] what began as a consensual, largely unregulated mechanism for transferring parentage (at any rate for the parties' lives), designed for de facto and baby adoptions,[126] has become a highly regulated procedure dealing with step-parent and public law adoptions. Together with increasing regulation, the organisation of adoption work also underwent considerable change, with the prohibition of private placements (other than with relatives) and the bulk of the work being done by local authorities (each of whom is bound to operate an 'adoption service') rather than by voluntary adoption agencies. Even the very notion of adoption changed, with the emphasis shifting from that of completely severing the child from his or her former family to that of securing a permanent home for the child without necessarily ending all the links with the birth family, nor ending the state obligation (through adoption agencies) to give continuing support to the adoptive family.

In summary, over the last half-century adoption was transformed from an essentially private law action to a predominantly public one aimed at providing a long-term stable home for children in care who cannot return to their birth family. Accompanying this change has been a shift of focus from the adults to the children and from what has been described as a gift/donation model to a contract/services model.[127]

Although this transformation is well-charted territory, it is worth adverting to, since it provides an interesting example of how this aspect of family law evolved against a background of changing social attitudes and values, a developing understanding of children's welfare and overt political pressure.

The rise and fall of private law adoptions

The 1960s witnessed an explosion of adoptions, rising from 15,019 in 1960 to a peak of 24,831 in 1968. What accounted for this rise was the increase of both baby adoptions (peaking in 1968) and of step-parent

---

[124] As described by the Report of the Departmental Committee on the Adoption of Children (Hurst Report) Cmd 9248 (1954), para 196 and adapted by T E James in R Graveson and F Crane (eds) *A Century of Family Law*, p 46 to refer to adopters as 'special guardians'.

[125] Lowe, op cit, pp 331–332.

[126] The term 'de facto adoptions' refers to orders made in favour of applicants who had been looking after children on a long-term basis but without any formal legal protection, which was a particular concern of the legislature in 1926. 'Baby adoptions' refers to adoptions of children under the age of 12 months.

[127] See N Lowe 'The Changing Face of Adoption – the gift/donation model versus the contract/services model' [1997] CFLQ 371.

adoptions (peaking in 1975). But this rise was short-lived. Baby adoptions fell from 12,641 (or 51% of all adoptions in 1968) to 4,548 in 1975 and to 969 in 1990 (15% of all adoptions). For the past decade there have been typically 150–200 baby adoptions per year, amounting to just 4% of all adoptions. Step-parent adoptions fell from 9,262 (or 43% of all adoptions) in 1975 to 1,107 (or 23% of all adoptions) in 2004.[128]

The decline in the number of babies available for adoption was noted as early as 1972 by the Houghton Committee,[129] which attributed the reduction to the increasing number of legal abortions (the Abortion Act 1967 came into force on 27 April 1968), more use of contraception, and the changing attitude to illegitimacy, inasmuch as unmarried mothers became less disadvantaged, while at the same time there was a 'significant increase in tolerance and understanding towards them and their children'. In contrast, the decline in step-parent adoptions was attributable to legal changes. Based on the concerns of the Houghton Committee that they were inappropriate, the 1975 Children Act included provisions[130] specifically designed to discourage step-parent adoptions.

The rise and rise of public law adoptions

Although public law adoptions were by no means unknown in the 1950s (in 1952, for example, there were 453, or 3.2% of all adoptions) and they had increased during successive years (in 1968, for example, there were 2,168, or 8.7% of all adoptions), a significant change took place in the 1970s when local authorities began to use adoption to secure the long-term welfare of older children and not just babies, in a practice known as 'permanency planning'. This practice had been stimulated in turn by the seminal work of Goldstein, Freud and Solnit *Beyond the Best Interests of the Child*, published in 1973,[131] which challenged the then prevailing view that biological and legal parenthood should take precedence over psychological parenthood, and strongly promoted the view that children from neglectful, disrupted or severely disordered families might often do much better if placed permanently with loving, secure, more stable families. Other research, particularly Rowe and Lambert's *Children Who Wait*,[132] also published in 1973, which emphasised the need for long-term planning for children in care, together with the Maria Colwell Inquiry,[133] reinforced the view that for certain abused or neglected children long-term care away from their families was

---

[128] *Judicial Statistics 2004* Annual Report, Table 5.4.
[129] The Report of the Departmental Committee on the Adoption of Children 1972 Cmnd 5107, para 20.
[130] See s 10(3), subsequently re-enacted as s 14(3) of the Adoption Act 1976, but subsequently repealed by the Children Act 1989, Sch 15.
[131] Free Press, New York.
[132] J Rowe and L Lambert *Children Who Wait* (ABAFA, 1973).
[133] Report of the Committee of Inquiry into the Care and Supervision provided in relation to Maria Colwell (HMSO, 1974).

in their best interests and that adoption was a key means of achieving this where the birth parents were opposed to it.

Although not everyone was swayed by the permanency argument (and in any event it was not infrequently bad social work practice rather than parental failure that had led to many children languishing in care) there were nevertheless lasting significant changes in adoption practice. Not the least of the changes has been the determined efforts by local authorities to secure adoption placements for so-called 'hard to place' children, even to the extent, unimaginable in the 1950s, of having extensive publicity campaigns focusing on particular children in need of adoption. The knock-on consequence of this change was an overall rise in the age of children adopted out of care and an increase of contested adoptions. The net overall result was that at a time when adoptions were falling, the number of children adopted out of care rose from 1,488 in 1979 to 2,605 in 1990.

Further impetus to expanding public law adoptions was given in the late 1990s following various initiatives of the newly incoming Labour Government, which took a keen interest in the issue, and placed pressure on local authorities to increase adoptions by making their number a performance indicator of good practice.[134]

Not surprisingly, in the wake of this overt government pressure, public law adoptions continued to rise. In 2001, for example, they reached 3,061, or 69% of all adoptions. But the government still pressed for further increases. Its declared intention[135] when introducing the Adoption and Children Act 2002 was to achieve a 40% and, if possible a 50%, increase in the number of children adopted out of care. Indeed, it was in pursuance of this policy (and not to improve 'Gay Rights') that in order to widen the pool of would-be adopters the 2002 Act permits joint adoptions by same-sex couples.[136] Again, this policy was reflected (initially, at any rate) by a further increase of adoptions of children out of care, rising to 3,600 in 2006.[137]

---

[134] See *The Government's Objectives for Children's Social Services* (Department of Health, 1999) and Performance Indicator C23.

[135] See the White Paper, *Adoption: a new approach* (2000) Cm 5017, p 5.

[136] See ss 49(1) and 144(4) (definition of a 'couple'). For an interesting ruling that notwithstanding art 14 of the Adoption (Northern Ireland) Order 1987, SI 1987/2203 (NI 22), which only permitted joint adoption by married couples, based on human rights considerations, an unmarried couple *were* entitled to apply to adopt a child: see *Re P (Adoption: Unmarried Couple)* [2008] UKHL 38, [2008] 2 FLR 1084. Query whether this ruling would permit same-sex couples to apply for adoption in Northern Ireland?

[137] See DfES *Children Looked-After Statistics* (2006), Table AJ. Since then they have dropped back a little to 3,200 in the year ending 31 March 2008: BAAF Statistics, 2008.

Broadening the concept of adoption

Traditionally, adoption was a secretive process based upon the notion of a complete and irrevocable transfer of parentage. As originally conceived, it aimed to protect unmarried mothers and their children from excessive stigma, whilst at the same time enabling childless couples to avoid the oppressive taint of infertility. Consequently, practice was designed to ensure that birth parents would generally have no knowledge of the adopters (and of course no further contact with their child) and adopters would be similarly ignorant of the birth parents' identity.[138] One result of this secrecy, however, was that adopters were encouraged in their belief that the child was 'theirs' and were generally reluctant to tell the child of his or her adoption. While this may have made some sense when the vast majority of adoptions by non-parents were of babies or toddlers, the legal fiction of a family transplant was clearly more difficult to sustain in the case of adoption of older children, which became more common from the 1970s onwards. It is therefore no surprise that two major developments permitting children to trace their birth parents and making provision for ongoing contact after adoption date from this period.

Following studies in the 1960s and 1970s, which had demonstrated the harmful effects upon adopted children of not knowing their identities,[139] the law was changed in 1975[140] to permit *adult* adopted children to obtain their original birth certificate and so be enabled to trace their birth parents. Since the introduction of this right, an Adoption Contact Register has been created which provides 'a safe and confidential way for birth parents and other relatives to assure an adopted person that contact would be welcome and to give a contact address'.[141]

Accompanying the ability to trace birth parents, albeit only after attaining adulthood, was the acceptance both in law and practice that adoption and ongoing contact with the birth family were not mutually exclusive. As a matter of principle this was established by the ground-breaking decision, *Re J (A Minor) (Adoption Order: Conditions)*,[142] and confirmed by the House of Lords in *Re C (A Minor) (Adoption Order: Conditions)*.[143] However, given that the courts have hitherto[144] been reluctant to *impose* a contact order on unwilling adopters, the more important development has

---

[138] See N Lowe 'English Adoption Law: Past, Present and Future', op cit n 123, at p 136.
[139] See A McWhinnie *Adopted Children: How They Grow Up* (Routledge and Kegan Paul, 1967) and J Triseliotis *In Search of Origins: The Experience of Adopted People* (Routledge and Kegan Paul, 1973).
[140] Following the implementation of s 26 of the Children Act 1975, which, controversially had retrospective effect. This provision was based upon the Houghton Committee's Recommendation 77.
[141] Dept of Health *The Children Act 1989: Guidance and Regulation*, Vol 9, 'Adoption Issues' (HMSO, 1991), para 3.2. See now the Adoption and Children Act 2002, s 80, replacing the Adoption Act 1976, s 51A.
[142] [1973] Fam 106.
[143] [1989] AC 1.
[144] Though query whether this position might change in the light of *Re P (Placement*

been the increasingly common adoption agency practice of providing for some form of ongoing contact, be it direct face-to-face contact, indirect contact or, more commonly, through the exchange of information, reports and photographs via a confidential adoption agency 'letter box' service. Some agencies go further and actively involve the birth parents in the process of selecting adopters. None of these developments could have realistically been imagined in 1957, let alone in 1927.

Further evidence of the changing face of adoption is the provision of post-adoption support. The conventional view of adoption was that it was an end in itself, such that the adoptive family were left to their own devices and resources to bring up the child. But that view sits uneasily with the adoption from care of older and vulnerable children, and it became increasingly recognised that adoption is not the end of the process but merely a part of an ongoing and often complex process of family development, and that in many cases the adoptive family will need ongoing support.[145]

A key part of post-adoption support is the payment of adoption allowances, which were first permitted in 1982[146] and expanded by the Children Act 1989.[147] But ongoing support is more than the payment of allowances and includes the organisation of post-adoption contact, payment for the provision of therapy, ongoing counselling for the adoptive (and birth) family including the child, the provision of updating information and the organisation of support groups. This more general obligation is now provided by the Adoption and Children Act 2002.[148]

Other changes made by the 2002 Act

The Adoption and Children Act 2002 also shifted focus onto the child and away from the interests of birth parents by importing the paramountcy principle into adoption decision-making.[149] This was significant because prior to this the child's welfare had always been expressed to be the *first* consideration, to provide a more balanced protection for the birth parent, given the draconian nature of an adoption order. Accompanying this change, and again emphasising the shift of

---

Orders: Parental Consent) [2008] EWCA Civ 535, [2008] 2 FLR 625, in which the court considered that the previous reluctance to impose contact orders needed to be 'revisited' in the light of the 2002 Act.

[145] See N Lowe 'The Changing Face of Adoption – the gift/donation model versus the contract/services model' [1997] CFLQ 371.

[146] Children Act 1975, s 32, subsequently re-enacted by s 56(4)–(7) of the Adoption Act 1976.

[147] Substituting s 57A for s 56(4)–(7) of the 1976 Act.

[148] Section 2(6) and by the Adoption Support Services Regulations 2005, SI 2005/691.

[149] Section 1(2).

focus, is the introduction of a welfare based ground for dispensing with parental consent, namely where 'the welfare of the child requires the consent to be dispensed with'.[150]

Prima facie, once it is decided that adoption is in the child's interests, it would seem that the birth parents' chances of successfully opposing the adoption are virtually non-existent. However, as has already been emphasised,[151] the welfare test under the 2002 Act is different from that under the Children Act 1989, since it refers to the child's welfare 'throughout his life'. Moreover, among the checklist of factors that the court is required to consider when coming to a decision relating to the adoption of a child is 'the likely effect on the child (throughout his life) of having ceased to be a member of the original family and become an adopted person'.[152]

Although this is still child-focused, it does provide some avenue for a birth parent opposed to the adoption to explore. A second way of balancing the residual interest of the birth parents was to replace the freeing for adoption provisions with placement orders, which local authorities are required to obtain as soon as the plan for the child in their care is for adoption. Although these provisions[153] have proved immensely complicated, by forcing authorities to obtain court sanction before placing the child for adoption, birth parents are afforded some protection inasmuch as court adjudication is required before placements become a fait accompli.

Another key change brought about by the 2002 Act was to provide further alternatives to adoption which would still secure long-term stability for the child. These included extending the parental responsibility provisions under the Children Act 1989[154] to allow step-parents to make parental responsibility agreements with their spouse or civil partner[155] and to permit courts to make parental responsibility orders in their favour. A second alternative was the introduction of 'special guardianship', which was intended to meet the needs of children for whom adoption is not appropriate (for example, older children who do not wish to be adopted), but who cannot return to their birth parents, yet who 'would benefit from the permanence provided by a legally secure family placement'.[156] It is ironic that these orders are called 'special guardianship orders', since, as has been seen, that is how adoption under the 1926 Act was originally perceived. The crucial difference is that whereas, even under the 1926 Act,

---

[150] Section 52(1)(b). The two other grounds, namely that the parent or guardian cannot be found or lacks capacity to give consent, replicate the earlier law.
[151] See *Re P (Placement Orders: Parental Consent)* [2008] EWCA Civ 535, [2008] 2 FLR 625.
[152] Section 1(4)(c).
[153] Sections 18–29.
[154] See s 4A inserted by s 112 of the Adoption and Children Act 2002.
[155] Note that this does not apply to an unmarried partner.
[156] See the Explanatory Notes to the 2002 Act, para 18.

adoption transferred parentage, special guardianship does not, although it does place special guardians in firm control[157] and, importantly, parents need court leave to seek the ending of an order and that leave cannot be given 'unless there has been a significant change in circumstances'.[158] Another difference is that whereas adoption is for the child's life, special guardianship ends upon the child attaining 18.

What of the future?

It is obviously a matter of conjecture how adoption might develop over the next half-century, but there are two milestones to look forward to. The year 2027 will mark the centenary of the availability of adoption in England and Wales and at about the same time, if the current numbers are maintained, the millionth adoption order will be made. Whether the current numbers will be maintained is doubtful. It seems likely, though, that for the foreseeable future public law adoptions will continue at roughly the same rates and that there is unlikely to be a significant rise in domestic private law adoptions. However, one area that could develop is intercountry adoptions (that is, where applicants seek to adopt children from abroad). In contrast to continental Europe, the number of intercountry adoptions is quite low in this jurisdiction, amounting on average to about 300 per year. Although in the past this low figure was thought to be attributable to the lack of specialist agencies,[159] even since their creation, originally by the Adoption (Intercountry Aspects) Act 1999, the numbers have remained static. Certainly, local authorities have not in the past been enthusiastic about such adoptions, but it may be, especially as such adoptions are now globally regulated by the 1993 Hague Convention on Intercountry Adoptions, which the UK ratified in 1999, that attitudes might change, leading to an increase in the number of applications.

Mention has just been made of the different pattern of adoption in the UK compared with continental Europe, where domestic adoptions are in the minority. The reason for this lies in the reluctance of continental systems to dispense with parental consent. It was for that reason that it had been speculated whether the domestic law on dispensing with parental consent would survive a Human Rights challenge. However, fears that it may not be were allayed by *Scott v UK*.[160] But whether our domestic law will continue to be immune to further challenges in the future can be debated. For example, could it be argued that the automatic severance of siblings' and grandparents' legal ties is in breach of their

---

[157] See Children Act 1989, s 14C(1)(b), which states that a special guardian 'is entitled to exercise parental responsibility to the exclusion of any other person with parental responsibility (apart from another special guardian)'.
[158] Section 14D(3) and (5).
[159] See the Adoption Law Review Discussion Paper No 4 (Dept of Health, 1992).
[160] [2000] 1 FLR 958, ECHR.

Art 8 rights? In other words, it is by no means a given that the current concept, which has so radically evolved over the last 85 years, will remain intact over the next 50.

CONCLUSION

This overview of family law, past, present and future will, we hope, have provided some background context to the chapters that follow. Viewing family law as in a process of evolution may help explain what has otherwise been characterised by Dewar as the 'normal chaos' of family law.[161] The apparent inconsistencies and contradictions between competing policies, decisions and trends may simply reflect the ongoing changes which family laws and policies have to confront. Some initiatives and responses will prove to be dead ends, others will have to adapt further if they are to prove useful in tackling the problems which families face in themselves adjusting to social and economic changes. As those who are challenging conjugality[162] as the keystone of family formation suggest, the very notion of 'family' that we currently share will no doubt change in response to new attitudes and modes of behaviour. We hope that this chapter and the contributions which follow will add to our understanding of the complexity of family change and to the role that family law and family scholarship have played in society's responses to it.

---

[161] J Dewar 'The Normal Chaos of Family Law' (1998) 61 MLR 467.
[162] See Freeman, Chapter 6 below.

CHAPTER 2

THE TROUBLEMAKERS: CRANKS, PSYCHIATRISTS AND OTHER MISCHIEVOUS NUISANCES – THEIR ROLE IN REFORM OF ENGLISH FAMILY LAW IN THE NINETEENTH AND TWENTIETH CENTURIES[1]

Stephen Cretney

INTRODUCTION

In 1956 A J P Taylor, himself something of a troublemaker, delivered the prestigious Ford Lectures at Oxford under the title *The Troublemakers, Dissent over Foreign Policy 1792–1939*. My own choice of title is a small gesture of homage to a great historian who believed that the 'one continuous thing in British policy ... is that there has always been disagreement, controversy about it', and that 'all change in history, all advance, comes from the nonconformists. If there had been no troublemakers, no dissenters, we should still be living in caves.'[2]

Today, of course, there is a huge investment in what we might call 'respectable' law reform conducted through the Law Commission, 'think tanks', researchers and so on. But for many years, it was the interest – often indeed the obsessions – of the dissenters, the troublemakers which most affected the process of change in respect of what we now call family law. Alan Taylor had a very simple reason[3] for taking an interest in these people: the dissenters 'existed: therefore they deserve to be put on record.' But there is another reason for taking in interest in their doings: very often the shape of our law is still dictated by the response made to the campaigns of cranks, psychiatrists and other troublemakers (the language is that of a Permanent Secretary in the Lord Chancellor's Department).

The perfect profile for a 'troublemaker' in the present context is someone with a clear cause or objective pursued by means respectable opinion regards as being, if not wholly unacceptable, at least disproportionate to

---

[1] This is the text of a lecture substantially as delivered at Cardiff Law School on 21 November 2007. Footnote references have been added.
[2] A J P Taylor *The Troublemakers, Dissent over Foreign Policy 1792–1939* (Oxford UP, 1957), p 14.
[3] At p 15.

the ends to be attained. There are of course many undoubted troublemakers whose objectives lack clarity or definition. These people too have often had an influence: for example, there is Mrs Georgina Weldon, a deranged vexatious litigant whose activities in the 1880s had a lasting impact on the law in at least three areas. First, she played a large part in bringing about reforms to the lunacy laws. Secondly, as a result of her getting an order committing her husband to prison for failure to comply literally with a restitution decree, a statute was hurriedly passed which in practice meant that a wife could immediately divorce her adulterous husband – a substantial move towards the equal treatment of man and wife in divorce not formally acknowledged until 1923. Thirdly, the legal action she brought against General Sir Henry de Bathe,[4] the Governor of the Lunatic Asylum to which her husband had tried to commit her, established that a married woman had the right to exclude her husband's agents from the house which he owned but she occupied. It was still being cited as authority nearly a century later[5] in the case law which led up to the enactment of the Matrimonial Homes Act in 1967. But this lecture focuses on men and women who were concerned with the effect of the law on the public. Of course, some of them had their own personal reasons for their interest in – to take an obvious example – divorce reform, but none of them was exclusively concerned with their own situation.

PRIORITIES FOR REFORM: DIVORCE OR PROPERTY?

One recurrent issue in law reform in general and family law in particular is to settle an order of priorities: which should come first, for example, reform of divorce or reform of family property law? This particular question was hotly debated in the nineteenth century. There was a highly influential group of women writers who certainly accepted that reform of the marriage laws (that is, the divorce laws) was important, but argued that it was the property laws (which meant, for instance, that the copyright of authors who happened to be married belonged not to the author but to the author's husband) were of much greater practical importance. Yet in 1857 Palmerston's Government (against fierce opposition) legislated on divorce, and refused to deal with property. What possessed them? As one eminent lawyer MP, Sir Erskine Perry – a committed supporter of property law reform until his death – put it, urging that something be done to meet the injustices detailed in a petition signed by 25,000 people, including 'the most distinguished names in literature art and society', not a single petition had been presented urging divorce reform.[6] You may doubt whether Perry was right in his view that

---

[4] *Weldon v de Bathe* (1884) 14 QBD 339, CA.
[5] See notably *National Provincial Bank Ltd v Ainsworth* [1965] AC 1175.
[6] For speculation on why Palmerston's Administration acted as it did, see S M Cretney *Family Law in the Twentieth Century, A History* (Oxford UP, 2003), pp 162–165.

reform of matrimonial property law would 'remove all demand or necessity for tampering with the indissolubility of marriage', but it is difficult to controvert the view that reluctance to deal with property entitlements became a characteristic of English law-making, and that we are still living with the consequences.

Edith Summerskill: married women's property

We were certainly living with them as World War II drew to a close. One Labour Member of Parliament was especially active in trying to get something done to remedy the fact that the law seemed often to leave the married woman out in the cold (sometimes literally so) when there were differences. In 1943 an official in the Lord Chancellor's Office, noting that some troublesome women were actually claiming that a housewife should have the right to an equal share in the family income 'in recognition of her services in the home and in the community', minuted his Permanent Secretary that there seemed to be an 'assumption that a wife who is a hard worker and an efficient manager is entitled to be rewarded on a cash basis'. What an idea! There were even fears that Labour ministers then in Churchill's Coalition Government would not quite understand the terrible legal difficulties which this preposterous notion would cause. But please don't think this is a matter of party politics: one MP recorded in his diary that a colleague was 'emotional, unintelligent, and governed in her political judgments almost entirely by personal experience'; another dismissed the same person in less reflective words: she was (he recorded) simply a 'cantankerous bitch'. Difficult, is it not, to identify in these assessments the cerebral high-mindedness usually associated with the products of Winchester and New College, yet these words are those used by Hugh Gaitskell (later Chancellor of the Exchequer and Leader of the Labour Party) and R H S Crossman (son of a Chancery judge; latterly Lord President of the Council and Secretary of State for Social Services) about their party colleague, Edith Summerskill.[7]

Dr Summerskill was a socialist. She believed in equality, as people did in those days. And not only economic equality for male trade unionists (at the time well represented on the Labour benches) in their dealings with management, but social equality, and not least equality between husband and wife: 'real sharing' within the home, 'where the wife and husband are legal partners'.[8] Her commitment to equality had become evident even before she was elected an MP in 1938: in 1935 she had been rebuffed by the electorate in Bury, Lancashire, and her defeat may have been partly attributable to the fact that she declined offers of support from the Roman Catholic priests in the constituency for what she thought was the

---

[7] See the excellent entry by John Stewart in the *Oxford Dictionary of National Biography* (2004, online edn, accessed 10 July 2007).
[8] *Hansard*, HC Deb, vol 391, col 597 (16 July 1943).

very good reason that in return they would make her give an undertaking never to advise anyone about birth control. On the Sunday before the poll she was denounced from the pulpits.

When Edith Summerskill was eventually elected to the Commons, one of the issues she pursued vigorously was that of the wife's rights to a share of the family income: the decision of the courts in the case of *Blackwell v Blackwell*,[9] that the husband was solely entitled to the money – £3,000 or so in today's values – which his wife (left 'a pathetic little figure' in a basement room 'helpless and homeless' and 'reduced to working as a waitress') had put into her savings account, was a focus for the Married Women's Association's campaign for reform.

Dr Summerskill (who had long been a member of the Association, and indeed was to become its President) led the troublemakers in Parliament. But progress there was none: Dr Summerskill became a Minister in the 1945 Attlee administration, and had to toe (more or less) the party line. And that was not sympathetic: when, during the closing days of the Attlee administration in 1951, the Conservative MP Irene Ward introduced a Deserted Wives Bill,[10] the Cabinet's Legislation Committee apparently thought it 'rather a joke' and officials solemnly recorded ministerial fears that husbands were in danger of becoming their wives' chattels.[11] But in the meantime all was not lost: in the same year Mrs Eirene White caused a great deal of trouble by introducing a Bill allowing divorce after seven years' separation: the Government kicked that issue into touch by setting up a Royal Commission on Marriage (as well as Divorce) with terms of reference broadened to extend specifically to 'the property rights of husband and wife, both during marriage and after its termination'.[12] No official decision had yet been taken about whether reform of divorce law or reform of property law were in principle desirable and, if so, whether they should be dealt with together or separately and, if separately, in what order.

The defeat of Dr Summerskill and the 'Women of England'

There were a few things on which the Royal Commission (chaired by the scarcely radical Law Lord, Lord Morton of Henryton) could agree: one was that (in effect) the *Blackwell* decision should be reversed by statute. Getting that onto the statute book took 9 years.[13] But Lady Summerskill (as she had become) continued to stir things up. The case law, culminating

---

[9] [1943] 2 All ER 579; see generally S M Cretney *Family Law in the Twentieth Century, A History* (2003), pp 114–117 and p 125, note 229.
[10] The measures proposed to protect the deserted wife were modest in the extreme, and the Government decided to condemn the Bill with faint praise whilst not rejecting it entirely: in the event it made no progress: see Cretney, op cit, n 9 above, p 117.
[11] Ibid.
[12] The background is complicated: see Cretney, op cit, n 9 above, pp 324–328.
[13] The Married Women's Property Act 1964 was blocked on several occasions: see Cretney, op cit, n 9 above, p 124, n 239.

in *National Provincial Bank v Ainsworth*[14] – an impeccable piece of property law analysis – demonstrated the fragility of a wife's right in the family home, and even the Morton Commission had recommended statutory reform. Lady Summerskill had extracted a promise of help from the incoming Labour Lord Chancellor, Gerald Gardiner. Then everything started to go badly wrong: the property lawyers raised all sorts of technicalities, and the newly created Law Commission – at that time anxious to secure a reputation for scientific and comprehensive codification – was anxious to hold itself publicly aloof from what it clearly regarded as a half-baked stop-gap prejudicial to the radical but scientific reform which (as the Lord Chancellor told the President of the Probate Divorce and Admiralty Division) they both wanted. Even so, a Matrimonial Homes Bill was produced by one of the Parliamentary counsel[15] seconded to the Law Commission. But it was not a Law Commission bill.[16] How wise the Commissioners were to hold their delicate noses: 'don't blame me, Gov' they were able to say (of course in rather less demotic language). And in some respects there was a lot for which someone could and perhaps should have been held 'accountable', as we say in the twenty-first century: 'something better – much better' was needed (said a High Court judge)[17] to remove the 'cumbersome uncertainties' which the Matrimonial Homes Act 1967 had produced 'to the peril of all', not least 'those of modest means'. But with the benefits of hindsight we can see there is quite a lot to be said in praise of the 1967 Act:[18] the Act has 'provided practical relief for countless families over the years'. Certainly, the Act, unusually for an English statute, *did* establish a clear principle from which it would be impossible subsequently to retreat: this was that the family had a *right* to security in their home which could be protected against commercial claims founded on traditional property rights.[19] But the downside was that the problems experienced in providing the technical machinery came to dominate all future thinking about matrimonial property: 'don't touch it, you'll get your fingers horribly burnt'.

And so it was. The order of priorities became fixed – not by rational assessment but really by what Victorian divorce lawyers would have called 'invincible repugnance' to getting ensnared in property law. This became clear in the events leading up to the Divorce Reform Act 1969. The

---

[14] [1965] AC 1175.
[15] Ellice Eadie (1912–2001): see the Entry by Ruth Deech in the *Oxford Dictionary of National Biography* (online edition, accessed 10 July, 2007).
[16] For the background to the Matrimonial Homes Act 1967, see Cretney, op cit, n 9 above, pp 123–131: n 251 on p 128 is especially revealing.
[17] *Wroth v Tyler* [1974] Ch 30 at 64, per Megarry J. Most of the defects in the 1967 Act were subsequently removed.
[18] Cretney, op cit, n 9 above, p 130.
[19] Defects in the 1967 Act were dealt with, after a thorough examination by the Law Commission (see *Third Report on Family Property (Co-ownership and Occupation Rights) and Household Goods*, Law Com No 86 (1978) by amendments effected by the Matrimonial Homes and Property Act 1981.

reformers had to face one great problem: how to protect the economically vulnerable and 'innocent' spouse from the hardship flowing from the loss of that status. There was, it seemed, a simple answer: as Lady Summerskill put it:[20] few men can afford to support two wives. That is why she branded the Divorce Reform Bill a 'Casanova's charter'. But (she promised) if 'they introduce an amendment offering community of property, I would accept the [Divorce] Bill'.[21]

And so, one Friday afternoon, the House of Commons gave a Second Reading to Mr Edward Bishop's Matrimonial Property Bill: on divorce, the court was to divide the couple's 'matrimonial property equally'. The Government realised Bishop and his associates could kill the divorce Bill if they wanted to. So there was a (no doubt tense) meeting in the Lord Chancellor's Room. Lord Chancellor Gardiner – who knew from personal experience the hardship the 'matrimonial offence' law could cause[22] – gave an undertaking to legislate on property matters before the divorce Bill came into force. Perhaps the Lord Chancellor was not entirely candid in describing the effect of his undertaking. Lady Summerskill certainly thought so: when she saw what the Government, on the advice of the Law Commission, in fact offered[23] she spoke scornfully of the 'rather miserable little Bill' as 'a confidence trick against the women of this country'.[24] Perhaps she was right: she thought she had been offered full blown and radical reform of property law and that is certainly not what she got.

True, there were still plenty of fine words around: in 1971 the Law Commission eloquently urged that a community system would be in harmony with the modern pattern of social development; and two years later the Commission reported a widespread belief that the introduction of community was indeed 'essential in the interests of justice and certainty' and that it was vital to accept the principle of deciding property rights 'in accordance with fixed principles'. But, they said – if co-ownership were applied to the matrimonial home, it would not really be necessary to go any further. And so they laboured on for more than five years on this limited form of co-ownership. When the Report with draft Bill was eventually published in 1978[25] it was certainly successful in demonstrating that co-ownership was indeed 'all very difficult'. Ten years later, another group of Commissioners returned to the issue;[26] they – or,

---

[20] As quoted in Cretney, op cit, n 9 above, p 133.
[21] She was not alone: see Cretney, ibid.
[22] Gardiner's second wife Muriel Box states in her biography, *Rebel Advocate* (Gollancz, 1983), that his first wife refused to divorce him and he was thus prevented from marrying the woman with whom he had fallen in love.
[23] That is, the Matrimonial Proceedings and Property Act 1970, the relevant provisions of which were subsequently consolidated in the Matrimonial Causes Act 1973.
[24] *Hansard*, HL Deb, vol 305, col 500 (6 November 1970).
[25] *Third Report on Family Property (Co-ownership and Occupation Rights) and Household Goods*, Law Com No 86 (1978).
[26] *Report on Family Law: Matrimonial Property* (1988, Law Com No 175).

rather, most of them, for this was one of the very few Law Commission Reports which incorporate a formal dissent – made a spirited defence to the community principle; but the truth is that it was no longer practical politics. After Mr Bishop's Bill in 1969, no attempt to introduce community of property by legislation got anywhere.[27]

On one view, it had all become an irrelevance, and you can argue that the House of Lords in its judicial capacity – in *White*[28] as interpreted in *Lambert*[29] and *Miller/McFarlane*[30] – may have done what Parliament was too timid to do. Certainly, if you were to ask Mr John Charman[31] whether English law is unfair *to women* when it comes to dividing up the family property, you would get a fairly clear answer: according to *The Daily Telegraph* he thinks the 48 million pounds his wife was to take from the family's assets excessive: indeed, that 'twenty million ... is enough for any wife'.[32]

What would Lady Summerskill think? I'm not sure she would be at all happy. You see, she believed that women should have definite property rights, not possible discretionary benefits granted in the secret exercise of a judicial discretion. But they have not got them. She also believed in Parliamentary democracy and might not be altogether at ease with the notion that fundamental issues of social policy should be decided from time to time by five eminent Law Lords, accountable to no one (and certainly not the electorate), no doubt as wise as Plato's guardians and certainly suffused with a proper appreciation of Dworkinian principles, but not susceptible to most of the processes normally associated with democratic decision taking.

Why did divorce come first?

How did it happen? One overriding difficulty was that very few people could really be confident that they understood what reform of property law was all about. In contrast, everyone knew (or at any rate almost everyone thought they knew) about divorce. And of course, many of them knew from personal experience what it was about: it was about being enabled to marry the person with whom they were living – at this period, an important matter. So it was not too difficult to build up a head of steam behind campaigns for reform. Even so, it took 80[33] years before there was reform of the ground for divorce which had been established in 1857 and another 32 before the Divorce Reform Act 1969 proclaimed that

---

[27] For the history, see Cretney, op cit, n 9 above, pp 136–141.
[28] *White v White* [2001] 1 AC 596, HL.
[29] *Lambert v Lambert* [2002] EWCA Civ 1685, [2003] Fam 103.
[30] *Miller v Miller; McFarlane v Mc Farlane* [2006] UKHL 24, [2006] 2 AC 618.
[31] *Charman v Charman (No 4)* [2007] EWCA Civ 503, [2007] 1 FLR 1246.
[32] *Daily Telegraph*, 25 May 2007.
[33] This is not intended to understate the significance of the Matrimonial Causes Act 1923, which, for all practical purposes, made the grounds the same irrespective of the petitioner's sex.

the sole ground for divorce should be that the marriage had broken down irretrievably.[34] Many, many, people played a part in the process which eventually produced the 1969 Act, and many of them were perhaps actuated to a significant extent by the impact of the law on their own relationships: consider the case of John Francis Stanley Russell, grandson of a Prime Minister (and himself to become a Minister of the Crown, albeit for a short period). Not really troublemaker material, you might have thought. But this is the man who, unimpressed by the 'beauties of English law' which denied him a divorce from the wife who had made his life impossible by harassing him with terrible allegations (for example, that he was a practising homosexual), went to the United States, obtained a divorce and married there, only to be arrested as soon as he stepped from the gangplank on his return, convicted (by his peers, of course)[35] of bigamy, and sent to prison for 6 months.

When he was released, he founded a Society for Promoting Reforms in Marriage and Divorce Laws; but its meetings were sparsely attended, and it seems some eminent persons (like Sir Frederick Pollock and A V Dicey) thought it was wrong for the Society to be run by a jailbird, albeit a Peer of the Realm. So he went like a gentleman: and a much more skilful and knowledgeable person – the Lincoln's Inn solicitor, Edmund Sydney Pollock Haynes – became the leading light of the Divorce Law Reform Union. Haynes had four characteristics especially significant in this respect. First, he had a detailed, insider's knowledge of how the divorce laws operated. Secondly, he was a superbly effective communicator – for example, briefing his own client Evelyn Waugh on the material Waugh needed to ridicule the working of the law in his novel *A Handful of Dust* – and ridicule was an especially powerful ingredient in the reformers' case. Thirdly, Haynes's belief in the need for reform was based, not on being himself a victim of the law but on a coherent philosophical position which emphasised personal liberty as against the powers of the state. (Hence, his almost obsessive attacks on the King's Proctor's role, not to mention his hostility to attempts, however well intentioned, to prohibit street gambling and consumption of alcohol). Finally, his professional skills enabled him to draft reforming Bills which themselves were the raw material on which a parliamentary campaign could be based. It was of course A P Herbert whose efforts both as an author of humorous novels and in Parliament as MP for Oxford University finally brought divorce reform onto the statute book, but it was entirely appropriate that Herbert's autobiographical account of how the Matrimonial Causes Act 1937 was brought to the statute book should have been dedicated to Haynes.[36]

---

[34] Divorce Reform Act 1969, s 2(1). This statement was not wholly accurate: see below.
[35] *The Trial of Earl Russell (Before the King in Parliament)* [1901] AC 446.
[36] The reader of the excellent biography of the late John Mortimer QC by Valerie Grove, *A Voyage Round John Mortimer* (Viking, 2007) might be surprised to read this favourable assessment of Haynes, described in her book (apparently in reliance on information supplied to her by the 'gentle wise and scholarly' poet, Michael Hamburger see p 498) as

Haynes was perhaps the first of the technocratic troublemakers. And I do ask the question whether, had someone with his combination of technical and negotiating skill been around to support property law reform in the 1960s and 1970s, things would have happened as they did. But everyone knew about divorce (or, in most cases erroneously, thought they did) and once that reform had been achieved everything else seemed, at least for a while, to be irrelevant. And it was achieved, in large part because the pent-up grievances of the victims of the system were transmuted into *effective* pressure by those we can perhaps describe as 'facilitators': the Parliamentary Draftsman, Ellice Eadie, and those at the Law Commission who, first, worked to achieve a 'concordat' with the Church based on the belief that the 'sole and comprehensive' ground for divorce would indeed be that the marriage had irretrievably broken down[37] and, secondly, to present the provisions of the Matrimonial Proceedings and Property Act 1970 as an adequate answer to those who had supported an 'entitlement' basis for the division of matrimonial property.[38] True, a huge amount of work was done by the Commission in grappling with property law reform; but their priorities were – as you can read in the files lodged in The National Archives[39] – very clear: it was to 'achieve the liberalisation of the grounds of divorce … *without the need to wait for the overhaul of family property*'. And once we had divorce reform on the statute book, family property quickly became 'oh, so boring'.

DO 'RIGHTS' MATTER? THE CASE OF THE GUARDIANSHIP LEGISLATION

There is another area in which it is temptingly easy to believe that legally enforceable rights are irrelevant. Surely, when we are dealing with a child's upbringing the only really important question is what we think will best serve the child's welfare. So there is often a certain amount of incredulity when I say that a significant part of the women's movement's claims in the period after World War I centred around precisely this issue. Feelings ran very high: Eleanor Rathbone – for nearly 20 years the leading proponent

---

a 'sinister, Rabelaisian ex-lawyer' who collected 'decadent and sado-masochistic pornography', which he liked to show to young male visitors – including Hamburger and the young Mortimer. According to Hamburger (see op cit, p 50) 'Haynes beat his dog and his manservant beat him'. But it seems that Mortimer 'got on like a house on fire with this filthy old man.' Perhaps Mortimer – well known for his progressive views on social matters and legal policy – would be saddened that his biographer gives no indication that the 'filthy old man' whom he befriended in his youth had made, over many years, so significant a contribution to the liberalisation of the law, especially in areas in which Mortimer himself had a special interest. Further information about Haynes can be found in the present author's contribution to the *Oxford Dictionary of National Biography* (2004) and the materials referred to therein.

[37] See above; and S M Cretney *Family Law in the Twentieth Century, A History* (Oxford UP, 2003), pp 363–374.
[38] See above; and see Cretney, op cit, n 37 above, pp 133–137.
[39] BC3/400.

of women's issues in the House of Commons – put it very clearly:[40] she admitted that comparatively few husbands abused their exclusive legal right to take decisions about their children's upbringing, but this was simply because the ordinary man's sense of justice refused to 'let him take seriously the monstrous legal fiction that a man has a primary right to the sole control of the children whom a woman has borne with great suffering and at the risk of her life and to whose care nature and custom require her to devote herself as the chief work of the best years of her life'. The case for reform is surely self-evident.

Not for Sir Claud Schuster, the Permanent Secretary in the Lord Chancellor's Office and a dominant figure in the Whitehall of his day. For him the principle of equal authority legislation was simply 'nonsense' because it would produce deadlock. And it was for Schuster no answer to say disputes could always be dealt with by the court: courts, he said, are concerned with the 'definite ascertainment' of rights and duties; but there are no rights here; it would be a question of discretion. 'To take a ridiculous instance, a dispute whether a child is to go to one school or to another school – how on earth is the Court going to deal with that?' It would simply be the judge applying his own personal ideology, which would be unacceptable. And on this occasion, the master of the compromise and the deal, stood firm: 'no compromise is possible'.[41]

But of course there was, up to a point, a compromise: as we all know, in 1925 the Guardianship of Infants Act established that courts should apply the principle that the child's welfare was to be the 'first and paramount' consideration in resolving disputes. But (as a few people did realise) this was not quite what the women's groups had wanted. As with the 1969/73 divorce legislation, there was perhaps a certain lack of candour in making the true position clear.

The 'troublemaker' who had carried most of the burden of persuading the Government to act was Eva Hubback. She had taken a first in Economics at Cambridge, was widowed in World War I, and then served for nearly a decade as Parliamentary Secretary to the National Union of Societies for Equal Citizenship. She was an outstanding lobbyist: her remarkable ability to grasp complex legal issues was one of the attributes which enabled her to gain the confidence of Schuster and other men at the centre of power. But it is possible to argue that by becoming so close to Schuster she became too ready to accept compromises which did not satisfy the expectations of her membership. Yet in this instance she was clearly right in believing that the 1925 Act would in due course provide a firm foundation for the true equal parental rights legislation ultimately enacted (after a campaign associated with the name of Dame Joan Vickers with cross-party and virtually unanimous support) in the

---

[40] *The Disinherited Family* (Edward Arnold, 1924), pp 91–92.
[41] The quotations in this paragraph are from a number of sources; all can be identified by reference to Cretney, op cit, n 37 above, pp 569–570.

Guardianship Act of 1973. Joan Vickers – daughter of Sir Winston Churchill's stockbroker, and described by Churchill as 'a very clever young lady ... a brilliant horsewoman and an independent and attractive spinster' and in her time a 'glamorous, extrovert debutante',[42] does not easily fit into any stereotype of the troublemaker. She may have become *in appearance* 'the epitome of the strident and mindless Conservative matron' (as the *Oxford Dictionary of National Biography* describes her) but in fact she believed that anti-feminism was as serious a problem as racism or any other prejudice, and she put that belief into practice before it became as widely accepted as perhaps it is today.

Today, few people would take Schuster's line that 'parental rights' (albeit now subsumed in the concept of 'parental responsibility') are largely irrelevant in the context of children's upbringing. The shifts in opinion about the legal status of the father of a child born to unmarried parents suggest the contrary. Indeed, the Secretary of State for Work and Pensions in Mr Gordon Brown's administration believes that getting the name of the father onto the birth certificate (and thus giving him the 'parental responsibility' he might not otherwise have) will 'embed a new culture in our society which places much more equal weight on the relationship of both parents with their children'.[43] It will certainly be a change from the view, forcefully and effectively urged on the Law Commission by the National Council for One-Parent Families in 1979, that automatically to vest parental authority in an unmeritorious (and unmarried) father would put both child and mother at risk. But that was nearly 30 years ago; and it may be that attitudes and perceptions have changed over that time. As A J P Taylor claimed, yesterday's dissent becomes today's orthodoxy.

CARING FOR DEPRIVED, NEGLECTED AND ABUSED CHILDREN

The year 2008 marked the centenary of the first 'children's charter', the Children Act 1908. This not only created the (for long much admired) juvenile court – albeit described by the Chief Metropolitan Magistrate[44] as 'the happy hunting ground of all the cranks, male and female, psycho-analysts, psychiatrists, and Christian Scientists' – but made provision for protecting abused children by removing them from their parents. But actually it was not the courts, which at the time had the greatest impact on the lives of disadvantaged children; it was the Poor Law. And in 2009 we mark the centenary of the publication of the Reports of the Royal Commission on the Poor Law. I say 'Reports'

---

[42] Entry by Patrick Cosgrave in the *Oxford Dictionary of National Biography* (online edition, accessed 10 July 2007).
[43] See the Ministerial Foreword to *Joint Birth Registration: promoting parental responsibility*, Cm 7160 (2007).
[44] Sir Chartres Biron *Without Prejudice* (Faber & Faber, 1936), p 259. But even Biron believed that juvenile courts had 'thoroughly justified their existence': ibid.

because, whilst the Majority Report is a no doubt worthy and humane document, it is the 716-page Minority Report which has had historically much the greater impact. The Minority Report is largely the work of Mrs Beatrice Webb (certainly a troublemaker, not least because she was always so well informed that it was virtually impossible to get the better of her in argument, and being always right is often not the best way of getting your way). Even today, the words leap off the page:[45] 'shocking defects' of the system for caring for children, the 'demoralising atmosphere' of the institutions provided for them, the 'stunted, debilitated and diseased children' lacking the necessities of life. What was needed was not only an efficient administration – that went without saying – but the creation of machinery to bring child destitution automatically to light to take the necessary action to relieve it. But even the creation of efficient 'machinery' was not enough. What was required was 'the steady and continuous guidance of a friend, able to suggest in what directions effective help' could be obtained. It took 40 years, and two World Wars to bring it about – or, more accurately, to set up the machinery intended to bring it about. And 'the War' is not just a date: the mass evacuation of children in 1939 'to live with strangers in country towns and villages' was certainly one of the biggest disturbances to family life in British history. This highlighted the need for child psychiatry and social work expertise; and it also created a considerable bureaucratic problem. What was to happen when the evacuation schemes were finally wound up?

This was only one of the problems which troubled Whitehall:[46] what exactly did it mean to 'abolish the poor law', for example? So there was a lot of activity. Possibly surprisingly, no word of this seems to have got into the public domain. However, Marjory Allen, widow of a socialist conscientious objector politician[47] had been shocked by the 'fat, flabby and listless' children in residential care whom she had observed dressed in 'heavy, ill-fitting clothes and boots so clumsy [the children] could only shuffle along'.[48] Disturbed by the fact that the problems of such children had not even been mentioned in published government reconstruction plans, in 1944 she sent a lengthy Memorandum to the Home Secretary. It took 3 months for her to get a reply. And when it came it was of the time hallowed 'this matter is already under consideration ...' kind.

---

[45] Sources for these quotations can be found in Cretney, op cit, n 37 above, pp 653–654.

[46] An attempt to analyse the complex strands in the emergence of the policies finally embodied in the Children Act 1948 is made in 'The State as a Parent', ch 9 of S M Cretney *Law, Law Reform and the Family* (Oxford UP, 1998).

[47] Clifford Allen (1889–1939), imprisoned 1916, Chairman of the Independent Labour Party 1923–1925, loyal to Ramsay McDonald as Prime Minister of the National Government formed in 1930, his acceptance of a peerage in 1932 damaged his reputation within the Labour Party: see Entry for Lord Allen of Hurtwood in the *Oxford Dictionary of National Biography* (online edition, accessed 10 July 2007).

[48] M Allen and M Nicholson *Memoirs of an Uneducated Lady* (Thames & Hudson, 1975), p 170.

Lady Allen knew what to do: she had already arranged to have a letter published in *The Times*.[49] The response was amazing: as the Permanent Under-Secretary of State at the Home Office noted to a colleague, the Government would 'have been very glad to postpone an enquiry of [the kind for which Lady Allen had asked] but the Home Secretary feels that in view of the correspondence in *The Times* and the pressure which will no doubt be exerted in Parliament ... it will probably be impracticable to avoid taking early action.' And so, eventually, the Report of the Curtis Committee on the *Care of Children*[50] was published, and the Children Act 1948 gave statutory effect to its recommendations. This is how Lady Allen described her role. 'At first', she said, she—

> 'had been much too timid in my manner of putting questions to civil servants: a polite letter obviously got nowhere. And why should I plead with them? They were there to serve the public, and as a member of the public I was entitled to be served. From this moment my whole attitude changed. Instead of writing to government departments, I arranged to see someone fairly high up. This method was much more successful. My new contacts were most willing to tell me what I wanted to know. The only difficulty was that they did not always know it themselves.'[51]

One final, unhappy, note about the Children Act 1948. On 9 January 1945 a 12-year-old boy in the care of a local authority was killed by his foster-father. There was an immense public outcry and (as the *Daily Mail* put it) this fanned the conscience of the British people. The decision to set up the Curtis Committee had already been taken, and the boy's death could not have had anything to do with that decision. But the evidence that it did have a great deal to do with the contents of the Committee's Report, and (critically) with the decision to legislate seems to me to be overwhelming.[52] Like it or not, the history of child abuse inquiries demonstrates over and over again that there is nothing like a scandal to generate the feeling that 'something must be done' – whether, in the event, that 'something' is likely to prevent a recurrence of what happened or not. Even so, it was the decision to set up a Committee, with wide terms of reference, which critically affected what that 'something' was, and the 'uneducated' Marjory Allen is entitled to a lot of the credit for that.

TRANSFORMING IDEAS INTO LAWS

In saying that all major structural law reform requires legislation I am not seeking to disparage the part played by judicial decision in bringing about change. The relationship between the two is complex and extremely interesting, but it is not the subject of this lecture. Ultimately all my troublemakers have been concerned to secure the passing of primary

---

[49] 15 July 1944.
[50] Cmd 6922 (1946).
[51] M Allen and M Nicholson, op cit, n 48 above, p 183.
[52] See Cretney, op cit, n 46 above, pp 212–216.

legislation, and under a constitution in which the executive controls the legislature that is not easily done, however clear the consensus in favour of change. In particular, governments will not wish to be associated with legislation raising moral issues on which sections of the electorate have strong views – especially if those sections include groups who traditionally support the governing party at elections. The history of divorce reform exemplifies this. Ultimately you need members of Parliament (which, remember, had and still has two Houses) who have the will to bring about reform, the organisational and personal skills needed to overcome the many obstacles to getting legislation with no place in a party manifesto, and even some legislation which is in a manifesto but which is possibly a vote-loser, onto the statute book.

Leo Abse: the most effective law reformer in twentieth-century Britain?

One man, Leo Abse, a Cardiff solicitor,[53] and a Labour Member of Parliament for Welsh Constituencies for nearly 30 years, was an outstanding example of such a person.[54] In *Family Law in the Twentieth Century, A History* I describe him as a 'brilliantly skilled master of parliamentary procedures' who 'probably had a greater influence on the development of law relating to family matters than any other MP in the twentieth century'. But that is wrong. The word 'probably' should be deleted.

One thing is quite clear: Leo Abse undoubtedly qualifies as a 'troublemaker'. The summary of his career he gave in *Who's Who* begins with the boast that his 'arrest for political activities' in 1944 whilst serving as an aircraftsman in the Royal Air Force 'precipitated a parliamentary debate'. Service personnel in Cairo had organised, with the goodwill of the authorities, a 'Forces Parliament', at which issues of the day (and especially the post-war future) such as the nationalisation of the banks were to be debated. But suddenly at the 'Parliament's' second meeting a Brigadier appeared. He promulgated an order that the word 'Parliament' should not be used, that no civilians or press were to be present, and – worst of all – that the subjects to be discussed were to be supervised by the Military authorities and controlled by them. 'Ringleaders' including Abse were immediately 'posted', some to what were described as 'really unpleasant places'.[55] Not perhaps a promising start. But once again 'look at the achievements'.

---

[53] The firm which he founded (now Leo Abse and Cohen) is now 150 strong, and practises from offices in Swansea and Newport, as well as in Cardiff.

[54] Leo Abse died in 2008, aged 91. He was a productive author well into old age, publishing books on literary, political and psycho-analytical topics.

[55] This account is based largely on *Hansard*, HC Deb, vol 401, col 1136 (5 July 1944); and vol 403, cols 1090–1100 (4 October 1944). See also L Abse *Private Member* (Macdonald, 1973), pp 40–41.

First, there is the Divorce Reform Act 1969. Leo Abse[56] (says a Professor of Politics) was the 'dominant figure' in organising support. 'His colourful personality, his boundless energy, his contacts with the press and his close acquaintance with some Ministers were all of great importance.'[57] Second, decriminalising homosexuality: it was his Bill, which on 27 July 1967 finally achieved what he and others had campaigned for over a decade and more. The long campaign meant that the arguments had all been repeated ad nauseam, there was nothing left to say, and the 'heat and vigour' of the controversy had faded. So the final stages depended on Abse's tactical skill in knowing when to compromise (notably by exempting the merchant shipping industry from the Bill and thus preventing their opposition bringing down the Bill). Professor Richards says that the eventual success 'depended largely upon Abse's crusading energy and his good personal relationships with some ministers'.[58] Third, the Children Act 1975: now, in the wake of the Children Act 1989 and the Adoption and Children Act 2002, almost forgotten. But it was Abse who vigorously lobbied Home Secretary Callaghan (and his wife)[59] to set up the Houghton Committee on Adoption,[60] promising Callaghan that he would secure a place in history as 'the man who had revolutionised Britain's Child Law'.[61] And it was the Houghton Report which led to acceptance of the idea of a nationwide comprehensive adoption service, to 'freeing for adoption', to an improved institutional framework for fostering and, perhaps most significant, the 'right to know' about adoption. And it was Abse who helped David Owen to produce a draft Bill[62] which became the catalyst for the 1975 Children Act. It was Abse who played a lead role in getting issues of assisted reproduction properly investigated, and thus to the Human Fertilisation and Embryology Act 1990.[63] And there is all the rest, not perhaps family law as traditionally understood: decriminalising suicide, provision of family planning, and so on.

James Callaghan was surely right to say[64] that Abse did 'much more good in terms of human happiness than 90% of the work done in Parliament on what is called "political issues"'; and that is surely a sufficient reason for marking – especially in Cardiff – Leo Abse's remarkable achievements. But there is another one: he had a deep understanding of what is possible

---

[56] See P G Richards *Parliament and Conscience* (Allen & Unwin, 1970), p 157.
[57] He appreciated that the Matrimonial Proceedings and Property Act 1970 was the price which had to be paid for reform of the ground for divorce.
[58] Who were persuaded to allow more time for votes to take place.
[59] See Abse, op cit, n 55 above, pp 243–247.
[60] *Report of the Departmental Committee on the Adoption of Children*, Cmnd 5107 (1972).
[61] See L Abse *Fellatio, Masochism, Politics and Love* (Robson Books, 2000), p 164.
[62] 'A remarkable achievement for a Private Member without official assistance': S M Cretney *Law, Law Reform and the Family* (Oxford UP, 1998), p 704; see also D Owen *Time to Declare* (Penguin Books, 1992), p 2; Abse, op cit, n 61 above, pp 163–165.
[63] See Abse's perceptive essay 'The Politics of In Vitro Fertilisation in Britain' in S Fishel and E M Symonds (eds) *In Vitro Fertilisation, Past, Present, Future* (IRL Press, 1986), pp 207–227.
[64] Abse, op cit, n 55 above, p 246.

within the constraints of the British Parliamentary system. First, he understood that a Member of Parliament must have an intuitive understanding of how far constituents are prepared for their MP to go. Take the perhaps trivial example of the Law Reform (Miscellaneous Provisions) Act 1970: the Law Commission, committed to the view that it was of 'overriding importance' to do away with litigation about who was to blame for ending a relationship, wanted to provide that a man be entitled to get back an engagement ring even if he had jilted his fiancée. But Abse thought it was quite wrong for 'over-logical lawyers' to trample on women's feelings. Public reaction was 'immediate, extensive and unanimous' in supporting him.[65] His 'exasperated' colleagues 'sensed the danger of a flood engulfing the whole Bill' and the Bill was accordingly amended:[66]

> 'My wife, and womankind, had their way: and jilted girls [sic] can now keep their ring, sell them, throw them in the river or at their faithless lovers.'[67]

You may not find this language entirely congenial; but surely it is of the essence of democracy that, up to a point, legislation should reflect not only 'informed opinion' but the views of others who are to be bound by it.

'Up to a point'. But the issue of where that point is to be placed – think of capital punishment – is of course vital and cannot easily be answered in general terms. Abse had at least a partial answer. Perhaps rather uncharacteristically – because as Professor Peter Richards[68] put it, Abse's basic philosophy was that 'the only way to achieve social reform in a parliamentary context is to persevere, to nag and nag, and to keep nagging away' – Abse also believed in the need for calm and patience in law reform. He saw the advantage of the long gestation period offered by the Law Commission's methods of first issuing a public and tentative consultation period, thus enabling the Commission to identify not only weaknesses in its own provisional view but to see where compromise may be needed to obtain consensus; and he noted that the technique also has 'a wide educational effect', prompting discussion both formal and informal. And it gives time to identify 'the strength or weakness of those who will sustain unremitting hostility to proposals and alerts those who wish to support [the proposals] to the nature of the recalcitrant opposition'. Putting it in the psycho-analytic framework which had so evident an influence on him, he saw the traditional role of the political process as being to 'obviate conflict by the reduction of tension levels in our society'. But he believed this to be under threat because of changes in the nature of the political process. In particular, what he described as the decay of Party and the growth of lobby – in effect that the Party tradition involved 'inevitable restraints' that must come with membership of a

---

[65] Abse, op cit, n 55 above, p 193.
[66] See S M Cretney (1970) 33 MLR 534.
[67] Abse, op cit, n 55 above, p 193.
[68] Richards, op cit, n 56 above, p 158.

party (always to some extent a coalition), whereas the growth of the single issue lobby has led to tunnel vision, the demand for instant results.[69] Certainly, a great deal of progress has been made by allowing time for attitudes to change, and even by allowing opponents of reform the opportunity to believe that the change is not quite as far-reaching as they fear, as perhaps has happened with 'breakdown' divorce and, indeed, civil partnership.

CONCLUSION

'Troublemakers' have had a huge influence on the development of family law. But do not misunderstand me: their activities have often – as I believe happened in the divorce/property area – purchased change at the price of pushing what is desirable off the agenda for all time. Perhaps we should not mourn the fact that the one man or one woman campaigner no longer has so important a role to play as once was the case. After all, the Civil Partnership Act 2004 got onto the statute book with none of the razzmatazz which I have described in relation to other much less significant reforms. Certainly the story of how that happened – and whether it will ever be transmuted into an unashamed statutory acceptance of same-sex marriage – will be a fascinating subject for research. But that must wait for many years. For the present, it is right simply to recognise, above all in a conference marking the fiftieth anniversary of the publication of Graveson and Crane,[70] that our lives are affected by the past, and that we certainly cannot understand the law as it has come to be without taking into account the way in which it came into being.

---

[69] L Abse, op cit, n 61 and n 54 above.
[70] R H Graveson and F R Crane (eds) *A Century of Family Law* (Sweet & Maxwell, 1957).

CHAPTER 3

LOOKING BACK ON THE OVERLOOKED: COHABITANTS AND THE LAW 1857–2007

Rebecca Probert

INTRODUCTION

'The past half-century has witnessed great changes, both social and individual, in attitudes towards sex and marriage.'[1] So wrote Eustace Chesser in 1956 – a useful reminder, perhaps, that we tend to focus on the changes of our own time, and give insufficient emphasis to the way in which previous generations experienced similar changes. Even so, it can be said with certainty that the past 30 or so years have witnessed great changes – social, individual, and legal – in the incidence of, and attitudes to, cohabitation. Fifty years ago, it was reasonable for *A Century of Family Law*[2] to take the husband-and-wife unit as the basis of discussion: few couples cohabited, and the whole trend of the reforms documented in that work was to treat married couples more like cohabiting couples than vice versa. Cohabiting couples were almost entirely overlooked by the various contributors. Today, by contrast, there are over two million cohabiting couples,[3] and the question of whether cohabiting couples should be treated more like married couples is a very live issue.

But when looking forward to reform, it is often useful to look back, to understand the past. Despite the evidence of widespread public support for reform, it is likely to be politically controversial and there is a danger that the truth may be sacrificed to what is politically expedient. As Peter Marshall has noted, history can easily 'become a political resource pack, a storeroom of weapons for fighting the battles of one's own age'.[4] But myths and misunderstandings are no basis for a coherent discussion of what the law has been, and how it should develop.

There is a widespread assumption among lawyers, historians and other commentators that cohabitation was prevalent in the past. One claim that has been widely accepted is John Gillis's estimate that in the late eighteenth and early nineteenth centuries up to one-fifth of the

---

[1] E Chesser *The Sexual, Marital and Family Relationships of the English Woman* (Hutchinson's Medical Publications, 1956), p 3.
[2] R Graveson and F Crane (eds) *A Century of Family Law* (Sweet & Maxwell, 1957).
[3] S Smallwood and B Wilson (eds) *Focus on Families* (ONS, 2007), p 4.
[4] P Marshall *Mother Leakey & the Bishop: A Ghost Story* (Oxford UP, 2007), p 239.

population may have cohabited at some point.[5] Parallels are drawn between the eighteenth century and the twenty-first,[6] or occasionally between the 1930s and the 1960s,[7] with the Victorian era and the 1950s, by contrast, being depicted as periods when a more conservative morality reigned. It is also widely assumed that before Lord Hardwicke's Act of 1753 cohabiting couples would enjoy the benefit of a 'common-law marriage', and be treated as if they had in fact married. Marriage in the eighteenth century is today often depicted as an institution for the rich, imposed on an unwilling populace who for the most part ignored its requirements.[8]

In fact, nothing could be further from the truth: the data on which Gillis relied for his estimate of cohabiting unions does not support (and sometimes contradicts) his inference;[9] all the demographic evidence indicates that the extent of cohabitation in England and Wales in the twenty-first century is unprecedented; the legal evidence shows clearly that the idea that cohabiting couples in the past enjoyed the protection of a 'common-law marriage' is just as much a myth as is the idea, still prevalent among cohabiting couples, that this is the case today;[10] and, in the eighteenth century, cohabitation was not only vanishingly rare,[11] but also the subject of legal and social disapproval. Far from cohabiting couples being equated to married couples, they ran the risk of being punished as fornicators by the ecclesiastical courts for living together unmarried.

It is necessary, therefore, to begin afresh and to examine the actual evidence of cohabitation. The terminal dates of this study – 1857 and 2007 – both constitute important landmarks in the history of cohabitation, but for very different reasons. 2007, of course, saw the publication of the Law Commission's proposals for reforming the rules applicable when a cohabiting relationship comes to an end.[12] The passage

---

[5] J Gillis *For Better, For Worse: British Marriages 1600 to the Present* (Oxford UP, 1985), p 219.

[6] S Parker 'The Marriage Act 1753: A Case Study in Family Law-making' (1987) 1 *International Journal of Law and the Family* 133; G Stewart 'The swinging 1700s were so like today' *The Times*, 24 February 2007, p 23.

[7] See eg S McRae (ed) *Changing Britain: Families and Households in the 1990s* (Oxford UP, 1999), p 2, who claimed that 'much of what we are seeing in Britain today is the continuation of trends briefly interrupted by the "ideal family" of the 1950s' but offered no data on key trends such as cohabitation or births outside marriage.

[8] See eg S Parker *Informal Marriage, Cohabitation and the Law, 1754–1989* (Macmillan, 1990), p 4; W Mansell, B Meteyard and A Thomson *A Critical Introduction to Law* (Cavendish, 3rd edn, 2004), p 84; A Diduck and F Kaganas *Family Law, Gender and the State: Text, Cases and Materials* (Hart Publishing, 2nd edn, 2005).

[9] See R Probert 'Chinese Whispers and Welsh Weddings' (2005) 20 *Continuity and Change* 211.

[10] See R Probert 'Common-law marriage: myths and misunderstandings' [2008] CFLQ 1.

[11] See R Probert and L D'Arcy Brown 'The Clandestine Marriages Act: Three Case Studies in Conformity' (2008) 23 *Continuity and Change* 309.

[12] Law Commission *The Financial Consequences of Relationship Breakdown*, Law Com No 307 (HMSO, 2007).

of the Divorce and Matrimonial Causes Act in 1857 is, at first sight, of less immediate relevance to cohabiting couples, but the case law and reports that it generated do provide a useful source of information about cohabiting couples, and an indication of the law's policy towards them, at a time when little other reliable evidence is available. There is, therefore, evidence that *some* couples cohabited, at least in the mid-nineteenth century; further, it is clear that the legal system could not but be aware of this fact.[13]

This chapter will first sketch out the history of cohabitation over the past 150 years – the extent of cohabitation and attitudes towards it – and will then show how the law has engaged with cohabiting couples in that period. It will focus on heterosexual cohabitants, since cohabitants of the same sex were not so much an overlooked as a hidden constituency before the decriminalisation of private homosexual behaviour in 1967, a fact which was reflected in social and legal attitudes towards such relationships.

THE EXTENT AND NATURE OF COHABITATION

Although it was not until the later part of the twentieth century that statistics as to the extent of cohabitation began to be collected,[14] some inferences as to the potential extent of cohabitation in earlier decades can be made from other evidence – for example, the marriage rate and the number and proportion of children born outside marriage.

If one examines the marriage rate from 1837 to 2003, both the crude marriage rate (marriages per 1,000 population) and the number of males marrying per 1,000 single, widowed and divorced males aged 16 and over show a long-term decline: at the start of the twenty-first century the crude marriage rate fell below 10 per 1,000 for the first time; while the number of males who are eligible to marry actually doing so has fallen far more precipitously, from 53 per 1,000 in the early 1980s to 28 per 1,000 in the twenty-first century.[15] Taking a longer-term perspective and considering the illegitimacy ratio[16] over the past 400 years, it is even clearer that modern trends have no historical precedent. The illegitimacy ratio has

---

[13] These are obvious enough points, but worth reiterating in the light of accounts that suggest that the authorities only 'discovered' cohabitation at the time of the First World War: see eg A Marwick *The Deluge: British Society and the First World War* (Penguin, 1967), p 113.

[14] The first national-level study was carried out in 1976, and a question about cohabitation was first included in the census in 1991.

[15] Source: ONS 'Marriages 1841–2003' available at http://www.statistics.gov.uk/statbase/ xsdataset.asp?vlnk=4103&More=Y.

[16] That is, the percentage of births outside marriage as a percentage of all births. In this case to calculate the proportion of births outside marriage in relation to the unmarried may be misleading, since many of those who produced illegitimate children were married women separated but not divorced from their husbands.

fluctuated over time, but it was not until the 1980s that it exceeded 10 per cent; today, by contrast, it is over 40 per cent.[17]

Of course, it should be borne in mind that a birth outside marriage does not necessarily denote a cohabiting relationship: even today, over one-third of mothers who have a child outside marriage are not living with the father at the time of the birth.[18] Nor can one project today's figures back into the past and conclude that two-thirds of mothers who had a child outside marriage were cohabiting: this percentage would inevitably have been influenced by the social acceptability (or otherwise) of cohabitation at the time. Indeed, earlier studies suggest that a far lower percentage of illegitimate births occurred in the context of cohabiting unions. For example, Steven King's study of several parishes in the early nineteenth century found that '[l]ess than one-third of all women bearing multiple bastards had all of their children by the same father, fewer than the 40 per cent of women who acknowledged four or more different fathers.'[19] Similarly, although there were a high number of illegitimate births in Culcheth, '... their mothers, even if they had more than one child, appear not to have been cohabiting with a man'.[20] Instead, they remained with their parents, a trend also evident in mid-nineteenth-century Colyton.[21] Ginger Frost, examining the experiences of illegitimate children in the late nineteenth and early twentieth centuries, confirms the importance of kin in caring for illegitimate children and notes that 'in the vast majority of cases, one or both of their natural parents were not part of the family circle.'[22] Even in the mid-twentieth century the percentage of illegitimate births that occurred in the context of cohabiting unions was lower than today: one study found that just under 6 per cent of a sample of 1,142 infants born in Newcastle in 1947 were illegitimate; of these 67 children, 27 were living with both parents 'as members of unofficial families'.[23] Similar findings emerged from a study carried out in Leicester in 1949.[24] This focused solely on illegitimate children and found that around half of the mothers were living with the father at the time that the

---

[17] 43 per cent in 2005: ONS *Social Trends 37* (HMSO, 2007), p 22. For earlier periods see P Laslett 'Introduction: comparing illegitimacy over time and between cultures', ch 1 in P Laslett, K Oosterveen and R Smith *Bastardy and its Comparative History* (Edward Arnold, 1980); ONS 'Live births, Age of mother occurrence within/outside marriage and sex', available at http://www.statistics.gov.uk/STATBASE/xsdataset.asp?vlnk=4270.

[18] K Kiernan and K Smith 'Unmarried parenthood: new insights from the Millennium Cohort Study' (2003) 114 *Population Trends* 26.

[19] S King 'The Bastardy Prone Sub-Society Again: Bastards and their Fathers and Mothers in Lancashire, Wiltshire, and Somerset, 1800–1840', in A Levene, T Nutt and S Williams (eds) *Illegitimacy in Britain, 1700–1920* (Palgrave Macmillan, 2005), p 80.

[20] G N Gandy 'Illegitimacy in a Handloom Weaving Community: Fertility Patterns in Culcheth, Lancashire, 1781–1860' (unpublished DPhil dissertation, 1978), p 21.

[21] J Robin 'Illegitimacy in Colyton, 1851–1881' (1987) 2 *Continuity and Change* 307.

[22] G Frost '"The Black Lamb of the Black Sheep": Illegitimacy in the English Working Class, 1850–1939' (2003) 37 *Journal of Social History* 293 at 309.

[23] J Spence et al *A Thousand Families in Newcastle upon Tyne* (Oxford UP, 1954), p 144.

[24] E K MacDonald 'Follow-up of Illegitimate Children' (14 December 1956) *The Medical Officer* 361.

child was conceived; five years later a high proportion – over 45 per cent – were still living with the father. This, however, is still lower than the proportion of births outside marriage that occur within the context of a cohabiting partnership today.[25] Any estimate of the extent of cohabitation must therefore treat the illegitimacy ratio as a maximum, while bearing in mind that it is likely to be considerably lower.

This is consistent with the evidence that, when rights – discussed further below – were conferred on cohabitants for a brief period in the early part of the twentieth century, there were few to take advantage of them. It has been suggested that mothers, rather than cohabitants, were the primary recipients of dependants' pensions in the First World War, with a mere 3 per cent of such pensions being paid to 'unmarried wives'.[26] Similarly, when dependants' benefits were provided to the cohabitants of unemployed men in the 1920s, only a tiny proportion of unemployed men – less than one per cent – claimed benefits for women living with them to whom they were not married.[27]

Put together, all the evidence supports the conclusion of demographers that cohabitation on a mass scale is unprecedented and was virtually unknown before the 1970s. As Kathleen Kiernan et al have noted, cohabitation was 'statistically and socially invisible' before the 1970s.[28] In a similar vein, Mike Murphy notes that 'under 1 per cent of women aged 18–49 were cohabiting until the late 1960s.'[29] Other commentators concur in dating the rise in cohabitation to this period.[30] One early study found that 9 per cent of women who had married between 1970 and 1975 reported that they had cohabited with their husbands-to-be; among those who had married between 1956 and 1960 it was only 1 per cent.[31] This is confirmed by research carried out by John Haskey, who found that of those born between 1925 and 1929, and therefore of an age to form partnerships in the late 1940s and early 1950s, only 1 per cent had cohabited before marriage, and a mere 0.4 per cent had cohabited without

---

[25] In 2005, 84 per cent of births outside marriage were jointly registered, and of these three-quarters were registered by parents living at the same address: ONS *Social Trends 37* (HMSO, 2007), p 22. In addition, 8 per cent of those mothers who alone registered the birth were cohabiting with the father at the time of the birth: S Smallwood 'Characteristics of sole registered births and the mothers who register them' (2004) 117 *Population Trends* 20, table 1.

[26] G Thomas 'State Maintenance for Women During the First World War: The Case of Separation Allowances and Pensions' (unpublished PhD thesis, University of Sussex, 1989).

[27] Ministry of Labour *Report on an Investigation into the Personal Circumstances and Industrial History of 9,748 Claimants to Unemployment Benefit, April 4th to 9th* (HMSO, 1928).

[28] K Kiernan, H Land and J Lewis *Lone Motherhood in Twentieth Century Britain* (Clarendon Press, 1998), p 40.

[29] M Murphy 'The evolution of cohabitation in Britain, 1960–95' (2000) 54 *Population Studies* 43 at 45.

[30] See eg C Haste *Rules of Desire: Sex in Britain: World War 1 to the Present* (Chatto & Windus, 1992), p 234.

[31] K Dunnell *Family Formation 1976* (OPCS, 1979), para 2.4.

marrying.[32] Cohabitation was not unknown, but it was rare, and any individual instances must therefore be set in the context of these general trends.

From the start of the 1970s, however, the numbers cohabiting began to grow. The 1979 General Household Survey found that 3 per cent of the women in its sample were living in a cohabiting relationship, although only 1.4 per cent of first unions were cohabitations, as opposed to the 16 per cent of second or later unions.[33] The percentage of couples who had lived together before marriage rose from 10 per cent in the 1970s to around 80 per cent in the twenty-first century. By the end of the century both men and women were more likely to cohabit than to marry in their first relationship, and those who had been divorced were also more likely to cohabit with a new partner rather than to embark on marriage again.[34] Cohabitation is now prevalent amongst all age groups: in 2005 almost a quarter of non-married men and women under the age of 60 were cohabiting with a partner.[35]

ATTITUDES TO COHABITATION

The low levels of cohabitation in previous generations are perhaps understandable if one examines social attitudes towards cohabitation in this period. In the mid-nineteenth century the writer George Eliot, despite her fame, was not received into society because of her relationship with the married George Lewes.[36] Frost has shown that some couples, unable to marry legally because one or both of them was already married, preferred the apparent respectability of bigamy to cohabitation: while the parties to such a marriage would, in strict legal terms, be no more than cohabitants (and criminals to boot), the extent of bigamy in the nineteenth century is a clear indication that cohabiting without a marriage ceremony was not an acceptable alternative for many couples.[37]

---

[32] J Haskey 'Cohabitational and marital histories of adults in Great Britain' (1999) *Population Trends* 13.

[33] See A Brown and K Kiernan 'Cohabitation in Great Britain: Evidence from the General Household Survey' (1981) 25 *Population Trends* 4.

[34] J Ermisch and M Francesconi 'Patterns of household and family formation' in R Berthoud and J Gershuny (eds) *Seven Years in the Lives of British Families* (The Policy Press, 2000).

[35] ONS *Social Trends 37* (HMSO, 2007), p 19.

[36] R Ashton *George Eliot: A Life* (Penguin, 1997), p 121. On the range of views expressed after Eliot's death, see T Mangum 'George Eliot and the Journalists: Making the Mistress Moral' in K Ottesen Garrigan (ed) *Victorian Scandals: Representations of Gender and Class* (Ohio University Press, 1992).

[37] See eg G Frost 'Bigamy and cohabitation in Victorian England' (1997) 22 *Journal of Family History* 286.

Cohabitation by choice was not unknown, but was generally limited to a small and disreputable minority.[38] Indeed, cohabitation was depicted by a number of commentators as almost synonymous with urban poverty and irreligion, as characteristic of 'outcast London'. In the 1880s Andrew Mearns suggested that inquiries regarding marital status would merely produce a smile in certain parts of London:

> 'Nobody knows. Nobody cares. Nobody expects that they are ... Those who appear to be married are often separated by a mere quarrel, and they do not hesitate to form similar companionships immediately. One man was pointed out who for some years had lived with a woman, the mother of his three children. She died and in less than a week he had taken another woman in her place.'[39]

Similarly, Henry Mayhew, writing in the 1850s, had claimed that '[o]nly one-tenth – at the outside one-tenth – of the couples living together and carrying on the costermonging trade, are married'.[40] Among patterers,[41] too, 'marriage is as little frequent as among the costermongers, with the exception of the older class, who were perhaps married before they took to the streets.'[42]

The accuracy of such claims is perhaps open to question: Mayhew's comments were based on qualitative rather than quantitative methods. Investigators who actually counted the unmarried found significantly lower levels of cohabitation: the London City Mission missionary for Deptford found one-third – rather than nine-tenths – of couples in one deprived area to be unmarried.[43] Interestingly, this was seen as confirming rather than contradicting Mayhew: for the moralist, the fact that *any* couples lived together unmarried was a problem, and the precise numbers did not matter too much.

By contrast, among the 'respectable' poor considerable importance was attached to marriage. As Ellen Ross has pointed out, marriage was a 'far more central part of adult life' for the working classes, who married earlier and more often than the middle-classes.[44] Marriage certificates were valued as a symbol of respectability and (more practically) might be made a precondition of assistance from parish visitors and poor law officials.[45]

---

[38] F M L Thompson *The Rise of Respectable Society: A Social History of Victorian Britain, 1830–1900* (Fontana Press, 1988), p 91.
[39] A Mearns *The Bitter Cry of Outcast London* (James Clarke & Co, 1883), p 7.
[40] H Mayhew *London Labour and the London Poor* (Frank Cass & Co Ltd, 1951), p 20.
[41] Patterers were street vendors who sold cheap booklets and broadsides. According to Flanders, their name derived from the fact that they 'sang through the songs on the broadside for any customer unacquainted with the tunes': J Flanders *Consuming Passions: Leisure and Pleasure in Victorian Britain* (Harper Perennial 2007), p 176.
[42] Mayhew, op cit, p 213.
[43] See eg the *London City Mission Magazine* (August 1855), Vol XX, p 188.
[44] E Ross *Love and Toil: Motherhood in Outcast London, 1870–1918* (Oxford UP, 1993).
[45] Ibid, p 64.

Towards the end of the nineteenth century, however, marriage and the family came under increasing criticism,[46] with alternatives to marriage being discussed amongst radical intellectuals and writers more widely than ever before.[47] A few suggested that marriage could be improved by allowing couples to test their compatibility before signing up to a life-long commitment, although they often stopped short of advocating pre-marital cohabitation.[48] In 1878, however, the feminist and socialist Annie Besant contended that 'women have a fairer chance of happiness and comfort in an unlegalised than in a legal marriage';[49] and this idea was echoed in a number of novels of the period.[50] The fate of the 'New Woman' who cohabited was not necessarily any better than that of the 'fallen' woman of mid-Victorian fiction: almost inevitably novels depicted disaster and death, rather than a 'happy-ever-after' ending. Yet, as Gail Cunningham has described, there was a difference between the two: in the case of the 'New Women', their fates were presented as a result of the fact that they were too advanced for the society in which they lived rather than as a form of punishment for transgressions.[51]

And it is fair to say that these fictional heroines *were* too advanced for the society of the time. Only a very few men and women actually put these ideas into practice. Most feminists of the time believed that the way forward was to reform the law of marriage and opposed free unions on the bases, first, that they offered too little protection to women, and, secondly, that impropriety might damage the women's cause.[52] In the 1870s, Elizabeth Wolstenholme Elmy was a rare example of a feminist who cohabited outside marriage and she was quickly persuaded to marry for fear that her situation would damage the feminist cause. Indeed, the fact that she is mentioned in a number of accounts suggests that she was practically the only prominent feminist to flout convention in this way.[53] Moreover, the social ostracism meted out to her dissuaded others from following in her footsteps: Emmeline Goulden, for example, initially proposed a free union with Richard Pankhurst, but in the light of Elmy's treatment was persuaded to marry for the good of the cause.[54] And the sad fate of Eleanor Marx stood as a warning: she cohabited with Edward

---

[46] See eg R Binion 'Fiction as Social Fantasy: Europe's Domestic Crisis of 1879–1914' (1993) 27 *Journal of Social History* 679.

[47] For earlier proponents, see eg M Mason *The Making of Victorian Sexual Attitudes* (Oxford UP, 1994).

[48] See eg E Ellis *A Noviciate for Marriage* (Haslemere, 1984); W Donisthorpe 'The Future of Marriage' (1892) 51 *Fortnightly Review* 258.

[49] Quoted in L Bland *Banishing the Beast: English Feminism and Sexual Morality 1885–1914* (Penguin, 1995), p 153.

[50] See eg G Allen *The Woman Who Did* (John Lane, 1895); T Hardy *Jude the Obscure* (Macmillan, 1895); H G Wells *Ann Veronica* (T Fisher Unwin, 1909).

[51] G Cunningham *The New Woman and the Victorian Novel* (Macmillan, 1978).

[52] L Bland *Banishing the Beast: English Feminism and Sexual Morality 1885–1914* (Penguin, 1995), pp 151–161.

[53] See eg Bland, op cit; J Walkowitz *Prostitution and Victorian Society: women, class and the state* (Cambridge UP, 1980), p 123.

[54] J Adams *Pankhurst* (Haus Publishing, 2003), p 10.

Aveling, and regarded herself as married to him. But even those in advanced circles objected to mixing with her;[55] worse still, it transpired that Edward had no objection to marriage, since he secretly married a young actress while continuing to visit, and to borrow money from, Eleanor. On learning of his defection, she committed suicide.[56]

Of course, more positive examples of cohabiting unions can be found – particularly among artists and writers of the early twentieth century. Free love was part of the Bohemian creed,[57] although its practitioners went beyond simply living together as husband and wife outside marriage. The Bloomsbury group has been described as 'a circle of people who lived in squares and loved in triangles',[58] and even those who married did not live conventional lives.

The examples set by individuals who were in any case on the intellectual extremes of society did little to alter the perceived irrespectability of cohabitation: Bohemians, after all, deliberately behaved in a way that would shock respectable society. Official attitudes, meanwhile, remained harsh. Police personnel records indicate that police officers might face dismissal if discovered to be cohabiting, and even when lighter penalties were imposed they were still expected to give up the relationship.[59] And other occupations were no less regulated: as one writer noted in the 1930s, '[t]here are a good many jobs to which you will not be appointed, or from which ... you may be dismissed' if living in sin.[60] The philosopher Bertrand Russell was equally pessimistic, arguing that:

> 'for economic reasons [cohabitation] is impossible in most cases. A doctor or a lawyer who attempted to live in open sin would lose all his patients or clients. A man engaged in any branch of the scholastic profession would lose his post at once.[61] Even if economic circumstances do not make open sin impossible, most people will be deterred by the social penalties.'[62]

In many ways, as Simon Szreter has argued, Britain did not cease to be 'Victorian' in terms of sexuality until the 1960s.[63] In the 1950s the novelist Margaret Forster had to pretend to be married to get accommodation

---

[55] Her membership of the Men and Women's Club was objected to by Maria Sharpe on this basis: J Walkowitz *City of Dreadful Delight: Narratives of Sexual Danger in Late-Victorian London* (The Virago Press, 1992), p 140.
[56] R Braddon *The new women and the old men: love, sex and the woman question* (Secker & Warburg, 1990).
[57] See eg V Nicholson *Among the Bohemians: Experiments in Living 1900–1939* (Penguin, 2003), p 34.
[58] Ibid, p 41.
[59] J Klein 'Irregular Marriages: Unorthodox Working-Class Domestic Life in Liverpool, Birmingham, and Manchester, 1900–1939' (2005) 30 *Journal of Family History* 210.
[60] M Cole *Marriage, Past and Present* (JM Dent & Sons Ltd, 1939), p 245.
[61] Unless, as Russell wryly noted, 'he happens to teach at one of the older universities and to be closely related to a peer who has been a Cabinet Minister.'
[62] B Russell *Marriage and Morals* (George Allen & Unwin Ltd, 1976), p 147.
[63] S Szreter 'Victorian Britain, 1831–1963: towards a social history of sexuality' (1996) 1 *Journal of Victorian Culture* 136.

with her boyfriend – when they told landlords they were not, doors were closed 'so in the end it had to be on with the Woolworths ring.'[64] In one 1950 survey, Geoffrey Gorer posed the rather coy question '[n]ot counting marriage, have you ever had a real love affair?' and half of his respondents replied that their only relationship had been with their spouse. The other half spoke variously of romance and sex, but a handful of those quoted mentioned cohabitation. In one case this had preceded marriage, in another it had ended with the death of the male partner, a soldier, during the Second World War, while a third boasted that he was 'defying convention in top neighbourhood'.[65] Depictions of 'common-law wives' in the media – when that term first began to be used in the 1960s – were largely negative.[66] And as late as 1979, when the General Household Survey included a question on cohabitation, over half of the women who were living in a cohabiting relationship initially described themselves as married, which suggests that cohabitation was still thought to carry a stigma.[67]

But as cohabitation increased, so attitudes towards it became more favourable. The proportion of respondents to the British Social Attitudes Survey believing that 'people who want children ought to get married' fell from 70 per cent in 1989 to 57 per cent in 1994 and to 54 per cent in 2000.[68] By the mid-1990s 64 per cent of the population 'strongly agreed' that it was 'OK to live together without marrying' and 58 per cent thought that it was 'a good idea to live together before marriage';[69] similar proportions were of the same view in 2000. And even the Church of England saw fit to argue that 'living in sin' was no longer sinful.[70]

THE LEGAL TREATMENT OF COHABITANTS

In the light of such attitudes, how did the legal system treat the few cohabitants that came to its notice? One difficulty in discussing the policy of the law towards cohabiting couples is that for much of the period under discussion there simply wasn't one.[71] Until the 1970s, cohabitants

---

[64] M Forster *Hidden Lives: A Family Memoir* (Penguin, 1995), p 251.
[65] G Gorer *Exploring English Character* (The Cresset Press, 1955), p 91.
[66] See R Probert 'Common-law marriage: myths and misunderstandings' [2008] CFLQ 1.
[67] See A Brown and K Kiernan 'Cohabitation in Great Britain: evidence from the General Household Survey' (1981) 25 *Population Trends* 4.
[68] A Barlow, S Duncan, G James and A Park 'Just a piece of paper? Marriage and cohabitation', in A Park, J Curtice, K Thomson, L Jarvis and C Bromley (eds) *British Social Attitudes: Public policy, social ties. The 18th Report* (Sage Publications, 2001), table 2.1.
[69] ONS *Social Focus on Families* (TSO, 1997), table 1.8.
[70] J Melkie 'Out with traditional sin as Church embraces modern values' *The Guardian* 7 June 1995, p 1.
[71] Michael Freeman notes the absence of discussion of cohabitation in Graveson and Crane's *A Century of Family Law* (Sweet & Maxwell, 1957): see 'Fifty years of family law: an opinionated review', below, Chapter 6.

could only make claims under the general law – whether of trusts, contract, or succession – and therefore everything depended on the precise context of the case.

For example, in the eighteenth and nineteenth centuries a woman was able to pledge the credit of the man with whom she was living, and the man would be liable to pay for any goods supplied to her on this basis.[72] This, however, was a rule dictated partly by convenience (recognising the difficulty that tradesmen would have in inquiring into the marital status of those giving them orders) and partly by policy (since, between the tradesman and the male partner who had allowed the woman to pass as his wife, it seemed fairer that the latter should bear the cost of the goods supplied). And a cohabitant – unlike a wife – had no power to pledge the man's credit once the relationship had come to an end, however straitened her circumstances.[73] In *Munro v De Chemant*[74] the parties had lived together for 17 years. The man then 'turned her away' and refused to pay for the coal that had been delivered to her in her new home. Such refusal was upheld by the court: according to Lord Ellenborough—

> '[h]ad the goods been furnished while the defendant was living with this lady, his representation that she was his wife would have been conclusive against him; but I think his liability for necessaries supplied to her after they had separated depends entirely upon whether he really has been lawfully married to her or not.'[75]

Yet in some contexts provision for a cohabitant would be upheld by the courts. In the context of succession law, for example, if a bereaved cohabitant claimed under a will that described her as a wife, the question for the court was whether the testator had meant to refer to her when using the word 'wife'. If he had, she would succeed in her claim: thus, in *Lepine v Bean*,[76] for example, the court held that the testator obviously intended his cohabitant to take under his will, since she was clearly identified by name as well as being described as his wife.[77] The same rule applied to gifts from outsiders who had believed the woman in question to be a wife.[78] But cases such as these merely reflected the general rule that judges would adopt the meaning intended – in so far as this was obvious – by the testator. It by no means indicated that the legal system as a whole equated the married and the unmarried, or even that judges would show

---

[72] *Watson v Threlkeld* (1798) 2 Esp 637, 5 RR 760; *Ryan v Sam* (1848) 12 QB 460, 116 ER 940.
[73] Unless the man had made an express contract for goods to be supplied to her: *Blades v Free* (1829) 9 B & C 168; 109 ER 63.
[74] (1815) 4 Camp 215.
[75] At 216.
[76] (1870) 10 LR Eq 160.
[77] See also *Re Brown* (1910) 26 TLR 257; *Re Hammond* [1911] 2 Ch 342; *Re Smalley* [1929] 2 Ch 112. Note also *Re Lynch* [1943] 1 All ER 168 (cohabitant entitled to take as wife even though, as his niece, she could not legally have married him).
[78] See eg *Re Lowe* (1892) 61 LJ Ch 415 and *Anderson v Berkley* [1902] 1 Ch 936, in which the testator believed the woman in question to be married to another legatee.

sympathy towards bereaved cohabitants. Positive assistance was not extended to cohabiting couples. In one case in 1890 Edward Cook applied for letters of administration in relation to the estate of Rebecca Miles, with whom he had lived for 27 years and who had borne him eight children.[79] The judge refused indignantly: 'I am not going out of my way to assist this sort of thing' and held that the next of kin should be cited. When counsel suggested that there would be nothing left of the estate if this course were adopted, Butt J's response was uncompromising: 'I do not much care in the present instance whether there will be or not.'

As for trusts in favour of cohabitants, these could be upheld if the necessary conditions for their creation had been observed. For those who did not wish to advertise their relationships, secret or half-secret trusts could be declared, although those who were too secretive might fail to create a trust at all, as in *Johnson v Ball*,[80] in which the testator's attempt to create a secret trust in favour of his cohabitant of 40 years' standing and their five children failed, as the relevant letter setting out the trust did not exist at the date the will was made; or in *Re Boyes*,[81] in which the trust in favour of the lady had not been communicated during the lifetime of the testator. An alternative way of making provision for an ex-cohabitant was to enter into a deed for the payment of a specific sum or annuity. The decision that past consideration was no consideration meant that promises of support *not* made by deed would be unenforceable,[82] unless consideration other than the past relationship between the parties could be found.[83] And a contract or deed agreeing on *future* cohabitation in return for support would be struck down as based on immoral consideration. But a deed promising support to an ex-cohabitant would be upheld.[84] Such rules obviously operated to the detriment of the woman – who was dependent on the willingness of the man to make provision for her when the relationship had come to an end – and therefore may have been intended to have a deterrent effect. Occasionally, however, it is possible to discern some sympathy for the – inevitably female – party trying to enforce such promises of provision. In *Re Vallance*, for example, the parties had cohabited for over 30 years, and the court adopted a generous interpretation of the facts of the case to uphold the bond in the lady's favour.[85]

---

[79] *In the Goods of Rebecca Miles (deceased)* (1890) 62 LT 607.
[80] (1851) 5 De & G Sm 85, 64 ER 1029.
[81] (1884) 26 Ch D 531.
[82] See eg *Beaumont v Reeve* (1846) 8 QB 483, 115 ER 958; *Parker v Rolls* (1854) 14 CB 691; 139 ER 284.
[83] See eg *Smith v Roche* (1859) 6 CB (NS) 223, 141 ER 440 (promise to care for the children of the relationship); *Re Plaskett's Estate* (1861) 4 LT 544 (promise to yield up custody of children); *Keenan v Handley* (1864) 2 De G J & S 282, 46 ER 384 (release of claims relating to promise of marriage).
[84] See eg *Benyon v Nettlefold* (1850) 3 M & G 94, 42 ER 196; *Ayerst v Jenkins* (1873) LR 16 Eq 275; *In re Wootton Isaacson; Sanders v Smiles* (1904) 21 TLR 89.
[85] (1884) 26 Ch D 353, and see C Barton *Cohabitation Contracts* (Gower, 1985), p 38.

What these disparate areas of the law had in common, however, was that the exact nature of the cohabiting relationship was effectively irrelevant. If the arrangement complied with the legal requirements for the creation of a valid will, trust, or deed, it did not matter whether the parties had been living together for 2 weeks or 20 years, or whether the relationship was adulterous. But there was one context in which the nature of cohabitation *did* have to be considered, namely that of divorce (which explains why 1857 was a significant year in the history of cohabitation law as well as the history of divorce). The Divorce and Matrimonial Causes Act 1857 had made it both cheaper and procedurally easier to divorce, and perhaps had enabled some cohabiting unions to be formalised. In 1858, 50 petitions were based on adulterous relationships that were continuing at the time of the petition,[86] at least some of which may have involved cohabitation, and from the reported cases it is clear that some respondents had set up home with the co-respondent.[87] But in addition to providing evidence of some cohabiting relationships, the cases show how the law's attitudes to cohabitation evolved between the 1857 Act and the Divorce Reform Act 1969.

One might imagine that the law would be on the side of a petitioner seeking to divorce a spouse who was cohabiting with another, but things were not always so straightforward. Of course, in some respects the fact that the respondent was cohabiting did make the task of the petitioner easier. The open nature of the adultery made it easier for the petitioner to prove. For a husband, this was all that had to be established; for a wife, there was the necessity of establishing that her husband had committed some further matrimonial offence, but where her husband had left the matrimonial home to cohabit with another woman she would (after 2 years) be able to obtain a divorce based on his adultery coupled with desertion.[88] But in other respects the fact that the respondent was cohabiting might make the task of the petitioner more difficult: the circumstances of the case might allow various defences to be mounted, either by the respondent or by the Queen's (or King's) Proctor.

Connivance, for example, was an absolute bar to a divorce,[89] and the making of arrangements as part of the reorganisation of households consequent upon one spouse's cohabiting with another person could be problematic. In *Thomas v Thomas* the fact that the wife had accepted an

---

[86] *Divorce and Matrimonial Causes: Further Returns PP 1862* (99) Vol XLIV, p 182.
[87] See eg *Heathcoat v Heathcoat* (1865) The Times, March 6, p 10; *Clark v Clark, Perrens and Cumins* (1865) The Times March 16, p 11; *Jennings v Jennings* (1865) LR 1 P & D 35; *Evans v Evans and Bird* (1865) 1 P & D 36; *Gatehouse v Gatehouse* (1867) LR 1 P & D 331; *Buckmaster v Buckmaster* (1869) LR 1 P & D 713; *Ousey v Ousey and Atkinson* (1874) LR 3 P & D 223; *Izard v Izard and Leslie* (1889) 14 PD 45.
[88] See eg *Nott v Nott* (1866) LR 1 P & D 251; *Drew v Drew* (1888) 13 PD 97; *Garcia v Garcia* (1888) 13 PD 216; and note also *Dickinson v Dickinson* (1889) 62 LT 330 (in which the husband was guilty of constructive desertion in bringing the woman to the matrimonial home).
[89] Divorce and Matrimonial Causes Act 1857, s 30.

allowance under a deed of separation was held to constitute her connivance in her husband's cohabiting relationship with their former lodger.[90] Similarly, the rule against condonation prevented George Henry Lewes from divorcing his wife Agnes: both freethinkers, they had agreed to have an open marriage,[91] and the fact that she went on to have several children by Thornton Hunt was therefore irrelevant.

A cohabiting spouse might also defend the petition on the basis that the petitioner had deserted him or her, or had been guilty of cruelty, or of neglect or misconduct that had conduced to the other's adultery.[92] This was a discretionary, rather than an absolute bar to a divorce. In this context, the fact that the respondent was cohabiting might highlight his or her need for support in the wake of abandonment. Such was the plea of the wife in *Baylis v Baylis, Teevan and Cooper*.[93] One might imagine that the court would have had little sympathy for a woman it described as being of 'loose character', who had cohabited with the husband before marriage, and who had 'made little concealment' of her adultery, 'saying she must have a protector, and would not live alone.'[94] But the court still refused to grant a decree of divorce to her husband, who, after a disagreement, had ordered her to live apart from him (in the chambers he had occupied as a bachelor), and had 'then watched her and detected her in adultery.' The court opined that a husband was bound to accord his wife the protection of his name and home – 'certainly not the less so where the previous life of his wife renders her peculiarly accessible to temptation.'[95] The husband's cruelty to his wife was held to be a bar to divorce in *Lempriere v Lempriere and Roebel*, the court noting that it was 'scarcely too much to say that his treatment of his wife drove her into cohabitation with another man.'[96] Similarly, in *Dagg v Dagg*,[97] the husband's petition for divorce was dismissed on the basis that he had deserted her. He had agreed to marry her after she became pregnant by him but insisted that she sign an agreement to the effect that they would not live together. The court stated that his desertion was probably the cause of her cohabitation with another man: 'knowing her frailty, it was his duty, when he became her husband, not to have left her to the chances of falling, to which, abandoned as she was by him, she must have been exposed.'[98] Nor was this a defence confined to cohabiting wives: in

---

[90] (1860) 2 Sw & Tr 113, 164 ER 935. Given that the separation agreement was entered into before 1857, this decision may appear harsh, but it should be noted that the wife was petitioning only for judicial separation – an option that would have been available to her before 1857.
[91] P Rose *Parallel Lives* (Vintage, 1994).
[92] Divorce and Matrimonial Causes Act 1857, s 31.
[93] (1867) 1 P & D 395.
[94] At 397.
[95] At 397.
[96] (1868) LR 1 P & D 569 at 570.
[97] (1882) 7 PD 17.
[98] At 18. See also *Heyes v Heyes and Mason* (1887) 13 PD 11; *Starbuck v Starbuck* (1889) 61 LT 876.

Boreham v Boreham a wife's cruelty to, and wilful separation from, her husband was held to have conduced to his adultery.[99]

A further discretionary bar to divorce was the petitioner's unreasonable delay in petitioning for divorce. Again, the fact that the respondent was cohabiting might be significant. In *Short v Short and Bolwell*,[100] for example, the wife had been cohabiting with the co-respondent since separating from her husband 15 years earlier. The husband's petition was dismissed on the basis that he 'has been content to see his wife living in adultery with the co-respondent for all these years.'[101]

A final discretionary bar to divorce was misconduct on the part of the petitioner, and it is in this context that the court had to assess the moral iniquity of his or her behaviour. In the early years the court took a very narrow view of its powers. In 1869 the court noted that it had only exercised its discretion to grant a divorce to an adulterous petitioner in three classes of cases: first, where the petitioner had believed the other spouse was dead and had remarried; secondly, where the wife had been compelled by the husband to lead a life of prostitution; and, thirdly, where the petitioner's act of adultery had been condoned by the respondent and had not conduced to the respondent's own adultery. It rejected the idea that a more general discretion would be appropriate:

> 'in cases where the adultery complained of has no special circumstances attending it, and no special features placing it in some category capable of distinct statement and recognition, there would, I think, be great mischief in this Court assuming to itself a right to grant or withhold a divorce upon the mere footing of the petitioner's adultery being, under the whole circumstances of each case, more or less pardonable or capable of excuse.'[102]

So the fact that the petitioner was cohabiting would bar a divorce – as in *Lautour v Her Majesty's Proctor*, upon it being discovered that the petitioner had himself been cohabiting with a woman for 25 years. Even one-off incidents of adultery that did not fall within the categories outlined above would bar a divorce.[103]

Towards the end of the century, however, the divorce courts began to demonstrate a little more leniency towards a petitioner who had been guilty of adultery. In *Whitworth v Whitworth and Thomasson* the parties had separated informally, signing an agreement that each was free to marry again.[104] The husband went through a ceremony of marriage with another woman and lived with her for 3 years before discovering that it

---

[99] (1866) LR 1 PD 77.
[100] (1874) LR 3 P & D 193.
[101] At 196.
[102] *Morgan v Morgan* (1869) LR 1 P & D 644.
[103] See eg *Clarke v Clarke and Clarke* (1865) The Times, March 16, at p 11 (wife living with husband's brother; husband had committed adultery after she left).
[104] [1893] P 85.

was not valid. He thereupon returned to his first wife. She does not appear to have welcomed this turn of events, since 3 months later she left him and went through a ceremony of marriage with the co-respondent. The court held – rather tenuously – that this was analogous to cases where one spouse had married after decree nisi but before a decree absolute had been granted,[105] on the basis that this was a case where the husband had been mistaken as to the law. It did note that it was difficult to credit that the husband had genuinely believed his first marriage was legally dissolved, but accepted his story on the basis that:

> '[h]e was a man in a humble rank of life; he knew nothing about law – according to his own counsel, he was a stupid man, he was entirely unable to understand his legal position, and he allowed himself to be misled.'[106]

Similarly, in *Symons v Symons*,[107] a divorce was granted to a wife who had been living with a man for 5 years, on the basis of her husband's adultery and desertion: the court held that her adultery had not conduced to the husband's adultery – he had left her long before to live with another woman – and that it was his cruelty and prolonged desertion that had conduced to her adultery.

The possibility of fallen women being 'reclaimed' through divorce and remarriage featured in a number of cases in the early twentieth century and was held to justify the court in overlooking evidence of a female petitioner's cohabiting relationship.[108] In this context the double standard operated to the advantage of female petitioners, and it was some years before the desirability of allowing a husband to obtain a divorce and marry his cohabitant was held to justify the court in exercising its discretion: as late as 1918 the court in *Hines v Hines and Burdett* refused to exercise its discretion in favour of a cohabiting husband.[109] The parties had separated in 1908, and the wife had gone to live with Burdett. At the time of the hearing they had been living together for 9 years and had had three children together. In the meantime, the husband had formed a connection with a young woman. His petition for divorce was, however, dismissed by McCardie J, despite the latter's recognition that this would simply perpetuate two cohabiting unions:

> 'I desire to say emphatically that I am under no illusion as to what will follow if I refuse this decree. The petitioner will ... continue his intimacy with Nellie Spencer and will become the father of more illegitimate children. The respondent ...will continue her cohabitation with Burdett (whom she loves), and as a result their illegitimate family will probably be increased. The refusal of a decree will then result in continued immorality by four people and the recurring procreation of bastard offspring ... If I am to

---

[105] See eg *Moore v Moore* [1892] P 382.
[106] At 88.
[107] [1897] P 167.
[108] *Burdon v Burdon* [1901] P 52 at 58–59; *Hampson v Hampson* [1914] P 105.
[109] *Hines v Hines and Burdett* [1918] P 364.

regard only the interests of the parties concerned in the case, I entertain no doubt that a decree of dissolution will benefit each of them ... But I cannot create new principles of divorce law administration, nor am I entitled to ignore the cogent weight of judicial precedents.'[110]

Yet only 2 years later the court proved itself willing to grant a divorce in a very similar case. In *Wilson v Wilson* the court exercised its discretion in favour of a husband who, on returning home from the war, had found his children in a neglected state and his wife having committed adultery.[111] He gave the children into the care of an old family friend, Amelia Brown, with whom a relationship then developed and with whom he was living at the time of the divorce petition. In stark contrast to *Hines v Hines*, the court considered the interests of not only the children, but also Amelia and the husband, and granted his divorce petition.

There was clearly increasing sympathy for petitioners who wished to regularise cohabiting relationships, although the court continued to be reluctant to exercise its discretion in favour of promiscuous petitioners, those who had attempted to conceal adulterous relationships from the court,[112] and those who had been guilty of delay.[113] In *Andrews v Andrews* the judge noted that:

> '[o]ver and over again I have had cases where discretion has been asked for, where there has been a long association, the birth of children, and where in every respect save the actual legal relationship a new home has been set up and is likely to continue indefinitely.'[114]

He exercised his discretion in favour of the husband, noting that 'it would be a misfortune if the prospect of this association turning into a happy married home were to be frustrated.'[115] Of course, if there was no prospect or possibility of the parties marrying, there was no ground for the court to exercise its discretion. In *White v White*,[116] for example, the court gave the petitioning husband short shrift: it noted that 'if it were the fact that he was anxious to be free so as to marry the woman with whom he lived for eight years, and who has borne him a child, that ... might have been a consideration of some cogency';[117] however, since he wanted his freedom 'to marry yet another woman', his petition was denied. Similarly, in *Price v Price*[118] the petition of a husband who was cohabiting with his

---

[110] At 365.
[111] [1920] P 20. See also *Pointon v Pointon* [1922] P 278.
[112] See e g *Apted v Apted and Bliss* [1930] P 246; *Bainbridge v Bainbridge* [1934] P 66; *Bull v Bull (Queen's Proctor Showing Cause)* [1968] P 618.
[113] See e g *Binney v Binney and Hill* [1936] P 178; *Lowe v Lowe* [1952] P 376; *Chalmers (orse Gunning) v Chalmers* [1964] P 61.
[114] [1940] P 184 at 185.
[115] At 186.
[116] [1952] P 395.
[117] At 398.
[118] (1947) 176 LT 10.

brother's former wife was denied, since as the law then stood a marriage between the parties would have been prohibited.[119]

Such cases underline the fact that the willingness of judges to exercise their discretion in favour of a cohabiting petition was not motivated by approval of cohabiting relationships. It was, rather, the *undesirability* of such relationships that made divorce and remarriage the lesser evil. Granting divorces to petitioners who wished to marry their cohabitants was justified 'in the interests of decency'.[120] Such attitudes continued well into the 1960s. If one reads the Law Commission's 1966 recommendations for reform of the law of divorce, there are striking parallels with the arguments advanced since the start of the twentieth century: reform – to the law of marriage, or of divorce – is advocated precisely because it is perceived that the alternative is cohabitation.[121] Even the language had changed but little: the Law Commission suggested that to allow broken marriages to be ended would enable the regularisation of existing 'illicit unions'. The report focused on the position of the children of such unions: it was suggested that if divorce were more widely available, 'about 180,000 living illegitimate children could be legitimated'; moreover, 'in each future year some 19,000 children who would otherwise be condemned to permanent illegitimacy might be born in wedlock or subsequently legitimated.'[122] The alternative of making changes to the law of illegitimacy was considered but rejected: even if public attitudes to illegitimacy could be changed, 'alleviating the lot of children would not remove all the undesirable social consequences of large numbers of permanently illicit unions masquerading, in many cases, as lawful marriages.'[123]

Given this desire that cohabiting unions should be converted into marriages wherever possible, and the fact that cohabitation was, for most of the period under review, relatively rare, it is not surprising that the legal system should have held back from conferring positive rights on cohabiting couples. There were exceptions – but these were inspired by exceptional circumstances. For example, in times of crisis provision might be made for cohabitants – such as the separation allowances provided for dependent cohabitants during both World Wars, and the unemployment benefits paid to unmarried wives in the 1920s.[124] But such provision was

---

[119] A man could marry his deceased brother's widow (by virtue of the Deceased Brother's Widow's Marriage Act 1921), but it was not until the Marriage (Enabling) Act 1960 that such a marriage could take place during the brother's lifetime: see S Cretney *Family Law in the Twentieth Century: A History* (Oxford UP, 2003), pp 49–52.
[120] *Herod v Herod* [1939] P 11 at 36.
[121] See eg Women's Co-operative Guild *Working Women and Divorce: An Account of Evidence Given on Behalf of the Women's Co-operative Guild Before the Royal Commission on Divorce* (David Nutt, 1911).
[122] Law Commission *Reform of the Grounds of Divorce: The Field of Choice* (1966), Cmnd 3123, p 36.
[123] Ibid, p 37.
[124] See R Probert '"Unmarried Wives" in War and Peace' [2005] CFLQ 1.

seen as appropriate only to an emergency: separation allowances were a necessary concession to soldiers who might otherwise have been unwilling to fight for King and country,[125] and unemployment benefits were seen as a temporary measure arising as a result of the war.[126] Even in this context distinctions were still made between the married and the unmarried: under the scheme of wartime separation allowances, 'unmarried wives' received a lesser allowance than legal wives;[127] while for the purposes of unemployment benefits they were bracketed with housekeepers rather than wives.[128]

Once the emergency was perceived to be past, matters reverted to normal, with no provision made for the unmarried wife. When war broke out in 1939, separation allowances and pensions were once again granted to the 'unmarried wives' of soldiers. Interestingly, there appears to have been more opposition to the term 'unmarried wife' than there had been the first time round. Letters to the editor of *The Times* argued that the unmarried wife was simply a mistress and 'that officialdom should try to tone down or obliterate this distinction is simply foolish and un-moral.'[129] In the wake of such protests the official term was changed to 'unmarried dependant living as a wife' or 'udlaw'. Moreover, despite the impact of the Second World War on the civilian population and the fact that many were required to perform war duties,[130] a sharp line was drawn between the soldier and the civilian. No pension was provided for the unmarried wife by the Personal Injuries (Civilians) Scheme, a fact that was challenged by an aggrieved cohabitant who stated that he would be reluctant to undertake his fire-fighting duties if the state was reluctant to underwrite his responsibilities.[131] The Ministry of Home Security would have been willing for the scheme to be changed, arguing that the distinction between soldiers and civilians could not be maintained where the latter were compelled to carry out war work;[132] the Minister of Pensions, however, was strongly opposed, and his view prevailed when the War Cabinet Home Policy Committee decided that there was no pressure for change.[133] Once again, when the war was over, allowances were no longer paid even to the unmarried wives of soldiers.

---

[125] PRO PIN 15/2573; PRO HO 186/2089. In practice, however, it appears that cohabitants were not the primary recipients of dependants' pensions: see G Thomas 'State Maintenance for Women During the First World War: The Case of Separation Allowances and Pensions' (unpublished PhD thesis, University of Sussex, 1989).
[126] See eg Ministry of Labour *Report on National Unemployment Insurance to July 1923* (London: HMSO, 1923); H Emmerson and E Lascelles *Guide to the Unemployment Insurance Acts* (Longmans, Green and Co Ltd, 1928), p 2.
[127] See R Probert '"Unmarried Wives" in War and Peace' [2005] CFLQ 1.
[128] Ibid.
[129] 'The Unmarried Wife' *The Times*, 30 January 1940, p 4.
[130] The National Service Act 1941 provided that men who were not liable for military service could be called up for the purposes of civil defence.
[131] PRO HO 186/2089: letter dated 18 March 1941 from Mr Frank Quinn to Herbert Morrison, Ministry of Home Security.
[132] PRO HO 186/2089: letter dated 22 April 1941.
[133] Ibid: minutes of meeting held on 17 June 1941.

More typical than these exceptional examples of positive provision – and more durable – were those legislative provisions that operated to the detriment of cohabiting couples. From the 1920s welfare legislation included provisions intended to ensure that the recipients of benefits did not obtain any advantage from the state by cohabiting rather than marrying. The 'cohabitation rule' had its origins in the war-time system of allowances and pensions,[134] and was first put on a statutory basis in the Widows', Orphans' and Old Age Contributory Pensions Act 1925.[135] This stipulated that a widow's weekly 10-shilling pension would be suspended if she began to cohabit; however, once widows ceased to cohabit, their entitlement to a pension would be revived.[136] It is clear from the debates that many saw the clause as punishing cohabitation. Those in favour of it emphasised the immorality of cohabitation;[137] others focused on the fact that the clause would prevent a widow from 'cheating the Fund by living with a man and not marrying him.'[138] Even those who challenged the clause shied away from appearing to endorse the decision to live together unmarried. The furthest that any speaker would go in opposing the rule was to argue that the widow's entitlement was based on her own National Insurance contributions and should not be affected by her conduct.[139]

But the post-war welfare state adopted the approach that entitlement to benefits *should* be affected by the recipient's conduct. The National Insurance Act 1946 provided that widow's benefit would not be paid for any period during which she was 'cohabiting with a man as his wife'[140] and the National Insurance (Industrial Injuries) Act 1946 provided that a cohabiting widow would be *permanently* disqualified from receiving benefit,[141] a provision that remained in force until 1961.[142] By contrast, the National Assistance Act 1948 did not refer to cohabitation as a specific ground for the withdrawal of benefit; in practice, however, the Board had discretion to make a deduction in 'special circumstances'[143] and they took the view that the resources of cohabitants should be aggregated so that they did not receive an advantage over married couples.[144] Exceptions might be made if there were children from a

---

[134] PRO PIN 15/149.
[135] Section 21(1).
[136] Widows', Orphans' and Old Age Contributory Pensions Act 1925, s 21(1).
[137] *Hansard*, HC Deb, vol 186, col 1176 (14 July 1925).
[138] *Hansard*, HC Deb, vol 186, col 1171 (14 July 1925).
[139] *Hansard*, HC Deb, vol 186, cols 1169 and 1184 (14 July 1925). This was a ground on which widow's pensions could have been distinguished from war pensions, which had been treated as a favour rather than a right.
[140] National Insurance Act 1946, s 17(2).
[141] National Insurance (Industrial Injuries) Act 1946, s 88(3).
[142] The Working Party on Industrial Death Benefit for Cohabiting Widows considered the issue in 1960 and recommended that a cohabiting widow should not be permanently disqualified from receiving the benefit: PRO PIN 21/367. Their proposals were enacted in the Family Allowances and National Insurance Act 1961, s 4.
[143] National Assistance (Determination of Need) Regulations 1948, SI 1948/1334, reg 3.
[144] In a letter dated 6 November 1950, Miss Hope-Wallace of the National Assistance Board noted that this was 'justified morally and politically by the argument that it would

previous relationship or the cohabitant was on a low income or the relationship was unstable and might be jeopardised by the decision of the Board.[145]

As the numbers of lone mothers applying for national assistance grew in the 1960s, there was growing concern that some were cohabiting with new partners and so obtaining benefits fraudulently.[146] Inquiries were carried out to ascertain the extent of the problem.[147] New rules issued in 1964 provided that it was no longer necessary to prove that the woman was being maintained by the man, only that she had not disclosed his presence in the house, to prosecute her for fraud.[148] By the end of 1964 the inquiry had revealed 1,937 cases of undisclosed cohabitation across 224 area offices.[149] As a result, when the social security system was reorganised by the Ministry of Social Security Act 1966,[150] it was specifically provided that assistance (renamed supplementary benefit) would not be payable to the cohabitant of a person in full-time work unless there were exceptional circumstances.[151]

Yet although the rule itself was thought to be necessary,[152] the way in which it was administered attracted criticism from social workers, pressure groups such as the Child Poverty Action Group, academics and MPs.[153] Lister, in a survey published in 1973, found that in many cases where benefit had been withdrawn, the parties could not be said to be cohabiting, still less forming an economic unit.[154] The Supplementary Benefits Commission subsequently agreed that the administration of the rule should change and issued additional guidance requiring officers to have regard to the financial interdependence of the parties and the

---

be wrong and undesirable that a properly married couple should be so much more severely treated than a couple who are living together without being married': PRO AST 20/11.

[145] See PRO AST 39/91 for the approach of the National Assistance Board and AST 7/1126 for examples of the way the system operated in practice.

[146] K Kiernan, H Land and J Lewis *Lone Motherhood in Twentieth Century Britain* (Clarendon Press, 1998), p 164.

[147] An experimental inquiry into 185 pre-selected cases found 42 cases of undisclosed cohabitation. The inquiry was extended nationally in June 1964. See PRO 7/1622.

[148] PRO AST 7/1622: Assistance (Supplementary) Circular (1964) No 3 AX.3/64. Detailed advice on observing the residence was included in Assistance (Supplementary) Circular (1965) No 2 AX.2/65.

[149] 61,413 casepapers had been examined, of which 28,544 had been selected for investigation: PRO AST 7/1622.

[150] The Act transferred the functions of the Ministry of Pensions and the National Assistance Board to the newly created Ministry of Social Security and replaced national assistance by supplementary benefit.

[151] Section 4(2) and Sch 2, para 3(1).

[152] *Report of the Committee on Abuse of Social Security Benefits* (HMSO, 1973), Cmnd 5228, para 328; *Report of the Committee on One-Parent Families* (HMSO, 1974), Cmnd 5629, para 5.269.

[153] PRO AST 36/80, Memo 121, circulated 15 January 1969.

[154] R Lister *As Man and Wife? A Study of the Cohabitation Rule* (CPAG, Poverty Research Series 2, 1973), pp 6–8.

longevity of the relationship. Since 'cohabiting as man and wife' had acquired pejorative overtones,[155] changes were also made to the terminology used in the legislation, the offending phrase being replaced by 'living together as husband and wife'.[156]

This less punitive approach – and the concern not to stigmatise cohabiting couples – occurred at a time when positive rights were being conferred on cohabitants at all levels. Initiatives such as the Inheritance (Provision for Family and Dependants) Act 1975 were intended to benefit the survivors of cohabiting relationships, even if they had to bring themselves within the generic term 'dependant'. The Law Commission had argued that one of the purposes of family provision law was to ensure that reasonable provision was made for those whom the deceased had been legally liable to maintain, but noted that the law also recognised moral obligations and that a failure to make provision may have been accidental.

> 'In these cases an order for financial provision would be doing for the deceased what he might reasonably be assumed to have wished to do himself. This argument carries particular weight where the "dependant" is a person with whom the deceased has been cohabiting.'[157]

From one perspective this was in line with earlier developments: cohabitants only benefited from generally applicable policies. Yet it was significant that within less than a decade the Law Commission had changed from recommendations designed to reduce the number of cohabiting couples to proposals that would alleviate their disadvantages. Even so, it shied away from describing such relationships as familial, pointing out, rather apologetically, that the term 'family provision' was in this context a convenient rather than an accurate description, in that the recommendations extended to persons who were not members of the deceased's family.[158]

A similar perception that cohabiting couples were not 'family' was revealed by the Select Committee on Domestic Violence in Marriage in the early 1970s. A memorandum submitted to the Committee by the National Women's Aid Federation expressed the hope that cohabiting couples would be included within the Committee's report,[159] but the Committee's reaction was that this would be controversial and that the task that it faced was daunting enough without extending its enquiry to

---

[155] Supplementary Benefits Commission *Living together as husband and wife* (HMSO, 1976), para 52.
[156] Social Security (Miscellaneous Provisions) Act 1977, s 14(7).
[157] Law Commission *Second Report on Family Property: Family Provision on Death*, Law Com No 61 (HMSO, 1974), para 90.
[158] Ibid, paras 10 and 90.
[159] Memorandum submitted by the National Women's Aid Federation: *Minutes of Evidence Taken Before the Select Committee on Violence in Marriage*, HC 553-ii (1974–5) Vol 2, p 59.

'those who are living together but not strictly as a family'.[160] However, the Bill that eventually became the Domestic Violence and Matrimonial Proceedings Act 1976 was not the product of the Committee but of the National Women's Aid Federation, introduced into Parliament as a Private Member's Bill.[161] The rather modest provision made for cohabitants in the initial draft[162] was enhanced at committee stage,[163] the bill's sponsor, Jo Richardson MP, noting that the extension of rights to cohabiting couples had widespread support.[164]

The courts, too, began to take a more generous attitude to cohabiting couples. Childless unmarried couples were accepted as 'family' for the purposes of the Rent Acts.[165] Bridge LJ commented that there had been 'a complete revolution in society's attitude to unmarried partnerships of the type under consideration.'[166] Cohabitants succeeded in establishing claims to the family home under the doctrines of constructive trust[167] or contractual licence,[168] and the courts used their powers under the new Domestic Violence and Matrimonial Proceedings Act 1976 to exclude violent male cohabitants from the family home.[169]

Yet this new approach to cohabitants was no more coherent than the old,[170] and equally dependent upon context. Cohabitants were dependants for the purpose of claiming inheritance from a deceased partner's estate, but not under the Fatal Accidents Act 1976. They could claim protection under the Domestic Violence and Matrimonial Proceedings Act 1976, but not under the Domestic Proceedings and Magistrates' Courts Act 1978. Different definitions were adopted in different pieces of legislation: the Consumer Credit Act 1974 and Pneumoconiosis (Workers' Compensation) Act 1979 referred to a 'reputed spouse',[171] while other legislation spoke of those 'living together as husband and wife'.[172] It is unsurprising that this hotchpotch of legal rules

---

[160] *Minutes of Evidence Taken Before the Select Committee on Violence in Marriage*, HC 553-ii (1974–5) Vol 2, p 70.
[161] S Maidment 'Domestic Violence and the law: the 1976 Act and its aftermath' in N Johnson (ed) *Marital Violence* (Routledge & Kegan Paul, 1985).
[162] Domestic Violence Bill, as published on 17 December 1975, clause 2(1)(a).
[163] Standing Committee F, *Minutes of Proceedings on the Domestic Violence Bill (changed to Domestic Violence and Matrimonial Proceedings Bill)* 1975–6 HC 548.
[164] *Official Report*, Standing Committee F, Domestic Violence Bill, 30/6/76, col 5.
[165] *Dyson Holdings Ltd v Fox* [1976] 1 QB 503. See D Bradley 'Meaning of "Family": Changing Morality and Changing Justice' (1976) 39 MLR 223.
[166] *Dyson Holdings Ltd v Fox* [1976] 1 QB 503 at 751. Although see *Helby v Rafferty* [1979] 1 WLR 13 (childless cohabitant who had wanted to retain her independence not a member of the tenant's family) and note the reluctance of the House of Lords in *Carrega Properties SA v Sharratt* [1979] 1 WLR 928 to express a view on the case.
[167] See eg *Cooke v Head* [1972] 2 All ER 38; *Eves v Eves* [1975] 1 WLR 1338.
[168] *Tanner v Tanner* [1975] 3 All ER 776; *Pascoe v Turner* [1979] 1 WLR 431.
[169] *Davis v Johnson* [1979] AC 264.
[170] See eg T Honoré *Sex Law* (Duckworth, 1978), p 48.
[171] Consumer Credit Act 1974, s 184(5); Pneumoconiosis (Workers' Compensation) Act 1979, s 3(1)(c).
[172] Domestic Violence and Matrimonial Proceedings Act 1976, s 1(2).

should have led many commentators to call for reform.[173] In view of the subsequent development of the law, their confidence that such reform would be forthcoming in the near future is worthy of note.[174]

But it was not to be. The Law Commission did at this time consider reviewing the legal position of unmarried couples,[175] but in the event no action was taken beyond commissioning a preliminary survey on the law relating to the enforceability of cohabiting contracts.[176] A decade or so later it was suggested that 'the time may now be ripe for a more systematic consideration of the subject as a whole',[177] but the project that was actually undertaken in the mid-1990s was both narrower and wider in scope, since it focused solely on property rights but encompassed all those who shared a home.[178]

And so, in the absence of any systematic review, the process of piecemeal reform continued. Bereaved cohabitants were included within the scope of the Fatal Accidents Act 1976 by the Administration of Justice Act 1982, and their entitlement to succeed to a tenancy in the name of the deceased was put on a statutory basis in 1988.[179] However, those living with a bankrupt partner were not given the same protection as married couples, despite the express recommendations of the Cork Report in 1982;[180] the scope of certain rights was narrowed, whether intentionally or not, by later developments;[181] and the ambit of others – for example, the ability of cohabitants to enter into a contract regulating their finances – remained a matter of debate.[182]

---

[173] J Eekelaar 'The Place of Divorce in Family Law's New Role' (1975) 38 MLR 241; J Dwyer 'Immoral Contracts' (1977) 93 LQR 386; D Oliver 'The Mistress in Law' (1978) Current Legal Problems 81; S Blake 'To Marry or Not to Marry' [1979] Fam Law 29.

[174] D Pearl 'Cohabitation in English Social Security and Supplementary Benefits Legislation' [1979] Fam Law 232.

[175] Law Commission Fourteenth Annual Report 1978–79 Law Com No 97 (HMSO, 1980), para 2.32; Seventeenth Annual Report 1981–82 Law Com No 119 (HMSO, 1983), para 2.45; Eighteenth Annual Report 1982–83 Law Com No 131 (1984), para 2.42; Nineteenth Annual Report 1983–84 Law Com No 140 (HMSO, 1985), para 2.35.

[176] The survey was carried out by Chris Barton and later published independently as Cohabitation Contracts (Gower, 1985).

[177] Law Commission Twenty-seventh Annual Report Law Com No 210 (HMSO, 1993), para 2.40.

[178] And, in the event, no proposals for reform were put forward: see Law Commission Sharing Homes: A Discussion Paper Law Com No 278 (HMSO, 2002).

[179] Rent Act 1977, Sch 1, para 2(2), as substituted by the Housing Act 1988, s 39 and Sch 4, Pt 1, para 2.

[180] Insolvency Law and Practice: Report of the Review Committee (HMSO, 1982), Cmnd 8558, para 1117.

[181] In the context of domestic violence (see e g D Hoath 'The Council Tenant and the Housing Act 1980: Some Implications for Members of His Family' [1981] Fam Law 95 and Lee v Lee [1984] FLR 243), and in that of rights to property (see e g Burns v Burns [1984] 2 WLR 582; for contemporary comments see N Lowe and A Smith 'The Cohabitant's Fate' (1984) 47 MLR 341 and D Parker 'Cohabitants, Their Homes and the Winds of Change' [1984] Fam Law 40.

[182] See e g the Cohabitation (Contract Enforcement) Bill.

Despite the lack of any coherent policy relating to cohabitants, certain themes can be identified in the debates of the 1980s and 1990s. First, there was – in contrast to the discussions of earlier decades – a recognition that couples were increasingly choosing to bring up families outside marriage, that changes to the law of marriage or of divorce had not had the hoped-for effect of encouraging couples to formalise their relationships, that couples would cohabit even if they had the opportunity to marry, and that the position of their children accordingly needed to be addressed by the law. The most significant changes affecting cohabitants in this period therefore related to their role as parents, with legal initiatives intended to eliminate, so far as possible, the status and disadvantages of illegitimacy.[183] Yet there was a distinction between redressing injustices to existing families and encouraging cohabiting couples to become parents, as was obvious during the debates on the Human Fertilisation and Embryology Bill 1990. The question was raised as to whether access should be denied to unmarried couples, single women or lesbian couples on the ground that the best interests of the child should be paramount.[184] The concern derived from the need of the child for a male role model, cohabitants being included with the all-female households because of the perception that they were 'not necessarily stable'.[185] There was a considerable degree of support for the proposed amendment to deny treatment,[186] and in the event it was rejected by a majority of only one.

This leads on to the second point, that despite the evidence that more couples were living together outside marriage, and for longer periods, there was no consensus as to what rights (if any) should be extended to such couples. The inclusion of cohabitants within any legislative scheme might come about as the result of a general reform,[187] but was by no means a foregone conclusion. In particular, proposals for parity of treatment were often a step too far. Thus the government was not responsive to suggestions that the welfare system should be amended to ensure equal treatment of married and cohabiting couples. During the passage of the Welfare Reform and Pensions Act 1999 it was proposed that there should be an equal treatment rule to ensure that the terms of pension schemes were no less favourable to unmarried partners than to spouses. The increased costs that this would entail meant that the amendment did not have support from the government and was withdrawn. A similar fate befell the suggestions that bereavement damages should be payable to cohabitants.[188]

---

[183] Family Law Reform Act 1987; Children Act 1989.
[184] *Hansard*, HL Deb, vol 513, col 1090 (7 December 1989).
[185] *Hansard*, HL Deb, vol 515, col 788 (6 February 1990).
[186] *Hansard*, HL Deb, vol 515, cols 793, 795–798 (6 February 1990).
[187] See e g the Law Reform (Succession) Act 1995, which improved the position of bereaved cohabitants but significantly did not confer on them the same rights that married couples enjoyed.
[188] As proposed by the Law Commission *Claims for Wrongful Death*, Law Com CP No 148 (HMSO, 1997); Law Com No 263 (HMSO, 1999).

Thirdly, the topic was one that was capable of attracting strong feelings, as was evident in the fate of the Family Homes and Domestic Violence Bill 1995. The Bill had passed most of its stages without occasioning much discussion, and those who did note its application to cohabiting couples generally considered the limited changes being made as a positive development.[189] However, shortly before the Bill was due to receive its third and final reading in the House of Commons, the alarm was raised about its effect. On Monday 23 October the *Daily Mail* carried two articles: 'Anger at Bill to "sabotage" marriage', on the front page, while a full-page spread inside queried 'How could MPs fail to spot this blow to marriage?'[190] A number of Conservative backbench MPs subsequently expressed their dissent: a small number, but still crucially larger than John Major's slim majority of five.[191] The problem was not that the Bill would fail without their support – since it enjoyed cross-party support – but that the rebels might vote against the Government on another matter that did not enjoy such support. While the main provisions of the Bill were brought back before Parliament and became law as Part IV of the Family Law Act 1996, certain amendments were made to conciliate those who had expressed concern about the special nature of marriage.

While the New Labour Government elected in 1997 did not seem particularly eager to confer rights on cohabiting couples,[192] recent years have seen a number of proposals for reform, both inside and outside Parliament.[193] The passage of the Civil Partnership Act 2004 led to suggestions that the position of those cohabitants who had not formalised a relationship should be ameliorated, and as a result the Law Commission was asked to undertake a review specifically devoted to cohabitation law.[194] Its subsequent consultation paper and final report made a convincing case for reform. There is now a recognition that couples will cohabit even if the law allows them to marry, and despite the lack of legal

---

[189] *Hansard*, HL Deb, vol 561, col 1264 (23 February 1995).

[190] The articles were written by Steve Doughty and William Oddie respectively: *Daily Mail*, 23 October 1995, pp 1 and 8.

[191] The figures given by different sources vary between eight and ten: the rebels included Roger Gale, Edward Leigh, Lady Olga Maitland, John Butterfill, John MacGregor and Julian Brazier, the last of whom had actually sat on the Standing Committee but acknowledged he had not read the Bill. See P Cowley 'Chaos or Cohesion? Major and the Conservative Parliamentary Party', in P Dorey (ed) *The Major Premiership* (Macmillan, 1999), for a discussion of the divisions within the Conservative party at this period.

[192] While the consultation paper issued in 1998 adopted neutral terminology, the preference was clearly for marriage over cohabitation: *Supporting Families* (Home Office, 1998), para 4.3.

[193] See eg Law Society 'Cohabitation: The case for clear law' (Law Society, 2002); and note the Relationships (Civil Registration) Bill 2001, introduced by Jane Griffiths MP and the Civil Partnerships Bill 2002 introduced by Lord Lester.

[194] Law Commission *Cohabitation: The Financial Consequences of Relationship Breakdown* Law Com CP No 179 (HMSO, 2006), p 19.

protection, and a growing consensus that reform is necessary.[195] As Harriet Harman put it in a Parliamentary debate:

> 'Not having protection for cohabiting couples who subsequently separate has not stopped people cohabiting; nor has it encouraged people to marry rather than cohabit ... We must address the situation as it is.'[196]

CONCLUSION

Looking back at the evidence of attitudes to cohabitation over the past 150 years, it can be seen that for most of this period the attitude of the legislature and the judiciary was in line with that of the general public: until the 1970s cohabitants were few in number, attracted social disapproval, and could expect little assistance from the law. If not entirely overlooked by the legal system, they were only taken notice of when it was unavoidable, either when an individual brought a claim before the court, or when pressing social conditions made provision for cohabitants expedient.

Indeed, given the evidence as to when cohabitation began to emerge as a significant social phenomenon, it would seem that Parliament was relatively quick off the mark in extending rights to cohabitants. The problem was that it did not do so consistently, and that many problems went unaddressed. Looking back, it is obvious that reform is long overdue. A whole generation has grown up, cohabited, and perhaps suffered from an absence of legal protection in the time since the Law Commission decided not to carry out a general review of the law relating to cohabiting couples in the early 1980s. Even the Commission's 2007 recommendations, while addressing the lack of any adjustive regime when a cohabiting relationship breaks down, do not constitute a comprehensive review of the law. Looking forward, what is needed is a single piece of legislation that addresses the rights and responsibilities of cohabitants in a clear, coherent, and comprehensive fashion. It is to be hoped that this is achieved before family law is very much older.

---

[195] Note, for example, the resolution of the General Synod of the Church of England that 'those whose relationships are not based on marriage may face issues of hardship and vulnerability that need to be addressed by the creation of new legal rights': *Report of Proceedings 2004: General Synod: February Group of Sessions* (Church House Publishing, 2004), p 322.
[196] *Hansard*, HC Deb, vol 450, col 129 WH (11 October 2006).

CHAPTER 4

REMOVING CHILDREN FROM THEIR FAMILIES – LAW AND POLICY BEFORE THE CHILDREN ACT 1989

Mary Hayes

INTRODUCTION

When I was invited to give a paper at this conference I had to decide what I would talk about. Looking back over 150 years of family law stirred so many thoughts about how the law used to be and how it has changed. The editors asked me to talk about child law. I am sure they did so because they know that I have always taken a particularly close interest in this area of family law. Yet, when I remember my student days, I find my choice of child law, and my particular close interest in child protection in the years preceding the Children Act 1989, somewhat surprising.

I was a student in the early 1960s. Child law was hardly mentioned on my undergraduate family law course. References in lectures to children tended to be accounts of esoteric rules about whether and when children could make contracts; or to involve imparting arcane and dry information about the nature of parental rights and duties. This was a time in my own life when, as a matter of law, I would remain a child for many purposes until I was 21.[1] But in reality I was leaving childhood behind and I found these rule-based descriptions of child law all rather tedious and boring. The antics of the adult world, as revealed in lectures on topics such as nullity and divorce, were far more attention-grabbing and intriguing, even if the case law did sometimes border on the prurient.

It was when I began to build up my family law course for undergraduate law students at Sheffield University in the late 1960s and early 1970s that I became fascinated by child law. Initially I mainly focused on private child law. In those days, when marriages were ended by decree, trial judges not only had to be satisfied about the arrangements made for the children, they also were insistent on embodying these arrangements in court orders. Trial judges sitting in county courts made decisions on custody, care and control, and access to children (the terminology then used in private law cases) and recorded their reasons. Sometimes these first instance decisions were appealed and the outcome of the appeal was reported. It was

---

[1] The age of majority was reduced from 21 to 18 by the Family Law Reform Act 1969, s 1.

therefore relatively easy to gain an understanding of how the higher courts approached private law disputes about children.

In contrast, in the 1960s and 70s, cases involving removal by the state of children from their families were rarely subjected to judicial scrutiny by High Court judges, or even by circuit judges. The entry of children into state care did, of course, routinely take place because, sadly, there were and always will be children who do not receive good enough parenting safely to be left in the care of their families. But in those days such removals usually took place with the agreement of the parents and without recourse to the courts. The lack of accountability of local authorities to the higher courts was a striking feature of pre-1989 child care law. Only in rare cases were the higher courts involved in scrutinising a local authority's decisions and actions. As a result, practices and procedures relating to child protection law, as well as the substantive law itself, did not normally receive close study and analysis by academic family lawyers.

Why was there this lack of scrutiny by professional judges into major interventions by the state into the private lives of families? The structure of the statutory child law framework was the dominant reason. In the first part of this chapter I describe that statutory framework and comment on its limitations and defects. I then explain the role of wardship in supplementing that framework. It was mainly in wardship that the High Court became involved in removing children from their families. However, as I explain, the judges exercised their inherent powers in a one-sided manner in order to assist local authorities; but they declined to use wardship to come to the assistance of an aggrieved parent, relative or foster parent.

I conclude with a story about a child called Sarah. She had been taken into the care of Hertfordshire County Council with the agreement of her parents, but without the knowledge or involvement of concerned and loving members of her wider family. I give an account of the reasoning that led the House of Lords to rule that the High Court's wardship jurisdiction could not be used to assess, on the merits, whether Sarah's wider family were better placed to look after her than third party adopters who were the choice of the local authority.[2] In my view, and as I explain in my conclusion, this was a ruling of which the House of Lords should have been ashamed.

---

[2] *Re W (A Minor) (Wardship: Jurisdiction)* [1985] AC 791, HL.

THE STATUTORY FRAMEWORK

Care proceedings: the grounds

Discussion in this paper will focus first on the statutory child protection framework that immediately preceded the Children Act 1989. Under the Children and Young Persons Act 1933, a child could be made the subject of a fit person order either because (s)he had committed an offence[3] or because the child was in need of care, protection or control. Subsequently this court route into state care was amended by the Children and Young Persons Act 1969 (CYPA 1969). That Act saw the introduction of care proceedings in respect of three types of children. Such children could loosely be categorised as the neglected and ill-treated; the troublesome and the truant; and the juvenile offender. Care proceedings were taken in a juvenile court. The burden on the applicant local authority[4] was to establish that one or more of seven specified primary conditions applied to the child *and* that the child was in need of care or control that (s)he was unlikely to receive unless the court made an order.[5]

The scope of these primary conditions was broad. The 1969 Act was a real attempt to respond properly to the difficult balance that must be achieved by draftsmen when formulating child protection legislation. In a liberal society, parents must be allowed to bring up their own children as they see fit. But children are autonomous beings. They too have independent rights and interests and must be protected from inadequate, incompetent, improper and cruel forms of care.[6]

---

[3] Punishable by imprisonment in the case of an adult. The use solely of the male personal pronoun in the drafting of child protection legislation in 1969 can cause trouble for academics writing in 2008. Hence my decision sometimes to insert (s) in brackets before 'he' or sometimes to write he/she. The now ubiquitous use of 'they' goes against the grain for those amongst us who had it drilled into us at school that the plural 'they' cannot be used as a substitute for 'he or she'.

[4] Any local authority, constable or authorised person (only the NSPCC was authorised) could bring a child before the court. Almost invariably the local authority was the applicant.

[5] Under the CYPA 1969, s 1(2), a child could be brought before a court in care proceedings where it was alleged that '(a) his proper development is being avoidably prevented or neglected or his health is being avoidably impaired or neglected or he is being ill-treated; or (b) it is probable that the condition set out in the preceding paragraph will be satisfied in his case, having regard to the fact that the court or another court has found that that condition is or was satisfied in the case of another child or young person who is or was a member of the household to which he belongs; or (bb) it is probable that the conditions set out in para (a) will be satisfied in his case, having regard to the fact that a person who has been convicted of an offence mentioned in Sch 1 to the CYPA 1933 ... is, or may become, a member of the same household of the child; or (c) he is exposed to moral danger; or (d) he is beyond the control of his parent or guardian; or (e) he is of compulsory school age ... and is not receiving efficient full-time education suitable to his age, ability and aptitude and to any special educational needs he may have; or (f) he is guilty of an offence, excluding homicide.'

[6] Then, as now, the degrees of risk acceptable to local authorities appeared to vary according to whether the child came from a deprived inner city area or from a more prosperous community. Similarly, there was a tension over when physical punishment

When setting standards in primary condition (a) in s 1(2) of the 1969 Act – requiring proof that the child's 'proper development is being avoidably prevented ... etc', the choice of the word 'avoidably' reflected this difficulty. 'Avoidably' lent itself to two opposing interpretations. It could have meant that there were grounds for intervention only where those causing harm to the child could avoid doing so by an effort of will. This interpretation would have led to the undesirable result that an application must be dismissed where the parent, because of a physical or mental disability, could not avoid treating the child in a damaging fashion. Or 'avoidably' could have meant that harm to the child could be avoided if he was treated differently, regardless of any parental culpability. The correct interpretation of 'avoidably' was never determined by the higher courts.[7]

It is probably the case that the latter view was the correct interpretation. The focus of care proceedings was on the condition of the child, and while this would often require proof of culpability on the part of the parent, parental fault should not have been essential. Where a child was being harmed, and where a parent could not 'avoid' what he or she was doing, it seems to me plain that Parliament would have intended that an order could be made where this was the only way for the child to be protected.[8]

The courts faced other difficulties when ruling on the correct interpretation of the primary conditions in s 1(2) of the 1969 Act. Condition (a) was drafted in the present tense: a child's 'proper development *is being* avoidably prevented ...' and made no reference either to past or to future events.[9] The courts interpreted this drafting

---

amounted to ill-treatment in a multi-cultural society that permitted corporal punishment of children: see *Re H (A Minor)* [1987] 2 FLR 12. However, the tolerance level of what amounted to acceptable parental chastisement has undoubtedly lowered since then. Nowadays there is a real possibility that, before long, assaults on children will no longer be regarded by society as tolerable.

[7] Probably because failed applications in care proceedings were taken to the High Court in wardship where the principle of the paramountcy of the child's welfare was applied. In *Salford CC v C* (1982) 3 FLR 153 magistrates' interpretation of avoidability as requiring parental culpability led them to discharge a care order. The High Court, reversing their decision in wardship, gave no ruling on the point.

[8] I had thought that the concept of the 'similar child' introduced into legislation by s 31(10) of the Children Act 1989, coupled with the requirement that significant harm to a child is attributable to a lack of *reasonable* parental care, reflected my view of the proper interpretation of 'avoidably' in the previous legislation. But see Hedley J's worrying reasoning in *Re L (Care: Threshold Criteria)* [2007] 1 FLR 2050 when expressing his view of the correct application of principle in relation to proof of the threshold test. This was a case where parents, because of their own limited abilities, were unable to avoid causing harm to their child. See, particularly, paras [50] and [51].

[9] Section 1(2)(b) and (bb) empowered a court to make an order where a child was at risk of harm rather than where the harm had already occurred. This power arose under (b) where harm under para (a) could be established in relation to another child in the same household as the child before the court, or under (bb) where a person convicted of a specified offence against a child 'is, or may become, a member of the same household of the child before the court'.

realistically. They refused to countenance the analysis that condition (a) could not be proved where the child before the court had been removed from home and was currently being properly looked after.[10] In *Re D (A Minor)*[11] a baby was born suffering from drug withdrawal symptoms caused by the mother's excessive drug taking during her pregnancy. The baby was kept in hospital and never allowed into the care of her mother. When care proceedings were taken, the child, since her birth, had never been out of the care of responsible agencies. The House of Lords endorsed as correct the construction of 'is being' as indicating a situation over a period of time sufficiently proximate to the date of the court hearing to indicate that it was the present and continuing set of circumstances which was descriptive of the child's position.[12] In what, for some, was a controversial judgment, their Lordships ruled that the juvenile court was entitled to look back to the period before the child was born when considering whether s 1(2)(a) was established. It held that the legislative purpose was best furthered in a case of this kind by allowing such an approach.

A child could be brought before a court under s 1(2)(c) where it was alleged that '(s)he is exposed to moral danger'. In the main this provision was non-controversial. Usually it was relied on to protect children and adolescents who were engaging in unlawful or risky sexual activity.[13] However, disagreement was caused by the interpretation of moral danger in *Alhaji Mohamed v Knott*.[14] This case involved married immigrants from Nigeria. The child bride had been brought before the court under s 1(2)(c). On appeal, the High Court ruled that in assessing whether a child is in moral danger the standards of 'English people' and the 'English way of life' should not be rigidly applied to people from other cultures where the behaviour in issue would be acceptable in the foreign country in which the parties have been brought up. This is a challenging statement of principle. Within the context and circumstances of a particular case it may, sometimes, properly influence a court's judgment. However, as applied to the facts in *Alhaji Mohamed v Knott* it was, in my view, unsustainable and wrong.[15] The 'wife' was a pre-pubertal 13-year-old girl and her husband, a man in his late twenties, was suffering from a venereal disease. While it may have been arguable that sexual intercourse between the couple may not have exposed this particular child to 'moral' danger,[16]

---

[10] *F v Suffolk CC* (1981) 2 FLR 208; *M v Westminster CC* [1985] FLR 325.
[11] [1987] AC 317, HL.
[12] *F v Suffolk CC* (1981) 2 FLR 208 and *M v Westminster CC* [1985] FLR 325.
[13] For example, where a young girl was engaged in prostitution, or a young boy became involved in homosexual activity with a much older man.
[14] [1969] 1 QB 1.
[15] There are circumstances where a society from which a child comes permits conduct that wholly offends against the canons and principles of English society, e g forced marriages and female circumcision.
[16] Though this concession, too, is undoubtedly contentious, as the child was between 2 and 3 years below the age of consent.

it undoubtedly put her health and development at serious risk, as the court should have acknowledged and from which it should have taken steps to protect her.[17]

Under the 1969 Act, as well as being satisfied of one or more of the specified primary conditions, the court had in addition to find that the child 'is in need of care or control which he is unlikely to receive unless the court makes an order.'[18] This provision was a forward-looking test that required the court to consider what would happen to the child if an order was not made. In practice, where the primary condition was proved, a court was almost invariably satisfied that it should make an order in respect of the child. It may, however, have been open to persuasion that a supervision order rather than a care order would afford the child sufficient care and control.[19]

Care proceedings: practice and procedures

Place of safety orders, empowering a local authority to secure the immediate removal of a child into care, were often granted to local authorities as a preliminary to care proceedings.[20] Place of safety orders could, and usually did, last for a maximum period of 28 days. At that stage the child's parents had no rights. They were not entitled to be heard when the place of safety order application was made; they could not appeal against the order; and, if the local authority denied them contact with their child during the subsistence of the place of safety order (which local authorities often did), the parents had no right to challenge that decision in a court.[21]

---

[17] The court could and in my view should, instead, have ruled that the child's condition fell within s 1(2)(a).
[18] Care included protection and guidance and control included discipline: s 70(1). In *Re S (A Minor) (Care order: Education)* [1978] QB 120 a well-behaved, well-disciplined and respectful boy aged 12 was not being sent to school because his parents had an implacable objection to comprehensive education. The Court of Appeal ruled that a child who is not receiving a proper education is in need of care or control within the meaning of the provision, and that magistrates had been correct to make a care order (in reliance on s 1(2)(e)).
[19] It can be seen that despite the different language used in the 1969 Act to identify when the state had grounds for intervention, the structure of the legislation governing applications brought in care proceedings did not differ markedly from important aspects of the structure and content of the reforming legislation governing the 'threshold test' under the Children Act 1989, s 31. The strength and brilliance of the 1989 Act was the manner in which it brought cohesion and consistency to family proceedings as a whole.
[20] Indeed, the excessive use of place of safety orders instantly to remove children from their homes was one of the many criticisms of the manner in which pre-1989 child protection procedures operated in practice.
[21] This absence of any right of challenge was made plain in two reported cases. When parents applied to a juvenile court for an interim order with the express purpose of obtaining the child's release from care, this was held to be an improper application and an abuse of the process of the court: *Nottinghamshire CC v Q* (1982) 3 FLR 305. So too

When an application came before a juvenile court in care proceedings, the only parties to the proceedings were the applicant local authority and the child. Parents were not parties. Indeed, when the CYPA 1969 first came into force, the right of a parent to participate in the hearing was severely limited. It was only after Divisional Court rulings that the position of parents was improved. These rulings permitted a juvenile court to conduct its proceedings with flexibility in order to further the interests of justice. So, in a 1979 case involving the Milton Keynes juvenile court, it was held that parents had a right to cross-examine witnesses;[22] and in a 1983 case involving the Gravesham juvenile court it was held that the juvenile court could allow parents to be legally represented.[23] These rulings eventually resulted in amendments being made to the Magistrates' Courts (Children and Young Persons Rules) 1970. Although parents continued not to be parties, the amended court rules gave them the right to meet any allegations made against them.[24]

The child, by contrast, was always a party to care proceedings because, in a purist sense, care proceedings were about the child, not the parents. The initial position of parents was that they were entitled to represent their child themselves. However, parents were often prevented from doing so. The Rules prevented representation of the child by a parent where the child was legally represented; where proceedings were brought at the parent's request on the ground that the child was beyond control; or where the child objected.[25] In addition and crucially, the court was given the power to disqualify parents from representing their child, or otherwise acting on the child's behalf, wherever it appeared to the court that there was, or might be, a conflict between the interests of the child and those of the parents.[26] And of course this conflict was normally found to exist where child abuse was alleged. As a consequence, in child protection care proceedings a guardian ad litem for the child should normally have been appointed.[27] The duty of the guardian ad litem was to safeguard the interests of the child before the court.

Initially, guardians ad litem for children were appointed only in circumstances where a court was hearing an unopposed application to discharge a care order. This, on its face, appears curious. An explanation is found in the tragic circumstances surrounding the non-accidental death

---

was an attempt by different parents to secure their child's release through making an application to the High Court in wardship: *Re E (Minors) (Wardship: Jurisdiction)* (1983) 4 FLR 668.
[22] *R v Milton Keynes Justices ex parte R* [1979] 1 WLR 1062.
[23] *R v Gravesham Juvenile Court ex parte B* (1983) 4 FLR 312.
[24] Magistrates' Courts (Children and Young Persons) Rules 1970 (as amended), r 18.
[25] Ibid, r 17(1).
[26] CYPA 1969, s 32A(1) (inserted by the Children Act 1975, s 64).
[27] Then, as now, there was a serious shortage of guardians ad litem in some parts of the country.

of a little girl named Maria Colwell.[28] A local authority decided not to resist an application by Maria's mother that Maria be returned to her care. This was despite the fact that Maria had spent several years in foster care, where she was happy and settled, and despite the local authority having reservations about the suitability of Maria's mother and stepfather properly to look after her. No investigation of the local authority's decision was conducted on behalf of Maria. No independent assessment was made of the applicant and her husband and no independent consideration was given to whether Maria would be at risk of ill-treatment if returned home. No one had the duty to tell the court about Maria's wishes and feelings and how she felt about being taken from her present carers whom she loved. One outcome of the report of the Committee of Inquiry into Maria's subsequent ill-treatment and death was a recognition of how critically important it was that an independent person was appointed to look into an unopposed application to discharge a child from care. Without such an investigation no one was in the position to alert a court to any risks such an order might present to the child. Consequently, a court would have been unlikely to query such an outcome where the local authority was in agreement to it being made.

Gradually, the appointment of guardians ad litem to safeguard and represent the interests of children was extended to other proceedings. This legal development was an important reform that undoubtedly benefited the child, but the introduction of the guardian ad litem had both positive and negative implications for the parents' rights.

The Rules did not require parents to be notified that an application was being made to disqualify them from representing their child. Parents appeared to have no entitlement to be heard on the matter.[29] Juvenile courts differed widely in the procedures they adopted when determining this preliminary issue. Some courts acted with due regard to the rules of natural justice. They conducted an official hearing, allowed the parents to be legally represented and decided whether to disqualify the parents in a formal judicial manner. But other courts did not treat the application as a judicial decision that required an inter partes hearing to be held in a prescribed manner. Instead, in some juvenile courts the justices' clerk arranged for a representative of the local authority to speak in private to a single magistrate, who then decided whether to make the disqualification order. Some courts went even further. The disqualification order was made by a justices' clerk after consultation with the local authority and with no involvement of the magistracy at all.

A disqualification order under s 32A had one beneficial outcome of great practical importance to parents: it made them automatic parties to the

---

[28] *Report of the Committee of Inquiry into the Care and Supervision provided in relation to Maria Colwell* (HMSO, 1974) (Chairman: T G Fisher QC).
[29] *R v Plymouth Juvenile Court ex parte F and F* [1987] 1 FLR 169.

proceedings and eligible for separate legal aid.[30] But the decision to disqualify parents from representing their child had a critical negative outcome for parents' appeal rights. Where a parent had represented the child in the juvenile court the parent could appeal on the child's behalf to the Crown Court against the making of a care order, or the refusal to discharge a care order.[31] But where a guardian ad litem for the child had been appointed, only the guardian ad litem could appeal on behalf of the child on these grounds. Where the guardian ad litem decided not to exercise this right of appeal, no other person could do so.[32]

The rights of appeal of the local authority and the guardian ad litem were also strictly limited. Neither could appeal a juvenile court's refusal to make a care order, or its decision to discharge an existing care order. They could not obtain a fresh hearing on the merits in the Crown Court. Their rights of appeal were restricted to appeals on a point of law by way of case stated.

What was the thinking behind this strict control of appeals? Children who had come to serious harm and children who had committed offences could both be brought before a court in care proceedings. This led to the misguided reasoning that an application in care proceedings was an attack on the child's liberty and, therefore, that a failed application for a care order must be treated as analogous to a failed prosecution.[33] This flawed logic had the potential for disastrous consequences for a child where that child was genuinely at risk of serious harm unless protective intervention was authorised by a court. Where a local authority's application had been badly presented in a juvenile court, or where the magistrates had proved incompetent as decision-makers, neither the local authority nor the guardian ad litem could obtain a fresh hearing in the Crown Court. One outcome of this was an increased use of wardship by local authorities where they took the view that the juvenile court's decision had put the child at serious risk. A local authority would either itself ward the child or would permit the guardian ad litem to do so.[34]

So, to summarise: few cases brought in care proceedings ever went beyond a hearing in the juvenile court. That court was a private court to which the press did not have access. It was staffed by lay magistrates who were not required to give reasons for their decisions. Appeals by a local authority or guardian ad litem were not permitted against the court's refusal to make a care order, and disqualified parents could not appeal against a

---

[30] Legal Aid Act 1974, s 28(6A).
[31] The appeal took the form of a rehearing before a judge and two magistrates.
[32] *A-R v Avon CC* [1985] FLR 252. Disqualified parents were not entitled to appeal a child's removal into care until late in the 1980s.
[33] In practice, offending children continued to be prosecuted in a juvenile court. Only a tiny percentage of alleged juvenile offenders were brought before a court in care proceedings.
[34] *Re D (A minor) (Justices' Decision: Review)* [1977] Fam 158; *Re C (A Minor)* (1981) 2 FLR 62.

care order being made. Very few appeals were taken on points of law. All of this meant that children were being removed from their families by orders made by lay decision-makers in the lowest court in the land. In those days, lay justices operated with little training and, because of the limited appeal structure, they received very little guidance on how to apply the law from experienced Family Division judges.

Reception into care

The other main method of separating children from their families before the Children Act 1989 was through reception into care, followed by the assumption of parental rights. The Children Act 1948, and subsequently the Child Care Act 1980, placed local authorities under a duty to receive a child into care. This duty arose where the provision of social work support, services and, in exceptional circumstances, cash did not make adequate provision for a child's needs.[35] Generally, of course, it was accepted that the welfare of children was normally best served by being looked after by their parents and wider family. However, where a child was orphaned, abandoned or lost, or where parents were 'prevented by reason of mental or bodily disease or infirmity or other incapacity or any other circumstances from providing for [the child's] proper accommodation, maintenance and upbringing' *and* where local authority intervention was necessary in the interests of the welfare of the child, the local authority was required to receive the child into care.[36]

Reception into care was a 'voluntary' arrangement. Voluntary is put in inverted commas because the reasons why parents were prepared to agree to give up their children into state care arose, in some cases, from circumstances over which they had little or no control. A particularly poignant example was when a parent was made homeless, and hence the powerful impact that *Cathy Come Home*, a play for television, had on the public conscience.[37] There is anecdotal evidence too that some parents were pressured into agreeing to their child's reception into care by a warning from social workers that, if the parent were to decline to co-operate, the alternative would be the initiation of care proceedings. Whilst such a warning may often have been realistic, it appeared to be the case that sometimes it was given in circumstances where probably there was not enough evidence to satisfy a juvenile court that there were sufficient grounds for a care order.[38]

---

[35] Child Care Act 1980, s 1 (hereafter, CCA 1980).

[36] CCA 1980, s 2.

[37] A drama about the failure of housing and social welfare systems to support families with children, written by Jeremy Sandford, produced by Tony Garnett, directed by Ken Loach and screened shortly before Christmas in 1966; cf *Attorney-General ex rel Tilley v Wandsworth LBC* (1981) 2 FLR 377, which held that a local authority should not fetter its discretion by adopting a rigid policy against refusing to house an intentionally homeless family.

[38] Because of the present-tense drafting of s 1(2)(a) of the CYPA 1969, care proceedings

The main reason, however, why some parents had reason to fear their child's reception into care was that a local authority might subsequently decide to turn a voluntary agreement into a compulsory arrangement without the need first to obtain the authority of a court to do so. All a local authority had to do was to declare that one or more of several specified grounds were established in relation to the child and to pass an administrative resolution to this effect. How did this situation arise? A local authority's primary duty towards a child, whether the child was in care as a result of a court order or voluntary reception, was to safeguard and promote the child's welfare throughout his or her childhood. However, the focus of working with the family of a child in voluntary care was (or should have been) to secure the child's safe return home. Moreover, a local authority had no right to keep a child in voluntary care against the wishes of a parent.[39] Theoretically, this structure was straightforward and entirely consistent with a voluntary framework. Factually, the position may not have been so straightforward.

Assumption of parental rights: the grounds

Assumption of parental rights and duties by resolution was a procedure that enabled a local authority to take over the rights and duties of each parent individually in respect of his or her child.[40] It was regarded by local authorities as a valuable procedure for safeguarding the position of a child where the need to protect the child had arisen since the child's reception into care. The main grounds, apart from where the parents were dead and where the child had no guardian or custodian,[41] were based on parental unfitness or incapacity to care. A resolution could be passed where a parent had abandoned the child;[42] where (s)he suffered from some permanent disability rendering her incapable of caring for the child; where (s)he suffered from a mental disorder rendering her unfit to have the care of the child; where (s)he was of such habits or mode of life as to be unfit to have the care of the child; and where (s)he had so consistently failed without reasonable cause to discharge the obligations of a parent as to be unfit to have the care of the child.[43] This resolution gave a local

---

could not be taken to anticipate threatened harm to a child, no matter how imminent the threatened harm may have been: see *Essex CC v TLR and KBR (Minors)* (1978) 9 Fam Law 15.

[39] 'Nothing in this section shall authorise a local authority to keep a child in their care under this section if any parent or guardian desires to take over the care of the child': CCA 1980, s 2(3).
[40] Initially under CA 1948, s 2 and subsequently under CCA 1980, s 3.
[41] CCA 1980, s 3(1)(a).
[42] Section 3(1)(b)(i). Abandonment required culpable conduct by the parent. In *Wheatley v London Borough of Waltham Forest* [1979] 2 WLR 543 a mother left her child in the care of his grandmother and disappeared. The Divisional Court found that she had been feckless and irresponsible, but that she did not thereby abandon her child. Moreover, it held that the child must have still been abandoned at the time the resolution was made, and this mother had visited her child regularly in the several months preceding the passing of the resolution.
[43] These five sub-paragraphs fell within s 3(1)(b). Section 3(1)(c) provided as an additional

authority the right to keep the child in care against the parents' wishes: thus, it had the same impact as a court order. In those few cases where the assumption of parental rights was challenged in the High Court, it was stressed that to divest a parent of his or her rights and duties was a very serious decision. The High Court held that proof that 'a parent has so consistently failed without reasonable cause to discharge the obligations of a parent as to be unfit to have the care of the child', on which the majority of the reported case law turned, required evidence of a high degree of culpability.[44]

The final, and conceptually different, basis for assuming parental rights was where a local authority relied on lapse of time. This power arose where a child had been in the care of the local authority under s 2 throughout the 3 years preceding the passing of the resolution.[45] There was no need to prove parental fault or unfitness to care. Consequently, reliance on this ground would have been less damaging to the parents' sense of self-esteem and may have been more acceptable to them than a resolution made on one of the other grounds. The 3-year provision served several purposes. It enabled plans to be made for a child who might otherwise have drifted in long-term care. Sometimes it was relied on as a preliminary to adoption proceedings, or occasionally a custodianship application.[46] Sometimes it was used as a protective measure having regard to the welfare of a child. In cases where the child had been in care for many years, often that child would never have enjoyed a real and close relationship with his or her natural parents. The child's deepest feelings, loyalties and attachments would have formed with others, especially where (s)he had lived throughout with the same foster carers. Any attempt by the parents to have taken the child from the foster home would have been traumatic and harmful to the child.[47] The assumption of parental rights

---

ground 'that a resolution under para (b) of this subsection is in force in relation to one parent of the child who is, or is likely to become, a member of the household comprising the child and his other parent.'

[44] A parent who was intellectually, psychologically or emotionally inadequate might not be culpable. The authorities differed on whether the test to be applied was objective or subjective. In *O'Dare Ai v South Glamorgan* (1982) 3 FLR 1, the Divisional Court held there must be proof of blameworthy conduct involving a subjective departure by the parent from a proper standard of conduct which can be regarded as morally reprehensible. In *M v Wigan MBC* (1980) 1 FLR 45, the Divisional Court ruled that an objective standard was appropriate. It held that the court must look to see whether the conduct was reasonable or unreasonable according to what a reasonable parent would have done in the circumstances. In my view, the latter approach was (and still is) appropriate, as the focus of the court should be on child protection, not parental fault. (See n 8 above, and the associated text, in relation to parental fault and care proceedings under the CYPA 1969, and proof of the threshold test under the CA 1989).

[45] Section 3(1)(d). The ground was also satisfied where the child had been partly in the care of a local authority and partly in the care of a voluntary organisation during this time.

[46] This latter method of securing a child's future was never popular with relatives and foster parents. It was abolished by the Children Act 1989, although a similar order – a 'special guardianship' order – was subsequently introduced: see Children Act 1989, s 14A (inserted by the Adoption and Children Act 2002).

[47] See, for example, *W v Nottinghamshire CC* (1982) 3 FLR 33.

could be used by local authorities to protect a child from removal from care after such a long lapse of time where this was believed to be against the child's best interests.

Some local authorities did not make proper use of their powers to pass a parental rights resolution in cases where they should have done so.[48] This could cause problems because a local authority had no right to keep a child in voluntary care under s 2 where a parent desired to take over the care of the child.[49] However, at the same time a parental rights resolution could only be passed in respect of a child who was currently in care under s 2. Once a parent presented herself to the local authority and demanded the immediate return of her child, the local authority no longer had the power to assume parental rights.[50] This sometimes resulted in children suddenly being removed from care without warning by parents who were not fit to look after them, or abruptly being taken from foster parents with whom they had lived since early childhood, and to whom they had become very closely attached.

A reform was inserted into the Child Care Act 1980 as a response to such threats to the security of children in voluntary care.[51] It was designed to facilitate two outcomes. The first was to secure the planned and phased return of children to their families; the second was to give local authorities a 'breathing space' in which to consider whether to take steps to prevent the child's removal from voluntary care at all. The new section provided that once a child had been in care for more than 6 months a parent had to give 28 days' notice of her desire to have her child back again. During this notice period a parental rights resolution could be passed bringing to an end the parent's absolute right to remove the child, or an application could be made in wardship. This change in the law afforded much needed protection for some children in long term care. However, it made serious inroads into the voluntary nature of reception into care and may have led to a loss of confidence in the care system by those parents likely to be affected by it.

Assumption of parental rights: policy and procedures

The decision to assume parental rights was usually made by a specialist subcommittee of the Social Services Committee of the local authority. A senior officer of the Social Services Department would put a report before the elected members stating the grounds relied on. Policy varied considerably. Some local authorities used parental rights resolutions as a

---

[48] In line with their duty to safeguard and promote the welfare of a child in care throughout his or her childhood: CCA 1980, s 18.
[49] CCA 1980, s 2(3).
[50] Cf *Lewisham LBC v Lewisham Juvenile Court Justices* [1980] AC 273, HL. Lord Salmon emphasised the point when stating that the local authority might well consider it to be their moral duty to keep the child long enough to make it a ward of court, but said (at 291) that this was 'all they could do to save the child'.
[51] CCA 1980, s 13(2).

last resort, such as where parents had lost all contact with their child, or where successive attempts at rehabilitation had failed. But other local authorities passed a resolution soon after the child was received into care; they saw it as a means of imposing a clean break and placing the child into long-term foster care, often with a view to adoption.

Procedures, like policies, also varied from one local authority to another. There was a disturbing absence of statutory safeguards for parents at the stage when the resolution was passed. The only right conferred by statute on parents was the right to object to the resolution *after* it had been passed. The conduct of the meeting to assume parental rights was also at the discretion of each local authority. Some social services committees permitted parents to attend all or part of the meeting and parents were allowed to address committee members. Other social services committees simply permitted parents to meet the chairman, and perhaps some committee members, in advance of the meeting. Some committees did not permit parents to attend at all and merely allowed them to make their views known in writing. It is disturbing to note that as late as 1984 (perhaps a symbolic year) the circular advice issued by the DHSS was to the effect that 'in devising procedures for such meetings, every effort should be made to achieve informality as far as possible and particularly to avoid the appearance of judicial function. The aim should be to avoid cross-questioning of each other by parents or social workers.'[52] In other words, local authorities were advised to adopt procedures devoid of the normal safeguards to ensure a fair hearing.

Parents had one month in which to serve a counter-notice in writing objecting to the resolution. But, of course, many parents did not know how to go about challenging a parental rights resolution, let alone how to do so in writing. Many parents did not realise that if they objected to the resolution, this would result in the resolution lapsing after 14 days unless the local authority made a complaint to a juvenile court. The burden would then be on the local authority to prove in a juvenile court that the grounds on which the local authority purported to pass the resolution were made out when the resolution was passed; that there continued to be grounds at the time of the hearing; and that it was in the interests of the child that the resolution should not lapse.[53] This initial flawed and inadequate safeguard against parents' rights being improperly assumed was itself very short-lived. After the month for service of a counter-notice had elapsed the position changed. The burden no longer lay on the local authority to prove its case. The assumption of parental rights was still open to challenge in a juvenile court, but it would be for the parent to make an application to the court for the resolution to be rescinded. The burden of proof was now on the parent to establish that there was no ground for making the resolution, or that it should now be determined in the interests of the child. Even where the parent could show that there

---

[52] LAC (84) 5, para 26.
[53] CCA 1980, s 3(6).

had been no proper legal basis for passing the initial resolution, the court was not bound to discharge it.[54] The parent's capacity or fitness to care was no longer the critical statutory criterion.[55] The court had also to be satisfied that it was in the interests of the child to determine the resolution.[56]

Access to children in care

An account of how the statutory framework operated cannot be concluded without brief reference to access to children in care, even though access[57] was not regulated by statute until shortly before the Children Act 1989 replaced the previous law. Unless a child in care maintains regular contact with his or her parents, or at least with members of the wider family, it is undoubtedly the case that it is most unlikely that such a child will ever be rehabilitated back to his or her home, with all the human rights implications that such an outcome has for both the child and for the child's parents. It is therefore astonishing and shocking to remember how local authorities used to exercise total power over access between children in care and their parents and families. Nowhere in statute was there any provision requiring local authorities to maintain access between parents and children. Nowhere in statute was there any provision giving parents the right to challenge a reduction in access, even where that access was denied in its entirety. Access was regarded as part of the day to day administration of the statutory control exercised by local authorities over children subject to care orders. In *Re W (Minors) (Wardship: Jurisdiction)*,[58] an unsuccessful attempt was made in wardship to challenge a local authority's denial of access by a mother to her two children in foster care. The Court of Appeal held that Parliament had confided such decisions to local authorities and that they had an exclusive jurisdiction from which there was no right of appeal. Treating access to a child in care as a largely unreviewable matter over which local authorities had an unfettered discretion was subsequently confirmed by the leading House of Lords ruling in *A v Liverpool CC*.[59]

---

[54] Section 5(4) provided: 'a juvenile court ... if satisfied that there was no ground for the making of the resolution or that the resolution should in the interests of the child be determined, *may* by order determine the resolution.' It is easy to understand why the court, at this stage, retained a discretion despite the fact that there had originally been no ground for passing the resolution. A lengthy period of time might have elapsed since the child's initial reception into care and other plans for the child may have been made, such as placement with foster parents with a view to adoption.

[55] Where lapse of time provided the basis for the resolution, proof of incapacity or unfitness was not necessary.

[56] See *K v Devon CC* [1987] Fam Law 348. See *Re L (AC) (An Infant)* [1971] 3 All ER 743 for a case where a parental rights resolution was handled in a procedurally incompetent manner.

[57] What is now called 'contact'.

[58] [1980] Fam 60.

[59] [1982] AC 363: see below.

Parliament did not alter the law until the mid 1980s.[60] This change in the law was limited in its scope, but its significance lay in opening the door for the first time to the review by courts of disagreements between parents and local authorities about access to children in care. A parent, guardian or custodian who was refused access, or whose access was terminated, was given the right to apply to a juvenile court for an order requiring the local authority to arrange access.[61] There was no such right of application where access had been varied only and local authorities retained considerable discretion on how much access they would allow. It was specifically provided that a local authority was not to be taken to have terminated access in a case where it proposed to substitute new arrangements for existing arrangements.[62] In *Re Y (Minors)* it was argued that a drastic reduction in access amounted, in reality, to termination, but this argument failed.[63]

The accompanying Code of Practice, however, was an important breakthrough in the guidance offered to local authorities on the approach they should take to access. Significantly, there was an assumption running through the Code that access to parents was for the benefit of the child. The Code offered commonsense guidance about all aspects of access arrangements and recommended that local authorities produce explanatory leaflets. It highlighted such matters as listening to the child's views, the benefits of regular communication with the parents, and considering access to the wider family.[64] It reminded local authorities of the need for speed in reaching decisions, a discipline emphasised too by the courts.[65] The Act was silent on the legal effect of the Code and it was not clear whether it was to be regarded as general guidance under the Local Authority Social Services Act 1970.[66] In contrasting opinions, the Court

---

[60] The familiarity of courts nowadays with the rights conferred by Art 8 of the European Convention on Human Rights and Fundamental Freedoms makes the approach of courts to access to children in care up until the mid-1980s particularly startling. Indeed, the law prior to the change was found in breach of Art 8 in *R v United Kingdom* (1988) 19 EHRR 74 (ECHR).

[61] Health and Social Services and Social Security Adjudications Act 1983, Sch 1 inserted ss 12A–12G into the Child Care Act 1980, supported by a Code of Practice.

[62] CCA 1980, s 12B(4).

[63] [1988] 1 FLR 299. Bush J found that it was impossible to draw the line at which access became so minimal that it amounted to termination or refusal. He held that if the court were to draw such a line it would be encroaching on decision-making that Parliament had expressly left to the discretion of local authorities. Bush J took the view that the only possible avenue open to parents would be in judicial review, and only where it was possible to prove that a particular local authority had kept access alive on a minimum basis solely for the purpose of preventing an application for access being made in the juvenile court. See too the obiter remarks in *M v Berkshire CC* [1985] FLR 257.

[64] Relatives such as grandparents were not included in those entitled to apply to a court, so could not take advantage of the new statutory provisions.

[65] In *R v Bolton MBC ex parte B* [1985] Fam Law 193, the court held that 14 days, and exceptionally 21 were sufficient for a local authority to make up its mind whether to terminate access. Refusal of access could properly take longer as the local authority may have needed to conduct investigations and to take psychiatric advice.

[66] Section 7(1).

of Appeal referred to the Code as 'an aid to construction' of the statute,[67] while the Divisional Court declined to use the Code as 'a guide to the proper meaning of the words of the statute'.[68]

THE PREROGATIVE JURISDICTION OF THE HIGH COURT

When wardship was available to local authorities

The potential for conflict between parents and local authorities, and the desire on the part of each to resort to wardship where there appeared to be defects in the two main statutory schemes,[69] is the subject of the final part of this paper. The grounds for a care order or for the assumption of parental rights had, of course, first to be established to the satisfaction of a juvenile court before a child could lawfully be taken away from his or her parents against their wishes. In wardship, by contrast, the paramountcy of the welfare of the child was (and is) the principle guiding the High Court and no grounds for intervention, as such, had first to be proved. The importance of wardship before the Children Act 1989 was in its use in coming to the assistance of local authorities. Local authorities turned to the High Court either because they had no statutory powers to intervene in a child's life, or because those powers had run their course. Wardship was variously described as a jurisdiction to supplement statutory powers or to fill gaps or lacunae in the law.

Case law on removing children from their families arose in a variety of contexts. It has been explained that where a local authority was unable to establish to a court's satisfaction that a parental rights resolution should not lapse, it was forced to return the child to the care of the parent. However, where after failing in the juvenile court a local authority made the child a ward of court, a High Court judge would apply the principle of the paramountcy of the child's welfare when examining the merits of the local authority's application.[70] Where the judge took the view that it would be in the child's best interests to remain a ward of court he could order that the child be placed in the care of the local authority. Similarly, it has been seen that neither the local authority nor the guardian ad litem could appeal against a court's refusal to make a care order, or against its decision to discharge a care order. Where a local authority took the view that the juvenile court's decision put the child at risk, it was able to invoke the wardship jurisdiction or permit the guardian ad litem to do so.[71] A

---

[67] *M v Berkshire CC* [1985] FLR 257.
[68] *R v Bolton MBC ex parte B* [1985] Fam Law 193.
[69] CYPA 1969 and CCA 1980.
[70] *O'Dare Ai v South Glamorgan CC* [1979] 2 WLR 543; *Crosby (A Minor) v Northumberland CC* (1982) Fam Law 92.
[71] *Re C (A Minor)* (1981) 2 FLR 62.

local authority could do this even where a parent had made a successful appeal on behalf of the child to the Crown Court.[72]

A rather different example arose where a local authority feared for the safety of a new-born child still at a maternity hospital. It has been explained that the main ground for care proceedings required a court to be satisfied that the child's 'proper development *is* being avoidably prevented or neglected or his health *is* being avoidably impaired or neglected or he *is* being ill-treated'.[73] Since this provision was couched in the present tense, and since the baby was not at risk at the hospital, protective intervention under the 1969 Act was unavailable. Yet there might be powerful evidence to suggest that once the child was removed from hospital it would be gravely at risk. Where the baby's mother would not co-operate with local authority intervention on a voluntary basis, the only way for the local authority to safeguard the child was through making him a ward of court.[74]

In *Re D (A Minor) (Justices' Decision: Review)*[75] Dunn J held that in situations where the statutory scheme was failing to protect the child it should be regarded as stepping aside, and that far from local authorities being discouraged from applying to the court in wardship, they should be encouraged to do so. In *Re R*[76] the Court of Appeal endorsed Dunn J's approach, and emphasised that a local authority must be at liberty to invoke wardship if and when it was deemed necessary in the interests of the child. Thus, it was undoubtedly the case that the inherent jurisdiction of the High Court was available where there were gaps or lacunae in the law.[77] However, case law reveals that the jurisdiction was more readily available than this. Local authorities appeared able to obtain assistance in wardship at will, and whether or not the statutory jurisdiction had been exhausted or had failed to protect the child.[78]

The unavailability of wardship to parents and others interested in a child

The lack of availability of wardship to parents, or others such as grandparents and foster parents with an interest in the welfare of a child was in stark contrast. It has been seen how local authorities possessed

---

[72] *Hertfordshire CC v Dolling* (1982) 3 FLR 423.
[73] CYPA 1969, s 1(2)(a), emphasis added.
[74] See too *Re C (A Minor) (Wardship: Surrogacy)* [1985] FLR 846, where a contract for surrogate parenthood was involved.
[75] [1977] Fam 158.
[76] [1987] 2 FLR 400.
[77] Confirmed by the House of Lords in *A v Liverpool CC* [1982] AC 363.
[78] See, for example, *Re LH* [1986] 2 FLR 306; *Re M* [1988] 1 FLR 35. In medical cases of particular difficulty, such as whether a disabled child should have life-saving treatment against the wishes of the parents, a local authority would normally immediately ward the child. Wardship was also used to supplement a local authority's powers, for example, to prevent a child's removal from the jurisdiction.

most of the parental rights and duties in relation to a child in their care. A local authority could decide about whether, where and how often access would be allowed between a child in care and his or her parents, grandparents or other members of the family.[79] The local authority could decide whether to place a child in institutional care or foster care. It could move a child from one foster placement to another. There was no mechanism within the statutory framework for challenging these decisions.[80] Anyone with a genuine interest in a child had the right to make the child a ward of court, but in all such cases the wardship was terminated without any investigation by the judge of the merits of the local authority's decision or the manner in which it had been reached. All attempts to persuade the High Court to review the way in which local authorities exercised their discretionary powers ended in failure.[81]

The principles that guided the High Court for nearly three decades were laid down in the judgment of the Court of Appeal in *Re M (An Infant)*.[82] A child had been received into care under the Children Act 1948 in April 1956 and on the same day was boarded out with foster parents. A year later the foster father died. Soon afterwards the local authority assumed the natural mother's parental rights. The child remained with the foster mother until June 1960, when the local authority decided that boarding the child out with the foster mother was not in the child's interests, so it asked her to return the child. She refused and made the child a ward of court. In his judgment, Lord Evershed MR examined the effect of the Children Act 1948 on the ancient prerogative jurisdiction of the High Court. He ruled that the Act had laid down a clear and comprehensive scheme involving positive duties imposed by Parliament on local authorities. A local authority was given an absolute discretion provided that it acted in good faith. Where the issue before the court was one that fell within the comprehensive provisions of the Act, the wardship jurisdiction must be treated as restricted. The power to make the child a ward was unaffected, but a judge would not exercise control in relation to duties or discretions vested by statute in a local authority. Therefore the only proper order for the court to make in the case of this child was to bring the wardship to an end.[83]

---

[79] It was only after the implementation of the Health and Social Services and Social Security Adjudications Act 1983, referred to above at n 61 that local authorities were required by the supporting Code of Practice to set up a machinery to hear grievances from parents about access.

[80] An application for judicial review where a local authority had acted illegally, with procedural impropriety or irrationally was theoretically available, but in practice rarely succeeded.

[81] See *Re AB (An Infant)* [1954] 2 All ER 287; *Re M (An Infant)* [1961] Ch 328; *Re T (AJJ) (An Infant)* [1970] 2 All ER 865; *Re W (Minors) (Wardship Jurisdiction)* [1980] Fam 60.

[82] [1961] Ch 328.

[83] In *Re T (AJJ) (An Infant)* [1970] 2 All ER 865, another failed wardship case concerning a foster child, the distress and anguish caused to the young girl when being forcibly separated from her foster mother, with whom she had lived for many years, was graphically captured on television news.

Re M (An Infant) and *Re T (AJJ) (An Infant)* each concerned foster parents. They, unlike parents, had not at any stage had parental rights and duties in relation to their foster children. But the principles applied in foster parent cases were applied in an identical manner to natural parents. In *Re W (Minors) (Wardship: Jurisdiction)*[84] a local authority decided that the mother of two children made subject to care orders under the Children and Young Persons Act 1969 should no longer have access to them. It formed the opinion that long-term fostering would be in the children's best interests with a view to their adoption by their foster parents. The mother made the children wards of court.[85] The Court of Appeal refused to reverse the trial judge's decision to discharge the wardship despite expressing real disquiet about the lack of appeal rights for parents.[86] It ruled that a court in wardship could not review the merits of what the local authority had decided, it could only exercise a supervisory jurisdiction as opposed to an appellate jurisdiction, and only where the local authority had acted improperly. Eventually the nature of the limits on the High Court's powers to intervene in wardship came before the House of Lords. In *A v Liverpool CC*[87] the local authority had obtained a care order in respect of a 2-year-old child. Initially the mother was allowed weekly access at the home of the foster parents. However, after 3 months her access was reduced to monthly supervised access for one hour at a day nursery. This change was made because the local authority had taken the view that it was not in the child's best interests to restore him to his mother's care and, consequently, that regular parental access to him was not desirable. The mother warded her son and asked the court to decide whether her access should be restricted in this manner. The House of Lords, following earlier authorities, confirmed the principle that, as a matter of law, where Parliament had by statute entrusted to local authorities the power and duty to make decisions as to the welfare of children, the High Court had no reviewing power in wardship over the exercise of that discretion.[88]

The ruling in *A v Liverpool CC* finally closed the door of the High Court in wardship to parents and others who disagreed with a local authority's plans for a child in care. For a brief period after *A v Liverpool CC* it

---

[84] [1979] 3 All ER 154.
[85] Her purpose was to obtain a review by the court of the local authority's decision to deny her access. She did not challenge the continuation of the care orders, but asserted that the High Court was entitled to review the manner in which the local authority was exercising its powers where the applicant was a parent.
[86] Ormrod LJ's anxiety is noteworthy. He said: 'Counsel for the mother has made a valid attempt, unsuccessfully I am sorry to say, to construct a mode of appeal for parents who are the subject of care orders ... Whether or not some other statutory form of appeal should be created is a matter which certainly requires consideration' ([1979] 3 All ER 154 at 163).
[87] [1982] AC 363.
[88] This meant that the mother's limited access to her child and the impact this would have on planning for his future remained an unreviewable and unappealable decision. Furthermore, at that time there were no internal grievance procedures to which the mother could turn.

appeared that wardship would still be available as an alternative to judicial review.[89] But the courts soon made it plain that an allegation of abuse of power as a means of access to wardship would be denied to parents and others.[90] They firmly stated that any legal confrontation about the manner in which a local authority was exercising its powers must be challenged through an application in judicial review. However, the nature and scope of this remedy had many disadvantages in children cases. An applicant first had to overcome the hurdle of obtaining the court's leave and at this preliminary stage was required to produce cogent evidence of misconduct. A judge would not grant leave on the basis that such evidence would come to light during the process of discovery.[91] As a result, many actions never got off the ground. Where leave was granted, the case could be reviewed, but it was almost impossible to persuade the High Court that a local authority had acted improperly.[92] *Re DM*[93] was a

---

[89] See *D v XCC (No 1)* [1985] FLR 275, a case of which this author is personally proud as she prepared legal argument that persuaded first Balcombe J and then Hollis J to accept that the High Court had jurisdiction to intervene in wardship despite the HL ruling in *A v Liverpool CC*. A juvenile court had failed to notify a grandmother of pending care proceedings in relation to her granddaughter contrary to a notice requirement in the CYP Rules 1988. The local authority's plan was adoption. The grandmother wished to look after her grandchild. Hollis J agreed with the author's submission that this breach of the Rules let in the High Court jurisdiction in wardship and that the case fell outside the limits imposed by *A v Liverpool CC*. The author followed up this ruling by attempting to arrange a meeting at which the child's future care would be discussed between the grandmother and members of the social services department in a non-confrontational manner. This proved unsuccessful. Instead it was astonishing and revealing to the author to hear the social worker responsible for the case describe the grandmother's character in highly negative terms despite the fact that he had only met her that day. His opinion of the grandmother's unfitness to care for her grandchild was derived from what the child's mother had told him (she was estranged at the time from the grandmother). He had made no attempt to verify the truth or otherwise of what he had been told. Yet the local authority's desire to exclude the grandmother was based mainly on this social worker's one-sided view of her character. At the subsequent hearing in wardship, the trial judge, Waite J, said that it was 'unfortunate' that the social worker did not speak to the grandmother and went on to describe her as 'a very fine and admirable woman'. He confirmed the wardship and gave the grandmother care and control of her grandchild: see *D v XCC (No 2)* [1985] FLR 279. For a further account of this case, see M Hayes 'Relatives, Care Proceedings and Wardship' [1984] Fam Law 234. Had this case come before the court later in the year, this outcome would almost certainly not have been achieved. Instead the High Court would have been compelled to decline jurisdiction in view of the House of Lords ruling in *W v Hertfordshire CC* [1985] 2 All ER 301: see below.

[90] *Re DM (A Minor) (Wardship: Jurisdiction)* [1986] 2 FLR 122; *Re RM and LM (Minors) (Wardship: Jurisdiction)* [1986] 2 FLR 205; *Re S (A Minor) (Care: Wardship)* [1987] 1 FLR 479.

[91] Unless court proceedings had been set in motion there could be no discovery of documents. Thus the applicant did not have access to the information on which to base a claim of impropriety. The problem for applicants was that they did not know how a particular decision had been arrived at.

[92] A successful application was made in *Re L (AC) (An Infant)* [1971] 3 All ER 743. But contrast *Re S* [1981] Fam Law 175. There was some evidence that a mother had been misled into agreeing to the assumption of her parental rights by resolution on the understanding that her child's foster parents would be changed and that she would be encouraged to have access (now 'contact'). This was held to be an insufficient allegation

particularly disturbing example of how difficult it was to prove irrationality or unreasonableness on the part of a local authority.

SARAH'S STORY

Child law only truly comes to life when we tell the stories that lie behind the case law. What did the House of Lords' judgment in *A v Liverpool CC* mean for one little girl called Sarah? The details of Sarah's story are told in *W v Hertfordshire CC*,[94] the final case brought before the House of Lords in wardship shortly before the Children Act 1989 brought to an end most of the injustices in child care law that have been described in this paper.

Sarah was one of three children who all lived with their mother and father. Sarah's mother loved and was a good parent to her two sons, but almost from the outset she had an aversion to her daughter. At the beginning of August 1984, when Sarah was three and a half, the mother's feelings towards Sarah erupted into violence: she bruised and bit her little girl. To the parents' credit they realised that this state of affairs could not be allowed to continue, so they asked the local authority (from whom they had sought help earlier in the year) to take Sarah into care. The local authority immediately obtained a place of safety order, and this was followed by an interim care order at the beginning of September. By this date[95] the parents and local authority had reached the conclusion, not only that a care order must be obtained, but also that steps must be taken to free Sarah for adoption. But Sarah was never rejected by the members of her wider family. None of the family, with the possible exception of an aunt, had any suspicion that Sarah's parents had made up their minds to place her in care with a view to adoption by strangers. The parents were at pains to prevent the wider family knowing what was going on. An officer of the local authority admitted that ordinarily he would have consulted members of the family, but in this case he did not because the parents asked him not to do so. When, in September, the family found out what had happened to Sarah, they immediately made her a ward of court and asked that her care and control be given to her uncle and aunt, with the grandparents having a right of access to her.

---

of impropriety to allow review by the court, despite the Court of Appeal stating that 'unquestionably justice was not seen to be done to the mother', despite the court stating that it would be better for access to be dealt with by a judge and despite it inviting the local authority to allow the wardship to continue by consent. (The outcome of this invitation is unknown).

[93] [1986] 2 FLR 122. Applicants to adopt were rejected by a local authority for no apparent reason. Their inability to find out why the local authority would not approve them as adopters meant that nothing could be done to prevent a one-year-old child who was thriving in the applicants' care, and had lived with them virtually since birth, being taken from them.

[94] [1985] 2 All ER 301.

[95] Less than a month after the injury to the child.

The case came before Ewbank J. He emphasised that members of the family had no right to be heard by the juvenile court in care proceedings. He found that the only consent needed to free the child for adoption was that of the parents and that the members of the wider family had no right to be heard at the adoption hearing. He found that if the parents did consent to Sarah's adoption, then the court would have no option but to make the freeing order. He found that the family were vehemently opposed to a final care order being made, wished to have access to Sarah and wanted to be heard on whether the local authority would be acting in Sarah's best interests if they decided to apply for a freeing order. He also expressed doubt about the speed at which the decision had been made and as to whether the parents really understood what they were doing in agreeing that Sarah should be made free for adoption. In view of these findings, Ewbank J held that the proposals of the uncle, aunt and grandparents should be heard by a court in the interests of the welfare of the child. He therefore held that the High Court should exercise its wardship powers. The local authority appealed. The majority of the Court of Appeal felt compelled by authority to allow the appeal.[96] The family appealed.

The Law Lords' speeches make fascinating but depressing reading. More information emerged about the family dynamics and the attitude of the local authority towards the family. The local authority offered no personal criticism of the uncle and aunt, but they continued to express the view that adoption outside the family was in the best interests of Sarah. A court welfare officer attached to the Family Division had described the appellants as 'a delightful, happy and close family'. The parents themselves had stated in an affidavit that if the local authority decided that Sarah should be adopted by the uncle and aunt, then they would *not* oppose that application. A level of antagonism had developed between the social workers and the family. Their Lordships were clearly troubled by this information and by the evidence of some ill-feeling by the local authority towards the family. Against this background more than one Law Lord expressed the view that the resolution of Sarah's future should more appropriately be a judicial decision. More than one Law Lord acknowledged that it could properly be said that the case called for an objective investigation, with the family having a right to be heard, a right that existed only in the High Court. However, despite their reservations, the five Law Lords were united. They held that the arbiter chosen by Parliament to make decisions about Sarah was the local authority. Their Lordships were not prepared to make an exception for Sarah, and therefore the family's appeal was dismissed.

In my opinion, the ruling in *W v Hertfordshire CC* was an example of the House of Lords at its least admirable. The local authority had reached a hasty decision. It had failed to consult with the family before planning Sarah's future and had adhered to its plans when the family made their

---

[96] Purchas LJ dissented.

presence known. There was enough worrying information to require an independent scrutiny by a judge of the local authority's decision. Instead, their Lordships based their reasoning on a reiteration of 'the profoundly important principle' that Parliament had intended that local authorities should always be the final arbiter of the welfare of a child in state care. In my view, this assertion of principle defied close analysis in Sarah's case. It presupposed that Parliament would have approved the local authority's handling of the case. It presupposed that Parliament would have disagreed with the opinion expressed by some of their Lordships that the planning for Sarah's future would have benefited from an objective investigation by a court. It made untested assumptions about how Parliament wanted children cases to be managed by courts.

Ewbank J had recognised that Sarah's case required judicial intervention. He had given clear reasons why neither the administrative nor the statutory structure provided adequate protection for Sarah's welfare. He had identified gaps and lacunae in the law that only wardship could fill. These would have had an important impact on the planned adoption proceedings. A judge hearing the freeing application would not have known that family members were offering to look after Sarah. The family had no right to take part in that (or any other) hearing, and it can be assumed that the local authority would not have informed the judge about the relatives' interest in the child. Consequently, the judge would not have been fully informed when reaching his otherwise inevitable decision to make a freeing order. He would not have known that there was family opposition to the freeing application. Such concealment of relevant information from a court was surely unacceptable. It was using the court as a rubber stamp for a local authority's decision.

Sarah's case gave the House of Lords an opportunity fully to evaluate the proper role of courts in reviewing cases involving children in care. Their Lordships must have been aware of other cases where judges had struggled with the rigidity of the body of precedent that prevented them from responding judicially to allegations that cried out for judicial investigation.[97] As the Supreme Court, the House of Lords could have carried out a close and careful review of the legal and administrative framework within which Sarah's future had been, and would be, decided. This was a legal framework from which Sarah's wider family would be excluded, and an administrative framework within which the family's full involvement, without bias against them, could not be guaranteed. Their Lordships could have reached the conclusion that such disturbing gaps in the management by law of children cases should be filled by wardship, as they could and would have done if the local authority was to have been

---

[97] Normally, a judge's only way around this had been to put pressure on a local authority to agree to an application being made or continued in wardship: see, for example, *Re S (A Minor)* [1981] Fam Law 175.

the applicant.[98] It could and should have been acknowledged that access to wardship was biased towards local authorities and against the clients of local authorities.

Instead, in *W v Hertfordshire CC* the House of Lords approved and further embedded an already rigid approach to judicial review of administrative action in children cases, an approach that had taken root 25 years earlier in *Re M (An Infant)*[99] and about which judges had on several occasions expressed anxiety.[100] Had their Lordships allowed their hearts as well as their heads to determine whether intervention in wardship should have been permitted, they might have arrived at a different outcome. Instead of approaching the case at a level of abstraction and blaming Parliament for their inability to intervene, they could usefully have asked themselves what Members of Parliament would actually have wished them to do. Had they asked themselves the question: 'Do Members of Parliament want judges to ensure that a child's future has been determined by a fully informed and careful investigation of all the facts followed by an unbiased application of the welfare principle to those facts?' they might have felt free to come to a different conclusion. But their Lordships, despite their own anxieties, chose instead to take a cowardly way out. They responded as a 'safe pair of hands' and chose to follow precedent, fearful, perhaps, of opening the flood gates, and mindful, perhaps, of that dominant but controversial principle of jurisprudence: 'hard cases make bad law'. That is why I asserted at the outset of this paper that this was a decision of which the House of Lords should have been ashamed.

CONCLUSION

This paper has inevitably concentrated on those aspects of child protection law that failed children and their families. When introducing new legislation with social implications, governments invariably claim that the new provisions will be reforming when, all too often, what transpires is often of dubious benefit to society as a whole. However, the Children Act 1989 was a genuine example of legislation that transformed child law, family proceedings and the guidance offered to local authorities. It laid to rest most of the defects in child protection law and practice on which this paper has concentrated. Other papers in this volume consider how the law in this area may develop in the future, in the light of the changes introduced by the 1989 Act.[101] I hope that this paper may provide a useful comparison and some assistance to those engaged in examining current law and practice in relation to removing children from their families. Child protection is a uniquely difficult area of law. Knowing what has

---

[98] See above.
[99] [1961] Ch 328.
[100] See, for example, *Re W (Minors) (Wardship: Jurisdiction)* [1980] Fam 60.
[101] See J Masson 'Caring for our future generations', below, Chapter 10, and R White 'The future of welfare law for children', below, Chapter 11.

gone before can help to ensure that future changes in law and practice relating to the removal of children from their families are well thought through and carefully constructed.

CHAPTER 5

CULTURAL CHANGE AND THE FAMILY JUSTICE SYSTEM

Mervyn Murch[1]

INTRODUCTION

The challenging brief for this chapter was to review the development of the interdisciplinary family justice system over the last 150 years.[2] I decided to adopt a broad-brush approach, looking at major cultural developments and their influence on the system's growth. In this way I intend to complement and avoid overlapping with scholarly historical analyses concerning the development of the substantive law made by other conference contributors.

My approach is an exploratory mix of the history of ideas with what Michel Foucault termed the archaeology of knowledge.[3] That is to say, instead of tracing the development of a particular set of ideas in chronological order, one should look back, as it were archaeologically, uncovering layers of interacting cultural, political, social and intellectual thinking at particular periods as they appear to have shaped and defined family law and influenced the legal institutions which administer it, particularly the courts and related welfare support services.

The chapter falls into two parts. In the first I outline the approach, dealing with some of its limitations and two tricky definition questions. I explain why I have chosen to focus particularly on the divided local family court structure. I suggest that this has always reflected two basic contradictory social values concerning the system's approach to the family; on the one hand an element of authoritarian surveillance and social control (ie covert policing) and on the other a desire to provide

---

[1] In preparing this chapter I have been greatly helped by my former Cardiff Law School colleague Julie Doughty, who has endeavoured to keep me up to date with policy and practice developments, and by Clare Pike, without whose word processing skills and patience I would have been sunk. I am of course solely responsible for the views expressed and for any errors and omissions it may contain.

[2] This chapter is based on a Conference paper given in November 2007. Accordingly, most of the sources referred to precede that date. Nevertheless, because the family justice system is subject to dynamic development, in certain places reference is made to more recent material.

[3] Michel Foucault *L'Archéologie du Savoir* (Editions Gallimard, 1969); see English translation by Alan Sheridan Smith *The Archaeology of Knowledge* (Routledge Classics Series, 2002).

support to families and children caught up in the complexities of litigation. I argue that historically these value systems wax and wane in relation to each other dependent on the prevailing cultural zeitgeist.

In the second part of the chapter I concentrate on the emergence of the family justice system as a distinct interdisciplinary branch of civil jurisprudence in the 'golden age' of late modernity that followed the Second World War. This was the period when the emphasis of social policy was on family support and the prospect of a unified local system of family courts. I contrast this with the more recent postmodern age of rapid economic, technical and social change during which the family court system is showing signs of reverting to a more traditional socially divided structure. We are again witnessing legislative provisions emphasising a tougher approach to welfare and the social control of those largely impoverished families who do not match up to a stereotypical image of 'responsible' parents.[4]

GROUND CLEARING

To begin with, it is important to offer a few cautionary remarks concerning the definition of the family justice system and the term 'cultural change'.

The family justice system

We have come to think of the family justice system as an organic, complex system of interdisciplinary juridical and quasi-juridical practice with deep historical roots (of which more later). Today's system is engaged on a massive scale with the realities of helping thousands of children and their parents navigate critical and often highly stressful transitions in their lives; doing so in situations where the family is often embroiled in conflict with the welfare institutions of the state – situations where the evidence may be hard to prove and where the courts are often called upon to take extremely difficult and emotionally taxing decisions.[5] These include separating children from one or both parents, providing vulnerable family members with protection, and where possible doing 'justice' to the parties in resolving conflicting interests.

Although fundamentally still based on the common law adversarial mode of justice, and applying the civil law's evidential test based on the balance of probabilities, the interdisciplinary family justice system has a number of features which distinguish it from the criminal and other civil

---

[4] C Piper *The Responsible Parent* (Harvester Wheatsheaf, 1993).
[5] See Mr Justice Hedley 'Isn't the Judge Human Too?' and Lord Justice Wall 'Child Sexual Abuse Hearings in Family Courts: The role of the judge and the value of the expert witness' in C Thorpe and J Trowell (eds) *Re-rooted Lives: Interdisciplinary work with the family justice system* (Family Law, 2007).

jurisdictions. Some of these were noted by the Law Commission in its response to the Consultation Paper of the Inter-Departmental Review of Family and Domestic Jurisdictions.[6] They include the following:

> 'Most important decisions involve not merely the findings of relevant fact but also the exercise of very wide discretion which is often more akin to the management of the family's future than to more traditional adjudication upon its past.'

> 'Unlike other legal actions a large part of the court's work with families consists of approving decisions already agreed between the parties, where the need for adjudication is minimal.'

> 'In disputes about family matters the emotions of everyone in the court (including the Tribunal) are likely to be more deeply engaged than in most other forms of litigation.'

Three other factors (discussed more fully elsewhere)[7] should be added to the above points.

First, the importance of respect for family privacy. Despite public and media pressure to open up the family justice system to greater public scrutiny, this generally means that the identities of children and parents are treated as confidential in court proceedings.

Second, family proceedings should have no stigmatic association with criminality. This was a principle strongly held by the Finer Committee on One Parent Families.[8] It was one of the reasons why that Committee argued for the removal of family proceedings from the magistrates' jurisdiction, which it saw as associated in the public mind with the taint of criminal proceedings.[9] Later I will argue that recent government measures introduced by the New Labour administration have tended to blur the vital distinction between criminal and civil jurisdictions, even though of course in child protection cases there is bound to be a close relationship between the two. Also, one has to acknowledge that there is an argument that it is against the public interest for the civil family courts to appear morally neutral when faced with social deviance considered harmful to children and other family members.[10]

---

[6] Lord Chancellor's Department *Interdepartmental Review of Family and Domestic Jurisdiction: A Consultation Paper* (LCD, 1986) cited in M Murch and D Hooper *The Family Justice System* (Family Law, 1992).
[7] See Murch and Hooper, op cit.
[8] 'Finer Report': *Report of the Committee on One Parent Families* Cmnd 5629 (HMSO, 1974).
[9] Ibid, para 4.353. But note that in arguing for a family court the Committee still saw a place for a lay magistracy to deal with less complex cases, but within a unified local structure.
[10] See M Murch and D Hooper *The Family Justice System* (Family Law, 1992), p 35.

Third, perhaps the most distinctive feature of all is the interdisciplinary character of the system. This, as Lord Justice Thorpe has observed, 'has helped free lawyers from over reliance on purely legal thinking.'[11] Indeed, as Lord Mackay, a former Lord Chancellor, noted in 1989, in family law 'the black letters of the law do not take one very far'.[12] Later, I shall outline how in the post-war period behavioural and social science thinking about the family and the nature of child development helped set the scene for the emergence of a distinct family justice system utilising a clear interdisciplinary approach.

Although one can identify the distinguishing features of the family justice system, there remains a problem of how one should define its boundaries – boundaries which separate it from other parts of the civil and criminal justice systems and from related health, welfare and educational services, practitioners from which periodically engage in family justice work. In this chapter, I focus primarily on courts of first instance and their related welfare support services, now principally provided by the Children and Family Court Advisory and Support Service (Cafcass). Thus I will largely omit reference to the important role played by the key gatekeepers to the system, ie solicitors and those mediators and conciliators involved in alternative dispute resolution.

The problem of defining 'cultural change'

'Culture' is a slippery, complex concept used in all sorts of ways. Adam Kuper, a social anthropologist, suggests that one should look at the context in which it is used and then try to deconstruct it.[13] In this way, instead of bundling up a mass of ideas, beliefs, moral values etc into a single package labelled 'culture', we should try to separate out different elements and then explore 'the changing configurations in which language, knowledge, technologies, political ideologies, religious beliefs, social rituals, commodities and so on appear related to each other'. If one couples this deconstructive approach with that concerning the archaeology of ideas advanced by Michel Foucault, one can, as it were, set the cultural stage upon which to better understand the part played by various key historical persons whose activities in the development of family law in England and Wales are brilliantly described by Stephen Cretney.[14]

In the context of this chapter, consideration of the family justice system means looking at the various changing ways in which the institutions of

---

[11] See C Thorpe and J Trowell (eds) *Re-rooted Lives: Interdisciplinary work with the family justice system* (Family Law, 2007), p vii.
[12] Lord Mackay (1989) 'The Joseph Jackson Memorial Lecture' (1989) 139 NLJ 505.
[13] A Kuper *Culture: The Anthropologists' Account* (Harvard University Press, 1999), p 245.
[14] S Cretney *Family Law in the Twentieth Century* (Oxford UP, 2003). See also 'The troublemakers: cranks, psychiatrists and other mischievous nuisances – their role in reform of English family law in the nineteenth and twentieth centuries', Chapter 2 above.

the family, parenthood and childhood have been socially constructed in response to socio-political, demographic, economic and technical change. It means grappling with often conflicting and evolving ideas about the way the law and social policies structure these institutions. It also means taking account of different interpretations by practitioners, policy makers and law reformers.

THE ROOTS OF THE SYSTEM

The roots of the court system and its supporting services are varied and penetrate deep into ancient cultures. We sometimes fail to appreciate that a tap root of our modern system can be traced far back into the Middle Ages. Of course, we now know from the study of court records,[15] both in relation to the institution of wardship and the Court of Wards (see further below) and from the study of Canon law,[16] the way families were regulated through the ecclesiastical courts.[17] But what is harder to grasp is the way this tied in with the cultural life of the 'common people', because their social history was less well recorded.[18]

It is possible to make three general propositions about some of the deep roots of the system which have significance for today's structures.

Rapid cultural and economic social change increase public anxiety and lead to authoritarian measures of social control

The first is that periods of relatively rapid cultural change, together with social and economic upheaval, invariably lead first to official measures of social control.[19] Jean Heywood's[20] classic text concerning State care for children contains several historical examples of how this tendency has

---

[15] R Helmholz *Marriage Litigation in Medieval England* (Cambridge University Press, 2007).

[16] See J A Brundage *Medieval Canon Law* (Longmans, 1995). See also J A Brundage *Law, Sex and Christian Society in Medieval Europe* (Chicago University Press, 1987).

[17] See M Antokolskaia *Harmonisation of Family Law in Europe: A historical perspective. A tale of two millennia* (Intersentia Antwerpen, 2006).

[18] C Gibson *Dissolving Wedlock* (Routledge, 1994), p 50. Gibson quotes Lord Bryce writing in 1901 'that to pass from the civil law of Rome to the ecclesiastical law of the dark and middle ages is like quitting the open country, intercepted by good roads, for a tract of mountains and forests where rough and torturous paths furnish the only means of transport'.

[19] J Brundage *Law, Sex and Christian Society in Medieval Europe* (Chicago University Press, 1987), p 487, writing of the period from 1348–1417 following the Black Death notes that it was an age of political turmoil and endemic warfare throughout western Europe. Sharp demographic changes resulted in a considerable measure of social realignment and stress. This was followed by increased Royal and municipal government regulation of sexual behaviour, particularly in relation to prostitution.

[20] J Heywood *Children in Care* (Routledge and Kegan Paul, 1959), pp 4–8. See also J Boswell *The Kindness of Strangers* (Allen Lane Publishers, 1988). Boswell shows that in this period most abandoned children were rescued and brought up as members of another household or employed as agricultural labourers of some sort.

occurred. For example, she shows how the church in the Middle Ages played an important support role in caring for deprived children and then recounts how this compassionate supportive concern for the disadvantaged broke down after the Reformation when major economic and religious changes were taking place. The famous Act of 1601, described by the Finer Committee[21] as forming part of the Tudor scheme for controlling and cushioning the social results of economic change, put legal sanctions, exercised by Justices of the Peace, behind the observance of what had previously been regarded as the ordinary obligations of kinship. As is well known, the Elizabethan Poor Law set the pattern for the system of relief of the poor which lasted until 1948. As McGregor[22] observed:

> 'A main function of the Poor Law was to enforce a distinction between the independent poor who earned their own subsistence and the paupers who did not. The family law imposed on this latter class comprised support obligations upon relatives; the denial or subordination of parental rights to the control or custody of children and the determination of education or occupational training; as well as the general regulation of familial relationships ... The Poor Law was not only a law about the poor but a law of the poor. It dealt with a condition and it governed a class.'

Periods of relative social stability facilitate the development of community based support services

My second proposition is that more benign measures of community social support tend to occur in relatively stable optimistic periods of social history. A good example is the late Victorian and Edwardian periods preceding the First World War, when the British Empire was at its height. This was an age of modernity and a developing culture of rational scientific thought in which the great nineteenth-century social reformers such as Lord Brougham,[23] John Ruskin, Charles Booth and, later, Joseph Rowntree set about exposing the social problems and injustices experienced by women and children in the largely patriarchal industrial society of Victorian England. The social history of the period paints a grim picture of exploited children taken from the workhouse for employment in factories, mills and mines – many orphaned and deserted by destitute and sick parents.

---

[21] See *Report of the Committee on One Parent Families*, Vol II, Cmnd 5629-1, (HMSO, 1974), p 112. Appendix 5, written by M Finer and O R McGregor is a readily accessible treatise on the history of the obligation to maintain and contains ample evidence about the elements of social control and the institutional stigmatic processes exercised by both local authorities and magistrates' courts.

[22] O R McGregor *Social History and Law Reform, Hamlyn Lectures* (Stevens, 1981), p 47.

[23] O R McGregor, ibid at p 20, recounts how Lord Brougham in 1857 convened a meeting of notables, several ladies amongst them, to establish the National Association for the Promotion of Social Sciences, which amalgamated with the Law Amendment Society in 1864.

Yet this period was also one of great philanthropic voluntary ventures such as Barnardos, the Shaftesbury Homes, and the NSPCC, so prominent in the child-saving movement which, in the ethical society of late Victorian England, generated pressure for child protection legislation. At the same time the developing feminist movement through, for example, the social investigations of Francis Power-Cobbe,[24] Matilda Blake[25] and others[26] highlighted the problem of domestic violence.

Because many of the principles and social values which underlay the nineteenth- and early twentieth-century legislation concerning women's rights and the protection of children still form the basis of much of our family law, we tend to take these developments for granted. But it is worth questioning why these vigorous social reform movements developed at the time and in the way that they did. What gave rise to the age of ethics and morality that became such a prevailing counterforce to the horrors of industrial production and patriarchal domination of family life? Legal historians provide the details, but I suggest we need to turn to sociologists such as Zygmunt Bauman to obtain a broader cultural perspective. He argues that, in addition to a prevailing protestant work ethic, it had much to do with the need to control the threat of social disorder and chaos that sprang from the very rapidity and extent of social change generated by the new technical industrial society. In Bauman's view[27] legislation and law:

> 'Stood between order and chaos, human existence and criminal free-for-all, the habitable and uninhabitable world, meaning and meaninglessness ... the incessant search for ethical principles was a part (an expectable and inexorable part) of legislative frenzy. People had to be told of the duty to do good and that doing their duty is goodness. And people needed to be prevailed upon to follow that line of duty, which without being taught or goaded or coerced they would hardly do. Modernity was, and had to be THE Age of Ethics – it would not be modernity otherwise.'

From priests to psychiatrists – the translation of 'spiritual wellbeing' into modern child welfare and mental health thinking

My third proposition traces a connection between the early ecclesiastical jurisdictions concerning marriage and the concept of the matrimonial offence with today's interdisciplinary approach to the family justice process in which mental health thinking has come to play an important ancillary support role.

---

[24] Frances Power-Cobbe 'Wife Torture in England' (1878) 32 *Contemporary Review* 55.
[25] M Blake 'Are Women Protected?' (1892) *The Westminster Review* 43.
[26] M Doggett *Marriage, Wife-Beating and the Law in Victorian England* (Weidenfeld and Nicholson, 1992).
[27] Z Bauman *Life in Fragments* (Blackwells, 1995), p 34.

Others[28] have charted the story of how the courts of common law and chancery cut back the ecclesiastical jurisdiction in matrimonial and related property matters. Clearly, the Matrimonial Causes Act 1857 and the creation of the Court for Divorce and Matrimonial Causes[29] is a milestone in that development. But in my view it would be a mistake to ignore the much earlier medieval origins of the ecclesiastical courts as well as the institution of wardship and the church-dominated culture from which they sprang. After all, because divorce law reform following the abortive Family Law Act 1996 was not implemented, we have not, as yet, entirely eliminated the last vestiges of the concept of the matrimonial offence. Moreover, the influence of Christian ethics in our childcare law, particularly its development in the late Victorian period, remains strong to this day.

The zeitgeist of the modernist age with its belief in social progress and the advance of Christian civilisation drove forward reform on many fronts, not least in the field of family justice. But it was not until the late twentieth century that mental health thinking began increasingly to influence practice in the juvenile and family courts, due largely to advances in the social and behavioural sciences which followed the Second World War and the 'golden age' of late modernity, the cultural era to which I turn next.

EMERGENCE AND CONVERGENCE OF THE FAMILY JUSTICE SYSTEM IN LATE MODERNITY

Except for those of us who lived through it, it is hard to appreciate what a cultural transformation occurred during the 30 or so years immediately following the Second World War. This was a period in which a really complex set of ideas about the social institution of the family and the administration of civil family law unfold together.

At the time *A Century of Family Law* was being written, the UK was finally emerging from the economic crises and restrictions in the aftermath of war. There was a spirit of optimism and a growing confidence in an expanding economy and the prospect of full employment. The war and military conscription, which did not end until 1962, had weakened traditional social divisions and contributed to a heightened sense of egalitarianism – of all being in it together. There was a strong belief in progress, the spur to post-war reforms in health, education and social welfare, particularly in the childcare field with the

---

[28] For example, see S Cretney *Family Law in the Twentieth Century* (Oxford UP, 2003).
[29] Matrimonial Causes Act 1857, s 6.

Children Act 1948.[30] This was also the era when social work, under the influence of advances in behavioural and social sciences, made increasing claims for professional status.[31]

It was an era of changing social values concerning the liberation of women from 'domestic incarceration'.[32] There was a growing belief in upward social mobility based on merit regardless of gender or inheritance. The enforced separations and stresses of war-strained marriages aggravated the housing shortage and contributed to the post-war divorce reform movement, particularly for those wishing to free 'couples manacled to long dead marriages by the clamp of fault'.[33] Even in a traditionally cautious profession such as the law, radical voices arguing for reform were becoming more influential through the activities, for example, of the Haldane Society, The Society of Labour Lawyers, and Justice (the British branch of the International Commission of Jurists).[34]

Prospects of a non-stigmatic unified system of family justice also began to emerge based on the following contributory factors.

Post-war conceptual advances in the behavioural and social sciences concerning the family

It is important to note the development during this period of a range of sometimes competing ideas and frameworks in the behavioural and social sciences, as they affected thinking about the family in the post-war period and helped to cultivate the conceptual ground out of which grew new thinking about family law and family justice as a unified system of judicial administration.

First there was the seminal influence of the British School of Psychoanalysis.[35] This developed after the war at that powerhouse of ideas, the Tavistock Institute of Human Relations. This was also the place where attachment theory was to be most clearly articulated by John Bowlby.[36] One important strand of psychoanalytic thinking concerned object-relations theory and the psychodynamics of marital interaction. In the 1960s this particularly influenced the civil work of the probation

---

[30] N Parton *Safeguarding Childhood – early intervention and surveillance in late modern society* (Palgrave/Macmillan, 2006), p 21.
[31] See S Cretney *Family Law in the Twentieth Century* (Oxford UP, 2003), ch 19, pp 671–737.
[32] See C Gibson *Dissolving Wedlock* (Routledge, 1994), p 123.
[33] Ibid, p 132.
[34] See J H Farrar 'Law Reform Now – A Comparative View' (1976) 25 *International and Comparative Law Quarterly* at 214–228.
[35] For a clear introductory account of the contribution of various thinkers in the British psychoanalytic movement, see E Raynor *The Independent Mind in British Psychoanalysis* (Free Association Books, 1991).
[36] J Bowlby *Attachment and Loss* (Hogarth Press, 1982). See also *A Secure Base – Clinical Application of Attachment Theory* (Routledge, 1988).

service and the then National Marriage Guidance Council (now RELATE). This line of approach was further researched and related to attachment theory by Christopher Clulow[37] and colleagues at the Tavistock Marital Studies Institute.

Yet as far as developments in family justice are concerned, it was the small American publication by Joseph Goldstein, Anna Freud and Albert Solnit,[38] rooted in Anna Freud's psychoanalytic knowledge of child development, which was to have the most seminal influence. Their interdisciplinary text, *Beyond the Best Interests of the Child* introduced the ideas of the psychological parent/child relationship as being of more importance than the mere blood tie of biological parents; the child's sense of time being different from that of an adult; and the concept of the least detrimental alternative as the key determinant in making child welfare decisions.

Thinking about the family as a dynamic interacting social system is now fully accepted in psychotherapeutic and social work circles and has been validated by a number of research studies in the increasingly important field of cognitive developmental psychology.[39] A key underlying principle is that of 'homeostasis'[40] – ie the adaptive capacity to stabilise the self in the face of continually shifting demands of life, a principle which operates at three levels: mind, body and society. In other words, it is the adaptive mechanism which establishes, regulates and controls a steady state.

This is a vital, if as yet little appreciated, concept in understanding psychological aspects of the family justice process. For example, one can apply this line of thought, which I have referred to elsewhere as 'participant justice',[41] to the way families and individual family members, who are involved in litigation and undergoing basic structural change, may interact during this process with practitioners working within the family justice system. I argue that the seeking of justice and/or fairness is to be understood, in part at least, as a means symbolically of trying to restore psychological balance following the emotional turmoil and disturbance associated with grief caused by the actual (or threat of) breakdown in family relationships.

---

[37] C Clulow *Adult Attachment and Couple Psychotherapy: The 'Secure Base' in Practice and Research* (Brunner/Routledge, 2001).

[38] J Goldstein, A Freud and A J Solnit *Beyond the Best Interests of the Child* (Free Press, 1973). See also J Goldstein and J Katz *The Family and the Law* (Free Press, 1965). This groundbreaking publication, arising from a major grant from the American National Institute of Mental Health to the Yale Law School was the result of an intensive 'elbow to elbow' collaboration between two different disciplines, law and psychoanalysis. The participants sought to understand and challenge each other's experiences, assumptions and knowledge in furtherance of a common task: the study of the family law process.

[39] See G T Harold and M Murch 'Interparental Conflict and Children's Adaptation to Separation and Divorce: theory, research and implications for family law practice and policy' [2005] CFLQ 185.

[40] N Ackerman *The Psychodynamics of Family Life* (Basic Books, 1958), pp 68–79.

[41] M Murch *Justice and Welfare in Divorce* (Sweet & Maxwell, 1980), ch 14.

Many family lawyers are still not accustomed to perceiving the family justice system as part of the complex of services which may provide families with a degree of social support while they undergo stressful life-changing events such as divorce, compulsory admission of children into care, adoption out of care etc. This is because until comparatively recently their training, which conditions their professional mindset, contained little or no social psychology. Yet in practice, from the moment an allegation of child neglect or abuse is notified to a local authority or in private law when a client enters a family lawyer's office and the family justice process begins to work on the legal and related welfare aspects of the case, a degree of psychosocial interaction between practitioner and a family or a client is inevitably set up.

The sociology of the institution of the family as it developed in the post-world-war era in some respects represented a challenging critique to the role of hospitals and courts in society. Even today, in much positivist psychology, the individual and the family remain curiously detached from their social context. By contrast, sociologists and radical social political theorists were more concerned with the public interface between the family and its socio-political context. They drew attention to societal power relationships, to the way established societal forces regulated and controlled social deviance, hitherto regarded by many social reformers and social workers as arising from a failure to learn the behaviours appropriate for a stable social order. Particularly influential in this field were the writings of the interactionist sociologists, Erving Goffman[42] and Howard Becker.[43] They saw the notion of deviance ('delinquent', 'feckless', 'irresponsible', 'immature') as not something that is inherent in the behaviour of certain individuals but as an ascriptive label conferred upon actors in certain social situations. Changing social values affect the way and strength with which such social labels are applied. In this view, asylums, prisons, the courts, medical and social work services are all social mechanisms by which such negative labels can be applied and, on occasion, removed. Indeed, in a family dispute a carefully thought out judgment praising the behaviour of parents and children coping with difficult circumstances can be experienced as a powerful way of boosting morale.

---

[42] E Goffman *Stigma: Notes on the Management of Spoiled Identity* (Prentice-Hall, 1968); *Presentation of Self in Everyday Life* (Penguin, 1959); *Asylums* (Anchor Publications, 1961).
[43] H S Becker *Outsiders – Studies in the sociology of deviants* (Free Press, 1966). He writes (at p 163), 'social groups create division by making the rules whose infraction constitutes deviants and by applying these rules to particular people and labelling them as outsiders ... the deviant is one to whom that label has been successfully applied; deviant behaviour is behaviour that people so label.'

THE DEVELOPMENT OF FAMILY-FOCUSED SOCIAL POLICY AND SOCIAL WORK

All these emerging conceptual frameworks in the behavioural and social sciences provided rich intellectual soil out of which grew the new supportive family-focused social policies and social work practice in the period between 1956 and the mid-1970s. All created an intellectual climate which stimulated 'progressive ideas' about family law and the concept of specialist family courts to administer it. I mention six key areas where one can trace this development.

The growth of university social work training

First there was the post-war growth of university based 'generic' professional social work training for psychiatric social workers, medical social workers, child care officers and probation officers, all part of the movement to improve the professional status of these emerging occupations. Until the mid-1970s, demand for postgraduate social work places, with generous grants provided by central and local government, outstripped supply, particularly as expansion of local authority social work departments provided new career paths, especially for women (see further below).

Social casework training in this period underwent a variety of doctrinal phases. It began with a largely psychoanalytic orientation, but from about the late 1960s onwards, sociological and social policy approaches provided something of a reaction to the psychoanalytic approach associated with the Tavistock Institute. Moreover, as local authorities developed large combined social services departments, following the recommendations in 1969 of the Seebohm Committee on Local Authority and Allied Personal Services,[44] generic social work training took an increased interest in sociology and in the psychodynamics of administrative and organisational behaviour.[45]

Post-war child care policy and practice

Child care practice in the post-war period, particularly in the new local authority children's departments, also emphasised the importance of early supportive preventive strategies and interventions aimed at dysfunctional 'problem' families. These were seen as the main breeding ground of child neglect, deprivation and delinquency. The post-war specialist Children's Departments had built upon the family support methods developed in war time by Quaker Family Service Units and the Family Welfare Association, each of which had focused on childcare and working with

---

[44] Implemented by the Local Authority Social Services Act 1970. See further below.
[45] Especially the work of W R Bion *Experiences in Groups* (Tavistock, 1961).

the whole family. Their aim was to establish a close working relationship with the family. As Nigel Parton[46] has written, the approach was—

> 'Essentially benign but paternalistic ... interventions in the family were not conceived as a source of antagonism between social worker and individual family members. Not only was it assumed that many problems had their genesis within the family but that their resolution resided there as well.'[47]

Thus, in the post-war reconstruction period there was an optimistic belief that skilled social workers would be able to form positive supportive partnership relationships with families so that children could be provided with appropriate conditions in which to develop.

Nowadays some look back on this approach as soft liberalism, but at the time in the 1960s this was a major departure from the tougher, less eligibility, deterrent approach adopted under the Poor Law and Public Assistance, which others would argue is creeping back into recent social policy.[48] Authoritarian, controlling intervention through the courts in order to 'police' families was seen very much as of secondary importance and as simply providing a mandate for therapeutic preventive intervention. Removal of children from their parents was a measure of last resort and even then seen as an interlude before rehabilitation, except in the most extreme battered child cases.[49]

This family support based approach was accepted by the Ingleby Committee,[50] whose recommendations were reflected in the preventive provisions of the Children and Young Persons Act 1963. Thus, s 1 imposed a duty on local authorities to make available 'such advice, guidance and assistance as may promote the welfare of children by diminishing the risk of taking children into care or keeping them in care ... or to bringing them before the juvenile court'.

---

[46] N Parton *Governing the Family: Childcare, Protection and the State* (Macmillan, 1991), p 20.
[47] It is also worth noting that in those days a probation officer's duty was to 'advise, assist and befriend', ie a benign supportive approach which more recently has been gradually replaced by a more authoritarian social control function in the supervision of offenders.
[48] B Jordan and C Jordan *Social Work and the Third Way: tough love as social policy* (Sage Publications, 2000); N Parton *Safeguarding Childhood – Early intervention and surveillance in late modern society* (Palgrave Macmillan, 2006).
[49] For a rather different perspective, see M Hayes 'Removing children from their families – law and policy before the Children Act 1989', at Chapter 4 above.
[50] Viscount Ingleby (Chairman) *Report of the Committee on Children and Young Persons* Cmnd 1191 (1960).

The Seebohm Committee and reorganisation of local authority social services

The establishment of comprehensive 'generic' local authority social service departments as recommended by the Seebohm Report[51] under the provisions of the Local Authority Social Services Act 1970 was widely regarded at the time as providing a community-based, family-focused professional social work service. Idealistically, Seebohm envisaged it as reaching 'far beyond the discovery and rescue of social casualties'. The role of the new service was to be primarily supportive and preventive, building on the good practice of post-war childcare services.[52] Yet, as Cretney observes, 'the day of the children's officer with a personal knowledge of all her charges, was unceremoniously dispatched into history'.[53] In its place came a large hierarchical bureaucracy. The Seebohm approach was largely based on the assumption that skilled supportive preventive work with families would forestall many social problems often associated with poverty. The hope was that the number of families affected by such problems would in turn continue to be much reduced, given a continuation of the relatively full employment levels of the 1950s and 1960s.

Yet all these aspirations were to be unfulfilled after the economic crises of the 1970s. The supply of well-trained social workers never matched the increasingly broad social demands on what became in effect a largely emergency social work service. This was reinforced when in the 1980s the Thatcher government adopted policies of welfare retrenchment aimed at 'rolling back' the frontiers of the state, policies which further cramped what local authorities could do.

From the late 1970s onwards there was a gradual loss of well-trained childcare expertise at the coal face as the more talented staff were promoted into senior administrative and supervisory positions. Subsequently, a culture of managerialism aimed at compensating for the lack of experience and professional skill in fieldwork staff, often unfortunately combined with poor supervision, sometimes by people with little experience of child care, was to reap a bitter harvest. Coinciding with these developments came a whole series of shocking child abuse inquiries.[54] These were critical of local authority childcare social work, called for closer inter-agency collaboration and led to a demand that

---

[51] *Report of the Committee on Local Authority and Allied Personal Social Services* (The Seebohm Report) Cmnd 3703 (1968).
[52] N Parton *Governing the Family: Childcare, Protection and the State* (Macmillan, 1991), p 19.
[53] S Cretney *Family Law in the Twentieth Century* (Oxford UP, 2003), p 698.
[54] See particularly inquiries concerning Maria Colwell (The Field Fisher Report, DHSS, 1974), Jasmine Beckford (The Beckford Report, London Borough of Brent, 1985), Tyra Henry and Kimberley Carlile (London Borough of Greenwich, 1987) and the Report of the Inquiry into Child Abuse in Cleveland, 1987 Cm 412 (1988). See also Department of Health *Report on Child Abuse Inquiries 1973–1981* (HMSO, 1982) and Volume 2 of

courts exercise their constitutional oversight of the Executive more strictly in order to better protect the rights of parents and children. The publicity given to these failures in social care damaged local authority staff morale and recruitment. Yet they were ultimately to lead to the major reforms of the Children Act 1989,[55] which advanced the concept of an interdisciplinary family justice system.

The post-war development of the probation service's civil work

From its inception in the early part of the twentieth century until the late 1990s,[56] the primary task of the probation service was the community treatment of offenders. Nevertheless, a subsidiary function in this post-war period was a certain amount of social work in the civil courts. In this respect there were in the 1950s and 1960s three key areas.

The first was juvenile court work involving the preparation of social enquiry reports and the supervision of young offenders and children deemed to be in need of care and protection, all of which involved a measure of 'family casework'. Subsequent to the Seebohm Report this area of work was to be taken over by local authorities. Secondly, there was civil matrimonial work in the domestic magistrates courts, mostly involving short-term advice and attempts at marital conciliation. This work declined rapidly in the 1970s when civil legal aid became available and much of the business transferred to the divorce court. Thirdly, in the 1950s, following the Denning Committee on Matrimonial Causes,[57] the probation service slowly began to extend its social enquiry function to the divorce court. This practice went against the policy of the Home Office, which wanted the service to concentrate on work for the criminal courts and prison welfare and aftercare.

Child Abuse: a study of inquiry reports 1980–1989 (HMSO, 1992). The first of these volumes covered 18 reports and the second 19.

[55] Thereafter highly publicised child abuse tragedies continued to occur, which highlighted the continuing failure of inter-agency collaboration between police, social services and health authorities. See the Victoria Climbié Inquiry *Report of an Inquiry by Lord Laming* Cmnd 5730 (TSO, 2003). For a fuller discussion of policy issues concerning child abuse inquiries, see N Parton *Safeguarding childhood – early intervention and surveillance in a late modern society* (Palgrave Macmillan Publishing, 2006), particularly pp 47–62.

[56] The probation service's civil work was finally removed by the provisions of the Criminal Justice and Courts Services Act 2000 as part of the New Labour Government move to make the criminal justice system more overtly punitive and accountable to central government. However, this Act also established the Children and Family Court Advisory and Support Service (Cafcass), taking over the functions of the family court welfare service previously provided by the probation service – see S Cretney *Family Law in the Twentieth Century* (Oxford UP, 2003), p 773.

[57] *Final Report of the Committee on Procedure on Matrimonial Causes* (The Denning Committee Report) Cmd 7024 (1947).

Unified local family courts – a feasible reality or mirage?

Another feature of the post-war 'golden age' was the idea of family law as a distinct interdisciplinary system of civil jurisprudence with a separate unified judicial structure to administer it. The family-minded thinking prevailing in the social welfare field prepared the ground for the idea of a corresponding system of local civil family courts. This was reflected in a whole series of publications and committee recommendations.[58]

The germ of the idea, according to McGregor,[59] can be traced as far back as 1909, when Lord Gorell, who chaired the Royal Commission on Divorce and Matrimonial Causes (the Gorrell Commission), suggested the removal of the magistrates' domestic jurisdiction to the superior courts. This was regarded as impracticable by the rest of the Commission. However, in 1951 the idea was again picked up by Jack Simon, later the President of the Family Division, in a suggestion to the Morton Commission (Royal Commission on Marriage and Divorce).[60] Simon wanted to see 'a system of specialist matrimonial and family courts'. Once again the idea was rejected. Yet it re-surfaced in the 1965 White Paper, *The Child, The Family and the Young Offender*.[61] This foresaw family courts developing out of the juvenile court and in the first instance dealing with delinquency. One might describe this as a social work proposal for family courts, heavily influenced as it was by a paternalistic child-saving/social control ethic.

A very different, lawyer's 'citizen's rights' view of family courts was advanced the following year by the first chairman of the Law Commission, Sir Leslie Scarman.[62] He suggested a family division of the Supreme Court,[63] with a supervisory and appellate jurisdiction over a system of regional family courts. These would have dealt with all kinds of family disputes which had nothing to do with the criminal law. A few years later, in similar vein, an experienced county court judge, Judge Jean Graham-Hall,[64] suggested a system of local family courts whereby the domestic jurisdiction of the county courts and magistrates' courts would be combined to complement the idea of a family division of the High Court. Her proposal influenced the setting up in 1971 of the joint Home

---

[58] For a more comprehensive account of these developments, see Cretney, op cit, n 56 above, at pp 741–745; O R McGregor *Social History of Law Reform* (Stevens, 1981), pp 43–66; and M Murch *Justice and Welfare in Divorce* (Sweet & Maxwell, 1980).
[59] O R McGregor, ibid, pp 50–51.
[60] *The Report of the Royal Commission on Marriage and Divorce* Cmd 9678 (1956).
[61] White Paper *The Child, The Family and the Young Offender* Cmnd 2742 (1965).
[62] The Hon Mr Justice Scarman *Family Law and Law Reform* (University of Bristol, 1966).
[63] Subsequently established by the Administration of Justice Act 1970.
[64] HH Judge Jean Graham-Hall *Proposal for a Family Court* (The National Council for One Parent Families, 1970). See also 'Outline of a Proposal for a Family Court' [1971] Fam Law 6.

Office/Law Commission Family Courts Working Party[65] chaired by Sir Leslie Scarman as part of the Law Commission's general programme of family law reform.

So one can see that in the five years between 1965 and 1970 something of a family court bandwagon developed, carried along by the prevailing national spirit of liberal optimism and reform. It was coupled with a sympathetic move on the part of the good and the great to understand better the stresses and strains of family life and to provide humane and supportive measures to deal with them through social welfare policies and a specialist branch of the civil law.

All this came together in 1974 in the socio-legal analysis made by the Departmental Committee on One Parent Families (Finer Committee).[66] This endorsed the concept of an independent local family court as a judicial institution administering family justice according to law, not as a branch of social welfare. Finer proposed the abolition of the magistrates' domestic jurisdiction because of its stigmatic association with criminality. In the Committee's view:

> 'To deal with people in matrimonial disputes and distress though a court which is almost entirely given over to the trial of criminal offences is to show a manifest disrespect for their needs and feelings.'[67]

Finer's family courts proposal was fiercely opposed by the Home Office (at that time responsible for the magistrates' courts) and by the Magistrates' Association. It was rejected by the then Secretary of State, Barbara Castle, on grounds of cost (although these were never quantified). But, coinciding with the oil crisis and a period of political turbulence, the tide of reform was on the ebb. Within a few years the concept of a unified system of local family courts turned out to be a mirage.

Even so, the Finer Committee gave a boost to the idea of conciliation linked to the courts[68] and may well have influenced the subsequent compromise solution of bringing the magistrates' family proceedings courts into closer association with the divorce county court – a measure which was facilitated some years later when the then Lord Chancellor, Lord Mackay of Clashfern, succeeded in transferring ministerial

---

[65] This Working Party failed to report, since its work was overtaken by the Finer Committee – see further below.
[66] *Report of the Committee on One Parent Families*, Vol 1, Cmnd 5629 (HMSO, 1974).
[67] Ibid, para 4.360.
[68] An ad hoc committee of lawyers and social workers, calling themselves the 'Finer Joint Action Committee' was set up in Bristol and succeeded in establishing with charitable funds the pioneering Bristol Family Courts Conciliation Service – an innovative model which was subsequently developed across the country. See J Westcott (ed) *Family Mediation: Past, Present and Future* (Bristol Family Mediation, 2003).

responsibility for magistrates' courts away from the Home Office to the Lord Chancellor's Department (as it then was).

The influence of socio-legal 'consumer' studies of the family jurisdictions

A passage in the Finer Committee's Report stated that:

> 'The doing of justice requires knowledge of the results of its own procedures. Legislators, judges, critics and citizens must have knowledge of the social consequences of legal actions without which a democratic society cannot keep its institutions under constant and open scrutiny.'[69]

No doubt drafted by McGregor,[70] this reflects his passionate commitment to sound statistics and social research as a means of providing feedback on the workings of the civil law. One can see this in his powerful attack on the Royal Commission on Marriage and Divorce, the Morton Commission's reactionary dismissal of social and behavioural science[71] and in the pioneering 'consumer' feedback study of the magistrates' matrimonial jurisdiction which he conducted with Louis Blom-Cooper and Colin Gibson.[72]

Similarly, one of Scarman's early objectives on becoming Chairman of the Law Commission was that it would harness the findings of social research to the process of law reform.[73] Unsurprisingly, this was a view that did not find much favour at the time with the senior officials in the Lord Chancellor's Department, who had a somewhat limited traditional mindset.

Nevertheless, if I may strike a personal note, Scarman and McGregor encouraged me to undertake my first empirical socio-legal investigation into the circumstances of families in undefended divorce proceedings. One early result was to show that undefended divorce petitions, then heard in open court, were an expensive ritual experienced by the majority of petitioners (mostly women) as a public degradation ceremony and totally ineffective as a child welfare check.[74] These findings were seized upon by the Lord Chancellor's Department to justify the introduction in 1973 of

---

[69] *Report of the Committee on One Parent Families* (The Finer Report) Cmnd 5629 (HMSO, 1974), para 4.417, p 220.
[70] Professor of Social Institutions at Bedford College, London, and first Director of the Socio-Legal Centre at Wolfson College, Oxford.
[71] O R McGregor *Divorce in England: A Centenary Study* (Heinemann, 1957).
[72] O R McGregor et al *Separated Spouses – a study of the matrimonial jurisdiction of magistrates courts* (Duckworth, 1970).
[73] See Law Commission (1965) *First Annual Report*.
[74] E Elston, J Fuller and M Murch 'Judicial Hearings of Undefended Divorce Petitions' (1975) 38 MLR 609 at 632. See further G Davis, A Macleod, M Murch 'Undefended Divorce: Should s 41 of the Matrimonial Causes Act 1973 be repealed?' (1983) 46 MLR 121.

the so-called 'Special Procedure'. Introduced by changes approved by the Rules Committee it obviated the need for open court hearing and permitted postal application for divorce. As this did not require legal aid for representation in court, the measure was estimated to have saved £6 million on the civil legal aid budget in its first year – a measure described by McGregor as 'the only fundamental change in divorce since it ceased to be obtained by act of Parliament'.[75]

This first empirical research into divorce proceedings proved to be a springboard for a whole series of further empirical family law studies. A number were to influence the drafting of the Children Act 1989 and other substantive law reforms concerning adoption, domestic violence and the like. Even so, while research findings in the 1980s may well have influenced the growth and form of mediation and conciliation services and the unification of court welfare services[76] which ultimately resulted in Cafcass, the core divided local court structure remained largely impervious to change.

FAMILY JUSTICE IN THE POSTMODERN AGE – FRAGMENTATION, REVERSION AND DECAY?

I leap now over a twenty-five-year gap from the late 1970s to our own postmodern age. I broadly accept Hobsbawm's view that the history of the twenty years following 1973 is 'that of a world which lost its bearings and slid into instability and crisis. And yet until the 1980s it was not clear how irretrievably the foundations of the "golden age" had crumbled'.[77] He called this period 'the landslide'. Its instability and uncertainty affected almost every aspect of our lives from international relations to the social norms and realities of intimate family relations.

Postmodernity and the family

Indeed, the 1980s and 1990s saw such a remarkable cultural change affecting the social construction of family life and childhood that law and social policy had to adapt and find solutions to these changes and to the problems they generated. Thus, while, as already mentioned, subsequent conservative governments under Margaret Thatcher and John Major generally pursued social and economic policies of retrenchment, they were not averse to family law reform, being particularly responsive to public concern about high divorce rates, domestic violence, the apparent

---

[75] O R McGregor *Social History of Law Reform* (Stevens, 1981), p 41. He further notes that 'the far-reaching nature of this development received neither parliamentary nor public discussion. It was in fact established by fiat of judges and officials, an example of the strong influence of procedure upon substantive law which in Maine's famous phrase has 'the look of being gradually secreted in the interstices of procedure'.

[76] See M Murch and D Hooper *The Family Justice System* (Family Law, 1992), pp 65–82.

[77] E Hobsbawm *The Age of Extremes: A History of the World 1914–1991* (Vintage, 1996).

fragmentation of family life and growing concern about child abuse connected with a series of child death scandals.

It was also a period which fostered a good deal of sociological thought. The leading commentators in this field, at least as they affect the western developed world, include Ulrick Beck,[78] Anthony Giddens,[79] Zigmunt Bauman[80] and Amitai Etzioni.[81] Bauman and others focus not only on the rapidity of social change, consumerism and the economics of the shifting global marketplace, but also associate it with a new age in which people are increasingly constrained to live in the present and to adopt flexible lifestyles in response. Consequent life strategies of those who appear economically successful depend on being fleet of foot, quick-witted and on the avoidance of being trapped in long-term commitments. Moreover, in an increasingly risk-averse society children are portrayed simultaneously as defenceless angels or dangerous young monsters. As Jackson and Scott[82] put it, 'childhood is increasingly being constructed as a precious realm under siege from those who would rob children of their childhoods, and as being subverted from within by children who refuse to remain childlike'.

A broad outline of the social changes affecting contemporary family life that have occurred over a single generation and in a very changed working and leisure world[83] reflects the fluidity and flux that seems to characterise postmodernity. They include the continued decline of patriarchy, the rise of serial monogamy as a mode of continuing intimate relations,[84] an increased variety of family forms, and historically low marriage rates. A significantly large majority of parents separate and form new partnerships, with consequent psychological discontinuities in their children's formative years. Cohabitation preceding marriage is virtually the norm. Almost half of all children are now born outside wedlock and

---

[78] U Beck and E Beck-Gernsheim *The Normal Chaos of Love* (Polity Press, 1995). See also *Risikogesellschaft: Auf dem Weg in eine andere Moderne* (Risks Society: Towards a New Modernity) (Suhrkamp Verlag, 1986).

[79] A Giddens *The Consequences of Modernity* (Polity Press, 1990); see also *Modernity and Self-Identity: Self and society in the late modern age* (Polity Press, 1991) and *The Third Way: The renewal of social democracy* (Polity Press, 1998).

[80] Z Bauman *Legislatures and Interpreters* (Polity Press, 1987). See also *Post Modern Ethics* (Polity Press, 1993) and *Life in Fragments – essays in post-modern morality* (Blackwell, 1995).

[81] A Etzioni *The New Golden Rule – Community and Morality in a Democratic Society* (Profile Books, 1997).

[82] See S Jackson and S Scott 'Risk, Anxiety and the Social Construction of Childhood' in D Lupton (ed) *Risk and Socio-Cultural Theory – New Directions and Perspectives* (Cambridge University Press,1986).

[83] S Dex *Families and Work in the Twenty-First Century* (Joseph Rowntree Foundation, 2003).

[84] ONS *Social Trends 37: 2007 Edition* (Office for National Statistics, 2007), p 19. Provisional figures for 2005 showed that remarriages accounted for two-fifths of all marriages.

25 per cent of children live with a single mother. Children live in an increasing variety of family structures, with step-families being generally larger than non step-families.[85]

Risk aversion, such a feature of postmodernity, extends particularly to the protection of children. Yet for all that, the high incidence of parental conflict, separation and re-partnering means that almost a third of all British children have lived through their parents' separation or divorce by the time they reach school leaving age of 16.[86] The government's Green Paper issued in 2004[87] cites various researches which suggest that, when compared with children with continuously married parents, children with divorced or separated parents perform less well on measures of academic achievement, general conduct, psychological adjustment and social relations. Other research, however, suggests that the impact of separation and divorce may be determined more by the level of conflict that exists between parents before, during and after breakdown of the parental relationship than the actual breakdown itself.[88]

Children, critical life transitions and the family justice system

One might think from the above sketch of the new postmodern culture and its impact on the institutions of childhood and the family that the consequences as far as the process of family justice is concerned are largely negative. This is emphatically not what I am suggesting. The picture might seem gloomy, but there are some encouraging chinks of light.

Thanks in part to a number of relatively recent socio-legal studies,[89] we have a much clearer idea of how children adapt to changes in their family

---

[85] Ibid, p 20.

[86] J Pryor and B Rogers *Children in Changing Families: Life after parental separation* (Blackwell, 2001); HM Government *Parental Separation – Children's Needs and Parents' Responsibilities: Next Steps* Report of the Responses to Consultation and Agenda for Action Cm 6452 (TSO, 2005).

[87] HM Government *Parental Separation – Children's Needs and Parents' Responsibilities* Cm 6273 (TSO, 2004), paras 32 and 35. Summarising these findings the Ministerial Forward states: 'Where the separation is handled well, the adverse impact on children is minimised. Where separation goes badly and in particular where children are drawn into parental conflict, then the effects can be profoundly damaging to children. Evidence shows that children in this situation are likely to do less well in life. They are more likely to do less well at school, to truant or run away from home. But these risks can be reduced if parents can resolve parenting issues in an amicable way.'

[88] See further G Harold and M Murch 'Interparental Conflict and Children's Adaptation to Separation and Divorce: theory, research and implications for family law, practice and policy' [2005] CFLQ 185.

[89] See, for example, C Lyon, E Surrey and J E Timms *Effective support services for children and young people when parental relationships break down* (Centre for the Study of the Child, Family and the Law, 1998); A Buchanan, J Hunt, H Bretherton, V Bream *Families in Conflict: perspectives of children and parents of the family court welfare service* (Policy Press, 2001); C Smart, B Neale, A Wade *The changing experience of childhood: families and divorce* (Polity Press, 2001); L Trinder, M Beek, J Connolly *Making Contact:*

life and what they expect of the family justice system. Children need reliable information to help them understand what is happening in their families and in any consequent litigation; the right to express their views and participate in proceedings, if they so wish; and psycho-social support from a reliable trustworthy person (sometimes referred to as a passage agent) to help them navigate critical family life transitions associated with legal proceedings and their aftermath.

This last point seems critical in helping children maintain or regain a measure of control over their own lives and a sense of stability. At least as far as family justice practitioners are concerned, it is recognised that the apparatus of family justice is one vital means by which to help children meet these needs, particularly through the agency of children's legal representatives, where they are appointed, and through the services of Cafcass officers. In this respect, as all practitioners know, courts have a duty to ascertain the 'wishes and feelings' of the child and to give due weight to them, having regard to the child's age and level of understanding. This applies in all adoption cases and in public law care proceedings and in contested child-related private law proceedings brought under the Children Act 1989. Moreover, in the last few decades, international law, particularly Art 12(2) of the United Nations Convention on the Rights of the Child 1989 and more recently in child abduction cases under the provisions of the Brussels II Revised Regulation ((EC) No 22001/2003), Art 11(2),[90] has increased the pressure on the UK government to give greater recognition to the principle of listening to the voice of the child, even though this is still in a number of respects a hotly debated issue.[91]

So, potentially at least, support mechanisms linked to the family justice systems are in place which give credibility to the ideas of continuity, coherence and protection in the regulation of family relations, which in the cultural conditions of postmodernity are often lacking. But in order to give them operational effect, much depends on the level of practitioners' professional understanding and skill, particularly on how lawyers and Cafcass officers appreciate the community mental health aspects of family justice. It also depends on a government willing to provide the system with adequate financial resources to its judiciary, the court support services and the civil legal aid scheme. Much of this will

---

how parents and children negotiate and experience contact after divorce (York Publishing Services, 2002); I Butler, L Scanlan, M Robinson, G Douglas, M Murch *Divorcing Children – Children's Experience of the Parents' Divorce* (Jessica Kingsley, 2003); G Douglas, M Murch, C Miles, L Scanlan *Research into the Operation of rule 9.5 of the Family Proceedings Rules 1991* (Department for Constitutional Affairs, 2006); C Thomas, V Beckford with N Lowe and M Murch *Adopted Children Speaking* (BAAF, 2000).

[90] On which, see N Lowe 'Where in the world is international family law going next?', Chapter 12 below.

[91] For a comprehensive review of the issues see Baroness Hale of Richmond 'The voice of the child' [2007] IFL 171.

hinge on the New Labour Government's priorities and how the Ministry of Justice approaches and resolves the fundamental surveillance/support dilemma. Here the omens are not good.

The surveillance and support dilemma

In the more turbulent, fast-moving, uncertain world of postmodernity, the balance is shifting back to a more authoritarian, socially controlling, risk-averse family justice regime. This is likely to be largely focused on parents in difficult cases, ie where they cannot be diverted away from the court system, either by being persuaded to settle their disputes privately themselves (with or without their solicitors) or by using alternative dispute mechanisms of mediation or conciliation.[92] It seems likely that, apart from 'big money' cases heard in the High Court, those cases that will still come before local family courts will be drawn predominantly from the ranks of the poor or from families where there is a perceived risk of domestic violence. What is the evidence for this?

Here one only has to look at a number of recent policy developments, largely driven by two major, if in some ways contradictory concerns: namely the need to protect children from the risk of harm and the Government's need to curb public expenditure.

The first of these has become closely associated with the historically recurrent social problem of domestic violence.[93] The publicity given during the 1980s and 1990s to child abuse tragedies, and growing risk aversion concerning children, have highlighted the effects of them witnessing inter-parental conflict. This has led to two major ways in which legislative and policy definitions of 'harm' and 'domestic violence' have been widened. First, s 120 of the Adoption and Children Act 2002 amends the Children Act 1989 to make more explicit the meaning of harm. This now includes 'impairment suffered from seeing or hearing the ill treatment of another', and has been added to the welfare checklist applied in all applications for s 4 and s 8 orders under the Children Act 1989. This is intended to emphasise the risk to children of witnessing domestic violence. There is no doubt that this can be traumatic, and even in a few tragic cases the result can be fatal, as a report by Lord Justice Wall for the Family Justice Council has shown.[94]

---

[92] Mediation is now taken to refer to those out of court services provided by voluntary organisations, while conciliation refers to ADR provided by Cafcass: see Cafcass *Pathway in Private Law Proceedings* (Cafcass, 2007). This introduced a policy termed 'extended dispute resolution', which shifted priorities in private law cases away from report writing for courts towards conciliation.

[93] 'Recurrent' because domestic violence has always been a feature of some intimate family relations. Over the last 150 years the issue has been forced periodically into public consciousness through the activities of the women's movement.

[94] Lord Justice Wall *A report to the President of the Family Division on the publication by the Women's Aid Federation of England entitled 'Twenty-nine child homicides: Lessons to be learnt on domestic violence and child protection'* with particular reference to the five

As far as the term 'domestic violence' is concerned, this too has been widened to include much more than physical violence. Until May 2008, there was no finally agreed definition in use in government departments,[95] but the new definition to be used across government and its agencies is now given as—

> 'any incident of threatening behaviour, violence or abuse (psychological, physical, sexual, financial or emotional) between other adults who are or have been intimate partners or family members, regardless of gender or sexuality.'[96]

In fact, in England, Cafcass have widened the definition even further. In their practitioners' toolkit concerning domestic violence, published in April 2007, it is defined as:

> 'Behaviour characterised by the misuse of power and control by one person or another within a family context both overt and subtle which can take the form of emotional, financial, physical, psychological or sexual abuse or any combination of these.'[97]

It can be argued that such a broad definition opens the door of professional discretion too wide to a range of subjective interpretations by Cafcass officers in their assessment of potential harm to children. Moreover, from a policy point of view, given such a wide definition, it will be hard to make accurate estimates of the incidence of domestic violence where inter-parental conflict occurs, since a degree of interparental conflict in this context must be considered as a natural and normal part of family life.[98]

Furthermore, following considerable public concern about child abuse, some of which occurs in relation to domestic violence and contact arrangements, and resulting from pressure group agitation,[99] a new s 16A of the Children Act 1989, as inserted by the Children and Adoption Act 2006, requires Cafcass officers and Welsh family proceedings officers

---

cases in which there was judicial involvement (Royal Courts of Justice), available at www.dca.gov.uk.judicial/judges.pubs.htm (2006). This report, as the title indicates, concerns twenty-nine children from thirteen families over a ten-year period. Lord Justice Wall examined all the available court files (five cases). It is worth noting that as he observed 'these cases, therefore, tragic as they are, represent a tiny proportion of the many thousands of contact orders which are made each year'.

[95] See N Lowe and G Douglas *Bromley's Family Law* (Oxford UP, 10th edn, 2007), p 208.
[96] http:www.crimereduction.homeoffice.gov.uk/dv/dv01.htm.
[97] Cafcass *Domestic Violence Toolkit – Version 2* (Cafcass, 2007), para 1.2.
[98] See G Harold and M Murch 'Interparental Conflict and Children's Adaptation to Separation and Divorce: theory, research and implications for family law, practice and policy' [2005] CFLQ 185 at 193.
[99] See Lord Justice Wall *A report to the President of the Family Division on the publication by the Women's Aid Federation of England entitled 'Twenty-nine child homicides: Lessons to be learnt on domestic violence and child protection'* with particular reference to the five cases in which there was judicial involvement (Royal Courts of Justice), available at www.dca.gov.uk.judicial/judges.pubs.htm (2006).

to carry out risk assessments where they consider there is cause to suspect that a child is at risk of harm (as defined above).[100] The officers then have a duty to inform the court of their findings.

Periodic inspectors' reports have been critical of a number of Cafcass officers who apparently have shown little awareness of the safety risks to women and children. It is understandable therefore that in England and Wales Cafcass should seek to remedy these criticisms by giving priority to improving risk assessment, and no one would wish to belittle the seriousness of domestic violence and its potentially adverse consequences for children. But crucial in all this are the qualities of good professional knowledge, sense of proportion and sound judgment on the part of Cafcass officers investigating the case. Much also depends on the practitioner's capacity to win the trust and confidence of the family members, adults and children alike. A faulty child risk assessment carries weighty risks for the professional practitioner who makes it: on the one hand a failure to safeguard the child and on the other unwarranted intrusion and threat to a family's integrity and stability. Thus, it would not be surprising if those Cafcass practitioners who were uncertain of their capabilities in these respects were to err on the side of caution and not take risks with the child's welfare, particularly since the toolkit currently available to English[101] Cafcass staff contains a huge array of possible risk factors, but gives very little guidance as to how the individual practitioner is to weigh or calculate them.[102]

The very nature of our postmodern risk averse culture carries within it two tendencies. The first is for small risks to become magnified in the public mind, particularly if they attract strong media interest. This in turn can provoke a disproportionate official response. The second is that those who campaign most vigorously for tighter regulation and the policing of families are often those special interest groups who stand to gain most from operating complex surveillance regimes. Moreover, when government finances are increasingly stretched, public services tend to make exaggerated claims about their effectiveness in order to justify the maintenance and increase in their publicly funded budgets. In this way,

---

[100] See also *Children and Adoption Act 2006 – Court Rules: Amendment to the Family Proceedings Rules 1991*, implemented in December 2008 in r 4.11AD of the FPR, which specifies duties of Cafcass Officers and Welsh Family Proceedings Officers, and lists various new duties concerning supervision of contact activity in addition to making a risk assessment under s 16A of the 1989 Act.

[101] See Cafcass *Domestic Violence Toolkit (Version 2)* (2007). Cf Wales, where Cafcass Cymru has commissioned the development of a specific psychometric instrument for use by practitioners as a child and adolescent welfare assessment pack aimed at identifying and assessing the psychological impact on children of witnessing inter-parental conflict and domestic violence.

[102] This unsatisfactory aspect of the English Cafcass toolkit prompted a pilot study to be made of its use. An evaluation report by Thangam Debbonaire, *The pilot of the Respect/Relate/CAFCASS domestic violence risk identification tool* (Cafcass, 2008) revealed that Cafcass officers were divided as to the value of the toolkit.

widened definitions concerning the risky side to family life lead inexorably to priority being given to family surveillance over the need for family support.

Enforcement in the family courts – blurring the distinction between the criminal and civil jurisdictions

For years family courts have had to struggle with the problem of what to do when faced with an apparently intransigent parent who stubbornly refuses to obey a court order, particularly over the question of contact in private law proceedings.[103] During the decade preceding the introduction of the Children and Adoption Act 2006 this issue received a good deal of public attention, in part fuelled by the activities of the pressure group Fathers4Justice. In March 2001 the Advisory Board on Family Law Children Act Sub-Committee, chaired by Lord Justice Wall, concluded that what was needed when they faced intransigent parents was a wider range of enforcement powers to bring greater flexibility into proceedings.[104] This was accepted by the government in 2004,[105] which undertook to legislate at the earliest opportunity and suggested a new set of provisions ranging from referral to counsellors and parenting programmes to the tougher imposition of community based orders and the award of financial compensation from one parent to another. The draft Bill published a year later included draconian sanctions such as curfews and electronic tagging, but in the event the new enforcement measures that were enacted were restricted to financial compensation and an order imposing an unpaid work requirement to be organised by the probation service up to a maximum of 200 hours, with the additional requirement for a Cafcass officer to monitor compliance and report to court.[106] This latter order effectively equates this aspect of the family justice system with the community treatment of offenders. It thus further blurs the distinction between the criminal and civil jurisdictions which in the 1970s was seen as such an important principle by the Finer Committee. This is accentuated because in enforcement proceedings the welfare of the child is *not* the paramount consideration, as were the

---

[103] For an exposition of enforcement powers in family proceedings, see N Lowe and G Douglas *Bromley's Family Law* (Oxford UP, 10th edn, 2007), pp 567–574.

[104] Advisory Board on Family Law Children Act Sub-Committee *Making Contact Work: A Report to the Lord Chancellor on the Facilitation of Arrangements for Contact Between Children and their Non-Residential Parents and the Enforcement of Court Orders for Contact* (2001), ch 14.

[105] See Green Paper, *Parental Separation: Children's needs and parents' responsibilities* Cm 6273 (TSO, 2004).

[106] See Children and Adoption Act 2006, Pt 1, inserting ss 11A–11P into the Children Act 1989.

original child-related proceedings.[107] Moreover, there is no obligation to appoint a guardian to protect the interests of the child.[108]

Official encouragement to make greater use of the magistrates' family proceedings court

Although New Labour in its 1997 manifesto mentioned the desirability of establishing a unified system of local family courts, successive governments have shied away from doing so. In so far as the concept remains on the official agenda, it is seen as a long term objective. Even so, it can be argued that a number of important preliminary steps have been taken to prepare the ground for such a reform – for example, the establishment in 2001 of Cafcass. Moreover, a Consultation Paper, *A Single Civil Court?*, was issued in February 2005.[109] In November of that year the Department for Constitutional Affairs issued a policy statement[110] in which the then Family Justice Minister, Baroness Ashton, stated that 'unifying a single family court is our long term objective but this will take time and require primary legislation'.

Thus, for the time being at least, it is clear that the government is against severing the magistrates' family proceedings court from its criminal jurisdiction counterpart. Instead, a number of measures have been set in train to improve links between the FPC, the county court and the High Court with a view to facilitating transfer of cases to the most appropriate forum and achieving a number of management objectives, such as a greater measure of judicial continuity and the need to avoid delay.

Such progress towards a unified structure as has been made might not have happened at all had it not been for the work of the House of Commons Constitutional Affairs Committee chaired by the Rt Hon Alan Beith MP. This Committee has kept a watchful parliamentary eye on developments in family justice since the initial managerial and staffing problems experienced in establishing Cafcass. For example, following serious concerns expressed by the Law Society, the Committee in its Sixth Report in Session 2005–06[111] addressed the continuing problems of delay in family courts and the extent to which such delays were due to a lack of adequate resources.

---

[107] See further *M v M (Breaches of Order: Committal)* [2005] EWCA Civ 1722, [2006] 1 FLR 1154.

[108] For discussion of this issue see G Douglas, M Murch, C Miles, L Scanlan *Research into the Operation of rule 9.5 of the Family Proceedings Rules 1991* (Department for Constitutional Affairs, 2006), pp 207–209.

[109] Department for Constitutional Affairs *A Single Civil Court? The scope for unifying the civil jurisdictions of the High Court, the county courts and the Family Proceedings Courts* Consultation Paper CP06/05 (2005).

[110] Department for Constitutional Affairs Press Release (21 November 2005) *Moving Towards a Single Family Court*, www.dca.uk/consult.

[111] House of Commons Constitutional Affairs Committee *Family Justice: The Operation of the Family Courts Revisited* HC 1086 (TSO, 2006).

On 2 May 2006 the Committee took evidence from the current President of the Family Division, Sir Mark Potter,[112] who told them that, as a result of the Judicial Resources Review published the previous year and financial cuts in the courts service,[113] the senior judiciary accepted it would be necessary to introduce a policy of 'cascading down' (ie cases from the higher courts to the FPC) in order to relieve workload pressures on judges in the High Court and county courts. Yet, in the same Committee session, Audrey Damazer of the Justices' Clerks Society recognised that there was an inbuilt tension between the magistrates' criminal and family jurisdictions. She told the Committee:

> 'There is so much political pressure in the criminal field that legal advisers (to the lay justices) and courtroom space are often needed for criminal work rather than family work.'

In other words, within the magistrates' court structure criminal work very often takes priority over civil family work, even where the interests of children are under consideration. Furthermore, there are other difficulties such as finding enough magistrates with sufficient experience and training in family work in many areas; the continuing unmet need to advance specialist training in family justice matters for legal advisers; and the problem of securing the availability of sufficient experienced magistrates to meet the requirements of judicial continuity in complex cases.[114] This is aggravated in the case of the FPC because of the requirement to convene a bench of three justices unless, as is the case in London at the Wells Street Court, a district judge (magistrates' courts) can be found.[115]

The emergent nature of the government's strategy for family justice

One can see that in the absence of a properly designed unified system of local family courts as envisaged years ago by the Finer Committee, the New Labour government has chosen 'to make do and mend', ie pragmatically taking a number of relatively small administrative measures in the hope of overcoming some of the more costly and pressing administrative problems in the existing system.

Politically this may be an astute strategy. It does not challenge the many established interests which have an investment in maintaining the status quo. It holds out a vague hope of root and branch structural reform to placate those liberal family law reformers imbued with the values of high

---

[112] Evidence taken on 2 May 2006.
[113] The budget for the following year 2007 required the Ministry of Justice to make cuts in expenditure of 3.5% year on year.
[114] These often involve more than a single day's hearing – a problem which extends, of course, to the county courts and High Courts as well.
[115] It should be noted that so far very few magistrates' courts have replicated this particular arrangement: personal communication in November 2008 with District Judge Nicholas Crichton of the Wells Street Court. See also his evidence to the Constitutional Affairs Committee (2 May 2006) Ev 4, Q16 and Q17.

modernity acquired during the 'Golden Age' of the 1960s and 1970s. It pays lip service to some of the criticisms of the court system voiced by the consumer pressure groups. But it largely ignores research feedback of more representative litigant experience revealed by various socio-legal researchers over the last few decades[116] – not least the views of children.[117]

Moreover, we know from research conducted in the 1980s for the Inter-Departmental Review for Family and Domestic Jurisdictions[118] that, when faced with a choice of jurisdictions, solicitors, the gatekeepers to the system, in most areas favoured the county court. They had more faith in professional judges than they had in the lay magistracy, whose decisions they saw as the less predictable. A further factor in their preference for the county court was the value of affidavit evidence over solely oral evidence. In hearings before magistrates this often introduced a greater element of uncertainty.

If these points still hold good – and as far as I know there is no recent research evidence pointing to the contrary – then, taken together with the risk-avoidance surveillance approach now operated by Cafcass whenever there are allegations of domestic violence, solicitors will have every incentive to encourage their private law clients to settle their child-related disputes without litigation and, when litigation is pursued, to advise their clients to commence proceedings in the county court. In other words, the deterrent factor of hearings before magistrates suits the government policy of encouraging settlement through alternative dispute resolution while acting as a covert rationing mechanism in order to reduce demand both on an apparently over-burdened judiciary and on the civil legal aid budget, which, as a result of the Carter proposals and recent changes in civil legal aid has, as we shall see, led to a loss of many experienced family solicitors.

Implementation of the Carter Review of Legal Aid

A number of the proposals in the Carter Report of Legal Aid,[119] published in July 2006, and in the subsequent government White Paper[120]

---

[116] See M Murch, M Borkowski, R Copner, K Griew *The Overlapping Family Jurisdiction of Magistrates' Courts and County Courts – a study for the Inter-Departmental Review of Family and Domestic Jurisdictions* (Socio-Legal Centre for Family Studies, University of Bristol, 1987); A Buchanan and J Hunt 'Disputed Contact Cases in the Courts' in A Bainham, B Lindley, M Richards and L Trinder (eds) *Children and their Families – Contact, Rights and* Welfare (Hart Publishing, 2003), pp 365–384; C Smart, V May, A Wade, C Furniss with K Sharman and J Strelitz *Residence and Contact Disputes in Court*, Vol 2, DCA Research Series 4/05 (Department for Constitutional Affairs, 2005).

[117] See sources cited at n 89 above.

[118] See M Murch et al, op cit, n 116 above, p 110 and pp 40–46.

[119] Report of Lord Carter of Coles, *Legal Aid: A market-based approach to reform* (2006) at www.legalaidprocurementreview.gov.uk. For comment focused on the implications for public child law, see R White 'The future of welfare law for children', at Chapter 11 below; J Masson 'Controlling costs and maintaining services – the reform of legal aid

caused consternation in the legal profession and amongst many leading commentators. As a result of these widespread concerns, the House of Commons Constitutional Affairs Committee examined the issues and published its own report.[121] While it acknowledged that overall legal aid expenditure had risen considerably, particularly in Crown Court defence work and public law children's cases, the Committee found that in a number of respects the government's proposals (ie to cease legal aid payment on an hourly basis and to introduce a transitional system of fixed and graduated fees as a way of preparing for a system of full competitive tendering for legal aid contracts by solicitors) were flawed and were likely to lead to more solicitors giving up legal aid work. Indeed, it found this was already having a serious impact on the availability and provision of legal aid in family justice work.

In relation to private law, two main criticisms are levelled at the Carter proposals. First, there is clear evidence that the number of solicitors holding civil legal aid contracts undertaking family work has declined steadily, from 4,039 in 2000/01 to 2,887 in 2005/06 – a drop of 32%, with a corresponding decrease in family cases being taken on from 410,916 in 2000/01 to 283,274 in 2005/06. As the Constitutional Affairs Committee observed:

> 'This represented a huge decline in access to justice for people with family problems as firms gave up legal aid work because of poor rates of pay, the bureaucracy of costs of administering legal aid contracts and difficulties in recruiting and retaining suitably qualified staff.'[122]

The Committee feared that the Carter reforms would lead to a further decline in the number of legal aid providers, with 'potentially severe effects on the provision and availability of publicly funded legal services'.

Various consequences were expected to follow from this state of affairs; not only a deflection away from the kind of help, advice and protection that experienced family lawyers can offer families experiencing family breakdown, but in cases which proceed to court an increase in the number of unrepresented litigants. As Professor Judith Masson said in her evidence to the Committee, this in turn will increase pressure on the courts and adjudicators:

---

fees for care proceedings' [2008] CFLQ 425; and A MacDonald 'The caustic dichotomy – Under-resourcing in the care system' [2009] CFLQ 29.

[120] Department for Constitutional Affairs/Legal Services Commission *Legal Aid Reform: The way ahead* Cm 6993 (HMSO, 2006).

[121] House of Commons Constitutional Affairs Committee *Implementation of the Carter Review of Legal Aid – Third Report of Session 2006–07, Vol 1 together with formal minutes* HC 223-1 (2007).

[122] Ibid, p 16, para 40.

'Without the restraining influence of settlement seeking and negotiation by experienced family lawyers there will be more protracted contested litigation.'[123]

She further criticised the government's general acceptance of the Carter proposals on the grounds that, particularly in public law care proceedings, there was an evident lack of understanding of the main cost drivers of these proceedings (ie the proliferation of parties, delays in appointing guardians, the greater use of experts etc). In this respect, criticism was levelled more at the Legal Services Commission than the Carter Review, whose terms of reference excluded consideration of the particular context and complexities of care proceedings. Moreover, in care proceedings the proposed transitional graduated fee scheme was based on average costs, which bore little relation to the realities or variability in the complexities of these cases, each of which of course requires careful preparation.

New Labour's stealthily emergent policy for family justice

So, if one puts together these various developments – extending the definitions of 'harm' and 'domestic violence'; focusing Cafcass priorities on risk assessment and surveillance; blurring the distinction between criminal and civil jurisdictions when it comes to enforcement powers; failing to introduce a unified system of local family courts and seeking to reactivate the magistrates' Family Proceedings Court; reducing the quantity and quality of a strong supplier base of family solicitors through the reorganisation of civil legal aid – one is driven to the conclusion that the New Labour Government has been determined to restrict the work of the family justice system. It seeks to sharpen up the system's social control/family policing function with a simplistic, and in some respects contradictory, mixture of cost-saving and child-saving measures.

Superficially, taken separately, each of these policy developments might appear as a series of individual ad hoc policy initiatives spread out over a number of years and responded to by various interest groups, sometimes favourably, as with the issue of domestic violence and risk to children, or with consternation, as in the case of the legal professions' response to the Carter proposals concerning legal aid reform. But, those who believe in government conspiracy might well argue that many of these measures reflect a longstanding New Labour distrust of so-called 'fat cats' in the legal profession and a resentment of the constitutional independence of the judiciary. They might even reveal ambivalent second thoughts about the value of the Human Rights Act as a measure to protect children and parents in their dealings with the state, ie the right to a fair trial and to respect for one's family life.

Conspiracy or not, it is clear that the Government's apparent strategy largely accords with the zeitgeist of the new postmodern culture: that is to

---

[123] Ibid, p 27.

say, it is pragmatic and responsive to media headlines, which are often fuelled by the activities of highly vocal pressure groups, such as those concerned about domestic violence and those fathers who feel discriminated against by the so-called 'secret' nature of procedures in family courts. It also reflects the culture's risk-averse approach to childhood, as well as a largely uninformed scepticism about the activities of family lawyers and the interdisciplinary nature of the family justice system. For those who believe that access to good quality family justice should be open to all, regardless of social status and wealth, the socially divisive effect of the Government's approach is a clear repudiation of the modernist philosophy which in the 1970s characterised the Finer Committee's proposals for a unified system of local family courts.

Some continuing positive support measures of family justice

Yet, reflecting on developments in the family justice system over the last decade, all is not gloom.

We have seen the creation of a unified family court welfare service in the shape of Cafcass, the title of which at least gives credence to the concepts of advice and support for children and parents, despite the current emphasis on risk assessment and surveillance.

In both private and public law, in appropriate cases, diversion away from costly litigation to private ordering through alternative dispute mechanisms has many advantages – but will probably apply to and benefit middle class families most. Where ADR is used in this respect by the judiciary in preliminary hearings without too much coercion, the results can be positive, even though children do not have much opportunity to voice their views because many conciliators and mediators still lack appropriate skill and understanding in working directly with them.

Another positive advance has been the concept of judicial continuity, ie the desirability of trying to ensure that as far as possible the same judge deals with the case throughout its various hearings. This has been advocated by the senior judiciary in a number of recent cases[124] and in a Practice Direction from the President of the Family Division.[125] It saves time by avoiding repetition and is more acceptable to parents.[126]

---

[124] See *Re O (Contact: Withdrawal of Application)* [2003] EWHC 3031 (Fam), [2004] 1 FLR 1258; *V v V Implacable Hostility* [2004] EWHC 1215 (Fam), [2004] 2 FLR 851; *Re D (Intractable Contact Dispute: Publicity)* [2004] EWHC 727 (Fam), [2004] 1 FLR 1226.

[125] President of the Family Division *The Private Law Programme – Guidance* (2005).

[126] See G Douglas, M Murch, C Miles, L Scanlan *Research into the Operation of rule 9.5 of the Family Proceedings Rules 1991* (Department for Constitutional Affairs, 2006), p 193. Of course, this is much more likely to be achieved by a single judge overseeing the various stages of litigation than by a bench of lay magistrates, which, as already mentioned, may well be difficult to reconvene without undue delay.

Perhaps the most significant of all developments in family justice in recent decades has been the widening of opportunities for children to have a voice in proceedings and the use of the so-called 'tandem model' by which a specialist children's lawyer and social worker collaborate in representing the child. Yet, while almost totally accepted in public law proceedings, the current practice in private law proceedings is limited to the occasional use of r 9.5 of the Family Proceedings Rules 1991. Nevertheless, judges and lawyers generally favour greater use of this provision, particularly in seriously contested disputes. As the 2007 Cafcass Annual Report observed,[127] evidence is coming through that r 9.5 is an effective measure in resolving disputes and supporting children in some of our most complex private law cases. By contrast, the government, although sponsoring research into the matter,[128] has largely, for economic reasons, so far been reluctant to see its use extended.

But it is not just a question of giving children a voice in proceedings that is important. As the researchers into the operation of r 9.5 concluded, what stood out from their study was the importance to children of having—

> 'a concerned impartial person accessible to them apart from their parents to support them and help them manage the critical family transitions following the breakdown of their parents' relationship.'[129]

This sort of 'passage agent' role is necessary for a great many children involved in family proceedings and of course is sometimes played by Cafcass officers preparing welfare reports or acting as a guardian and/or by a specially appointed children's legal representative in a r 9.5 case. So the potential exists to extend this role to many more children caught up in family conflict or litigation, but that will not be fulfilled while overwhelming priority is given to risk assessment or diversion to ADR.[130]

Another fairly recent positive development has been the creation, with government support, of the National Family Justice Council and its supporting network of regional family justice councils. The primary purpose of these organisations is to promote an interdisciplinary approach to family justice. Established in July 2004 as a non-statutory non-departmental public body, the FJC aims to:

---

[127] See Cafcass *Annual Report and Accounts 2006–07* HC 781 (TSO, 2007), p 7. This shows that the number of such cases increased from 1,035 in 2005–06 to 1,206 in 2006–07, while requests for welfare reports decreased from 26,144 to 23,942 in the corresponding periods.
[128] See G Douglas et al, op cit, n 126 above.
[129] Ibid, para 7.14.
[130] For more detailed discussion of the policy and practice issues, see G Douglas, M Murch and A Perry 'Supporting children when parents separate – a neglected family justice or mental health issue?' [1996] CFLQ 121.

'Facilitate the delivery of better and quicker outcomes for families and children who use the family justice system.'[131]

As an independent body, chaired ex officio by the President of the Family Division, it organises a bi-annual interdisciplinary conference, responds to various consultation documents issued by government, and attempts to monitor through consultation and research how effectively the system is working. Overall, it aims to promote inter-professional collaboration and understanding of family justice issues in a fast changing society.

Unfortunately, it does not as yet have a well funded and established research budget, so its attempts to keep a finger on the pulse of the system and to ensure a reliable stream of consumer feedback from parents and children are limited. Thus, its influence on government policy may be relatively weak. The danger is that government will dismiss it as comprising mainly conservatively minded self-interested professional groups. Moreover, the FJC could quite easily 'be put to sleep' if it appears too critical of government policies, as has been the case in the past with the Lord Chancellor's Legal Aid Advisory Committee, the Children Act Advisory Committee and, more recently, the Advisory Board on Family Law. Nevertheless, within its own terms, it is regarded as authoritative and influential in professional circles. It embodies both actually and symbolically the concept of interdisciplinarity concerning law, medicine and the social sciences and their relationship to the social institution of the family. If appropriately resourced with a research commissioning facility, it could help to adapt family justice to the needs of children and parents in an ever-changing society.

CONCLUSION

There is a paradox in all this: the more individualised, fragmented and subject to rapid social change our postmodern culture becomes, with its stresses and strains on family life, the more people yearn for stability. The overwhelming evidence from social research concerning families and child development is that coherence, continuity and stability provided in the context of supportive family relationships is of primary importance. As an ESRC study[132] of contemporary life reported in 2004:

> 'Although relationships may be changing shape these changes have not undermined people's sense of commitment to one another. When faced with dilemmas people generally negotiate "the proper thing to do" in and through such commitments, especially with reference to the wellbeing of their children. The picture of people as individualised and freed from the

---

[131] Family Justice Council *Annual Report and Accounts for 2006–07* (2008). See Appendix A for Terms of Reference set by the Secretary of State and Lord Chancellor.
[132] F Williams and the ESRC Cava Research Group *Rethinking Families* (Calouste Gulbenkian Foundation, 2004), p 41.

older constraints of marriage does not account for this connectedness and the influence it has on the choices people exercise in their family lives and personal relationships.'

It follows from this that social policy and family law, as far as possible, should be supportive of conflicted families and their children, rather than merely seeking to control them with heavy-handed surveillance backed implicitly by the threat of traumatic removal of children into care, where in any case past research evidence suggests that their futures may well be further blighted.[133]

To achieve this within the requirements of substantive law, family justice practitioners and court staff need to see themselves as working *with* parents and children on an essentially shared task of resolving conflicting interests fairly while protecting the vulnerable. After all, in the last resort the family justice process cannot be viewed simply in legalistic terms. It also has to be seen from a child welfare and community mental health perspective. Unfortunately, the traditional way of viewing the family justice process still largely marginalises the psycho-social aspects of this task. Instead, the prevailing mindset, reinforced by many court procedures, conditions many policy makers and practitioners to think in paternalistic terms of either an adversarial or inquisitorial approach to family justice. The former risks polarising family conflict, while the latter risks driving those on the receiving end into unhelpful defensive positions. Yet, as has been pointed out elsewhere,[134] the effectiveness of our family court welfare system will ultimately have to be judged by 'whether or not it promotes the interests of children and the attainment of emotional balance and stability in family relationships.'

Despite the Government's tougher restrictive and socially controlling approach, if progress towards a more participant interdisciplinary system of civil family justice is to be achieved, well informed and trained practitioners will have to go on driving home to politicians and officials the reasons for this approach and arguing the need to fund it properly. Then we may finally arrive at a unified civil system of child-friendly local family courts open to all citizens and their children alike and no longer constructed along socially divisive lines.

---

[133] See Department for Education and Skills *Care Matters: Transforming the Lives of Children and Young People in Care* Cm 6932 (2006), in which the Government acknowledges that children leaving care face very poor outcomes.

[134] G Douglas, M Murch and A Perry G Douglas, M Murch and A Perry 'Supporting Children when Parents Separate – a neglected family justice or mental health issue' [1996] CFLQ 121.

CHAPTER 6

FIFTY YEARS OF FAMILY LAW: AN OPINIONATED REVIEW

Michael Freeman

1957 AND ALL THAT

I have an involvement with family law which goes back nearly 50 years. I studied family law in 1964–1965, and first taught it in 1967, the year in which I also got married. The syllabus I studied in the mid-1960s was divorce-centric – the perimeters of cruelty were under scrutiny.[1] There was an unhealthy dose of nullity – volumes of the All England Reports opened at the relevant pages more naturally than, it seems, did some wives, and pages attracted marginal comments like 'he should have used a pencil sharpener'.[2] The only issues relating to children that were discussed were legitimacy (or rather illegitimacy) and adoption.

There were no refuges for victims of domestic violence[3] or contact centres. The closest we got to gender reassignment was the 'pantomime dame'. The radical suggestion as regards homosexuals was not, as now, that they should be allowed to marry,[4] but that they should be spared the sanction of the criminal law.[5] If you had spied a case called 'Up Yaws' in 1957[6] it would most probably have been about a conspiracy to corrupt public morals.[7] Abortion would not be legally permitted – it still has not been decriminalised[8] – for another 10 years,[9] but of course the 'Vera Drakes' were on hand to assist women in distress, and, as that film so graphically illustrated, 'rich girls' had no difficulty in finding doctors to terminate

---

[1] The cases of the moment were *Gollins v Gollins* [1964] AC 644 and *Williams v Williams* [1964] AC 698.
[2] In relation to *S v S (otherwise C)* [1956] P 1.
[3] Which only became (or rather became again) a 'social problem' in the early 1970s. The first refuge in Chiswick was established in 1971.
[4] As I argued in M Freeman 'Not Such A Queer Idea: Is There a case for Same Sex Marriages?' (1999) 16 *Journal of Applied Philosophy* 1.
[5] The *Report of the Committee on Homosexual Offences and Prostitution* Cmnd 247 (HMSO, 1957) – the Wolfenden Report, which so argued, was published in 1957. The government resisted its recommendation. It was another 10 years before homosexual sex was decriminalised.
[6] See *The 'Up Yaws'* [2007] 2 FLR 444.
[7] A crime resurrected in 1961. See *Shaw v DPP* [1962] AC 220, HL.
[8] The grounds for termination remain exceptions to the crime set out in the Offences Against the Person Act 1861, ss 57 and 58.
[9] Abortion Act 1967.

their pregnancies.[10] Because of the barriers to abortion – as well, of course, as poor contraception[11] and the low threshold of tolerance towards unmarried mothers – the infertile (who were fewer in number than today) had babies to adopt. We were not to hear of fertility treatment ('test-tube' babies) for another 20 years.[12] There was donor insemination – then called AID before concern was expressed that so called it might be confused with AIDS[13] – but discussion about this centred on such matters as whether it should be criminalised,[14] and whether if it was without the husband's consent it amounted to adultery.[15]

Children were barely seen, let alone heard. There was, of course, no child abuse.[16] The Kempes first wrote of the 'battered baby syndrome' in 1962.[17] The first articles on the subject appeared in England in 1963.[18] Hugh Bevan was, I think, the first lawyer to address the issue – in his 'Inaugural' in 1970.[19] For the 'discovery' of sexual abuse we had to await another quarter of a century. Given the opportunity to recognise the social problem in the 1920s we had missed it: children's voices had not been heard.[20]

Fifty years ago there was no discussion of children's rights:[21] *Gillick* was still 28 years away,[22] but the UN Declaration on the Rights of the Child was to come out in only 2 years.[23] There was no sense of this in England.

---

[10] I refer to Mike Leigh's film *Vera Drake* (2004).
[11] The contraceptive pill only became an option in the mid-1960s.
[12] Louise Brown was born in 1978.
[13] HIV/AIDS was first brought to our attention in 1981.
[14] See the Feversham Committee report, *Report of the Departmental Committee on Human Insemination* Cmnd 1105 (HMSO, 1960).
[15] In Scotland it was held not to do so: *Maclennan v Maclennan 1958 SLT 12*. Cf Canada: *Orford v Orford* (1921) 58 DLR 251. The Morton Royal Commission on Marriage and Divorce Cmd 9678 (HMSO, 1956) considered it should constitute a new ground of divorce (see para 90).
[16] A good discussion is N Parton *The Politics of Child Abuse* (Macmillan, 1985) particularly ch 3. See also B Corby *Child Abuse: Towards A Knowledge Base* (Open University Press, 2000), ch 3.
[17] CH Kempe et al 'The battered-child syndrome' (1962) 181 *Journal of the American Medical Association* 17.
[18] By D L Griffiths and F J Moynihan 'Multiple Epiphysial Injuries in Babies ("Battered Baby" Syndrome)' (1963) *British Medical Journal* (No 5372) 1558.
[19] *Child Protection and the Law* (University of Hull, 1970).
[20] See C Smart 'A History of Ambivalence and Conflict in the Discursive Construction of the "Child Victim" of Sexual Abuse' (1999) 8 *Social and Legal Studies* 391.
[21] The 'child liberation' movement, associated with Richard Farson (*Birthrights* 1978, Penguin) and John Holt (*Escape from Childhood* (Dutton, 1975)) emerged in the mid-1970s.
[22] *Gillick v West Norfolk and Wisbech AHA* [1986] AC 112.
[23] There is a full discussion of this in P Veerman *The Rights of the Child and the Changing Image of Childhood* (Martinus Nijhoff, 1992), pp 159–180. It is of interest that the proposal of Israel and Poland that discrimination against illegitimate children was wrong got virtually no support. That Israel's main support came from Iraq tells us something about the era – but I'm not sure what!

This was the era of *Billy Bunter*[24] and Jimmy Edwards' *Whacko!*[25] Edwards was one of a number of comedians to try to get into Parliament as a Tory MP – one, Gyles Brandreth, even succeeded, and gave us the 1994 Marriage Act![26] I've often wondered what our laws would look like if they were made by comedians! In 1957 there were, of course, no ASBOs,[27] but there was the slipper and the cane.[28] It was unthinkable then that corporal punishment would be abolished in schools: indeed, I remember in the early 1970s when the campaign to rid schools of the cane began, critics thought the abolitionists were a lunatic fringe.[29] Perhaps they were, but it took less than 30 years for their views to prevail.[30] The campaign to make it unlawful to hit children began in the late 1980s[31] and only a Canute (or a Blair)[32] would expect it to take as long to succeed. In 1957 even Sweden allowed children to be corporally chastised.[33]

But what I have said about children's rights can be generalised. We were not a rights-conscious society in 1957.[34] The European Convention on Human Rights was 7 years old, but it had had no impact on English law. It would be another 40 years before its rights were brought home.[35] Without it, one of its most famous critics – the Prince of Wales – would not have been able to marry Camilla[36] (though arguably he was already

---

[24] There were innumerable books by Frank Richards about Greyfriars. I doubt if any failed to include a caning of the fat anti-hero by Mr Quelch. And in the 1950s the BBC was regularly screening children's TV dramatisations of the Bunter books.

[25] Where there was more overt sexuality. This continued well beyond the 1950s: examples can be found in *Blackadder*. Nor should serialisations of serious classics like D H Lawrence's *The Rainbow* (on BBC TV in 1989) be overlooked.

[26] He thought he would be remembered for piloting this: *The Times*, 21 January 2003.

[27] A total of 5,110 were issued to children between April 1999 and December 2006 out of a total of 12,675 such orders: see http://www.crimereduction.homeoffice.gov.uk/asbos/asbos2.htm (accessed 24 October 2008).

[28] I was last caned in 1958 for 'bunking' off school to watch England play Spain at Wembley. The goals (England won 4–2) were more enjoyable than the punishment – a stroke for each goal!

[29] See P Newell (ed) *A Last Resort?* (Penguin, 1972).

[30] Corporal punishment in schools being finally abolished in 1998: School Standards and Framework Act 1998, s 131 – this actually removes the defence of justification, rather than making it unlawful as such, but it amounts to the same thing.

[31] I was instrumental in this: it led Barbara Amiel into castigating me in *The Times* for what she called the 'smack of statism'.

[32] Tony Blair, who may have been the oldest boy to have been caned at his public school, remained a virulent opponent of anti-smacking laws, using phrases like 'loving smack' and 'safe smack'. His imprint is firmly embedded in the so-called Department of Health Consultation Paper, *Protecting Children, Supporting Parents* (2000), which ruled out abolition and then purported to consult.

[33] Sweden's anti-smacking law was passed in 1979.

[34] This was the era of 'you've never had it so good' (Macmillian's speech was on 20 July 1957): see P Hennessy *Having It So Good* (Allen Lane, 2006) – rights/human rights etc do not figure in the Index at all. He attributes our interest in 'rights' to Herbert Hart assuming the Jurisprudence Chair at Oxford.

[35] By the Human Rights Act 1998.

[36] See R Probert 'The Wedding of The Prince of Wales: Royal Privileges and Human Rights' [2005] CFLQ 363.

married to her, Lord Hardwicke's Act not applying to him!).[37] No discussion of family law today can omit discussion of rights.[38] Contrast this with *A Century of Family Law* in 1957: royal marriages are discussed (the 1772 Act is, of course, not questioned)[39] and so is *renvoi*,[40] but rights are not indexed. Nor are human rights, women's rights or children's rights. None of this is in the slightest surprising. Feminism (or at least 'The Feminist movement') is – the discussion is by Norman St John-Stevas who detected 'minor inequalities' in 1957.[41] He was not over-concerned about unequal pay for equal work,[42] but then few were[43] – and equal pay has still not been achieved, despite legislation enacted in 1970.[44]

It is striking that none of the contributors to the collection *A Century of Family Law* are women – Olive Stone was across the road[45] – and that none of them is known as a family lawyer. The book is edited by a 'conflicts' lawyer (Ronald Graveson) and a property law scholar (Roger Crane). A cursory glance at the book provides firm evidence of how much the territory of family law has changed. Instead of chapters on financial provision on divorce, domestic violence, child abuse, children and local authorities, international child abduction, assisted reproduction, we find tort, contract, evidence and criminal law. And tort is not discussed in the context of a domestic violence remedy – it hardly could be, since husbands and wives could not sue each other in tort and anyway domestic violence was not then thought to exist.[46] Contract is not discussed in relation to pre-nuptials[47] or cohabitation contracts[48] – cohabitation is not a subject which would then have been thought to be within 'family law',[49] *Balfour v Balfour*[50] is discussed, but not critically.[51] The marital rape

---

[37] Did he therefore have a true 'common law' marriage with her?
[38] In particular, discussion of Art 8 of the European Convention on Human Rights.
[39] A good discussion is S Cretney 'The Royal Marriages Act 1772: A Footnote' (1995) 16 *Statute Law Review* 195.
[40] Which may have a role to play in choosing the law to apply to questions of formal validity of marriage.
[41] N St John-Stevas 'Woman In Public Law' in R H Graveson and F R Crane *A Century of Family Law* (Sweet and Maxwell, 1957), p 288.
[42] He discusses this at pp 285–286.
[43] A resolution favouring equal pay was, however, passed in the House of Commons as early as 1920 and in 1944 Parliament decided that female teachers should be paid the same as male ones: the vote was reversed at the instigation of Winston Churchill.
[44] Equal Pay Act 1970. Women now earn on average 87 per cent of male earnings: see ONS *Social Trends 38* (TSO, 2008), p 68.
[45] At LSE.
[46] But C A Morrison's chapter on 'tort' does not mention the tort of battery. It was 1962 before the law of tort could be invoked in a married domestic violence context.
[47] As yet not held to be binding. See B Clark 'Should Greater Prominence be given to Pre-nuptial contracts in the law of Ancillary Relief?' [2004] CFLQ 399.
[48] On which see E Kingdom 'Cohabitation Contracts and the Democratization of Personal Relations' (2000) 8 *Feminist Legal Studies* 5.
[49] I seem to remember an edition of *Bromley* which offered an 'appendix' on cohabitation!
[50] [1919] 2 KB 571.
[51] Critiques are M Freeman 'Contracting in the Haven: *Balfour v Balfour* Revisited' in R Halson (ed) *Exploring The Boundaries of Contract* (Dartmouth, 1996) and

immunity – which survived another 35 years[52] – is discussed by Mendes da Costa in the criminal law chapter – but there is no suggestion that it is unacceptable.[53] Of course, these are criticisms of what passed for legal scholarship in the mid-1950s. Black-letter law has very limited value. But family law, as a nascent discipline, was very much one of the poor relations and aped its models.

It would be comforting to dismiss this as merely the work of the 'Strand Polytechnic',[54] but things were no better – they were arguably worse – at the 'Godless institution of Gower Street'![55] Coincidentally – I refuse to believe it was a calculated decision – the Bentham Presidential lecture in 1957 was given by the leading family law judge, Charles Hodson.[56] He offers a conservative critique of the Morton Royal Commission[57] – but at least it is a critique. He is critical of the concept of irretrievable breakdown because it would take control away from the state and judges would have no function to perform. It would lead 'logically' he says to the Soviet Russia model. This slippery slope would end in Moscow! The *Current Legal Problems* volume for 1957 also published an article by the Catholic barrister Richard O'Sullivan[58] which, if summarised in a word, was to the effect that 100 years of family law had all been 'a mistake'.[59]

Family law in 1957 lacked a journal of its own. But both the *Law Quarterly Review* and the *Modern Law Review* published family law-related articles. In 1957 we had C K Allen on matrimonial cruelty[60] – the Law Reports of this era bulge with cases on cruelty.[61] The leading French lawyer, Marc Ancel, has an article in the LQR on *crime passionel* (of which we hear less today).[62] And there are articles in the LQR by Hugh Bevan,[63] Zelman Cowen,[64] Tony Guest[65] and Louis Blom-Cooper.[66] The *Modern Law Review* had less – perhaps surprisingly, since I believe LSE was the first university to teach family law. Louis Blom-Cooper is

---

J Wightman 'Intimate Relationships, Relational Contract Theory, and the Reach of Contract' (2000) 8 *Feminist Legal Studies* 93.

[52] Until *R v R* [1992] 1 AC 599 and Criminal Justice and Public Order Act 1994, s 142. See also *CR v United Kingdom; SW v United Kingdom* [1996] 1 FLR 434.

[53] See Michael D A Freeman 'Doing His Best to Sustain The Sanctity of Marriage' in N Johnson (ed) *Marital Violence* (Routledge & Kegan Paul, 1985), pp 124–146.

[54] As UCL students call it!

[55] The Kings' jibe at UCL. In 1957 Kings still insisted on compulsory chapel for students!

[56] C Hodson 'Some Aspects of Divorce Law and Practice' (1957) 10 CLP 1.

[57] Royal Commission on Marriage and Divorce, Cmd 9678 (HMSO, 1956).

[58] R O'Sullivan 'The Century of Divorce Jurisdiction' (1957) 10 CLP 12.

[59] Ibid, 35.

[60] C K Allen 'Matrimonial Cruelty' (1957) 73 LQR 316 at 512.

[61] For example, *Forbes v Forbes* [1956] P 16; *Crawford v Crawford* [1956] P 195; *Waters v Waters* [1956] P 344; *Thompson v Thompson* [1957] P 19; *Cade v Cade* [1957] 1 All ER 609.

[62] M Ancel 'Le Crime Passionnel' (1957) 73 LQR 36.

[63] H K Bevan 'Belief in the Other Spouse's Adultery' (1957) 73 LQR 225.

[64] Z Cowen 'Choice of Law Provisions in Matrimonial Causes' (1957) 73 LQR 350.

[65] A G Guest 'Family Provision and the *Legitima Portio*' (1957) 73 LQR 74.

[66] L J Blom-Cooper 'Obiter Dicta – A Proper Valuation' (1957) 73 LQR 453.

found here too, writing on adoption and parental responsibility:[67] it is salutary to be reminded that parental responsibility emerged in this context long before it found its way into the Children Act of 1989. There is a note by Olive Stone (on the Matrimonial Causes Rules 1957) and this is ahead of its time in expressing a concern for the status of children on divorce.[68] The main article in the MLR on a family law-related theme is on nullity jurisdiction (by Grodecki).[69] There is a lot of interest at this time in the private international law of the family: Cowen's article in the LQR on choice of law in matrimonial causes is an impressive piece which stands the test of time.

The Law Reports of 1957 are also worth excavating. Excavation is what it is about, because there is only one case in the Probate reports for 1957 that I still teach (or remember!). It is *Taczanowska v Taczanowki*[70] – it is very useful if you want to correct students who think they know what a common law marriage is. It is also a good example of the use (or possible use) of *renvoi* in family law – just in case any student sees the references to *renvoi* in *The Century of Family Law*'s index! The family law cases of 1957 otherwise are buried in the mists of history. The odd one is still footnoted. Can a 12-year-old commit adultery is one issue raised.[71] One wonders after *Gillick*,[72] and *Thompson and Venables* (the Bulger case)[73] whether we would come to the same answer today.

What is striking is that there are 26 cases reported in the Probate reports for 1957 (would that we today only had 26 new cases to read each year!), and that none of them relates specifically to child law issues. There is a case on paternity,[74] but it is marginal to such concerns as the right to know one's identity. Another case is about school fees,[75] but it is hardly about a child. Divorce issues dominate, and resonate the concerns of a bygone era, making it all the more anomalous that the fault lines survive in contemporary divorce law.[76]

1957 is not untypical of the era. Look at the Probate reports for 1956 or 1958 and the same picture emerges: divorce and conflicts issues dominate. In 1956 there is one 'child' case – *Re Wilby* on the recognition of a foreign

---

[67] L J Blom-Cooper 'Adoption Applications and Parental Responsibility' (1957) 20 MLR 473.
[68] O Stone 'Matrimonial Causes Rules 1957' (1957) 20 MLR 415.
[69] J Grodecki 'Recent Developments in Nullity Jurisdiction' (1957) 20 MLR 566.
[70] [1957] P 301.
[71] *Barnett v Barnett* [1957] P 78.
[72] *Gillick v West Norfolk and Wisbech AHA* [1986] AC112.
[73] On which see M Freeman 'The James Bulger Tragedy: Childish Innocence and the Construction of Guilt' in M Freeman *The Moral Status of Children* (Martinus Nijhoff, 1997), p 235. See also S Asquith 'When Children Kill Children' (1996) 3 *Childhood* 99.
[74] *Nokes v Nokes* [1957] P 213.
[75] *Farrant v Farrant* [1957] P 188.
[76] With the demise of the 1996 reforms.

adoption:[77] in 1958 there is also one case about children, concerning wards of court.[78] The Chancery reports of the era are also not reporting cases centring on children.

FAMILY LAW AS A DISCRETE ENTITY

1957 was also, it should not be forgotten, the year of *Bromley*, the first textbook on family law. It was firmly rooted within a positivistic and legalistic framework. Family 'law' was a discrete entity, not part of a social continuum.[79] Of course, viewing the discipline in this way had a number of consequences.

The law was seen apart from the values it embodied, and helped to structure and restructure – and it is by no means a one-way process. Thus, to take an example, and indeed a central one, the relationship between law and patriarchy, so central to an understanding of family law, was not understood.[80] It is difficult to forget Lord Denning's famous justification for the resurrection of the one-third rule in *Wachtel v Wachtel*,[81] or his reasoning in the two cases of *Button v Button*[82] and *Cooke v Head*.[83] Ignore the values involved, and these two cases may be readily distinguished. But it is important to look at the values. In *Button* the argument was that 'a wife does not get a share in the house simply because she cleans the walls or works in the garden or helps her husband with the painting and decorating'.[84] In *Cooke v Head*, by contrast, where the female cohabitant (as we now call her) did 'quite an unusual amount of work for a woman' – she used a sledgehammer to demolish old buildings, worked a cement mixer and did other 'male' activities, thus demonstrating that she was a crafts*man* – her work was richly rewarded.[85] The message was clear: what woman are expected to do has no economic value, but 'real' work has to be compensated.

Family law's image of the family

A further consequence of the way family law as a discipline developed was that what emerged as family law, in the eyes of most family lawyers,

---

[77] [1956] P 174.
[78] *Andrews v Andrews and Sullivan and Sullivan* [1958] P 217.
[79] And see generally Judith Shklar *Legalism* (Harvard UP, 1964).
[80] On which see Michael D A Freeman 'Legal Ideologies, Patriarchal Precedents, and Domestic Violence' in Michael D A Freeman (ed) *State, Law and Family: Critical Perspectives* (Tavistock, 1984), pp 51–78. See also Alison Diduck and Katherine O'Donovan *Feminist Perspectives on Family Law* (Routledge-Cavendish, 2006).
[81] [1973] Fam 72 at 94.
[82] [1968] 1 All ER 1064.
[83] [1972] 2 All ER 38.
[84] [1968] 1 All ER 1064 at 1067.
[85] [1972] 2 All ER 38 at 40.

academics and practitioners, was a narrow and distorted image both of the subject of the discipline – the family – and of the processes which regulate the family.

Looking at this first in relation to 'the family', we may observe that family law is about husbands and wives (or those who live in relationships 'like' husbands and wives) and the children they produce. Of course, this in part is true, but only in part. Why is it that we take it for granted that the family revolves around a sexual tie? Why is the 'sexual family' invested by our culture – including our legal culture – and society with exclusive legitimacy? Why is it, as Martha Fineman puts it, the 'foundational institution'?[86] The sexual tie may not be a marital bond, it may even exist between members of the same sex, but it remains at the core of our understanding of intimacy and family connection. In these terms, to take an example, single mothers are deviant: we never talk of married mothers, because mothers are assumed to be married or to be in equivalent relationships. We define children, even today, in terms of the relationships between their parents. The terms 'legitimate' and 'illegitimate' no longer exist[87] – this is a distinction few would have questioned in 1957 – and the legislation eschews terms like 'marital' and 'non-marital' (contrary to Law Commission advice).[88] Nevertheless, the relationship between a child and his/her father still depends on the father's relationship with the mother.[89] Step-children are only children of the family when 'treated' as such by both their parent and the person to whom the parent is now married (or is in a civil partnership with).[90] Anything less will not do. But isn't this odd: are the 'couple' and their children not a family? Is this not as they would conceptualise it?[91] Relationships between parents and adult children, even adult dependent children – think of the many in their 20s or even 30s who remain 'at home' or have returned to the nest – fit ill within conventional concepts of the family: this is well-illustrated by the discomfort the law feels when confronted by a family provision application by an adult child.[92] We are in a period of 'shifting familiarity',[93] as Alison Diduck has pointed out, but the core remains essentially tied to the sexual family.

---

[86] *The Neutered Mother, The Sexual Family and other Twentieth Century Tragedies* (Routledge, 1995).
[87] Family Law Reform Act 1987, s 1.
[88] Law Commission *Illegitimacy* (Law Com No 118) (1982), para 4. It has been 'abolished' in Scotland: see Family Law (Scotland) Act 1985, s 21.
[89] Unmarried fathers do not automatically have parental responsibility.
[90] Matrimonial Causes Act 1973, s 52(1).
[91] E Jackson 'What is a Parent?' in A Diduck and K O'Donovan (eds) *Feminist Perspectives on Family Law* (Routledge-Cavendish, 2006), pp 59–74.
[92] For example, *Re Jennings (Deceased)* [1994] 1 FLR 536 and *Garland v Morris* [2007] 2 FLR 528. For a comparison with New Zealand see N Peart and A Borkowski 'Provision for Adult Children on Death – the Lesson from New Zealand' [2000] CFLQ 333.
[93] See A Diduck 'Shifting Familiarity' (2005) 58 CLP 235.

Family law and social control

If the image of the family was narrow, so too was our understanding of the law's involvement with it. As with other areas of law, we saw the law's involvement – and thus also the state's – only at the point of breakdown.[94] It is true that the law refrains from intervention in ongoing relationships, though this can be over-emphasised.[95] This relative abstinence is said to reflect the values we place on autonomy, integrity and privacy.[96] But, in seeing the law as occupying a central hegemonic position, we overlook the ways in which the family is controlled by other than legal rules and principles. Order is not just constructed by law. Of course, attempts to shift from law to other forms of social control do not always work – or work well. The transfer of child maintenance to a regulatory body – the Child Support Agency – has been a dismal failure.[97] And I see no reason to hope for better from C-MEC.[98] The abortive attempt to reform divorce law in 1996 is a further illustration of resistance to new forms of dispute resolution.[99] But, if we had not totally immersed ourselves in law reports, we would have seen the subtle and less than subtle ways in which family interactions were socially controlled. As Richard Sennett saw it, the boundaries between what is intimate and what is public have become blurred.[100] Marriage has become 'medicalised', subjected to expert knowledge, guidance and intervention. We are expected to divorce 'responsibly'[101] and also to meet our caring responsibilities.[102] As Val Gillies put it in a recent article: 'Reasonable, rational moral citizens ... seek to do the best for their children'.[103]

Marriage and its discourses

There are two discourses on marriage. One emphasises social control, the other autonomy. The social control discourse is dominated by a view of

---

[94] See O Kahn-Freund, Editorial introduction to John Eekelaar *Family Security and Family Breakdown* (Penguin, 1971), p 7.
[95] As in J Eekelaar *Family Security and Family Breakdown* (Penguin, 1971), p 76. See also his *Family and Social Policy* (Weidenfeld and Nicolson, 1978) and now *Family Law and Personal Life* (Oxford UP, 2006). Contrast my 'Inaugural': 'Towards A Critical Theory of Family Law' (1985) 38 CLP 153.
[96] But see Carole Pateman *The Disorder of Women* (Polity Press, 1989), ch 6, and Freeman, op cit, n 95 above, at p 166.
[97] David Blunkett MP, when a government Minister, described it as a 'shambles'.
[98] The Child Maintenance and Enforcement Commission.
[99] Though the mediation pilot was quite successful (see G Davis et al *Monitoring Publicly Funded Mediation* Legal Services Commission, 2001); the information meeting pilot, by contrast, showed no real support for such meetings (see J Walker et al *Information Meetings and Associated Provisions within the Family Law Act 1996: Final Evaluation Report* DCA, 2001).
[100] *The Fall of Public Man* (Routledge, 1992), p 112.
[101] See Helen Reece *Divorcing Responsibly* (Hart, 2003).
[102] See Val Gillies 'Meeting Parents' Needs? Discourses of "Support" and "Inclusion" in Family Policy' (2005) 25 *Critical Social Policy* 70.
[103] Ibid at 75.

marriage as an institution involving constraints, clear and prescribed social roles, and penalties for those who break the conventions and norms governing marital relations. The autonomy discourse emphasises choice and depicts the social actor as a rational person empowered to shape family life in accordance with his/her life prospects. These discourses express 'ideal – types': they are ends of a continuum, and marriage and those who work with marriage – institutions ranging from the courts to mediators and counsellors and social workers – operate in the space between these polar positions.

If we narrow our focus, as the discipline of family law has tended to do, to family legislation and to what the courts are doing, it is easy to conclude that the autonomy discourse is in the ascendancy. Yes, we got away without the divorce reforms of 1996 – surely the first legislation in history to mandate 'thinking' (reflection and consideration). And yes there is a more relaxed attitude to whom one may marry, as a result of the Marriage (Prohibited Degrees of Relationship) Act 1986, and to where one may marry.[104] But do we need restrictions based on affinity at all?[105] Or even based on consanguinity?[106] And why shouldn't religious ceremonies be allowed in castles and hotels, or even in the open air?[107] Jews have long married in this way without the earth opening up! There is also greater tolerance of polygamy,[108] even of polygamous ceremonies abroad by those domiciled in this country.[109] But the tolerance only goes so far: do we not need rational debate on whether a plurality of spouses should be allowed at all?[110] And if we persist with civil partnership – in my opinion an absurd half-way house – why should monogamy be imposed on the gay? We can also now change our gender and marry, or enter into a civil partnership, in the new one.[111] Even here there are controls: you must be 18 (but you can, of course, marry at 16[112] and consent to medical treatment at 16,[113] or less if *Gillick* competent),[114] and you must satisfy a panel that you have or have had gender dysphoria, have lived in the

---

[104] See Marriage Act 1994.
[105] Australia does not have these prohibitions: see H Finlay 'Farewell to Affinity and the Celebration of Kinship' (1976) 5 *University of Tasmania LR* 10.
[106] Though public opinion would not, I think, support a change. See the case of twins separated at birth who married, whose annulment was widely reported on 12 January 2008 (eg *The Guardian*).
[107] The Marriage Act 1994 does not allow these: what can be said or sung is controlled, if loosely.
[108] This began after the Second World War with *Baindail v Baindail* [1946] P 122. And see P Shah 'Attitudes to Polygamy in English Law' (2003) 52 ICLQ 369.
[109] Private International Law (Miscellaneous Provisions) Act 1995, s 5.
[110] On these debates in Africa see F Banda *Women, Law and Human Rights – An African Perspective* (Hart, 2005).
[111] Gender Recognition Act 2004.
[112] Marriage Act 1949, s 1.
[113] Family Law Reform Act 1969, s 8(1).
[114] But whether a *Gillick* competent child could consent to a gender change is debatable. See the Australian decisions of *Re A* (1993) 16 Fam LR 715 and *Re Alex* [2004] Fam CA 297.

acquired gender for 2 years and intend to do so until death.[115] And how is one to interpret the growth of cohabitation law? As an enhancement of autonomy to shape relationships or as the imposition of 'marriage-like' consequences on those who may have wished to avoid marriage?[116]

Family law's neglect of family issues

A third consequence of the way family law has developed has been its continuing neglect of areas of life and social regulation, without an understanding of which it is not really possible to grasp what are generally agreed to be its central features. This is less so now of housing law or homelessness legislation or social security law than it was – certainly in 1957 family law did not embrace these areas – but it remains the case with what is euphemistically called 'community care'.[117] Perhaps because family law has revolved around a sexual tie, it has been easy to overlook the elderly.[118] In an ageing world, should not family law embrace family relationships with, and responsibilities towards the elderly? Herring's textbook, *Family Law*, is conspicuous for recognising this, and for penetrating beyond the question of elder abuse.[119] In relation to such abuse the textbook writers are behind the legislature for, though this has not specifically targeted elder abuse, the concept of 'associated persons'[120] is wide enough to embrace violence against the elderly in the typical family setting.

Of greater significance is family law's neglect of community care. Community care could not be more inappropriately labelled: it is care by the family, in effect disproportionately care by women (daughters and daughters-in-law in the main).[121] It raises important questions which family law has barely begun to address. If the state is imposing responsibility for caring for the elderly onto daughters and daughters-in-law, should it not consider giving them status? Ought we to consider the rights and responsibilities involved in this caring relationship? It is

---

[115] See Gender Recognition Act 2004.
[116] See, further, R Probert 'Looking back on the overlooked: cohabitants and the law 1857–2007' in this volume.
[117] Richard Titmuss referred to its 'comforting appellation' in *Commitment To Welfare* (Allen and Unwin, 1968), p 104.
[118] Yet 18.5 per cent of the population is over the retirement age: see National Statistics *Focus on Older People* (National Statistics, 2005). See further J Herring 'Older People and the Law' (2007) 60 CLP 148 and J Herring 'The Place of Carers' in M Freeman (ed) *Law and Bioethics* (Oxford UP, 2008). See also *B Borough Council v S (By the Official Solicitor)* [2007] 1 FLR 1600.
[119] J Herring *Family Law* (Pearson Longman, 3rd edn, 2007), ch 12. He does, of course, deal with elder abuse, a subject to which I devoted a couple of pages back in 1979: *Violence In The Home – A Socio-Legal Study* (Gower, 1979), pp 237–239 (but, oh dear, I called it 'granny bashing').
[120] Family Law Act 1996, s 62(3).
[121] See J Finch and D Groves 'Community Care and the Family: A Case for Equal Opportunities' (1980) 9 *Journal of Social Policy* 487; C Ungerson *Policy is Personal: Sex, Gender and Informal Care* (Tavistock, 1987).

perhaps a relationship best understood by reference to, or at least by analogy with, the trust relationship. The implications of extending a woman's home caring role, particularly if she has to give up work – for yet a further time – similarly need consideration. In terms of property interests and financial provision, should any significance be attached to whose parents – his or hers – she is expected to look after? (It is to be assumed that it is a contribution to the welfare of the family,[122] even of this is to give 'family' a broader meaning than it usually has.) 'Community care' raises all sorts of issues about state regulation and social control, as social workers become increasingly involved with 'normal' as opposed to deviant families, traditionally their clientele. This makes us ask whether they could yet become entangled with the lives of 'normal' families outside this context – yet another step towards the 'triumph of the therapeutic'.[123]

CONTRASTS WITH 1957

What would Lord Hodson[124] or Richard O'Sullivan[125] make of today's family law issues? What would Norman St John-Stevas[126] make of *White v White*[127] or *Miller/McFarlane*?[128] Or, for example, of the emancipation of divorce?[129] Was the failure of the 1996 Act the last throes of the reins of paternalism? What would the commentators of 1957 make of the secularisation of marriage, its decline, the huge increase in civil marriages, the replacement of marriage by cohabitation, the 'norm' of divorce? Marriage has become a terminable contact, broken and repudiated as often as other contracts, perhaps more so. There has been an ideological shift in which marriage has come to be seen as a social relation dependent on satisfactions and rewards.[130] It has freed itself from the traditional influences which used to shape it, such as tradition, religious dogma, and kin bargaining. Ironically, this has occurred in a period of history in which there has been substantial growth in population of people with Asian backgrounds, many of whom live their lives against the backdrop of the very traditional influences rejected by the majority. English courts,

---

[122] Matrimonial Causes Act 1973, s 25(2)(f): of which this is only of value where there is a divorce etc. See, further, J Twigg 'Carers, Families, Relatives: Socio-Legal Conceptions of Care-giving Relationships' (1994) JSWFL 279.
[123] Philip Rieff's phrase in his book of that title, *The Triumph of the Therapeutic: Uses of Faith after Freud* (Intercollegiate Studies Institute, 2006).
[124] C Hodson 'Some Aspects of Divorce Law and Practice' (1957) 10 CLP 1.
[125] R O'Sullivan 'The Century of Divorce Jurisdiction' (1957) 10 CLP 12.
[126] N St John-Stevas 'Woman In Public Law' in R H Graveson and F R Crane *A Century of Family Law* (Sweet and Maxwell, 1957), p 288.
[127] [2001] 1 AC 596.
[128] [2006] UKHL 24, [2006] 2 AC 618.
[129] This is not total, of course: total might involve the disintegration of the family, as in early Soviet experiments described in O Figes *The Whisperers: Private Life in Stalin's Russia* (Metropolitan Books, 2007).
[130] See A Giddens *Modernity and Self-Identity* (Polity Press, 1991), p 244. See also J Finch and D Morgan 'Marriage in the 1980s: A New Sense of Realism' in D Clark *Domestic Life and Social Change* (Routledge 1991), p 55.

which once – but long before 1957 – met the challenges of arranged (and sometimes forced) marriages are now having to forge remedies to protect young women caught in this clash of cultures.[131] Multiculturalism[132] was unheard of in 1957 – it was called private international law and this sorted out Polish marriages.[133] We may soon get a sense of déja vu as *'ska' v 'ski'* returns! Perhaps, more s 5 defences will be raised by Catholics of Polish origin?[134]

The real 'shock of the new' would be the way that family law reaches to those who deviate from the norm, who are gay or who have gender dysphoria. In 1957 the gay were more likely to find their way to Reading gaol than its register office.[135] In 1957 I doubt if the first sex change operation had yet taken place: the early ones, you may remember, were in Casablanca.[136] In relation to the latter we have gone from Ormrod J's biological determinism,[137] via the ambivalence of permitting sex changes on the NHS whilst having a legal system which refused to accept the results,[138] to Gender Recognition Panels[139] in a third of a century. Other countries moved more swiftly. There are still panels and therefore controls. As far as the gay are concerned, marriage is still not allowed. Civil partnership – the legislation of a 'separate but equal' policy which would be unacceptable in any other context – is.[140] The media comments on its popularity, but the truth is that few gay couples are knotting the tie, and few will. Gay marriage is not such a queer idea, and it will come.[141] Perhaps we should open a book on it! We are not, it should not be forgotten, very fussy about who we allow to marry. You only have to be 16 – and you can't even buy cigarettes until you are 18. We allow murderers and rapists to marry, even those who have murdered or raped previous

---

[131] *Re SK (an Adult) (Forced Marriage: Appropriate Relief)* [2006] 1 WLR 81; *Re SA (Vulnerable Adult with Capacity: Marriage)* [2006] 1 FLR 867.

[132] So issues such as whether it is bad for women or children were not raised. On the former see S M Okin *Is Multiculturalism Bad for Women?* (Princeton UP, 1999). On the latter, see M Freeman 'The Morality of Cultural Pluralism' (1995) 3 *International Journal of Children's Rights* 1.

[133] Such as *Taczanowska v Taczanowski* [1957] P 301. There were a whole series of cases involving Polish nationals who married in displaced persons camps etc in the turmoil following the end of the Second World War. One is reported the following year: *Kochanski v Kochanska* [1958] P 147.

[134] Matrimonial Causes Act 1973, s 5: refusal of decree of divorce in 5-year separation cases, on ground of grave hardship to the respondent. The only fully reported case, thus far, concerns a Sicilian Catholic woman: see *Rukat v Rukat* [1975] Fam 63.

[135] Following in Oscar Wilde's footsteps: for discussion of the trial see R Ellmann *Oscar Wilde* (Hamish Hamilton, 1987), ch xvii. See S Cretney 'The troublemakers: cranks, psychiatrists and other mischievous nuisances' – their role in reform of English family law in the nineteenth and twentieth centuries', Chapter 2 above.

[136] April Ashley's took place there: *Corbett v Corbett* [1971] P 83.

[137] In *Corbett v Corbett*, ibid.

[138] *Sheffield and Horsham v United Kingdom* [1998] 2 FLR 928 comments on this incongruence.

[139] Established by the Gender Recognition Act 2004.

[140] On this 'apartheid' see P Tatchell 'Civil Partnerships Are Divorced from Reality' *The Guardian*, 19 December 2005.

[141] See M Freeman *Understanding Family Law* (Sweet and Maxwell, 2007), pp 21–26.

spouses. We even facilitate such marriages in prisons. We allow child abusers to marry. Sadists, masochists and fetishists. Those on their death-bed. Transvestites – the groom may if he wishes wear a bridal dress. And, furthermore, there is no law requiring persons wishing to marry to prove that they are heterosexual: homosexuals may marry women – and do – and lesbian women may marry men. Indeed, gay men may marry gay women. Critics often invoke – rather as Lord Hodson did – the slippery slope. One,[142] in language reminiscent of Lord Hodson, thought homosexuality was more dangerous than communism! (Lord Devlin virtually equated them.) Another[143] wondered where it would end – marriage with pets, or even worse, polygamy!

There are huge contrasts too in the way financial responsibilities are viewed on divorce. The concept 'financial provision' did not exist in 1957[144] and therefore it does not figure in *A Century of Family Law*. But what looks incongruous to us today is how little attention was focused on the question. The book devotes only a few pages to the issues. The law reports suggest there was little to contend about. There are cases on alimony pending suit,[145] wilful neglect to maintain[146] and the meaning of ante-nuptial settlement.[147] There is one distinguishing *Hyman v Hyman*,[148] and one on secured periodical payments.[149] À propos of *Hyman*, Barton remarks that the incidents of the marriage relationship are a matter of public concern, and cannot be altered by a private agreement.[150] This is worth quoting, for we will find little recognition of the private-public divide and its implications then – or, for that matter, now.[151] Lacey's comment[152] that:

> 'the ideology of the public/private dichotomy allows government to clean its hands of any *responsibility* for the state of the "private" world and *depoliticizes* the disadvantages which inevitably spill over the alleged divide by affecting the position of the "privately" disadvantaged in the "public" world.'

---

[142] H Arkes 'The Closet Stranger' *National Review*, 5 July 1993, p 45.
[143] H Jaffa 'Our Ancient Faith: A Reply to Professor Anastaplo' in *Original Intent and the Framers of the Constitution* (Regnery, 1994), p 383.
[144] It is used first after the Matrimonial Proceedings and Property Act 1970.
[145] *Taylor v National Assistance Board* [1957] P 101; *Sterne v Sterne* [1957] P 168; *Waller v Waller* [1956] P 300.
[146] *Piggott v Piggott* [1958] P 1.
[147] *Best v Best* [1956] P 76; *Hindley v Hindley* [1957] 2 All ER 653; *Prescott (formerly Fellowes) v Fellowes* [1958] P 260.
[148] *Russell v Russell* [1956] P 283.
[149] *Bradley v Bradley* [1956] P 326.
[150] J C Barton 'The Enforcement of Financial Provisions' in R H Graveson and F R Crane *A Century of Family Law* (Sweet and Maxwell, 1957), p 367.
[151] But see K O'Donovan *Sexual Divisions in Law* (Weidenfeld and Nicolson, 1985).
[152] N Lacey 'Theory into Practice? Pornography and the Public/Private Dichotomy' (1993) 20 *Journal of Law and Society* 93 at 97.

is as true now as it was when she wrote this in 1993 and as applicable to the financial consequences of divorce as to pornography (which is what it was written in relation to).

Most reactions to the *White v White* and *Miller/McFarlane* decisions have been favourable.[153] And so they should be. The law is attempting to redress an imbalance in the economic power of husbands and wives (or at least most of them). We can see the pension reforms of 1995 and 1999 as similarly focused.[154] But the law, and in particular the private law associated with marriage, divorce and its consequences, can only achieve so much. As long as women's earnings are less – the impact of the Equal Pay Act has been disappointing[155] – and women's working lives are punctuated by having and bringing up children, as long as they remain the primary homemakers, many of them will suffer if their marriages break down. Lady Sorrell[156] and Mrs Charman[157] are typical. We cannot concentrate exclusively on private support law: we cannot avoid 'asking the more basic questions around the division of responsibilities among men, women and society, and around the greater issues of sex equality in the economy generally'.[158] Pamela Symes pointed out, as long ago as 1985, that in very few cases does financial provision on divorce 'adequately recompense an ex-wife for the many disadvantages she suffers when her marriage ends, and distinguishing between specifically marriage-related disabilities and the more general ones is not always a simple exercise'.[159] The law must deal, as Diduck and Orton note, 'with the society it has helped to create and play its part in shaping ideologies it helps to support'.[160] It is important that we are now talking about equality and fairness. But we are still situating these concepts within a private relationship. It is as if it is none of the state's business, as if private adjustment can ignore public inequality. Maintenance after divorce has the effect of containing 'the problem' within the private issue, a personal conflict, and not a matter of public policy.[161] Can a private law of maintenance ever be anything other than unfair? It is predicated on sex roles and sex ranks. Child-rearing and homemaking are perceived as second-class activities, and those who fulfil these functions (mainly women) are marginalised. The decisions in *White* and in *Miller/McFarlane* are important because they recognise these tasks as valuable,

---

[153] There are critics, eg S Cretney 'A Community of Property System Imposed Judicial Decision' (2003) 119 LQR 349; J Eekelaar 'Shared Income after Divorce: A Step Too Far' (2005) 121 LQR 1.
[154] Pensions Act 1995, s 166 and Welfare Reform and Pensions Act 1999.
[155] Since the implementation of the Equal Pay Act women's wages have increased from two-thirds of the average male wage to 87 per cent: see ONS *Social Trends 38* (TSO, 2008), p 68.
[156] [2006] 1 FLR 497.
[157] [2007] 1 FLR 1246.
[158] Per A Diduck and H Orton 'Equality and Support for Spouses (1994) 57 MLR 681 at 686.
[159] 'Indissolubility and the Clean Break' (1985) 48 MLR 44 at 51.
[160] Diduck and Orton, op cit, at 687.
[161] See C Smart *The Ties That Bind* (Routledge, 1984).

but attentive reading of the judgments makes it clear they are nevertheless secondary, to be measured against the more primary money-earning role. The 'yardstick of equality'[162] demands more than the adjustment of a private relationship. Equality cannot be achieved without true equality in the workplace – the end of discrimination, equal pay, family-friendly workplaces, good quality and affordable child-care. *White* and *Miller/McFarlane* address marriage-related disabilities, but not the more general handicaps faced by women.

The gulf between 1957 and today is even more striking when we look at children. Read a passage like the following (written by P H Pettit) and you find it difficult to believe that it represents the thinking of the mid–1950s:

> 'Where ... a father is prima facie entitled to custody but the court considers it undesirable that the child should be separated from its [sic] mother, it may decree that the child shall not be removed from the care and control of the mother until further order.'[163]

This is done, he adds, 'particularly where the child is very young'. Although the 'first and paramountcy' test is mentioned, there is no discussion of it. Although Bowlby's thesis about maternal deprivation had already been popularised in *Child Care and the Growth of Love*,[164] there is no understanding of the implications of attachment. The child is an 'it', a piece of property, a package to be moved about (in Dame Elizabeth Butler-Sloss's memorable put-down).[165] There is no attention whatsoever to the child as a person who may, therefore, have views. There is a discussion too of 'subsidiary' parental rights: religion, education and marriage (and in that order). Most of the 'rights' relating to education are of course 'responsibilities'. The concept of parental responsibility has not yet emerged, but nor as yet has any thinking as to how it is to be regarded. In 1957 the liberal paradigm was implicit. In the period under review it became dominant, only to be eclipsed as post-liberalism (in particular communitarianism and the feminist ethics of care) has taken root. As Helen Reece explains:

> 'post-liberal responsibility is no longer about discrete decisions; responsible behaviour has become a way of being, a mode of thought; the focus has shifted from the content of the decision to the process of making the decision.'[166]

---

[162] As formulated in *White v White* [2001] 1 AC 596.
[163] P H Pettit 'Parental Control and Guardianship' in R H Graveson and F R Crane *A Century of Family Law* (Sweet and Maxwell, 1957), p 74.
[164] J Bowlby *Child Care and the Growth of Love* (Penguin, 1953). It was published earlier as a WHO publication.
[165] In *Re B (A Minor) (Residence Order: Ex Parte)* [1992] 2 FLR 1 at 5.
[166] See H Reece 'From Parental Responsibility to Parenting Responsibly' in M Freeman (ed) *Law and Sociology* (Oxford UP, 2006), p 459.

At the same time parental responsibility has expanded, and has been redefined. From being about authority, current governmental initiatives identify parental responsibility with accountability.[167] The 'good' parent is constructed as resourceful and ethically responsible, 'able to recognise or learn what is best for their children and tailor their behaviour accordingly'.[168] And so we have got the parenting order, targeted of course at anti-social behaviour of children and not the abusive behaviour of parents (for example at abuse or neglect).[169]

In 1957 children were of course abused, physically, sexually and emotionally. This is skirted over in *A Century of Family Law*.[170] Indeed, legislation targeted at child cruelty had been resisted as late as 1889, though it was passed in that year.[171] The sponsor of the 1889 Act was 'anxious that we should give children almost the same protection that we give ... domestic animals'.[172] The resistance is explicable because such legislation was thought to undermine the sacred rights of parents, in particular fathers.[173] The 1889 Act seemed to have had an effect. By World War I, although more cases were being brought to the attention of the NSPCC, the percentage of prosecutions was in decline.[174] Why? The Home Office said children were being better cared for. But more likely it was a decline in the birth rate, the war and depression diverting attention from the issue, and complacency – misplaced confidence. And, as Dingwall et al point out, child protection (save at the end of the nineteenth century) had never been a major concern of the state. Its real worry was the threat provided by inadequate moral socialisation of children to the social order.[175] Whatever the reason, violence was de-emphasised, and child neglect, which it was thought led to delinquency, became the focus. And over sexual abuse a discreet veil was

---

[167] See L Koffman 'Holding Parents To Account: Tough on Children, Tough on the Causes of Children' (2008) 35 *Journal of Law and Society* 113.

[168] See V Gillies 'Meeting Parents' Needs? Discourses of "Support" and "Inclusion" in Family Policy' (2005) 25 *Critical Social Policy* 70 at 75.

[169] For an argument that parenting orders should be used with child abusers see M Freeman 'Family Values and Family Justice' (1997) 50 CLP 315.

[170] Child cruelty legislation is briefly referred to (see P H Pettit 'Parental Control and Guardianship' in R H Graveson and F R Crane *A Century of Family Law* (Sweet and Maxwell, 1957), p 70).

[171] Prevention of Cruelty to, and Protection of, Children Act 1889, and see G Behlmer *Child Abuse and Moral Reform in England 1870–1908* (Stanford University Press, 1982).

[172] Philip Mundella MP, *Hansard*, HC Deb, vol 337, col 229. There are striking parallels in the USA (the Mary Ellen Wilson case). This is documented in E Shelman and S Lazoritz *The Mary Ellen Wilson Abuse Case and the Beginning of Children's Rights in 19th Century America* (McFarland, 2005).

[173] This argument was used by the Attorney-General in 1889 to counter the move to criminalise child cruelty. See *Hansard*, HC Deb, vol 337, col 227. On the sacredness of father's rights see *Re Agar-Ellis* (1883) 24 Ch D 317. As Behlmer *Child Abuse and Moral Reform in England 1870–1908* puts it (at p 9): 'to patrol the home was a sacrilege'.

[174] According to the Home Office, because children of the poorer classes were being better cared for: *Report of The Work of The Children's Branch* (HMSO, 1923), pp 19–70.

[175] R Dingwall, J Eekelaar and T Murray 'Childhood as a Social Problem: A Survey of the History of Legal Regulation' (1984) 11 *Journal of Law and Society* 207.

drawn. Child sexual abuse within the family was not discussed publicly. It was thought to be exclusively a vice of the poor.[176] Incest became a crime only in 1908,[177] but there were few prosecutions.[178] A Royal Commission on Venereal Diseases in 1916[179] – there are contemporary echoes in South Africa[180] – reported as a 'fact' that sex with a virgin would cure a man of venereal disease. And so, Smart reminds us, it was neither abuse nor rape, but 'misdirected medical effort'.[181] There were calls for legal reforms in the 1920s and 1930s:[182] these were long forgotten by 1957. The legal response was to blame the victim.[183] Children did not matter: their abusers, adult men did. It was they, not the girls, who were recognised as legal subjects.[184] When, more than 60 years later, the Butler-Sloss report into sexual abuse in Cleveland looked forward to a time when children would be persons in their own right and not merely objects of concern, what may have been overlooked was that in relation to sexual abuse – indeed much else – they had hardly become even objects of concern.[185]

And so child abuse was only discovered (or rediscovered) in the early 1960s and it took the Maria Colwell case of 1973–1974 to draw it to public (and legislative) attention.[186] And it was more than a decade later that child sexual abuse was recognised as the social problem it is.[187]

---

[176] A good account (in relation to the USA) is L Gordon *Heroes of Their Own Lives: the Politics and History of Family Violence* (Virago, 1989), p 215.

[177] Punishment of Incest Act 1908. Incest was replaced by new offences in the Sexual Offences Act 2003, ss 25 and 26. That the new legislation is 'over the top' is graphically pointed out by John Spencer 'The Shameful Sex Crimes of Adrian Mole Aged 13¾', *The Times*, 7 October 2003.

[178] 24 in the first year; 516 in 1987, the year of Cleveland: see B Corby *Child Abuse: Towards A Knowledge Base* (Open University Press, 1993), p 162.

[179] *Final Report* Cd 8189 (HMSO, 1916).

[180] Where HIV infection is believed to be cured similarly, this has led to the rape of babies. See Amnesty International 'Kenya: Rape – The Invisible Crime' AJ Index: AFR 32/001/2002, 15.

[181] C Smart 'A History of Ambivalence and Conflict in the Discursive Construction of the "Child Victim" of Sexual Abuse' (1999) 8 *Social and Legal Studies* 391 at 397–398.

[182] Ibid. Reforms followed the Pigot Report – *Report of the Advisory Group on Video-Recorded Evidence* (Home Office, 1989): see Criminal Justice Act 1991 and J Morgan and L Zedner *Child Victims: Crime, Impact and Criminal justice* (Oxford University Press, 1992).

[183] Cf W Ryan *Blaming The Victim* (Vintage Books, 1976).

[184] C Smart 'A History of Ambivalence and Conflict in the Discursive Construction of the "Child Victim" of Sexual Abuse' (1999) 8 *Social and Legal Studies* 391 at 403.

[185] *Report of the Inquiry into Child Abuse in Cleveland 1987* (HMSO, 1988), p 245. See also P Newell 'Children's Rights After Cleveland' (1988) 2 *Children and Society* 199.

[186] On the Colwell case see DHSS *Report of Committee of Inquiry into Care and Supervision Provided in Relation to Maria Colwell* (HMSO, 197). See also J Howells *Remember Maria* (Butterworths, 1974). The case had a profound effect on the Children Act 1975. On comparisons with the Climbié case of 2002–2003 see N Parton 'From Maria Colwell to Victoria Climbié: Reflections on Public Inquiries into Child Abuse a Generation Apart' (2004) 13 *Child Abuse Review* 80. See further, M Hayes 'Removing children from their families – law and policy before the Children Act 1989' in this volume.

[187] See M Freeman 'Cleveland, Butler-Sloss and Beyond: How Are We To React To The Sexual Abuse of Children?' (1989) 42 CLP 85.

Someone must 'blow the whistle':[188] it seems there were no moral entrepreneurs in 1957. A best-seller of 1956, *Peyton Place*, describes sexual abuse by a father and names it as such – the victim was kept quiet by a threat that she (aged 14) and her little brother would be killed if 'she went to the law'.[189] This has been described as an 'extraordinary glimpse at what was happening in that most prosperous and complacent decade in American history',[190] for which we can read 'you've never had it so good'.[191] It took the impact of feminism to interpret unequal sexual relationships within the family as abusive.[192] A generation earlier Kinsey described sexual abuse but did not so label it.[193] He did not think that these early sexual experiences were necessarily a bad thing.

One of the reasons why physical abuse of children provoked so little concern in 1957 was the prevalence of institutionalised abuse in schools. The state sanctioned the beating of children. Children first protested in 1669:[194] it was another 300 years before Cardiff became the first education authority to abolish corporal punishment – in its primary schools for a trial period of one year.[195] It was restored after protests from teaching unions.[196]

Corporal punishment was finally abolished in schools in 1998.[197] It was removed from children's homes in 2001,[198] foster parents were banned from using it in 2002,[199] and nurseries and child-minders had the power taken away from them in 2003.[200] But debate rages fiercely over whether parents (and others with parental responsibility) should retain the liberty to smack children. Punishment/discipline is not one of the subsidiary rights discussed by Pettit – its existence was uncontroversial in 1957. But

---

[188] See H Becker *Outsiders* (Free Press, 1963). See, more pertinently, D K Weisberg 'The 'Discovery' of Sexual Abuse: Experts' Roles in Legal Policy Formulation' (1984) 18 *University of California Davis LR* 1.

[189] Grace Metalious *Peyton Place* (J Messner, 1956), p 347.

[190] So described by I Hacking *The Social Construction of What?* (Harvard University Press, 1999), p 139.

[191] See P Hennessy *Having It So Good* (Allen Lane, 2006).

[192] See J Herman and L Hirschman 'Father-Daughter Incest' (1977) 2 *Signs* 735.

[193] Kinsey discovered nearly a quarter of girls were being what we would now call 'sexually abused' in 1953. See A C Kinsey, W B Pomeroy, C E Martin and P H Gebhard *Sexual Behaviour in the Human Female* (Saunders, 1953): 24 per cent of their sample (of volunteers) of 4,444 adult women reported a sexual experience with an adult when they were children.

[194] The 'Children's Petition' is discussed by C B Freeman (1966) 14 *British Journal of Educational Studies* 216.

[195] In 1968: see P Newell (ed) *A Last Resort?* (Penguin, 1972) pp 72–75.

[196] Who claimed that the incidence of juvenile delinquency was greater in Cardiff than in many cities of comparable size: eg it was twice as high as in Bristol. Corporal punishment was restored within 2 months.

[197] School Standards and Framework Act 1998, s 131.

[198] Children's Homes Regulations 2001, SI 2001/3967, reg 17(5)(a).

[199] Fostering Services Regulations 2002, SI 2002/57, reg 28(5)(b).

[200] Day Care and Child Minding (National Standards) (England) Regulations 2003, SI 2003/1996, reg 5.

not so now. The campaign to make it unlawful for parents to hit children started in the UK in the late 1980s.[201] We now, 20 years on, have a compromise – it is hardly a solution.[202] Reasonable punishment' is no longer a defence to wounding and causing grievous bodily harm, assault occasioning actual bodily harm and cruelty to persons under 16, but the defence remains available where the offence is common assault or where the battery does not occasion actual bodily harm (in common parlance does not leave a mark).

No one is satisfied by this. Those calling for an outright ban continue to do so – the Government again rejected this in late 2007.[203] Those who see the legislation as unnecessary meddling with parents' rights to rear children as they see fit are critical of bungling interference by a nanny state. The police are unhappy too: do they charge with ABH only to be told that common assault only has been committed? And what can we tell parents – and let us not forget children? What message is conveyed by the new law? You may hit your children – but 'not hard', 'not too hard'. Can they still use an implement? (A slipper on a clothed bottom is unlikely to leave a mark.) These questions are about as valuable as medieval enquiries as to how many angels could perch on a pin-head. And they don't advance the debate. It is more important that we debate the status of children – whether for example hitting them enhances their personality and dignity. It will take a lot – probably a cultural revolution – to rid ourselves of child abuse.[204] Making it unlawful to hit children – now the preferred solution in more than 25 countries,[205] including now in New Zealand, the only English-speaking country – is a necessary first step. Of course, it will work only as part of a package.[206] Legislation aimed at social engineering never works in isolation.[207] But its knock-on effect will be profound: not just on abuse (sexual[208] as well as physical), but on the way we think about children and their lives, about participation[209] (the

---

[201] M Freeman 'Time To Stop Hitting Our Children' (1988) 51 *Childright* 5. A much earlier – and neglected – article is A Samuels 'Never Hit A Child' [1977] Fam Law 119.

[202] In Children Act 2004, s 58. And see M Freeman *Understanding Family Law* (Sweet and Maxwell, 2007), p 197.

[203] *Section 58 of the Children Act 2004 Review (Consultation): Analysis of Responses To The Consultation Document*, DCSF, 2007; *The Guardian*, 20 October 2007. The reasonable chastisement defence was due for debate in the House of Commons again in October 2008, but there was insufficient time to hold it.

[204] As I argued in M Freeman *The Rights and Wrongs of Children* (Frances Pinter, 1983) and at the ISPCAN conference in Hong Kong in September 2008 ('Can We Conquer Child Abuse If We Don't Outlaw Physical Chastisement of Children?').

[205] Sweden being the first (in 1979). A detailed account is S Bitensky *Corporal Punishment of Children: a Human Rights Violation* (Transnational Publishers, 2006).

[206] A point made strongly by Joan Durrant and G M Olsen 'Parenting and Public Policy: Contextualizing the Swedish Corporal Punishment Ban' (1997) 19 *Journal of Social Welfare and Family Law* 443.

[207] See M Freeman *The Legal Structure* (Longmans, 1974), p 64.

[208] On which see N King, T Butt and L Green 'Spanking and the Corporal Punishment of Children: the Sexual Story' (2003) 11 *International Journal of Children's Rights* 199.

[209] See UN Convention on the Rights of The Child 1989, Art 12.

implication of *Gillick*,[210] for example), education[211] (of which they are the consumers, but are often seen as the objects) and poverty (which will not be eliminated, as promised, by 2020).[212]

Looking back at 1957 now, it is the absence and silence of children that is so conspicuous. The only chapter on children in *A Century of Family Law* couples the 'illegitimate and deprived child'.[213] The joinder is made as if the association was unproblematic. Most of the chapter is on adoption (which was only introduced two-thirds of the way through the 1857–1957 period).[214] Adoption – then, of course, an absolutely closed institution[215] – is the solution. There is no discussion of alternatives, for there were none: custodianship was to come (and go swiftly)[216] and today's alternatives, special guardianship, residence orders and enhanced residence orders[217] were not yet contemplated and nor, of course, was assisted reproduction.[218] The law was pathological: it cleared up the mess. It did not prevent it arising or attempt to do so: the first steps towards prevention were 6 years away:[219] its fuller articulation was to await the Children Act 1989[220] and subsequent legislation.[221] Adoption was to reach its apogee of popularity in the late 1960s.[222] It has declined since,

---

[210] *Gillick v West Norfolk and Wisbech AHA* [1986] AC 112. And see M Freeman 'Rethinking Gillick' (2005) 13 *International Journal of Children's Rights* 201.

[211] See M Freeman 'Children's Education: A Test-Case for Best Interests and Autonomy' in R Davie and D Galloway (eds) *Listening to Children in Education* (David Fulton Publishers, 1996), p 29.

[212] See D Hirsch 'Ending Child Poverty' (2006) 125 *Poverty* 11. A particular concern is the poverty of children who have parents in work: see T Branigan 'Anti-Poverty Drive is Failing Working Families', *The Guardian*, 3 January 2008, p 10.

[213] By T E James, R H Graveson and F R Crane *A Century of Family Law* (Sweet and Maxwell, 1957), p 39. There is also Pettit's chapter on 'Parental Control and Guardianship'.

[214] In 1927, as a result of the Adoption of Children Act 1926. There were earlier attempts to legislate: see N Lowe 'English Adoption Law: Past, Present and Future' in S Katz, J Eekelaar and M Maclean (eds) *Cross Currents* (Oxford UP, 2000).

[215] And see J Triseliotis *In Search of Origins* (Routledge, 1973). See also Mike Leigh's film, *Secrets and Lies* (1996).

[216] I was foolish enough to write a book on it: M Freeman *The Law and Practice of Custodianship* (Sweet and Maxwell, 1986). Sweet and Maxwell more so, in that they asked me to do a second edition!

[217] On enhanced residence orders see Adoption and Children Act 2002, s 114; on Special Guardianship orders see Adoption and Children Act 2002, s 115.

[218] As noted above (fn 12) the first IVF baby, Louise Brown, was born in 1978. On the birth and reaction to it see R Deech and A Smajdor *From IVF to Immorality* (Oxford UP, 2007).

[219] Children and Young Persons Act 1963, s 1.

[220] Part III. See my full discussion in M Freeman *Children, Their Families and the Law* (Macmillan, 1992), ch 4.

[221] Children Act 2004 and Children Act 2006. And see Children's Rights Director for England *Children's Messages on Care* (Ofsted, 2007). Further developments are anticipated in the Children and Young Persons Bill 2007–2008.

[222] In 1968 there were 24,831 orders: ONS *Marriage, Divorce and Adoption Statistics 2002* Series FM2, No 30, Table 6.16.

for reasons already given. It seems unlikely that, whatever political initiatives are taken, it has much of a future. Indeed, it may be predicted that 50 years on it won't exist at all.

A Century of Family Law is oblivious to children's rights. There is a short section on criminal responsibility.[223] Mendes da Costa concedes that the age of 8 is 'an arbitrary choice'[224] (it was 7 until 1933), but he is not critical of this. In 1957 there was a *doli incapax* presumption (not mentioned by Mendes da Costa).[225] The age of criminal responsibility is now 10, an age far lower than that set by 37 other European states,[226] and the *doli incapax* presumption has been abolished.[227] The presumption may not have had much practical effect – it was rebutted relatively easily, as the *Bulger* trial demonstrated.[228] But, as Gelsthorpe and Morris point out, the importance of the presumption lay in its symbolism – it was 'a statement about the nature of childhood'.[229] The Government's explanation for the abolition of the presumption (and the right of silence in the dock) beggars belief: it contributes to 'the right of children appearing [in court] to develop responsibility for themselves'.[230] It is curious how the language of rights is used to defend the indefensible. Another example is found in the Court of Appeal decision in *Re M (Child's Upbringing)* (the 'Zulu boy' case). The boy, who was 10, was adamant he didn't wish to return to South Africa, but Neill LJ stated '... he has the right to be reunited with his Zulu parents and with his extended family in South Africa'.[231]

There is no discussion of children's rights in *A Century of Family Law*. This is not entirely surprising, though there were such issues waiting to be uncovered in 1957. The UN Declaration of 1959 passed family lawyers by – it is safe to assume that had it been in 1955 it would not have been noticed by the authors of *A Century of Family Law*. The period since has seen us taking children's rights more seriously.[232] True, this country thought a convention premature, but like the rest of the world, except

---

[223] D Mendes da Costa 'Criminal Law' in R H Graveson and F R Crane *A Century of Family Law* (Sweet and Maxwell, 1957), p 165.
[224] Ibid, p 194.
[225] There is a useful discussion in D Archard *Children – Rights and Childhood* (Routledge, 2004), pp 127–132. A good defence of the doctrine is G Douglas 'The Child's Right To Make Mistakes: Criminal Responsibility and the Immature Minor' in G Douglas and L Sebba (eds) *Children's Rights and Traditional Values* (Ashgate, 1998), p 264.
[226] See J Fortin *Children's Rights and the Developing Law* (LexisNexis, 2003), p 550.
[227] Crime and Disorder Act 1998, s 34.
[228] See M Freeman *The Moral Status of Children* (Martinus Nijhoff, 1997), ch 12.
[229] L Gelsthorpe and A Morris 'Much Ado About Nothing – A Critical Comment on Key Provisions relating to children in the Crime and Disorder Act 1998' [1999] CFLQ 209 at 213.
[230] Department of Health *2nd Report to the UN Committee on the Rights of The Child by the United Kingdom*, 1999, para 10.30.1.
[231] [1996] 2 FLR 441.
[232] But insufficiently so: see M Freeman 'Why it Remains Important To Take Children's Rights Seriously' (2007) 15 *International Journal of Children's Rights* 5.

Somalia and the USA,[233] it swiftly ratified it. It entered significant reservations[234] and remains in breach of a number of Articles.[235] The convention is important – it is my hope that we will take it to heart, and one day even incorporate it into our legal structure. Why shouldn't children's rights really be brought home too?[236]

Our judges began to talk about children's rights sporadically in the 1970s: for example, access was described as a child's right in 1972.[237] We didn't get a *Gault*[238] or a *Tinker*,[239] but in 1985 with little warning – only in retrospect can we see *Hewer v Bryant* in 1970[240] as pointing in this direction – we get the House of Lords' ruling in *Gillick v West Norfolk and Wisbech Area Health Authority*.[241] Although specifically about competence to consent to contraceptive advice and treatment, the principle it established extends to all forms of medical treatment, and beyond. Whether a *Gillick* competent child can be punished – less of an issue now that corporal punishment has been removed from schools – is dubious.[242] Or forced to stay on at school – is the Government's proposal to raise the school-leaving age to 18[243] compatible with *Gillick*? Whether a *Gillick* competent child attends classes of religious instruction and sex-education classes is surely now her decision, though legislation curiously gives the right to opt-out children to their parents.[244] Initially, the *Gillick* decision seemed to have an impact, for example, on some provisions in the Children Act 1989.[245] But it has proved a false dawn. There are too few examples of it being applied,[246] and there is, as is well known, a retreat from *Gillick* in a series of cases holding that even a *Gillick*-competent child cannot refuse medical treatment.[247] It is arguable that a mature adolescent, even one of 17, cannot refuse to do anything that a parent believes is in her best interests. So, for example, if a parent believes it is in

---

[233] M Guggenheim in *What's Wrong With Children's Rights* (Harvard University Press, 2005) says it would make no difference if the USA ratified the Convention.

[234] On which, see now Department of Health, *2nd Report to the UN Committee on the Rights of The Child by the United Kingdom*, 1999, para 1.8.

[235] See M Freeman 'Children's Rights Ten Years After Ratification' in B Franklin (ed) *The New Handbook of Children's Rights* (Routledge, 2002), p 97.

[236] And see J Fortin 'Rights Brought Home for Children' (1999) 62 MLR 350.

[237] *M v M (Child: Access)* [1973] 2 All ER 81.

[238] *Re Gault* 387 US 1 (1967).

[239] *Tinker v Des Moines School District* 393 US 503 (1969).

[240] [1970] 1 QB 357.

[241] [1986] AC 112.

[242] See J Eekelaar 'Parents' Rights to Punish – Further Limits After *Gillick*' (1986) 28 *Childright* 9.

[243] Proposal in 2007.

[244] See A Bainham *Children: The Modern Law* (Family Law, 3rd edn, 2005), p 714.

[245] Viz ss 38(6), 43(8), 44(7) and Sch 3, paras 4(4)(a) and 5(5)(b). But see *South Glamorgan CC v W and B* [1993] 1 FLR 574.

[246] See *Re Roddy (A Child) (Identification: Restriction on Publication)* [2004] 2 FLR 949; *R (Axon) v Secretary of State for Health and the Family Planning Association* [2006] 2 FLR 206.

[247] Notably *Re R (Wardship: Consent to Treatment)* [1992] Fam 11 and *Re W (Medical Treatment: Court's Jurisdiction)* [1993] Fam 64.

the best interests of a 16-year-old to leave school and go to work, the child cannot refuse to do this. As this happened to me,[248] I take this cutting down of a mature adolescent's rights to say 'no' rather personally. Such an affront to a child's dignity could not have been anticipated in the heady and exciting days of *Gillick*.

But why would one expect in a country that imprisons more children than almost any other European country, in which a quarter or more of children live in poverty (at least this figure is coming down, or was doing so), where restraint in secure training centres is such that in the years 2005–2006 oxygen had to be given to five children, where handcuffs are used on children as young as 10, and where it is a crime for a child excluded from school to be in a public place during the first 5 days of their exclusion (this would include a library or a museum)?[249] We remain in breach of so many of the provisions of the UN Convention on the Rights of the Child, even that most basic of Articles which mandates States Parties to ensure children are not subjected to torture or inhuman and degrading treatment.[250]

CONCLUSION – AND SO TO 2057

I would exceed my brief if I looked forward to 2057. Developments I have not discussed will have had a huge impact on the family and so on family law: for example, the internationalisation of family law,[251] rapid advances in human assisted reproduction, including reprogenetics,[252] greater sensitivity to the demands of those with disabilities.[253] Some changes are easy to predict: greater recognition of the institution of cohabitation – or more likely an assimilation of marriage to cohabitation;[254] gay marriage (though if the previous prediction is correct it will make little or no difference); it will become unlawful to hit children, but whether children's lives will improve or, as I fear, get worse is not certain. There will be more

---

[248] I was 15 years and 8 months when my parents attempted to get me to leave school.

[249] I take these examples from Children's Rights Alliance for England *State of Children's Rights in England Report 2007* (CRAE, 2007) published to coincide with the 18th anniversary of the UN Convention.

[250] Thus there are children living as domestic slaves in England today: see Debbie Arigo 'The 21st Century Slaves in the UK' *Community Care*, 13 December 2007, p 24. And see *Children and Society*, vol 22(3) (2008) Special Issue on *Child Slavery Worldwide*. No one has ever been prosecuted in the UK for child domestic slavery.

[251] See N Lowe 'Where in the world is international family law going next?', at Chapter 12 below.

[252] L Knowles and G Kaebnick *Reprogenetics – Law, Policy and Ethical Issues* (Johns Hopkins University Press, 2007); S McLean *Modern Dilemmas – Choosing Children* (Capercaillie Books, 2006).

[253] See Disability Discrimination Act 1995. When will family law texts address disabled families? In M Freeman *Understanding Family Law* (Sweet and Maxwell, 2007) I discuss children with disabilities (see p 161).

[254] Hitherto, the assimilation process has been towards treating cohabitation more and more like marriage: see M Freeman and C Lyon *Cohabitation without Marriage* (Gower, 1983).

rights for women, making the yardstick of equality on divorce more acceptable – perhaps even to men (if not there could be a backlash).[255] There will even be divorce reform. If society continues to polarise – a religious 'Right' and a secular 'Left' – we may get, as has happened in parts of the USA, different forms of marriage.[256] But we may transcend conjugality entirely.[257] Other changes are more difficult to predict, and could affect those just described. We could become increasingly secularised – but equally there might be a religious resurgence as our churches fill with immigrants (probably Catholics) and the Muslim population increases. The impact of this on abortion, divorce, gay rights etc would be enormous, and an enormity. But bigger than any of these changes is that our understanding of what it is to be 'human' may change. Rather than lament our 'post-human future', as Fukuyama has done,[258] I suggest we prepare for it. Think, for example, of the implications of enhancement for parent-child relations, for parental responsibility.[259] Is 'procreative beneficence', as Savulescu has dubbed it,[260] to be feared, or regulated? This takes me way beyond my remit – but it demonstrates, I think, that we could see much bigger changes in the next 50 years than in the last 50. What would the gentlemen at King's College London make of it?

---

[255] See E Cooke 'The future for ancillary relief', at Chapter 9 below.
[256] On covenant marriage see L Sanchez et al 'The Implementation of Covenant Marriage in Louisiana' (2000) 9 *Virginia Journal of Social Policy and Law* 192.
[257] See Law Commission of Canada *Beyond Conjugality – Recognizing and Supporting Close Personal Adult Relationships* (Law Commission of Canada, 2002). See also B Cossman and B Ryder 'What is Marriage-Like like? The Irrelevance of Conjugality' (2001) 18 *Canadian Journal of Family Law* 269.
[258] F Fukuyama *Our Posthuman Future* (Profile Books, 2002).
[259] See D Davis *Genetic Dilemmas* (Routledge, 2001); cf E B Schmidt 'The Parental Obligation To Expand a Child's Range of Open Futures When Making Genetic Trait Selections for Their Child' (2007) 21 *Bioethics* 191.
[260] J Savulescu 'Procreative Beneficence: Why We Should Select The Best Children' (2001) 15 *Bioethics* 413.

CHAPTER 7

LAW, FAMILY AND COMMUNITY

John Eekelaar

INDIVIDUALISM

It is fashionable to berate modern 'individualism'. Among many recent examples is Richard Layard, who in his recent book on *Happiness* twice attaches the epithet 'rampant' to it, as if it were a virus, and once 'unrestrained', as if all social bonds had disappeared.[1] Against this it is usual to set the virtues of community. This juxtaposition is of concern for family law, for families are a kind of community. Many say they are the primary form of community. The predominant view seems to be that the individual is being prized to the neglect of the collectivity. Individualism is perceived to be a key factor in contemporary social ills. Policies are designed to restore individuals to their communities and to their families.

It is indeed possible to point to selfish behaviour: a good deal of it. This could be related to the contemporary dominance of competitive market economics, and I wish to say nothing about that. But I want to argue that the greater threat lies in the opposite direction from individualism. There is a danger of overlooking the growing range of new communities. These include peer groups, which increasingly exert influence over individuals, and communities based on ethnic and religious affiliation. And families, in various guises, remain. It is a complex landscape, but one in which it is becoming all the more important to protect individuals from their communities, and to give them safe ways of detaching themselves from them.

Since it is easy to misrepresent this position as being somehow insensitive to the virtues of community, I must say at once that I fully accept the importance of the mutual interdependence of individuals and the value of communities. Who could not? Individuals need social interaction to survive and flourish. But I am concerned about the use of coercive power, especially through law. For, while law does have a role in the furtherance of communal objectives, it is often a dangerous way of achieving those objectives. It should therefore be only a restrained and secondary means

---

[1] Richard Layard *Happiness: Lessons from a New Science* (Penguin Books, 2005), pp 5, 91 and 229.

by which the positive obligations of community are brought about. But when it comes to protecting people against the community, it is primary and irreplaceable.

COMMUNITIES AND POWER

In *Family Law and Personal Life* I focused on the pervasiveness of power, both institutional and socially diffused, particularly in family structures.[2] This power is likely to serve primarily the interests of those who hold it. Ascribed roles within communities are not manifestations of acts of nature: they represent the script for sanctioned behaviour. The question is: who writes the script? Amartya Sen has vividly demonstrated the destructive consequences of supposing that most individuals have a single over-arching identity, which binds them closely with particular communities, particularly religious communities.[3] This not only falsely confers all the attributes associated with a single community on individuals who may accept only some of them; it also allows communities to claim, and exercise, control over the identity which individuals might wish to develop for themselves.

The key elements in the interrelationship are the roles of force or coercion, and of law. *Family Law and Personal Life* argues that community control over individuals within the group should be limited by the prerequisites for the existence of an open society and by values believed to be of universal character (in practice, human rights norms). The first requirement means that every individual (and every new generation) should have the responsibility to determine for themselves the nature of the moral decisions they embrace, guided by, but not controlled by, the pronouncements of those who went before them. The second requires adherence to claims supported by widespread international subscription.[4] This paper is centrally concerned with examining how these requirements can be met.

THE ROLE OF RIGHTS

Family Law and Personal Life argues that the assertion of rights is a significant mode through which restraints on intra-communal power-relations can emerge. Rights are seen, not *solely* as claims for the exercise of individual power, but as claims by individuals or groups of individuals for the social recognition of sectional interests within the community against a wider community as a matter of entitlement.[5] This account is therefore hostile to the notion that communities or groups have rights *qua* communities, except in so far as a community or group forms the social

---

[2] *Family Law and Personal Life* (Oxford UP, 2006 and 2007), chs 1 and 6.
[3] Amartya Sen *Identity and Violence: The Illusion of Destiny* (Allen Lane, 2006).
[4] *Family Law and Personal Life*, pp 164–173.
[5] *Family Law and Personal Life*, ch 6.

base of individual claims. The group exists for the individual, not the individual for the group. There is, however, a long history of resistance against such assertions of rights in the name of upholding community-based values, such as the sanctity of family life. These interventions do indeed raise serious issues, which may bring about more harm than benefit. But they do not suggest that intervention disrespects the privileged sphere, for unwanted oppression demands no respect.

There is another danger of intervention, though. Oppression by the family may be replaced by oppression by the wider community. There are many examples. It occurs when what is deemed to be marital wrongdoing is met by social ostracism; where homosexual intimates become outcasts; where decisions about entering marriage are dictated by the community. This can come about through the mechanisms of law, or without them. These actions are manifestations of a major function of community: to disseminate norms of behaviour and ensure their observance. But communities seldom act as organic wholes. Rather, they are constituted of a variety of internal groupings which exercise varying degrees of power. So who knows what the dominant power group may choose, and mutually reinforce, as being the way of living which qualifies the subject for membership of the group? Children to be struck or not to be struck? Non-marital children to be disowned or not to be disowned? Non-marital relationships to be condemned or to be tolerated? Mothers to stay at home or to go out to work? Beards to be worn, or not to be worn? Women to be veiled or not to be veiled? Boys and girls to be genitally cut or not to be cut?

CARE AND POWER

But, it is said, communities are a source of care for individuals, and communitarian ethics stress the interconnectedness of people. Is this not an unalloyed good?

The trouble is that to exercise care is *also* to exercise power. We hope that it is a beneficent exercise of power, but there are many examples where people do great harm with good intentions. The welfarism thesis set out in *Family Law and Personal Life* argues, and, it is hoped, demonstrates, that this could occur beyond individual relationships, and extend to social policy.[6] But the problem is deeper still than that. It centres on the question: what indeed *is* beneficial to the individual? Is the answer to be found only by reference to the opinion of the carer, or the caring community? No. Too much havoc has been wrought by policies fashioned by assertions of the powerful over what they believed to be in the best interests of the subjects of their power. But for concepts of rights to operate effectively as constraints on this power, at least two conditions

---

[6] *Family Law and Personal Life*, pp 9–17.

must be satisfied. One is to maintain access to the truth.[7] The truth can provide a constraint upon those whose power would be enhanced by concealing the truth. If the powerful can manipulate the truth, its restraining force is lost. Another potential constraint on power, allied to the first, is the ability of subjects to express their viewpoint, and for this to be taken seriously. Without this possibility, rights cannot be claimed. For this possibility to become reality requires the existence of secure institutions and processes through which the voice of individuals can be heard in contradistinction to that of the community.

SILENCING THE VOICE

There are many examples where the individual voice has been silenced. Here are a few. Within the Roman legal system it was taken for granted that slaves did not have access to institutional mechanisms, whether political or legal. Their case, if it was to be made at all, had to be through claims for benevolence or by revolt. Even citizens who were of low rank, or of little wealth, were unable to use the civil litigation system to assert rights which in theory should have been theirs against the more powerful and privileged.[8] In the English legal system the immunity granted to the Crown deprived subjects of the opportunity to develop appropriate legal remedies against government actions until the later part of the twentieth century. In the same way, the legal unity of husband and wife restricted the scope by which married women could use the law to protect their interests against husbands. These restraints were exacerbated by the costs of litigation. It is very unlikely that the developments in the law of matrimonial property so greatly influenced by Lord Denning in the 1950s and 1960s[9] could have occurred without the greater access to the courts which legal aid provided at that time, or that the divorce law would have been reformed in 1969 if it were not for the pressures these developments placed on the existing system. Of course, the use of human rights law in the courts has been a major influence on the recent direction of personal law.

In a study in the 1990s of individual responses to events perceived to 'raise legal issues', Hazel Genn found that people who experienced a problem of that kind within family relationships were more likely to seek advice than were people who experienced such a problem in any other context (for example, concerning faulty goods, employment difficulties, accidents or property issues). With family relationships, people were the least likely to do nothing ('lump it').[10] This does not mean that family problems constituted the major source of potential legal issues experienced by individuals; at 6% it came in below faulty goods or services (11%) and money problems generally (9%). But it does show that,

---

[7] See *Family Law and Personal Life*, ch 2.
[8] J M Kelly *Roman Litigation* (Clarendon Press, 1976), chs 1–2.
[9] See *Family Law and Personal Life*, pp 143–144.
[10] Hazel Genn *Paths to Justice* (Hart Publishing, 1999).

when such problems do occur, people strongly feel the need to look to 'external' sources for advice. What is more, across all income groups, the advice was most often sought from a solicitor.[11] It seems that people experiencing serious family problems have a general need for external support of some kind and that the very fact that a problem of this nature has arisen indicates that the parties involved are not able easily to resolve matters between themselves. Other family members, who could have conflicting loyalties, may not be able to help much, and in some cases will bring into play strong communal pressures which could stifle the individuals' opportunity to resolve the problem themselves.

So what is the nature of the institutions which can give individuals protection against the wider community, and against communities (like families) within that community? There must be a range of institutions independent of government but ordinarily enjoying some form of governmental support or recognition which can function as a setting for protection, advice, support and a safe route of exit for individuals who are in discord with their own communities. *Those institutions are of the community, but not identical with it.* There are many examples, ranging from individual legal practitioners, citizens' advice centres, domestic violence refuges, religious institutions and, very powerfully, the courts. Of course, the extent to which any or all of these are able to fulfil that function varies between societies. In some, they may be no more than outworks of the power of the community. But without institutional networks of some such kind, the chances of escape from the community are slim indeed.

HEARING THE VOICE

We therefore need to look at some of the types of institutions which can serve this purpose.

Community legal and advice services

Community law centres presently handle only about 5% of family work. Mostly they deal with issues concerning debt and welfare benefits.[12] The Carter Report, which the government has endorsed, favours expanding these in various ways, such as by developing community 'networks', which might include practitioners using the internet to communicate with one another.[13] There are many kinds of advice service, such as organisations dealing with troubled children and individuals under domestic stress. They all deal with individuals who are experiencing some form of difficulty with the 'community' in which they are, or have been, living.

---

[11] Ibid, p 86.
[12] Lord Carter of Coles *Legal Aid: A market-based approach to reform* (Department for Constitutional Affairs, July 2006) (Carter Report), ch 2, para 141.
[13] Carter Report, ch 3, para 101.

They may aim to restore the individual to that community, or to alter the nature of the community, or even assist the individual to exit from it. The tension between these objectives is found in the newly created Family Relationship Centres in Australia. Patrick Parkinson has described their role in this way:

> 'First and foremost, they are an early intervention initiative to help parents work out post-separation parenting arrangements in the aftermath of separation, managing the very difficult transition from parenting together to parenting apart. They will provide an educational, support and counselling role to parents going through separation, with the goal of helping parents to understand and focus upon children's needs, providing them with initial information about such matters as child support and welfare benefits, and negotiating workable agreements about partnering after separation. They will also be available to help ongoing conflicts and difficulties as circumstances change. They will not only be a resource for parents but for grandparents as well.
>
> The FRCs will not only have a role in helping parents after separation. They will also play a role in strengthening intact relationships by offering an accessible source for information and referral on marriage and parenting issues, providing a gateway to other government and non-government services to support families.'[14]

We can see here the potential for mechanisms like the FRCs both to give individuals support against their communities, sometimes by removing themselves from the community, but also to reinforce the demands of community, making modification of community practices more difficult, and blocking off ways by which the individual can escape from them. If they assume the latter role, they could become an ally of the oppressive aspects of community.

Individuals in families which are embedded within minority communities are enfolded by at least two levels of community within the third, wider, community: their own family and the community of their ethnic or religious group (though these may not be identical). Sonia Shah-Kazemi has examined the experiences of Muslim women with regard to divorce. She reports that all three of those of her interviewees who had experience of the police and domestic violence units considered that those agencies had been instrumental in assisting them to 'escape' from violent situations.[15] Shah-Kazemi's research was mainly focused on the role of the Muslim Law Shariah Council (MLSC), to which many Muslim women turned when their marriages broke down. Although only the husband could pronounce divorce, the Council has power under Shariah

---

[14] Patrick Parkinson 'Keeping on contact: the role of family relationship centres in Australia' [2006] CFLQ 157 at 159.

[15] Sonia Shah-Kazemi *Untying the Knot: Muslim Women, Divorce and the Shariah* (The Signal Press, 2001), p 60.

law to dissolve the marriage contract if the husband refused to take that step. Shah-Kazemi explains how important it was to the women to be able to communicate with the Council:

> 'The fact that the MLSC insist in all cases on communicating directly with the woman, even if she is not the one who first approaches the organisation, is distinctly to the advantage of these women. It allows her to be independent from her family, and to a certain extent also saves her family from the difficulties associated with unsuccessful negotiations ... Of course, there are a number of women whose families are determinedly hostile to them and their needs, and for these women independent access to the MLSC processes is of critical importance, such access empowering them within the framework of their faith.'[16]

Shah-Kazemi comments on how important it was that the women were prepared to have resort to people 'outside' the family group to assist them, something which she has noted is not true for all minority communities.[17]

The operation of the MLSC illustrates how an institution that is strongly related to certain cultural communities, but not necessarily identical with any one of them, can act as a protective instrument which mediates between the individual and various constituents of the communities that surround them. There is, however, evidence that the younger generation in various ethnic communities is tending to prioritise identification with religion over identification with a cultural group.[18] This replaces identification with one community with another, and transfers power from one community to another. The religious community might be more varied and open-ended than the ethnic community. But those of a fundamentalist nature will be more restrictive. The Government has reacted to this by seeming to want to enhance the propagation of what it believes to be 'sound' religious beliefs through manipulation of education or of religious actors.[19] Governments should not become involved in evaluating which religious beliefs are sound and which are not. It would do better for it to concentrate on ensuring that religious groups do not use their religious status to prejudice the interests of individuals who do not identify with them, and that channels remain open for individuals within those groups who wish to do so to choose other affiliations with safety.

---

[16] Ibid, p 36.
[17] See Sonia Nourin Shah-Kazemi 'Cross-Cultural Mediation: A Critical View of the Dynamics of Culture in Family Disputes' (2000) 14 *International Journal of Law, Policy & Family* 302.
[18] Yunas Samad and John Eade *Community Perceptions of Forced Marriage* (University of Bradford and University of Surrey Roehampton, for Community Liaison Unit of the Foreign and Commonwealth Office, 2003), pp 86–87. Available at http://www.fco.gov.uk/Files/kfile/clureport.pdf.
[19] See HM Government *Preventing Violent Extremism* (May 2008) (available at http://security.homeoffice.gov.uk/news-publications/publication-search/prevent-strategy/preventing-violent-extremism?view=Binary) (accessed 9 November 2008).

Solicitors and barristers

As has been observed, Genn's research showed that family members were likely to have recourse to a solicitor where serious problems arose within family settings. In our observations of the practical work of 'family' solicitors, Mavis Maclean and I saw many examples of the way solicitors provided support for clients. One was to give 'reassurance'. This could be simply through listening to the client, a chance to hear the voice: 'The very fact of listening sympathetically to a client might be counted as providing "emotional" support'.[20] It might simply be by calming the client down, and outlining the legal position. Often the support extended into advice on other practicalities, such as on how to go about seeking alternative accommodation, how to 'get a grip' on their financial situation and make ends meet – or where best to go to find advice on such things. Cases were observed where a solicitor acted as an intermediary through whom parties communicated with one another during a period of estrangement, after which they came together again;[21] and where the solicitor protected the interests of a vulnerable client who had suffered mental illness against pressures from the wider family.[22]

Since clients in these situations often lack economic independence (and this makes them more vulnerable to the pressures of their immediate community, since they are also largely dependent on it), it was important that the solicitors obtained funding from the legal aid system. Yet in the late 1990s, when the research was carried out, we noted that 'legal aid work which involves relatively low hourly fees together with restrictions about the nature of the work which can be charged for, was almost universally regarded as requiring considerable amounts of unpaid or poorly paid work.'[23] Firms were therefore taking on more private client work, and the availability of solicitors offering legally aided services was declining. Significant changes in the public funding of legal services provided by solicitors have taken place since 1998.[24] The ultimate goal seems to be a 'market-based' system in which firms compete against each other when tendering for public funding, and for the funding to be granted on the basis of an assessment of the quality, quantity and efficiency of the services to be provided to the client.[25] It is no easy matter to construct a good way to secure the provision of a public service through the private sector, and, as has been noted, problems were experienced prior to these measures. The most likely outcome of the new approach, though, is that publicly funded work will only be sustainable by

---

[20] John Eekelaar, Mavis Maclean and Sarah Beinart *Family Lawyers: The Divorce Work of Solicitors* (Hart, 2000), pp 81–82.
[21] *Family Lawyers*, op cit, pp 104–105.
[22] *Family Lawyers*, pp 106–108.
[23] *Family Lawyers*, p 194. See the examples on p 195.
[24] *Modernising Justice* (Lord Chancellor's Department, December 1998); see Access to Justice Act 1999.
[25] Lord Carter of Coles *Legal Aid: A market-based approach to reform* (Department for Constitutional Affairs, July 2006) (Carter Report), ch 2.

firms which can turn over a large number of cases. The firms providing it will therefore become larger and fewer, and therefore less accessible, though it is also possible, of course, that a large firm may be able to develop smaller branches dispersed within the community.

In the divided legal profession of England and Wales, barristers too have an important role in providing individuals with protection against the pressures of family or other communal institutions. Their part in formulating legal arguments which are presented to the highest courts is only the most well known. But Mavis Maclean has observed the less visible side. Family conflicts which reach the stage of formal adjudication are invariably those where hostility is most deeply embedded. These cases simply will not settle through normal discussion or negotiation. Maclean has observed[26] how, on the day of the hearing, barristers can be the only source of guidance, support and comfort to clients embarking on what is a form of proxy battle. The barristers could spend much more time trying to resolve the matter in the corridors outside the formal courtroom hearing than they spent in the courtroom. They would have face to face discussions with the barrister for the other party, with court officials, with welfare personnel and even with the judge. It is difficult to see how people could manage these serious conflicts with their immediate community without professional assistance of the kind provided by a barrister.

Children

Children are the individuals who are most vulnerable to misuse and oppression from their communities. This is why I argue in *Family Law and Personal Life* that the relationship between parents and children should, in principle, always be subject to external scrutiny.[27] Here I wish to consider briefly the opportunities for children to make their views heard in circumstances of significant conflict within the family. Organisations such as Childline and the Children's Legal Centre, now supplemented by the Commissioners for Children, can play an important role. Children can of course approach the legal profession if they know how. But can they play any part in legal proceedings?

A child can seek the court's leave to make an application for a 'section 8 order', such as an order determining with whom he or she should live.[28] Yet the courts have not welcomed such applications, which can be considered only by the High Court.[29] The more usual way for a child to be represented is where the court appoints a Child and Family Reporter in disputes between adults (usually a child's parents) in a matter concerning

---

[26] Mavis Maclean 'Family Lawyers: the work of the English family bar in contact cases: policy, mythology and data', Paper given to the Working Group on the Legal professions, Berlin, July 2007.
[27] *Family Law and Personal Life* (Oxford UP, 2006 and 2007), pp 90–92.
[28] Children Act 1989, ss 8 and 10.
[29] *Practice Direction (Application by Children: Leave)* [1993] 1 WLR 313.

the child. The Reporter should consult the child and provide evidence about the child's welfare to the court. But the child's voice will only be heard, if at all, through that of the Reporter. However, the Reporter must consider whether the child's interests demand that the child be made a party in the proceedings, and the Family Proceedings Rules 1991, r 9.5 allows a court to make a child a party if it thinks that this would be in the child's best interests. In that case, a guardian, normally a welfare professional, would be appointed and the guardian would normally instruct a solicitor, who might in serious cases also instruct a barrister. This occurs in fewer than 10% of cases.[30]

But that does not enhance the child's voice much. Research by Douglas et al[31] found that the procedure tended to be used in order to supplement information about the child's interests for the court rather than as a means to provide a 'voice' for the child. If the child does not want his position to be represented through the eyes of the guardian, they may seek to have the guardian discharged and instruct a solicitor alone, but the solicitor needs to make a judgment whether to take instruction from the child or not. If the solicitor refuses, the child can ask the court to be allowed to instruct a solicitor. Although the courts have been reluctant to allow this, either holding children to high levels of competence, or judging it would be against their interests, in *Mabon v Mabon*[32] the Court of Appeal said that the courts should give great weight to the importance of older children having an independent voice in private law proceedings which would affect them significantly. The former Department for Constitutional Affairs (now Ministry of Justice), however, has seemed to promote a narrower view, saying that separate representation should be allowed only where there was a legal reason for giving the child an independent voice, for example, to make a distinct legal submission, or to present evidence not otherwise available.[33]

Mediation

The virtues of mediation are similar to the virtues of community. It allows the parties to introduce any matter they consider relevant into the discussion, unlike the legal approach, which tends to isolate facts from their background and render personal factors irrelevant to the

---

[30] G Douglas, M Murch, C Miles and L Scanlan *Research into the Operation of Rule 9.5 of the Family Proceedings Rules 1991: Report to the Department of Constitutional Affairs* (2006).
[31] See n 30 above.
[32] [2005] EWCA Civ 634, [2005] Fam 366.
[33] Department for Constitutional Affairs *Separate Representation of Children* CP 20/06, 1 September 2006. However, the Department also mentioned the right of the child under Art 6 of the European Convention on Human Rights to access to a fair hearing, which suggests that it may be willing to consider the claim of a child to put his or her own case as a possible ground for allowing separate representation.

legal issues invisible.[34] In mediation, it is said, participants are encouraged to think less of their own interests, and more of those of others, including the group (the family) as a whole. As a consequence, worries about mediation correspond to anxieties about the way individuals may be overborne by their communities. It seems a consistent and common finding that, in family matters, men are more dissatisfied with the adversarial process than women are.[35] The likely explanation is that legal rights, fulfilling their usual role of providing a corrective against the exercise of power,[36] tend to favour women by restricting the usually dominant economic (and often physical) position of men when relationships break down. Although men and women seem to view mediation in much the same way,[37] there are concerns that women do not pursue their own interests as vigorously in mediation as men do.[38] The risks to women in cases of domestic violence have long been recognised,[39] and this seems to be just an extreme case of the effects of removing, or reducing, legal entitlements designed to counteract de facto exercises of power.

The UK Government was initially attracted to mediation in family cases because of its perceived potential to save public money.[40] The Government declared that it did not wish to make mediation compulsory, but only to encourage it. However, the Funding Code under the Access to Justice Act 1999 requires any person seeking legal help for representation for most family disputes to have attended a meeting with a mediator. Only if the mediator decides that the matter is not appropriate for mediation will public funding be granted.[41] There are exemptions, for example where domestic violence is suspected. And nothing can be done if the other party does not wish to participate. But apart from those cases, unless an individual can afford to fund the legal process themselves, they must attend the meeting.

---

[34] See John Eekelaar, Mavis Maclean and Sarah Beinart *Family Lawyers: The Divorce Work of Solicitors* (Hart, 2000), p 193.

[35] Jessica Pearson 'A Forum for Every Fuss: The Growth of Court Services and ADR Treatments for Family Law Cases in the United States' in Sanford N Katz, John Eekelaar and Mavis Maclean (eds) *Cross Currents: Family Law and Policy in the US and England* (Oxford UP, 2000), ch 23.

[36] John Eekelaar *Family Law and Personal Life* (Oxford UP, 2006 and 2007), pp vii and 133.

[37] Susan Tilley 'Recognising Gender Differences in All Issues Mediation' [2007] Fam Law 352.

[38] Susan Tilley, ibid.

[39] Trina Grillo 'The Mediation Alternative: Process Dangers for Women' (1991) 100 *Yale LJ* 1545; Robert Rubinson and Jane Murphy 'Domestic Violence and Mediation: Responding to the Challenges of Crafting Effective Screens' (2005) 39 *Family Law Quarterly* 53.

[40] See the Consultation and White Papers, both entitled *Looking to the Future: Mediation and the Ground for Divorce* (1993) Cm 2424 and (1995) Cm 2799, discussed in Eekelaar, Maclean and Beinart *Family Lawyers: The Divorce Work of Solicitors* (Hart, 2000), ch 1.

[41] See Jill Black, Jane Bridge and Tina Bond *A Practical Approach to Family Law* (Blackstone Press, 2000), pp 22–23.

It may be said that that there is little harm, and perhaps some benefit, in requiring an initial meeting so that an option not previously considered is investigated by the individual. But it may not be that simple. Even if a party has the right to walk away, it may be difficult to do that once discussions have started. If you did, you could lose moral credit, and prejudice your position in future negotiation, or even in litigation, and exacerbate conflict. So it is likely that people will feel pressured into agreement. This is what Liz Trinder found in a study of cases which had been processed through some form of 'in-court' mediation process as regards child contact.[42] Of course, it is true that there can be no such thing as totally free agreement, especially in this context. A negotiating party will almost always be weighing the advantages and disadvantages of any potential settlement to himself or herself. Hard choices are part of life. But here institutional pressure is added to the other pressures already present: personal, psychological and social. It is designed to produce positive action by compromising legal entitlements, or an individual's perception of their own or their children interests. I will conclude by suggesting why this is undesirable.

COMMUNITIES, LAW AND RESPONSIBILITY

The reason why law should not be used in this way forms part of the general nature of the role law should play with respect to individuals and their communities. Let me summarise. It is generally good that individuals interact in a positive way with their communities, whether the community is the family or a wider group. Social norms will guide such conduct, and in normal circumstances the responsible individual will fulfil these norms, and more, for the benefit of the community. Community spirit and love for partners and children are not creatures of the law. Law, though, can have a limited role in supporting these positive behaviours. Legal measures may be needed to provide mechanisms for discharging social duties more effectively. Tax and environmental laws are examples.[43] Law may also sometimes need to create, and enforce, substitute obligations if individuals fail to interact positively. Family support obligations are an obvious case. In fact, it is probable that such legal obligations have only been created when failures of positive interaction became serious.[44]

But, while the enforcement of such obligations may properly be justified on grounds of justice, society should be extremely reluctant to try to coerce individuals to engage in positive interaction with others. That is only partly because reluctant behaviour under compulsion is unlikely to produce positive results, and may even be damaging to others. More

---

[42] Liz Trinder and Joanne Kellett 'Fairness, efficiency and effectiveness in court-based dispute resolution schemes in England' (2007) 21 *International Journal of Law, Policy & Family* 323.

[43] See Tony Honoré 'The Dependence of Morality on Law' (1993) 13 *Oxford Journal of Legal Studies* 1.

[44] John Eekelaar *Family Law and Personal Life* (Oxford UP, 2006 and 2007), p 119.

importantly, the types of behaviour in question normally affect the way an individual chooses to live his or her life in a very deep way. They could involve the conduct of personal relationships, manifestations of strongly personal beliefs, and so on. This threatens to invade the privileged sphere,[45] and may even be inconsistent with the proper functioning of the open society. None of this is to say that programmes extolling the virtues of communal, including of course family, co-operation and harmony, and indicating how these may be achieved or maintained, should not be promoted, as Liz Trinder observes in the case of contact between non-resident parents and children, citing the Family Resolutions pilot.[46] Law can create frameworks and institutions which can promote intra-communal collaboration.

But I have also argued that law and related institutions can have a more critical role in protecting individuals *against* the communities (including families) in which they are involved. This may include providing a means by which individuals can bring about a modification of community norms or practice. In other cases, it may create an escape route from them. In the case of families, this could include norms for, and enforcement of, fair settlements on divorce, or police protection against honour killing. For broader communities, they include promotion of freedom of religion and the whole apparatus of civil society which allows individuals to move between communities and establish identities of their own. For group hostility, or the cruelty that can be inflicted within families, can be terrible things. In those cases, it is *only* legal or kindred institutions that can counterbalance those forces, and often that is difficult enough. Communities may have changed their form, and become more complex. They have not gone away. The need for the protective role of the law may be greater now than ever.

---

[45] *Family Law and Personal Life*, p 82ff.
[46] Liz Trinder and Joanne Kellett 'Fairness, efficiency and effectiveness in court-based dispute resolution schemes in England' (2007) 21 *International Journal of Law, Policy & Family* 323.

CHAPTER 8

THE FUTURE OF MARRIAGE

Brenda Hale

INTRODUCTION

We are here to celebrate the 150th anniversary of the beginnings of modern divorce and family law in the Matrimonial Causes Act 1857 and the 50th anniversary of the publication which celebrated its centenary, *A Century of Family Law 1857–1957*, edited by Ronald Graveson and Roger Crane.[1] It is difficult now to realise just how few academic books on Family Law there were in those days. Apart from the practitioners' text-books, there were O R McGregor's socio-legal study of *Divorce in England – A Centenary Study*[2] and Peter Bromley's pioneering academic legal text on *Family Law*, both also published in 1957.[3] The explosion in academic writing by family lawyers took off in 1971, with John Eekelaar's *Family security and family breakdown*.[4] So, although today is about the future, a little retrospection seems in order.

WHAT IS THE LEGAL INSTITUTION OF MARRIAGE FOR? THE INDIVIDUALS OR THE STATE?

Any discussion about whether marriage has a future has to ask what the legal institution is for. The great Dicey saw it as an instance of the struggle between the interests of the individual and the interests of the state:[5]

> 'If marriage be looked upon mainly as a contract between man and wife it is obviously reasonable to put an end to a marriage of two persons when it causes deep unhappiness to both, or when it causes misery to one party and gives very little happiness to the other ... But if divorce be looked upon mainly from the point of view of a sane collectivist, the question whether divorce should be facilitated becomes an inquiry far more difficult to answer. Marriage, he will argue, when treated as a union which hardly admits of

---

[1] (Sweet & Maxwell, 1957).
[2] (Heinemann, 1957).
[3] (Butterworths, 1957).
[4] (Penguin Books, 1971).
[5] A V Dicey 'Introduction to the Second Edition', *Law and Public Opinion in England during the Nineteenth Century* (Macmillan, 2nd edn, 1914), p lxxix.

dissolution, confers great benefits upon the State ... [For him] the relief which divorce may give to an individual suffering from an unhappy marriage cannot be a decisive consideration.'

Why should the indissolubility of marriage have been seen as conferring great benefits upon the state? There are two obvious answers to the question of what *legal* marriage is for. First, as John Eekelaar has put it, 'Humans need a way to ensure that wealth and power pass from one generation on its demise to the newly born'.[6] In patrilineal societies like ours, they want to ensure reliable descent through the male line. They also mind about the quality of the line and about forging alliances with other suitable lines. So a marriage with a suitable woman is arranged, after which it is presumed that all the children she has are her husband's children. This necessarily entails a strong obligation of fidelity in the wife, though not necessarily in the husband.[7] Nor does it necessarily entail a lifelong union. If the business is done, the heir and the spare supplied, the wife can be dispensed with. If the business is not done at all, she can be dispensed with too.

The state's interest in a lifelong union must stem from something other than the dynastic needs of the rich and powerful. The conjugal family is its own little social security system, a private space, separate from the public world, within which the parties are expected to look after one another and their children. The more the private family can look after its own, the less the state will have to do so. So of course the sane collectivist will want to strengthen family ties and to reinforce family responsibilities. As the first Lord Chancellor Hailsham put it in *Hyman v Hyman*,[8] the power of the court to secure sufficient provision for a wife when her marriage was dissolved was not only in her interests, but in the interests of the public: hence the parties' inability to oust the jurisdiction of the court in a private agreement.

The sane collectivist may therefore deplore the increasing dissolubility of marriage. But he should welcome two other trends in modern family law. These are, first, the great improvements in its treatment of the married home-maker and care-giver since 1957; and secondly, the more recent moves to extend some of that tenderness to relationships outside marriage. Of course, if you are the sort of collectivist who subscribes to the vision of a welfare state which supports us all from cradle to grave,

---

[6] *Family Law and Personal Life* (Oxford UP, 2006), p 57.
[7] Finer and McGregor 'History of the Obligation to Maintain, Appendix 5 to the Report of the Finer Committee on One-Parent Families, Cmnd 5629 (1974) assert that the strength of the wifely obligation depended upon the family's inheritance practices. In a system of primogeniture, as practised by the landed aristocracy and gentry, spurious children did not radically affect the source of the family's status and power; it was enough for the wife to produce 'the heir and the spare' before playing away. In a system of partible inheritance, as practised by the commercial middle classes, spurious children were a much greater threat, and adultery consequently disapproved.
[8] [1929] AC 601 at 614.

you will have misgivings about anything which may look like an excuse for the state to withdraw or reduce its support as well as imposing dominant relationship norms on people who want to choose a different way of life.[9] Expanding the scope and content of private family responsibilities can be threatening both to socialists and to individualists alike. But for most of us, when the going gets rough, the family is our first port of call for support of all kinds, some of it financial.

But even if there is indeed a role for private family responsibilities, that does not answer the question of where the legal institution of marriage fits into the picture. Eric Clive and I both raised this question at the Conference of the International Society on Family Law in Uppsala in 1979.[10] His paper was much more radical than mine, and he was soon to become a member of the Scottish Law Commission, but I was the one who got the flak from certain sections of the press when I repeated the paper more than a decade later.[11] My purpose then was to demonstrate how and why the question had to be asked. If we wanted the family to look after those who for one reason or another could not compete in the market place on equal terms, how much should it matter whether or not the adults were married to one another? My purpose now is to suggest that there is still a case for privileging the status of marriage; but that does depend upon what sort of an institution it is. Old-fashioned patriarchy is one thing; a modern partnership of equals is quite another. Nor should retaining a privileged status, whether marriage or civil partnership, rule out extending some of its functions to other forms of family arrangement.

THE RISE OF MARRIAGE AS AN EQUAL PARTNERSHIP

When Graveson and Crane published their retrospective, marriage was still firmly rooted in the old patriarchal system, albeit overlaid with what can historically be regarded as the kinder approach of the Christian Church. Families consisted of people related by consanguinity or affinity, blood or marriage. Stephen Cretney has already pointed out that in 1974 the Law Commission did not regard cohabitation as a 'family' relationship.[12] Blood relationships rarely counted for anything unless they were traced through marriage. The child of unmarried parents was not legally related to his father or his father's family (although his father might be made to contribute small sums towards his maintenance) and his

---

[9] For example, A Diduck 'Shifting Familiarity' (2005) 58 *Current Legal Problems* 235.
[10] E Clive 'Marriage: An Unnecessary Legal Concept?'; B Hoggett 'Ends and Means: The Utility of Marriage as a Legal Institution' in J M Eekelaar and S N Katz *Marriage and Cohabitation in Contemporary Societies: Areas of Legal, Social and Ethical Change* (Butterworths, 1980).
[11] At a seminar in a series organised by Relate at the Nuffield Foundation on 9 March 1994.
[12] Law Commission *Family Law, Second Report on Family Property: Family Provision on Death*, Law Com No 61 (HMSO, 1974), para 10.

relationship with his mother's family was very limited. The presumption that a child born to a married woman was her husband's child was extremely difficult to rebut. The fault-based system of divorce was seen as a strong incentive to both parties to stay together, but the incentive operated much more strongly upon the wife than upon the husband. A wife's marital behaviour was central to what she might expect if the couple parted. If she was judged at fault she risked losing her home, her livelihood and even her children. If he was at fault, he could keep his home, the major part of his income, and still expect a fatherly relationship with his children. For the vast majority of women, who had little choice but to adopt the traditional gender role, these were powerful incentives to stay at home and in line.

The criticism that developed during the 1950s and 1960s, led by Lord Denning, was that the law was not kind enough to the traditional female role. But his efforts to improve the protection given to the good wife and mother were largely rebuffed by the House of Lords. Parliament began to step in. Over the two decades beginning with the Matrimonial Homes Act 1967,[13] family law was theoretically transformed, although Stephen Cretney has taught us how slow the practitioners were to catch up with this.[14] It became sex-neutral, in that the same rules and remedies applied both to husbands and to wives. The law could now contemplate a househusband, in theory at least, or the equal sharing of homemaking and breadwinning roles, or swapping between the two as circumstances changed.

It also became much kinder to the homemaker and care-giver. The remedies available to her both during and after the relationship were vastly improved. The 'statutory objective' of the law of ancillary relief on divorce, later to be repealed, assumed that the divorce had not taken place. This meant that the parties would have continued to enjoy much the same standard of living. It therefore meant an equality of outcome of sorts, even if only an equality of misery. It also meant an equality of treatment of their respective marital behaviour. If all their property, both individually and jointly owned, was in principle up for sharing on the principle of equal misery, then their conduct should only affect the distribution if there had been a gross disparity between them. No longer was the guilty husband being stripped of some of his assets to support his blameless wife. No longer would the woman lose out if she had not been and did not remain 100% blameless. These principles were clearly recognised in the landmark case of *Wachtel v Wachtel*,[15] much maligned though it later became.[16]

---

[13] Not technically a Law Commission project, but the precursor of many others.
[14] *Family Law in the Twentieth Century, A History* (Oxford UP, 2003), especially ch 10.
[15] [1973] Fam 72, CA.
[16] For example, *Dart v Dart* [1996] 2 FLR 286, CA at 294, per Thorpe LJ: 'the reality is that it has been consistently rejected as a case of general application'.

However, before the new law came into force in 1971, the profession had largely focused on need, and afterwards they continued to focus on need, now rather more generously defined as 'reasonable requirements'. The improved remedies made it easier to preserve a roof over the mother's and children's heads, which was recognised as the first priority.[17] But this was still not true equality. Talk of earning a share in the family's assets, in some of the early cases in the 1970s,[18] soon gave way to the reasonable requirements approach.[19]

Eventually, the House of Lords stepped in, first in *White v White*[20] and then in *Miller v Miller; McFarlane v McFarlane*.[21] In *White*, their lordships insisted that the court's powers were not there only to cater for the wife and her children's needs or 'reasonable requirements'; they should also reflect an egalitarian norm of sharing within marriage; and that the differing contributions of the spouses, whether in home-making or money-making, were to be regarded as equally valuable. The overarching theme was fairness, but fairness meaning equality: equality of esteem for the differing contributions which each had made to the welfare of the family over time and equality of result as the yardstick against which the outcome of weighing the relevant factors listed in s 25 of the Matrimonial Causes Act 1973 should be measured. Those themes were reinforced in *Miller/McFarlane*, where there was a more extended discussion of the principles underlying the redistribution of assets on divorce. There was also some acknowledgement of the difference between equality of division and equality of outcome, which are rather different things.[22]

No one can blame the cranks, the troublemakers or extravagant feminist ambition for these developments. They were largely the work of serious men born in the 1930s and married well before the arrival of women's liberation in the 1960s.[23] The more cautious voices in *Miller/McFarlane*

---

[17] *Scott v Scott* [1978] 3 All ER 65.
[18] Not only *Wachtel v Wachtel* [1973] Fam 72; see e g *Trippas v Trippas* [1973] Fam 134, CA at 146, where Scarman LJ stated that 'there is nothing either in the so-called one third rule or in the language of the Act of 1970 which precludes this court from doing rough justice on the basis of approximate equality'.
[19] *O'D v O'D* [1976] Fam 83, CA; the high-water mark may be *Page v Page* (1981) 2 FLR 198, CA, but *Dart v Dart* [1996] 2 FLR 286, CA is a serious competitor.
[20] [2001] 1 AC 596.
[21] [2006] UKHL 24, [2006] 2 AC 618.
[22] [2006] UKHL 24, [2006] 2 AC 618 at [142], per Baroness Hale: 'Too strict an adherence to equal sharing and the clean break can lead to a rapid decrease in the primary carer's standard of living and a rapid increase in the breadwinner's'.
[23] Lord Nicholls, born 1933, married 1960; Lord Hoffmann, born 1934, married 1957; Lord Cooke, born 1926, married 1952; Lord Hope, born 1938, married 1966; Lord Hutton, born 1931, married 1975.

were the two 'youngest' judges,[24] born in the 1940s and married during or after the advent of 'women's liberation' in *The Feminine Mystique*[25] and *The Female Eunuch*.[26]

Other things had flowed from the developing recognition of equality within marriage. Married mothers at long last gained a status equal to that of married fathers while the parents were together[27] and in practice became a good deal more powerful once they were apart. This was because of the importance attached to keeping the children in a stable home with their primary care-giver, still in the great majority of cases the children's mother.

So now we had an institution that was no longer indissoluble but was in principle a great deal better at looking after its weaker members when things went wrong. There may, of course, have been a link between the two. Lord Evershed, in his Foreword to *A Century of Family Law*, stated that 'the two things, the multiplicity of divorces and the emancipated status of women have necessarily gone hand in hand'.[28] It is not entirely clear whether he meant that women had to be emancipated because men were abandoning their traditional responsibilities or whether he meant that women's freedom in the outside world made them increasingly willing to abandon theirs. Perhaps he meant both. But he was clearly deeply suspicious of the idea that 'husband and wife in law and in form would become ... partners in the firm of marriage. If such were the end, then clearly Lord Penzance's definition of marriage would cease to have significance and the family could no longer survive as the essential unit of society'.[29] Over the last 50 years, marriage law has indeed moved from patriarchy to equality. Marriage is no longer 'the voluntary union for life of one man and one woman to the exclusion of all others', although that is still what people hope and contract for when they marry. But the family still survives as the essential unit of society and I would argue that it is better and stronger as a result.

THE FLIGHT FROM MARRIAGE: IS EQUALITY TO BLAME?

Alongside these developments in marriage law were equally important developments in child law. The child of unmarried parents is now related to both his mother's and his father's families in the same way as if they were married. References to relationships are to be construed without regard to whether or not the parents of anyone through whom the

---

[24] Lady Hale, born 1945, married 1968; Lord Mance, born 1943, married 1973; but Lord Hoffmann agreed with them.
[25] Betty Friedan *The Feminine Mystique* (Victor Gollancz, 1963).
[26] Germaine Greer *The Female Eunuch* (MacGibbon & Kee, 1970).
[27] Guardianship Act 1973.
[28] Op cit, p xi.
[29] Op cit, p xvi.

relationship is traced were married to one another.[30] Almost all the remaining differences in the law's treatment of the child have gone. So too has the assumption that fatherhood is hard to prove. A father can have the same legal relationship with his children as does a married father, whether by court order, agreement with the mother, or (for births registered on or after 1 December 2003) by registration, irrespective of whether or not he is living with the family.[31]

These legal developments have been accompanied by a developing trend away from marriage and towards living together without marrying. The great story in the 1970s and 1980s was the increasing percentage of lone parent families: this more than tripled from 1972 to 2006, but has risen much more slowly over the last decade than it did over the preceding two. The proportion of all families which is headed by a lone parent rose less than one per cent from 1996 to 2006. The great story of the 1990s and the present century is the increasing percentage of cohabiting couples: from 9% of all families in 1996 to 14% in 2006. There are now as many cohabiting couple families as there are lone mother families. Some of those lone mothers may well be in long term relationships. There is a phenomenon, well know to family judges but not yet caught by the statistics, known as 'living apart together'. Married couples are still the great majority of families, but have dropped from 76% to 71% over the same period.[32]

So how to explain this apparent flight from marriage? Some may be inclined to blame it on the law. If so, there could be more than one culprit. The first is the equal partnership view of marriage. After *Miller/McFarlane*, the cry went up from sections of the popular press that equality would be the death of marriage. This was not for the first time. I am fond of quoting a warning given by Tony Honoré, better known as Regius Professor of Law in the University of Oxford, in his Hamlyn lectures,[33] published in 1982:

> 'In our pursuit of security for the weak we have overlooked the paradoxical fact that the interests of the weakest often depend upon the security of the strong.'

In other words, if I understand him aright, you will only persuade the strong to give their protection to the weak if their own security is not too much endangered by doing so. He predicted that the more protection marriage gave to wives, the more reluctant men would be to become husbands. He did acknowledge the near impossibility of proving this, but the figures quoted above may give him some support.

---

[30] Family Law Reform Act 1987, s 1.
[31] Children Act 1989, s 4, as amended by the Adoption and Children Act 2002, s 111.
[32] National Statistics Online. See further, Chapter 1 above.
[33] *The Quest for Security: Employees, Tenants, Wives* (Stevens, 1982), p 117.

But post hoc does not necessarily mean propter hoc. The acceptance of cohabitation was already well established before *White* and *Miller/ McFarlane*. In the 2006 survey of British Social Attitudes,[34] two-thirds believed that 'there is little difference socially between being married and living together' and only a fifth disagreed. Both in 2000 and 2006, only 28% agreed that married couples make better parents than unmarried ones, and 40% disagreed. There is now widespread acceptance of living together and having children outside marriage. But living together is seen as very like marriage. In their qualitative study, Anne Barlow and her colleagues[35] found that cohabiting people had three broad attitudes to the relationship:

(1) cohabitation as a prelude to marriage;

(2) cohabitation as a variety of marriage; and

(3) cohabitation as an alternative to marriage.

Only the third amounts to a deliberate rejection of marriage. They found two main reasons for doing this.[36]

The first was 'a principled desire to escape patriarchy, where marriage was seen as first and foremost a patriarchal institution'. To a lawyer's eyes, this is no longer obviously rational. There is nothing in marriage law these days which imposes gendered roles on either spouse. In theory they are free to decide for themselves who will do what and how they will run their lives. But that does not rob this view of its validity. Whatever the law may say, people may still conduct their lives in gendered ways and may even assume that they should. There is still quite enough discrimination in the workplace to make it rational for many couples to agree that the man will concentrate on breadwinning and the woman on home-making. Even when the woman is working full time outside the home, there are still must-do household tasks which the men are reluctant to undertake.[37] There is still considerable pressure on mothers to stay at home with their babies in the early days. Anyone who leaves the workplace for any length of time loses, not only salary, but pension contributions which are hard to make up at a later date.[38]

It is also possible that, whatever the law may in theory say, courts and judges up and down the country still make decisions based upon the gender stereotypes which held so firm until comparatively recently. After

---

[34] A Park et al (eds) *British Social Attitudes, The 24th Report* (Sage, 2008).

[35] A Barlow, S Duncan, G James and A Park *Cohabitation, Marriage and the Law* (Hart, 2005).

[36] Ibid, p 72.

[37] R Crompton and C Lyonette 'Who does the housework? The division of labour within the home', in A Park et al, op cit.

[38] J Ginn and D Price 'Do divorced women catch up in pension building?' [2002] CFLQ 157.

all, one very senior judge has recently declared that 'mothers are special'.[39] He may not be alone in that view. This is undoubtedly the perception of many fathers when they encounter the family justice system. If the courts do still consciously or unconsciously apply stereotypical assumptions when making their decisions, then women as well as men may feel that this is an institution which they do not want to join. However, recent evidence compiled by Joan Hunt and Alison Macleod makes this view much less tenable.[40]

The second reason for rejecting marriage found by Barlow and her colleagues was 'disillusion with marriage as an effective institution'. This makes much more sense. I was constantly amazed by the popular expectation that the law could force people to live together. The cohabitants who were disillusioned with marriage were strongly influenced by their experience of divorce, either their own or others' within their families. So the marital relationship was seen as fragile and the ending messy. Divorce itself may be simple to obtain, but the financial consequences can be difficult and expensive to disentangle. They can result in the one who owns or earns the most losing a good share of his assets to the other.

This disillusion can affect both sexes. To a much greater extent than Tony Honoré might have predicted in 1982, and despite all the workplace difficulties referred to earlier, the economically more powerful partner may well be the woman, especially at the outset of the relationship before children come along. More and more women see themselves as economically independent and are reluctant to give this up. They may no longer be prepared to risk relying on a man. Mavis Maclean and John Eekelaar, in their study of risk-taking in partner relationships,[41] were surprised to find an—

> 'almost universal awareness of the economic vulnerability of women, and the feeling that women should take steps to protect themselves, whether they were married or not. This vulnerability was firmly linked to gender and child care responsibilities.'

It is not only that women may be reluctant to surrender their independence. Women who are economically independent may not yet have developed the traditional protective responsibility towards their less powerful partners that the best of men have had for centuries. If Mrs Cowan had been the one to make money out of the bag on a roll,[42] would she have wanted to share the profits with a househusband? If both

---

[39] *Re G (Children) (Residence: Same-sex Partner)* [2006] UKHL 43, [2006] 1 WLR 2305 at [3], per Lord Scott of Foscote.
[40] J Hunt and A Macleod *Outcomes of applications to court for contact orders after parental separation and divorce* (Ministry of Justice, 2008).
[41] 'Taking the plunge: perceptions of risk-taking associated with formal and informal partner relations' [2005] CFLQ 247 at 257.
[42] *Cowan v Cowan* [2001] EWCA Civ 679, [2002] Fam 97, CA.

men and women are behaving like economic man, then it would not be surprising if the most independent and successful of them were increasingly reluctant to marry.

The second possible culprit could be the reform of child law, coupled with the scientific advances which made it possible. A man can now identify and have a full legal relationship with his children irrespective of whether or not he is married to their mother. That was not so until the reforms which began with the Family Law Reform Act 1969. Although he is still not in exactly the same position as a married father, his position now is radically different from what it was, and the remaining differences will become less and less important now that parental responsibility depends upon registration. I may not be the only one to have argued that, if a man can now have what used to be the principal legal benefit to be gained from getting married, a legal as well as an emotional relationship with his children, and without undertaking the concomitant legal responsibilities towards a wife, why should he bother to get married?

On the whole, however, the research evidence does not support either the Honoré or the Hale hypothesis. People do not choose between marriage and cohabitation in such a coldly rational way. Anne Barlow and her colleagues call this the 'policy makers' rationality mistake'.[43] Most cohabitants are not specifically rejecting marriage. Those who cohabit as a prelude to marriage are trying it out, either with a view to marriage if it works out as they hope, or in the vague expectation that they will marry some time in the future. The catalyst for setting up home together may be an unplanned pregnancy – the shotgun cohabitation having replaced the shotgun marriage. But this trial may well drift on for a considerable time, turning into 'cohabitation as a variety of marriage'. These cohabitants saw themselves 'as good as married'. They were as committed to one another and their lives together as any married people. They simply had not yet got round to marrying. Often this was because they did not see the point of a cheap and simple wedding. People do seem to confuse marriage with the wedding. If they got married at all, they wanted something altogether more expensive and elaborate. For these people, marriage might still be seen as an ideal arrangement, but too soon, too expensive or too important for them undertake just yet. This fits in well with the suggestion from US research that people tend to defer marriage until they feel financially secure: that 'people marry now less for the social benefits that marriages provides than for the personal achievements it represents'.[44]

These findings are borne out by the 2006 British Social Attitudes survey. Very few people think that 'there is no point in getting married – it's only

---

[43] A Barlow, S Duncan, G James and A Park *Cohabitation, Marriage and the Law* (Hart, 2005).

[44] A Cherlin 'The deinstitutionalization of American marriage' (2004) 66 *Journal of Marriage and the Family* 848 at 857.

a piece of paper'. More than half still believe that 'even though it might not work out for some people, marriage is still the best kind of relationship'.[45] Similar views were echoed in John Eekelaar and Mavis Maclean's smaller study,[46] which also asked why people had married. For a few it was primarily pragmatic – because they wanted to work abroad or save inheritance tax; for others it was to conform to religious norms, parental expectations, or social or cultural practice; for a similar number, it was to confirm, complete or embark upon a personal commitment to the other person.

Another reason to doubt both the Honoré and the Hale hypotheses is that there is little evidence that even the people who deliberately reject marriage know much about the different legal consequences of marriage and cohabitation. People very rarely take legal advice before doing either. Very few cohabitants have taken the obvious steps, which they ought to take if they do not intend to marry, such as making a will, a written agreement about ownership of the home or a parental responsibility agreement about the children. Belief in the myth of the 'common law marriage' is still widespread. The 2000 British Social Attitudes Survey[47] found that 56% of the population believed that people who lived together for some time without being married had the same legal rights as married couples. The proportion was even higher, 59%, among parents, both married and unmarried, and current cohabitants, although these were the people most likely to be adversely affected by their mistake. The 2006 survey showed no increase in the proportion of non-believers, but a decrease in the proportion of believers, to 51% and 53% respectively, and a corresponding increase in the 'don't knows'. Even so, just over half the population still believe.[48] Other studies made similar findings.[49] The one thing that does seem to have changed is that, in 2006, 61% of people believed that 'marriage gives couples more financial security than living together', whereas only 48% did so in 2000. It may be that the publicity given to *White v White* and some of the cases following it has contributed to this. But this view was held by slightly less than half of cohabitants, compared with two-thirds of married people.[50] So it seems that many cohabitants are still falsely optimistic about their legal position, despite the government's publicity campaign aimed at dispelling the myth.

---

[45] S Duncan and M Phillips 'New families? Tradition and change in modern relationships' in A Park et al (eds) *British Social Attitudes, The 24th Report* (Sage, 2008), p 8.

[46] 'Marriage and the Moral Bases of Personal Relationships' (2004) 31 JLS 510.

[47] Reported by A Barlow, S Duncan, G James and A Park *Cohabitation, Marriage and the Law* (Hart, 2005) and elsewhere.

[48] A Barlow et al 'Cohabitation and the law: myths, money and the media' in A Park et al (eds), op cit, p 41.

[49] For example, Ros Pickford's small qualitative study of unmarried parents, *Fathers, Marriage and the Law* (Family Policy Studies Centre/JRF, 1999); and J Eekelaar and M Maclean 'Taking the plunge: perceptions of risk-taking associated with formal and informal partner relations' [2005] CFLQ 247.

[50] A Barlow et al, loc cit, in A Park et al, op cit, p 35.

Perhaps we should not be surprised that people make decisions about intimate personal relationships for sentimental rather than instrumental reasons. How many of us, when deciding whether to move in together or whether to marry gave much thought to the legal position? It seems, then, that the allegation that equality will be the death of marriage cannot be proved. Surely equality should be celebrated rather than condemned? But that hard-won principle does seem to be under threat from several quarters.

THREATS TO THE EQUAL PARTNERSHIP

The first challenge has come from the judiciary themselves. *Charman v Charman*[51] was the first case to reach the Court of Appeal after *Miller/McFarlane*. In an extended postscript to their judgment, the court went out of their way to call for a review of the law, a call which had received a much less enthusiastic response from the family judiciary while 'reasonable requirements' still held sway.[52] The Family Justice Council has asked the Law Commission to include the reform of s 25 in its forthcoming programme of law reform. The Commission has, however, declined that invitation.[53]

Maybe these judges believe that they are closer to public opinion. Maybe they are, though we all know that big money cases are not what the world is really about, and in *Miller/McFarlane* we did take account of the attitudes to financial provision revealed by Sue Arthur and her colleagues in *Settling Up*.[54] Nor do the attitudes to financial provision for cohabitants revealed by the 2006 British Social Attitudes survey give them much comfort.[55] Almost certainly the judges are closer to the views of the legal profession, which, as always, are slow to change. And it was those views that led to the travesty which was the first instance decision in *White v White*. Even in a genuine economic partnership between husband and wife, 'reasonable requirements' worked in a discriminatory way. But I take some comfort from a prominent member of the profession who has recently told me that clients can understand and even accept the three principles identified in *Miller/McFarlane*.

One nagging doubt may be whether economic contributions should indeed be regarded on the same level as other contributions. The idea that they are incommensurable and must therefore be presumptively equal may not find universal favour, and not only from the big money makers. A wife who has gone out to work all her married life, borne and brought up the

---

[51] [2007] EWCA Civ 503, [2007] 1 FLR 1246, CA.
[52] *Report to the Lord Chancellor by the Ancillary Relief Advisory Group* (1998).
[53] Law Commission *Tenth Programme of Law Reform*, Law Com No 311 (TSO, 2008), paras 5.4–5.9.
[54] S Arthur et al *Settling Up: making financial arrangements after divorce or separation* (National Centre for Social Research, 2002).
[55] A Barlow et al, loc cit, in A Park et al (eds), op cit, 2008, pp 44–47.

children, and done her share of the household chores, may well feel that she deserves more out of the family cake than a wife who has not tried to do it all.[56] There is some hint of this in *Miller/McFarlane*, with the suggestion that the sharing principle might not apply to couples who have kept their finances generally separate and have no need to make calls upon one another.[57] But if that were so, the lower earning one in that family might end up less well off than the stay at home wife in another family.

This leads on to the second challenge to equality. How much weight should we give, not only to how the couple have arranged their finances during the marriage, but also to what they have agreed should happen if it ends? We are told that *Miller/McFarlane* has already led to an increased demand for pre-nuptial agreements from those with most to lose from the new approach. The Solicitors Family Law Association, now known as Resolution, has already recommended that:

> 'any agreement entered into between the parties to the marriage, in contemplation of, or after the marriage for the purpose of regulating their affairs on the breakdown of their marriage, ... shall be considered binding upon them unless to do so will cause significant injustice to either party or to any ... minor child of the family.'[58]

The courts have already moved some way in the same direction. In *MacLeod v MacLeod*[59] the Judicial Committee of the Privy Council held valid a post-nuptial agreement even though it covered what should happen in the event of a future separation or divorce, which had previously been thought contrary to public policy. But legislation would be necessary to make pre-nuptial agreements valid. Even though they are not strictly enforceable, the courts dealing with financial provision on divorce may well take them into account in deciding what is fair. In *Crossley v Crossley*[60] the couple were just the sort of people for whom pre-nups might have been invented: aged 60 and 50, independently wealthy, previously married with children from their previous relationships. Furthermore, they were just the sort of couple to whom, on the face of it, the various rationales for redistribution might not apply: a short, childless marriage, during which no extra wealth had been accumulated and no relationship-related detriment suffered. But it is hard to imagine that it would have occurred either to Mr and Mrs Cowan or to Mr and Mrs Charman to make a pre-nup when they married; or, more significantly, that what they might have agreed then would have had much

---

[56] One suspects that this was how the woman felt in *Stack v Dowden* [2007] UKHL 17; [2007] 2 AC 432.
[57] [2006] 2 AC 618 at [25], per Lord Nicholls; at [153], per Baroness Hale; at [170], per Lord Mance.
[58] Solicitors Family Law Association *A more certain future, Recognition of pre-marital agreements in England and Wales* (2004), para 7.7.
[59] [2008] UKPC 64, [2008] WLR (D) 402.
[60] [2007] EWCA Civ 1491, [2008] 1 FLR 1467.

relevance to what would have been the just solution many years later when they had acquired not only several children but also significant wealth. Nevertheless, as Thorpe LJ commented, 'It does seem to me that the role of contractual dealing, the opportunity for the autonomy of the parties, is becoming increasingly important'.[61] The Law Commission plan to begin work on marital property agreements in September 2009.[62]

A third challenge may emerge when the courts have to deal with the dissolution of civil partnerships. Professor Ken Norrie, for example, has argued that it is inappropriate to project the standards and values of heterosexual relationships onto relationships which have some important differences.[63] Aside from what he suggests is a significantly different approach to sexual fidelity, he argues that the partners to a homosexual relationship are likely to be economically independent of one another to a much greater degree than are most heterosexual partners, so that remedies and assumptions based upon economic as well as social and emotional interdependence may not be appropriate. Once again, how much weight should be given to the ways in which the partners themselves have chosen to run their affairs? Or should we say that, if they choose to contract into the status of civil partnership, they contract into the principles of equality which come with it?

The fourth challenge is even more sensitive. If we start accepting that the different values and attitudes of same sex couples should colour our approach to ancillary relief, what should we say about the different values and attitudes of couples from different religious or ethnic backgrounds? In his controversial lecture,[64] the Archbishop of Canterbury was indeed arguing for a greater legal recognition of differing religious and cultural identities:

> 'I have been arguing that a defence of an unqualified secular legal monopoly in terms of the need for a universalist doctrine of human rights or dignity is to misunderstand the circumstances in which that doctrine emerged, and that the essential liberating (and religiously informed) vision it represents is not imperilled by a loosening of the monopolistic framework.'

Quite what he means by a 'loosening of the monopolistic framework', when he also contemplates 'a scheme in which individuals retain the liberty to choose the jurisdiction under which they will seek to resolve certain carefully specified matters', may not be clear. But he does say that—

---

[61] At [17].
[62] Law Commission *Tenth Programme of Law Reform*, Law Com No 311 (TSO, 2008), paras 2.1 and 2.17–2.20.
[63] 'Marriage is for heterosexuals – may the rest of us be saved from it' [2000] CFLQ 363.
[64] 'Civil and Religious Law in England: a Religious Perspective' (Royal Courts of Justice, 7 February 2008).

'It would be a pity if the immense advances in the recognition of human rights led, because of a misconception about legal universality, to a situation where a person was defined primarily as a possessor of a set of abstract liberties and the law's function was accordingly seen as nothing but the securing of those liberties irrespective of the custom and conscience of those groups which concretely compose a plural modern democracy.'

I do not think that he is arguing for separate personal laws for the adherents of different religions. That would be hard to square with his support for individual choice. But he might be arguing for the conscious opting out, not only from the ordinary courts of law, but also from the ordinary principles of the law. To some extent that is already happening, with some people choosing not to marry according to the laws of the land but only according to their own religion. He might also be arguing for the ordinary law, where it has a choice, to give weight to the religious and cultural context within which the couple led their lives.

Is this just another aspect of the weight to be given to the choices the couple themselves have made about themselves? Or is it to take the first step along the slippery slope away from the universal principle of equality between the spouses, towards accepting that because the wife is not regarded as her husband's equal in some communities, she should not be regarded as his equal by the ordinary law of the land? Some might think that the construction of the slippery slope has already begun, with the provisions which make the giving of a religious divorce a condition of obtaining a civil release.[65] These were inserted for the humane purpose of relieving the situation of orthodox Jewish women who, although divorced in civil law, could not remarry and have legitimate children according to their religious law unless their husbands agreed to give them a 'get'. The motive is laudable but the principle of adapting secular law to mitigate the rigid requirements of an unchangeable religious law is dangerous.

DOES MARRIAGE HAVE A FUTURE?

I sincerely hope that the legal institution of marriage does have a future. But that future should retain the hard-won principle that marriage is a partnership of equals. Hitherto, our law has taken the view that, if you contract into the privileged legal status of marriage, you contract into the legal consequences which the state has prescribed for it. Individual autonomy has, to some extent, to give way to the collective good. If you do not want that privileged legal status, you may be able to make your own contractual arrangements, but you will inevitably forgo some of the privileges which go with the status. We have just about reached the point where the status brings with it the principle of equality. We should, in my view, be very wary of allowing the parties to contract out of that principle unless we are very sure that the contract is itself a manifestation of their truly equal status in the relationship. Equality is the distinctive principle

---

[65] Matrimonial Causes Act 1973, s 10A.

which the legal institution of marriage has to offer. Without it, we might just as well fall back on cohabitation contracts and the minimal compensatory scheme which the Law Commission has recently recommended.[66]

Marriage, as an increasingly equal partnership, has so far survived despite the dire predictions of Lord Evershed, so perhaps it does indeed have a future. But if it loses that vital principle, then perhaps it does not deserve one.

---

[66] Law Commission *Cohabitation: The Financial Consequences of Relationship Breakdown*, Law Com No 307, Cm 7182 (2007). Cf Resolution *Reforming the law for people who live together. A Consultation Paper* (September 2008).

CHAPTER 9

THE FUTURE FOR ANCILLARY RELIEF

Elizabeth Cooke[1]

INTRODUCTION

A natural starting point for my paper might be the recent judicial developments in this area; the shift from the 'yardstick of equality' to the 'sharing principle'; and the discretionary characteristics of non-matrimonial property. These are exciting developments, and the aftermath of *White v White*,[2] *Miller v Miller; McFarlane v McFarlane*,[3] and *Charman v Charman*[4] will keep the courts busy for a long time. Although I will return later to some of these issues, I want to look broadly at the context and nature of ancillary relief. My starting point, therefore, will be Dr Cretney's paper, in which he explained the pressure exerted in the 1960s for a move to community of property,[5] followed by the Law Commission's more limited advocacy in the 1970s for statutory co-ownership of the matrimonial home. The legislature might have chosen, in the 1960s and 1970s, to do something with a very continental European flavour. It had the opportunity to opt for community of property, or something very like it, but for a variety of reasons did not do so.

What I would like to suggest, as we look forward to the next 50 years, is that we ask two questions. First, how 'European' is the law of ancillary relief? And second, how European should it become?

If the first of those two questions had been asked in 1970, the answer would have been 'not at all'. Until 1970 we did have something that a continental European lawyer might accurately have described as a regime of separation of property. But from then onwards we had ancillary relief based upon discretionary property adjustment, which is quite foreign to continental European law and practice. From the point when the Matrimonial Proceedings and Property Act 1970 came into force,

---

[1] Professor of Law, University of Reading. By the time this paper is published I shall be serving as Law Commissioner; but of course the paper gestated before that appointment was made, and it is not written from a Law Commission point of view.
[2] *White v White* [2001] 1 AC 596.
[3] [2006] UKHL 24, [2006] 2 AC 618.
[4] [2007] EWCA Civ 503, [2007] 1 FLR 1246.
[5] In particular, Edith Summerskill's promise to support the Divorce Reform Bill if community of property were introduced; see S Cretney at Chapter 2 above.

ancillary relief belonged squarely in the common law tradition of equitable distribution[6] and was as thoroughly divorced from mainstream European matrimonial property law as could be imagined.

Now is a good time to ask how European is the law of ancillary relief today, partly because it has undergone some dramatic changes recently which have something of a European look about them; and partly because the publication of the European Commission's Green Paper on Matrimonial Property Regimes,[7] and the responses thereto,[8] means that we have an opportunity to look afresh at the way continental Europeans describe their law of matrimonial property. It also means that our system is under some European pressure, and there is quite a pressing need to think how we relate to and fit into European matrimonial property law, if at all. In order to answer that question I would like first to comment, briefly, on mainstream European matrimonial property law; then to examine some aspects of ancillary relief that have a distinctly European flavour to them; and thirdly to look at the UK's response to the European Commission's initiatives in private international law in this context. In the light of those points we can get a sense of how European, if at all, ancillary relief is; only then can we address the second question: how European should it become? And to that I am going to give only a partial answer, followed by some suggestions about research that needs to be done before we can answer it properly.

MATRIMONIAL REGIMES

First, a little about matrimonial property law in continental European jurisdictions.

It is often said that the vast majority of European jurisdictions, some American states,[9] and a number elsewhere,[10] impose upon married couples[11] (and, in some cases, registered partners)[12] regimes of

---

[6] See text at n 18 below.
[7] EU Commission *Green Paper on Conflict of Laws in Matters concerning Matrimonial Property Regimes, including the Question of Jurisdiction and Mutual Recognition*, COM (2006) 400 final (SEC (2006) 952).
[8] Available at http://ec.europa.eu/justice_home/news/consulting_public/matrimonial_property/news_contributions_matrimonial_property_en.htm.
[9] Eight American states are known as the 'community property states', whose family property law derives from the Spanish legal system: Washington, Idaho, Nevada, California, Arizona, New Mexico, Texas, and Louisiana. Note the linguistic quirk that Europeans refer to 'community of property' whereas Americans refer to 'community property'.
[10] Of which the most influential is perhaps South Africa.
[11] I use the term 'marriage' etc to include civil partnership, or its equivalent, in jurisdictions like ours that do not allow same-sex marriage but allow something very similar for same-sex partners.
[12] As in the Netherlands. In France, the default regime for couples who enter a *Pacs* is separation of property: law of 23 June 2006. See J Godard 'Pacs seven years on' (2007)

community of property.[13] However, closer examination reveals that what the continental European states do is to offer to such couples a number of possibilities into which they can opt by agreement, whilst imposing community and or some other matrimonial regime as what we might call a default option – the French call it the *régime légal* and the Swiss call it the *régime matrimonial ordinaire*. I refer to the legal systems that do this as regime-based jurisdictions. The default options, and those constructed by contract, might be any of a number of possibilities. There are regimes of immediate community (amounting to a form of joint ownership quite different from anything known here, because it involves a form of joint liability for debt). There are deferred community regimes that change nothing during marriage but define a community of property that must be divided when the marriage ends on death or divorce. There are accruals systems[14] that maintain separation of property during marriage but share, on death or divorce, the value that has accrued to either spouse's property during the marriage. And there are systems of separate property where marriage has no effect upon property rights. In a regime of separation each party continues to own their own property, including shares of property that the two choose to own jointly, during marriage and on divorce; on death the deceased's property falls into his or her estate, to be disposed of subject to the rules that we rather disparagingly call 'forced heirship'. And we have to say 'regimes' or 'systems' each time, because there are many different variants upon each of these themes: the default regime of immediate community system of France is different from that of the Netherlands, and different again from an immediate community regime that a French couple might construct by contract. '*Les régimes matrimoniaux ont plus de variétés que l'arc-en-ciel n'a de couleurs fondamentales.*'[15]

And it is that patchwork of possibilities that led the European Commission, in its Green Paper on Matrimonial Property Regimes (on which more later), to define a matrimonial property regime as 'the sets of

---

21 IJLP & F 310. For simplicity I do not make any further reference to registered partnerships or to the *Pacs*, but there is a fruitful field of inquiry here.

[13] For a comparison of regimes, see A Agell 'The division of property upon divorce from a European perspective' in M Meulders-Klein (ed) *Droit Comparé des personnes et de la famille* (Bruylant, 1998), p 17; and G Steenhof 'A matrimonial system for the EU?' [2005] IFL 74. For a general discussion, an updating (in ch 1) of some of the financial examples that Agell gives, and for much of the research that lies behind my thinking in this paper, see E Cooke, A Barlow and T Callus *Community of Property – a Regime for England and Wales?* (The Nuffield Foundation, 2006).

[14] This is the South African label; the French term is *participation aux acquests*, and refers to the German *Zugewinngemeinschaft* and to the French equivalent (since this is one of the options that French couples may adopt by contract).

[15] B Beignier *Les régimes matrimoniaux* (Presses Universitaires de France, 1999), p 4. The possible contractual variations are infinite, since where a form of community is elected the contract may state the range of property to be included and the proportions in which it is eventually to be shared – even the idea of 50% sharing is only a default option. Most jurisdictions do not allow couples a free choice, but make available a limited range of contractual options; whereas the rule in France seems to be that couples have complete contractual freedom. As to the requirements for valid agreements, see below.

legal rules relating to the spouses' financial relationships resulting from their marriage, both with each other and with third parties, in particular their creditors'.[16] That definition is content-neutral; it requires a set of rules, but it does not determine what they must be. A couple will get the default regime or one that they have chosen; either way what they get is a set of rules. Thus, the label 'community property states' for the civil-law-based American states does not mean that all married couples in those states own their property in community, but that community is the default regime where the couple have not chosen one of separation.[17]

The enactment of the Married Women's Property Act 1882 left us, in England and Wales, operating a system of separation of property which looked very much like the mainstream European concept of separation. Accordingly, up to 1970 it would have been quite reasonable to say that we operated a matrimonial regime, albeit without the ability to choose one's regime by contract. There was no automatic joint ownership, no provision for sharing property on divorce, and actually rather less regulation of devolution on death than would be experienced by a French couple *séparés de biens*. Until 1970, we may have seemed very distinct from our European neighbours in not having a community of property system; but if we look at the pre-1970 world through today's spectacles, in the light of a broad range of available regimes, we were at that stage not so very foreign. Our law of matrimonial property would have fitted nicely into the European Commission's definition of a matrimonial regime.

But of course all changed in 1970 when we moved to a discretionary system, which the Americans call 'equitable distribution'.[18] Such systems were adopted in most American and Commonwealth countries; the systems current in Ireland and Northern Ireland derive from our own. What now separated us from the regime-based jurisdictions across the channel was the absence of a 'set of rules' from which one might discover who owns what during marriage, on divorce and on death. During marriage we do indeed have separation of property. But on divorce there were no rules, and on death testamentary freedom is modified by the family provision legislation which, again, is discretionary.[19]

I do not suggest that there is a black-and-white dichotomy between rules and discretion, them and us. The concept of the matrimonial regime is perhaps more like a spectrum than a unitary concept: systems vary as to the rigidity of the 'set of rules'. In some community systems there is a

---

[16] See the definitions section; the Green paper can be found at:http://eur-lex.europa.eu/LexUriServ/LexUriServ.do?uri=COM:2006:0400:FIN:EN:DOC.

[17] I have not said anything here about the other noticeable element of the definition, namely that the rules determine the couple's relationship with their creditors; as to this, see below.

[18] M A Glendon *The New Family and the New Property* (Butterworths, 1981), p 63; G G Blumberg *Community Property in California* (Aspen, 2003), p 2ff.

[19] Inheritance (Provision for Family and Dependants) Act 1975, s 1(2).

potential for add-on discretion, in particular in the Nordic countries.[20] And in France there is the possibility of either spouse being awarded a *prestation compensatoire*, a compensatory capital payment for any disadvantage suffered as a result of the marriage, so that capital may not be equally divided after all. But even so, the starting point is equal distribution (or indeed distribution in whatever shares the couple have decided by contract), and equal distribution remains the overriding expectation. Thus, there are some grey areas;[21] but the dichotomy between the two types of system – regime-based and those operating equitable distribution – is uncontroversial.

SOME EUROPEAN FEATURES OF ANCILLARY RELIEF TODAY

Our law of matrimonial property became distinctively alien to Europe with the introduction of ancillary relief in 1970. But things have been changing recently. Some of the changes look distinctly European. So, has the answer to that first question changed?

Most obviously, the introduction in *White* of the yardstick of equality that so quickly became a sharing principle,[22] transformed ancillary relief into something that now looks much more like a community of property system. Inevitably, the comparison has been drawn.[23] But while there is indeed a similarity, this development does not in fact amount to community of property. Equal division is only really for the rich and, to some extent for the childless; it is primarily justified by an assessment of the value of contributions,[24] and therefore the way is left open for

---

[20] J Scherpe 'A comparative view of pre-nuptial agreements' [2007] IFL 18. There is considerable discretion in the Norwegian system; much less in Sweden. I am grateful to Dr Scherpe for discussing this with me.

[21] There are some grey jurisdictions. Does Scotland have a regime, with its starting point of equal division subject to adjustment, and its civil law legal roots? Probably not; the scope for adjustment is too great (see Family Law (Scotland) Act 1985, s 9). Certainly Scottish lawyers do not regard their system as a regime. New Zealand, however, with a much stronger expectation of equality, and clear scope for private ordering, probably should be said to have a regime, despite having a squarely common law legal tradition (see the Property (Relationships) Act 1976, s 11).

[22] S Cretney, in 'The Family and the Law: Status or Contract?' [2003] CFLQ 403, expresses the view that it was the Court of Appeal in *Lambert v Lambert* [2002] EWCA Civ 1685, [2003] 1 FLR 139 that took the decisive step into a *principle* of equal division. See also the references by Lord Nicholls in *Miller/McFarlane* to the 'equal sharing principle' and the 'sharing entitlement' [2006] UKHL 24, [2006] 2 AC 618 at [20] and [29]; cf Potter P in *Charman v Charman* [2007] EWCA Civ 503, [2007] 1 FLR 1246 at [65]: 'we take "the sharing principle" to mean that property should be shared in equal proportions unless there is good reason to depart from such proportions'.

[23] Stephen Cretney, in 'Community of property imposed by judicial decision' (2003) 119 LQR 349.

[24] [2001] AC 596, HL; the basis of equality in the valuation of contributions stems from Lord Nicholls's words: 'In seeking to achieve a fair outcome, there is no place for discrimination between husband and wife and their respective roles ... whatever the division of labour chosen by the husband and wife, or forced upon them by

discretionary departure on the basis of exceptional contribution.[25] This is selective equality with discretionary variants; it has a European flavour, but it does not amount to a regime.

The other dramatic move in *White* was the introduction of the concept of non-matrimonial property. Jurisdictions that operate a default system of community of acquests[26] recognise significant proportions of spousal property as non-matrimonial; even the Netherlands and the Nordic countries, where the default community regimes encompass very nearly the whole of a couple's property, recognise small categories of exceptions. And most regime-based systems allow couples married in community considerable freedom to decide the scope of non-matrimonial property by contract. Thus, the idea of non-matrimonial property could be said to be fundamental to community of property systems. And in most European regime-based systems, non-matrimonial property is not for sharing. Certainly, so far as I can discover, there is no question of non-matrimonial property in such jurisdictions becoming matrimonial over time.

Non-matrimonial property in ancillary relief, by contrast, may well be shared.[27] The Court of Appeal in *Charman* stressed this:

> 'To what property does the sharing principle apply? ... We consider ... that, subject to the exceptions identified in *Miller* [relating to short marriages] ... the principle applies to all the parties' property but, to the extent that their property is non-matrimonial, there is likely to be better reason for departure from equality.'[28]

In fact, the concept of non-matrimonial property is familiar in the American common-law states; and some of them allow such property to be divided, while some do not.[29] So the concept of non-matrimonial property is not even unique to regime-based systems, and is closer to the American concept in being divisible at the court's discretion. The English concept is unique, so far as I am aware, in its facility for non-matrimonial property to become matrimonial over time.[30] Thus, closer examination shows that the move towards the demarcation of non-matrimonial

---

circumstances, fairness requires that this should not prejudice or advantage either party when considering para (f), relating to the parties' contributions.'

[25] The endeavours of the Court of Appeal in *Charman* to set some limits to the range of departures from equality leave open a considerable range of possibilities: [2007] EWCA Civ 503, [2007] 1 FLR 1246 at [90].

[26] This is the majority default regime in Europe, whereby property acquired after the marriage falls into the community.

[27] See the explanation in *Miller v Miller; McFarlane v McFarlane* [2006] UKHL 24, [2006] 2 AC 618 at [147] per Baroness Hale.

[28] *Charman v Charman* [2007] EWCA Civ 503, [2007] 1 FLR 1246 at [66] per Potter P.

[29] T Walker 'Family Law in the Fifty States' (2007) 41 Fam LQ 309; see in particular table IV at 445. And see G G Blumberg *Community Property in California* (Aspen, 2003), p 4, n 11, quoting the statutory provision for Minnesota.

[30] See, for example, dicta of Lord Nicholls in *Miller/McFarlane* at [22].

property is, again, a move made by the judiciary that makes us think about community regimes, and therefore about Europe, but does not take us there.

The same can be said of what we normally call pre-nups, but to which I will refer as marital property agreements, for reasons that will appear. They were brought dramatically into the spotlight with *Crossley*,[31] but were already a focus of interest as a result of some powerful obiter dicta about private ordering[32] and the plea for reform at the close of the Court of Appeal's judgment in *Charman*.[33] And it is well known that such agreements are a feature of regime-based systems, which all, as explained above, allow couples to contract out of the default system, or *régime légal*, by agreement before or at any time during the marriage. The ability to make enforceable marital property agreements is not, of course, a logically necessary feature of a regime-based system. It would be possible to legislate to the effect that marriage means community and that it is not possible to contract out. But in fact, so far as I can discover, all the European regime-based jurisdictions allow this, to a greater or lesser extent.[34]

So again, developments here feel European. I would like to discuss marital property agreements in a little more detail because there is a lot to be said about the difference between our approach to them and the continental European approach. I suggest that the gulf in thinking is enormous, perhaps even more so than that which exists between the European and English concepts of equal division and of non-matrimonial property. This is so particularly in three respects.

First, their purpose. Marital property agreements in the regime-based systems of Europe are not primarily about divorce planning. The folk who live across the channel are not really so dissimilar to us; if we feel an antipathy to discussing divorce while getting married, so do they. But marital property agreements are made as a way of organising the property of the two people concerned so as to manage debt, and to manage

---

[31] *Crossley v Crossley* [2007] EWCA] Civ 1491, [2008] 1 FLR 1467.
[32] In *Parra v Parra* [2002] EWCA Civ 1886, [2003] 1 FLR 942, Thorpe LJ said: 'The parties had, perhaps unusually, ordered their affairs during the marriage to achieve equality and to eliminate any potential for gender discrimination. They had in effect elected for a marital regime of community of property. In such circumstances what is the need for the court's discretionary adjustive powers?'; and see the importance placed in *Miller/McFarlane* at [153] upon 'the way the couple have run their lives', per Baroness Hale.
[33] [2007] EWCA Civ 503, [2007] 1 FLR 1246 at [124] per Potter P: 'If, unlike the rest of Europe, the property consequences of divorce are to be regulated by the principles of needs, compensation and sharing, should not the parties to the marriage, or the projected marriage, have at least the opportunity to order their own affairs otherwise by a nuptial contract?'
[34] All the continental European jurisdictions described in C Hamilton and A Perry (eds) *Family Law in Europe* (Tottel, 2nd edn, 2002) allow the couple to agree an alternative regime before marriage and most allow this after marriage as well.

inheritance. Take a group of French couples. Without a marital property agreement, they will marry in an immediate community of acquests. Everything they acquire after the marriage will be jointly owned, whether or not transferred to the two of them; and the whole of that community of property may be taken in execution of the debts of either of them.[35] That may suit them; but if they take advice they may find that they prefer a different arrangement. The following examples are taken from a pamphlet produced by the *Conseils par des Notaires*,[36] and so form part of an advertisement for business by the French notaires; but that the principles are sound is clear from more academic texts.[37]

- *Couple A* plan a traditional businessman/housewife marriage. The default regime of community of property acquired after the marriage is tailor-made for this couple; it will enable them to share the fruits of the husband's earning while keeping separate any inherited or gifted property.[38]

- *Couple B*: both are earning; he owns a business while she has a secure salaried position. Both have their own homes. Community is not a good idea for this couple; they should opt into a regime of separation, thus protecting the wife's property from the debts incurred by her husband in the course of his business.[39] Note that if the couple's plan changes and either decides to give up work – perhaps if they have children – they should change their regime to one of community; separation of property is not advisable for the housewife/house-husband marriage.

- *Couple C* are a widow and a widower, both with children from their previous marriages. Each is comfortably off; each wants their own property to go to their own children. This is another case where the couple would be well advised to opt for a regime of separation.

- *Couple D*; again, one of the spouses is going to run a business. But in this case they would like to be able to share in the success of the business, without running the risks of immediate community. An

---

[35] *Code Civil*, art 1413. It is this feature of community of property that is so unfamiliar to common law systems; this form of joint ownership is literally impossible in England and Wales.

[36] See the writer's translation, at http://www.reading.ac.uk/nmsruntime/saveasdialog. asp?IID=7017&sID=34870of J Bernard *Choisir son contrat de marriage* (2002), one of the series *Les memos: conseils par des notaires*, which is a very helpful summary of some of the options available in France.

[37] See, for example, P Malaurie and L Aynès *Les Régimes Matrimoniaux* (Defrénois, 2004), Livre II.

[38] *Code Civil*, art 1401ff. Before 1966, the *régime legal* was the *communauté de meubles et acquêts*, whereby the spouses' movable property, as well as any property acquired after the marriage, fell within the community. This is still available as an option, but scarcely used: *Code Civil*, art 1498.

[39] *Code Civil*, art 1536.

option for them is *participation aux acquests*,[40] the default regime for Switzerland and Germany. When the regime comes to an end on divorce or death, each spouse keeps his or her own property; but the enrichment of each party is calculated, and shared equally. Sometimes the couple's contract is drafted so as to exclude the actual business assets from the calculation – thus avoiding the risk that the sharing of their enrichment will actually destroy the business.

- *Couple E* are in their sixties and retired. They have no children or near relatives. They are relatively well-off and hope that the survivor of the two of them will succeed to the other's wealth. For them, a regime of total community is appropriate (ie not limited, as is the *régime legal* to acquisitions after the marriage), with a provision that the whole of the community accrues to the survivor (thereby saving substantial inheritance tax). This regime is not a good idea where there are children, because substantial tax will of course be payable when the second spouse dies.[41]

None of these couples is thinking about divorce. And none of the decisions they have made can be replicated in English law.[42] For us, marital property agreements could only amount to divorce planning; even if we could rely on their effect, the take-up would be extremely small in the absence of other changes in the law.[43] But it is easy to see a constructive use for marital property agreements among very rich couples to agree a demarcation of non-matrimonial property; the point was made by Thorpe LJ in *Crossley*[44] that this saves court resources.

Second, the European approach to formalities is very foreign to us. It is not simply that 'they', across the Channel, have notaries. Solicitors could surely do what notaries do. But it is what they do that we find so hard to cope with: how can one notary advise both the parties to a marital property agreement, when there is so obviously a conflict of interest between the two parties? The answer, from the point of view of the French *notaires* advising the couples discussed above, is that they are giving advice in the interests of the family; they do not see it as a conflict, and indeed we would have to agree that there is no conflict in the examples just discussed.[45] The notarial view of their advisory role is as follows:

---

[40] *Code Civil*, art 1569.
[41] *Code Civil*, art 1525. The position of the surviving spouse under French inheritance law has been notoriously weak, but it was strengthened by the Law of 3 December 2001. However, the contractual arrangement described here would still be beneficial for the couple described.
[42] Not all are replicated in regimes of deferred community.
[43] For example, the possibility of enforceable agreements to avoid the effects of the Inheritance (Provision for Family and Dependants) Act 1975.
[44] *Crossley v Crossley* [2007] EWCA] Civ 1491, [2008] 1 FLR 1467.
[45] *Choisir son contrat de mariage* (see n 36 above), p 20.

'Choosing a marriage contract necessitates an interview with a notary. He will talk to the engaged couple about their family and financial situation, their plans, and their current and future professional activity. This enables the couple to make an informed choice on the basis of full information about the different regimes available to them and the effect of all the possible contractual provisions.'

But shared legal advice for an English marital property agreement, where there may be agreement but those features of mutual benefit are absent, is not possible; the giving of advice about such an agreement is much more like the advice that has to be given to one spouse guaranteeing another's debt,[46] or to one spouse planning to give away a large amount of capital by buying a house as beneficial joint tenants.[47] The spouse needs to be advised precisely because they are giving something up, or taking on a risk, or otherwise being disadvantaged. The advice must be given separately, and it would have to be extremely thorough. And that means that it cannot be regarded as an affordable or even a normal option for ordinary people, as it can in the regime-based jurisdictions of Europe.

Third, their effect. This is familiar territory; it is well-established that there is no guarantee that a marital property agreement will be enforced by the courts in England and Wales, but that the more clearly it can be seen that the spouse who seeks to invoke the discretion of the Matrimonial Causes Act 1973 has had independent advice, the more likely it is that he or she will fail and will be held to the agreement.[48] That is all the more so since *Crossley*.[49] But, even so, there is no certainty. In the absence of statutory reform, the best a solicitor can say of a marital property agreement is that it will probably work. By contrast, a marital property agreement in most of the European regime-based systems, properly notarised,[50] will be enforceable. Again, there are variations between systems, and in the Nordic countries the courts have a discretion to set them aside; it is no coincidence that in these jurisdictions notarisation is not required.[51] There is certainly a correlation between the strength of advice given – independent advice it must be, in this jurisdiction – and the likelihood that an agreement will be upheld; but an English couple cannot have the certainty that a French or German couple has that their agreement will 'stick'.

---

[46] Which takes us into the whole troubled area of law surrounding *Royal Bank of Scotland v Etridge (No 2)* [2001] 3 WLR 1021.

[47] Consider the case of Frank, in G Douglas, H Pearce and J Woodward *A failure of trust: resolving property disputes on cohabitation breakdown* (Cardiff Law School Research paper, 2007, available at http://www.law.cf.ac.uk/researchpapers/papers/1.pdf), para 4.51.

[48] The pre-*Crossley* developments are traced in R Todd 'The inevitable triumph of the ante-nuptial contract' [2006] Fam Law 539; the writer argues that in the absence of undue influence the parties should be held to their bargains, but that is not the law.

[49] [2007] EWCA] Civ 1491, [2008] 1 FLR 1467. Now see *Macleod v Macleod* [2008] UKPC 64, [2008] WLR (D) 402.

[50] Except in the Nordic countries, where notaries are unknown.

[51] See J Scherpe 'A comparative view of pre-nuptial agreements' [2007] IFL 18.

It is worth examining the Law Commission report on *Cohabitation: the financial consequences of relationship breakdown*[52] for a very English view of something very like marital property agreements, in the context of cohabitation. In Part 6 the Commission noted the desirability of private ordering and of a way for cohabitants to 'opt out' of the recommended scheme for financial relief. To that end, the Commission noted the correlation between levels of advice and likelihood of enforceability in the Report on the financial consequences of relationship breakdown for cohabitants. It is worth noting that the Law Commission did not find it possible to recommend shared legal advice; nor was it able to recommend 'cast-iron enforceability'.[53] Their view of 'opt-outs', for cohabitants, from their recommended scheme for financial relief, would function very much like marital property agreements, and the arrangements recommended for them are, appropriately, very English. We cannot 'do' shared advice or guaranteed enforceability in the context of an agreement about relationship property which is only ever going to be called upon in the event of divorce. We are a long way from the general financial planning of the couples that a French notary might advise about their *contrat de mariage*.

The American Uniform Premarital Agreement Act[54] does, by contrast, offer something almost cast-iron. It is therefore rather more European than anything we have devised, although unlike the European marital property agreements, the American 'pre-nups' really are about planning for divorce. It does not require that legal advice be taken, but there is a strong expectation that the parties will have been independently advised.[55]

Thus, in the invention of equal division and non-matrimonial property, and the increased focus on marital property agreements, we have a number of factors that seem to correspond to very characteristic features of European regimes. But on closer examination they can be seen to be hybrids; they resemble the legal toolbox used in regime-based systems, but in fact they are something rather different, with a distinctively common-law and somewhat American flavour. The adoption of these features makes ancillary relief *look* more European than it did in 1970; but I am not sure that they really take us much nearer.

---

[52] Law Com No 307 (2007).
[53] Ibid at [5.27], [5.28].
[54] http://www.law.upenn.edu/bll/archives/ulc/fnact99/1980s/upaa83.htm.
[55] The commentary states 'Nothing in Section 6 makes the absence of assistance of independent legal counsel a condition for the unenforceability of a premarital agreement. However, lack of that assistance may well be a factor in determining whether the conditions stated in Section 6 may have existed (see eg *Del Vecchio v Del Vecchio, 143 So 2d 17 (Fla 1962)*).'

EUROPEAN INITIATIVES

Aside from domestic developments, the other factor that brings that choice to our attention is the increased level of European initiatives in this area, and in particular in the area of the conflict of laws. The European Commission, in pursuit of free movement,[56] has set itself the ambitious objective of harmonising the conflicts rules applicable to divorce and to family property. Its concept of the latter is very wide, encompassing the financial consequences of marriage, or divorce, and of death. The idea is to ensure that wherever a conflict of laws arises about these matters, because the parties are from more than one state in Europe, there will be a relatively wide choice of jurisdictions in which to litigate, but there will be rules to ensure that whatever court is approached, there will be no difference in the choice of law to be applied.

As things stand, jurisdiction in divorce is dependant upon the rules in Brussels II Revised,[57] including the notorious 'first seized' rule of Art 19. Thus, for any divorce with a cross-border element, there tends to be a choice of court; but choice of law in the chosen court depends upon national conflicts rules. In the English courts, that choice remains the *lex fori*; a couple divorcing in this country will get the divorce law contained in the Matrimonial Causes Act 1973, and will also get ancillary relief, because that comes as part of the package. Other European states have various different rules and many of them take an applicable law approach, confidently applying law that is not their own.[58] That confidence may not be entirely appropriate; there is considerable anecdotal evidence that in interpreting and applying what they conceive to be English matrimonial property law, courts elsewhere in Europe may be getting it wrong. A French judge looking at an English couple can say *séparation des biens*, and if the assets happen to be in the husband's name the wife gets nothing.[59]

The Commission's plan is to ensure that in matters of divorce, financial provision and matrimonial property there should continue to be a range of possible jurisdictions (including an option for the couple themselves to agree jurisdiction is they can), but for there to be a hierarchy of conflicts rules so that the law applied will be the same wherever proceedings take place. Thus, what is known as the 'Maintenance Green paper' proposes

---

[56] See N Lowe 'The growing influence of the European Union on International Family Law: a view from the boundary' in (2003) 56 *Current Legal Problems* 439; also C McGlynn *Families and the European Union* (Cambridge UP, 2006).

[57] Council Regulation (EC) No 2201/2003 of November 2003 concerning jurisdiction and the recognition and enforcement of judgments in matrimonial matters and the matters of parental responsibility, repealing Regulation (EC) No 1347/2000.

[58] See the examples given by E Ries 'Pre-marital agreements and European law: where do we start' [2005] IFL 165.

[59] My evidence for this is anecdotal, deriving from practitioners, and there is considerable scope for research here.

that the applicable law shall always be that of the maintenance creditor.[60] The Commission has also proposed that there shall be a hierarchy of applicable law options for divorce (this is the proposed instrument known as 'Rome III'; though, at the time of writing, it seems unlikely that the proposed instrument will come into being).[61] The Green Paper on Matrimonial Property[62] appears to envisage the same idea for matrimonial property matters; as does the proposal for Succession and Wills.[63]

The United Kingdom has the right to choose whether or not to join in these measures. So far, it has not opted into the maintenance regulation; nor into 'Rome III'. We do not know what will be the UK's answer to the Wills and Succession instrument, when there is one. Its initial response was negative in the extreme, to the extent of simply denying that there was any difficulty to be addressed.[64] A hearing of a House of Lords Select Committee in November[65] took evidence about the sort of thing the Commission wanted to do, and enunciated some 'red line' areas: the dislike of forced heirship was very much in evidence, as was a horror of the idea of 'claw-back'.[66] Negotiations continue, which is why nothing is being heard from the Ministry of Justice (MoJ) about the Matrimonial Property Green Paper at the moment. The UK government's response to the latter was also very negative;[67] it stated rather tersely that the paper is inappropriate to the UK because of the absence of a regime here, and promised a further paper to explain the position. Professor Chris Clarkson and I were engaged to help draft that additional response,[68] as were academics in Scotland; but the assembling from those drafts of a paper from the UK has not taken place yet, apparently because of the MoJ's preoccupation with the Wills and Succession paper. Meanwhile responses from other jurisdictions and from professional bodies have been posted on the Commission's website: the Commission's summary reports:

---

[60] *Proposal for a Council Regulation on jurisdiction, applicable law, recognition and enforcement of decisions and co-operation in matters relating to maintenance obligations*, COM (2005) 649 final.

[61] *Proposal for a Council Regulation amending Regulation (EC) 2201/2003 as regards jurisdiction and introducing rules concerning applicable law in matrimonial matters* (2007).

[62] EU Commission *Green Paper on Conflict of Laws in Matters concerning Matrimonial Property Regimes, including the Question of Jurisdiction and Mutual Recognition*, COM (2006) 400 final (SEC (2006) 952).

[63] European Commission *Green Paper on Succession and Wills*, COM (2005) 65; SEC (2005) 270.

[64] Available, with other published responses, at http://ec.europa.eu/justice_home/news/consulting_public/successions/contributions/contribution_uk_en.pdf.

[65] The Report of a House of Lords Select Committee is at http://www.publications.parliament.uk/pa/ld200708/ldselect/ldeucom/12/7101001.htm; and the report of the hearing is at http://www.publications.parliament.uk/pa/ld200708/ldselect/ldeucom/12/7101001.htm.

[66] That is, the idea that lifetime gifts might be reversed in order to satisfy the 'forced heirship' requirements of civil law.

[67] See the published responses at n 64 above.

[68] See E Cooke and C M V Clarkson 'Matrimonial Property: Harmony in Europe?' [2007] Fam Law 920.

> 'In general, the Green paper received a warm welcome. Despite certain comments considering this project to be too ambitious or drafted without a proper understanding of the legal traditions of certain Common law systems – it being recalled that England and Wales do not have a matrimonial property regime as understood in continental Europe – the content of the Green Paper and the usefulness of a Community initiative on this issue was not contested.'[69]

So this is a game we are not joining in, at present, although the claim made by the Commission is that everyone else wants to play.

THE FIRST QUESTION

So to my first question the answer is undramatic. We have some new features in ancillary relief, since the turn of the century, which are certainly important ones in regime-based systems. But on closer examination they have brought us no nearer to matrimonial property regimes, and therefore no nearer to mainstream European matrimonial property law; they bear much resemblance to features of the American equitable distribution systems, and indeed in some respects are even more discretionary than the latter. And despite encouragement and pressure from Brussels, there is deep disquiet about any suggestion that the English courts might apply the law of other European states with regard to matrimonial property. How European is the law of ancillary relief? Not very.

THE SECOND QUESTION

I have so far ducked my task of crystal ball gazing; I am supposed to be looking forwards but the future is difficult to discern. How European should ancillary relief become? As promised earlier, I am going to suggest only a partial answer. I do so under two headings: the conflicts problem and then ancillary relief itself.

The conflicts problem

The response of the UK so far to this pressure has been extremely negative. Could we become a little more European – perhaps a little more at home in Europe – by responding a little more positively to the moves in the private international law of matrimonial property?

There are a number of different possible responses to the Green Paper on Matrimonial Property Regimes. There is a view that it is a non-starter; that because we do not have a regime, the instrument envisaged in the paper simply cannot make any sense in this jurisdiction at all. There is

---

[69] See the response at http://ec.europa.eu/civiljustice/news/whatsnew_en.htm, p 2.

also a view[70] that the entirety of the law of ancillary relief falls within the definition of 'maintenance', already covered by Brussels I[71] and in the proposed maintenance regulation, so that there is nothing for the proposed instrument on matrimonial property to bite on. My own view is that that really cannot be correct in so far as there are assets available in excess of what is required to meet the parties' needs. Even if that view were tenable pre-*White*, it is no longer correct. There is also a view that it must always be inappropriate for the courts in England and Wales to apply foreign law in the context of matrimonial property because of the expense, for the parties, of proving foreign law. I would like to suggest that these views are extreme, and that we can and should manage something more constructive, for a number of reasons. English courts do observe foreign rules of matrimonial property in the context of succession; it is well known that if you have a French holiday home, you have to take on board the operation of French matrimonial property regime for the purpose of succession.[72] Couples who move here from continental Europe will have a matrimonial regime, by default or by agreement; for either of them to seek to step outside that regime and seek ancillary relief may raise serious questions about legitimate expectations, or indeed about the peaceful enjoyment of possessions (since a regime of immediate community creates vested rights).[73] And the courts in European states, with different conflicts rules from our own, are indeed applying English matrimonial property law to divorcing couples in cases where they have jurisdiction.[74] The conclusion to which I am led is that different European states *can* apply each other's law of matrimonial property, but that it is difficult, and that it may be better to engage in constructive dialogue and to try to achieve a better understanding than simply to dig our heels in and refuse to play.

It is worth adding that the answer to the conflicts problem is not for the law of ancillary relief to be reformed so as to produce an English matrimonial regime. There might be reasons for doing that, but the resolution of the conflicts problem is not one of them. For the English courts to impose upon foreign couples a *lex fori* consisting of a particular regime chosen by the English legislature would be as inappropriate for most European couples as would be the present system of ancillary relief, simply because of the multitude of available regimes.[75]

---

[70] See the response of the Bar Council of England and Wales at http://ec.europa.eu/justice_home/news/consulting_public/matrimonial_property/contributions/others/bar_council_england_wales_en.pdf.

[71] Council Regulation (EC) No 44/2001 of 22 December 2000 on Jurisdiction and Recognition and Enforcement of Judgments in Civil and Commercial Matters.

[72] Because the English courts apply the *lex situs* for immoveables.

[73] Consider Art 1 of the First Protocol to the European Convention on Human Rights and Fundamental Freedoms.

[74] As the Spanish court would have done in *Moore v Moore* [2007] EWCA Civ 361, [2007] 2 FLR 339. As has been remarked above, foreign courts may be more confident than they should be when it comes to English matrimonial property.

[75] See text at n 15 above.

A better approach must be to look at the conflicts problem from the point of view of the experience of litigants who become involved in it. In particular, we should examine the American experience. There we find decades of expertise in sorting out conflicts, in the context of a majority of states operating equitable distribution and a substantial minority of community property states. It has not been suggested that those states should unify their internal law; nor even that they should unify their conflicts law. What would be helpful in this jurisdiction would be to tap into some of the American scholarship on the point, and to think through the advantages and disadvantages of *lex fori*/applicable law approaches from a point of view that focuses more on the effect upon individuals of the various ways of dealing with conflicts. A paper by Thomas Oldham[76] looks in detail at the various options available for choice of laws, and considers the effect upon the parties of total immutability (the parties stay with their regime at the time of marriage); partial mutability (property is owned subject to the law of the state where the parties acquired it); and total mutability (where the state applies the *lex fori*). He observes that the first two approaches require courts to operate the law of more than one jurisdiction;[77] that partial mutability may best meet the expectations of the parties; and that the *lex fori* approach generates forum shopping (a matter about which the English Court of Appeal has indeed complained).[78]

There is more thinking to be done here. The European Commission may be going too far in trying to unify the conflicts laws; our own conflicts rules may perhaps be too rigid.

The future for ancillary relief

Leaving aside conflicts, then, should ancillary relief itself become any more European over the next 50 years? Such a trend might be seen in a move to something that really is a matrimonial regime, with opportunities to contract out. Or it might be expressed in less dramatic steps, such as firming up the definition of non-matrimonial property and firming up its consequences (perhaps by developing a rule that it can never be shared); or perhaps by reforming, and thereby firming up, the law on marital property agreements.

Prediction is impossible. One only has to recall[79] the apparent long-term reluctance to reform ancillary relief, despite heavy pressure upon the government in the 1990s to do so, and indeed what seemed to be a

---

[76] T Oldham 'What if the Beckhams move to LA and then divorce? Marital property rights of mobile spouses when they divorce in the US' (2008) 42 Fam LQ 263.
[77] Note that this is less of a problem in the USA, where everything is in one language. Oldham cites on this point N Dethloff 'Arguments for the Unification and Harmonisation of Family Law in Europe' in K Boele-Woelki (ed) *Perspectives for the Unification and Harmonisation of Family Law in Europe* (Intersentia, 2003).
[78] See the dicta of Potter P in *Charman*: n 33 above.
[79] See n 33 above.

government commitment to do so. The government's response to the Law Commission's recommendations on cohabitation might be taken to indicate a deep reluctance to legislate in this area; and arguably the need to do *something* for cohabitants is stronger than any need to reform ancillary relief. If I am right that wholesale reform is unlikely, it seems to me that in this of all gatherings we should regard that as an opportunity; if reform is not imminent, then we should use the intervening time as an opportunity for research, so that when reform does happen, it will be informed by accurate data. I would like to suggest three areas that should be thoroughly researched before any fundamental change is made to the law of ancillary relief.

One area should be economic analysis. As Dr Cretney recalled in his paper,[80] it was women who were campaigning in the 1960s for community of property, and who were bitterly disappointed when what they got was the discretionary regime of the Matrimonial Causes Act 1973. Today, the argument might go the other way: equality has moved on, but we are conscious that childbearing inevitably involves an economic consequence; and in the light of that, an equal share of the family's assets for all but the very rich may not be enough. Of course, the effect of the yardstick of equality was not, I think, supposed to 'trickle down' to the 'ordinary' divorce. But there is evidence that this may be happening.[81] In particular, there is considerable anecdotal evidence that the decision in *White* has had an effect upon very ordinary cases in England and Wales involving quite restricted assets, where there is a *Mesher* order[82] requiring the house not to be sold until the children leave home. The division of the proceeds of sale at that point has been seen in the past to be a question about the meeting of needs. But after *White*, it seems, there is considerable pressure for proceeds to be split equally. This can be disastrous for a party who has sacrificed earnings and mortgage capacity in order to look after the children. It is hard to resist, because of the ambiguous relationship between the demands of s 25(2)(a) of the Matrimonial Causes Act 1973 and the demands of the yardstick of equality. This needs more investigation.

Second, any change must be examined in terms of its litigation effects. Will it keep people out of court? There is of course a trend towards private ordering; the child support system is moving swiftly in that direction. And we know that litigation wastes resources. Very few ancillary relief disputes go to trial; and a system that was designed for court-based solutions is having to support a system of bargaining in the shadow of the law. Could it be reformed so as to make that bargaining

---

[80] See Chapter 2 above.
[81] Lucinda Fisher, in 'The unexpected impact of *White*' [2002] Fam Law 108, presents some important and quite disturbing findings. Research by Emma Hitchings (see 'Everyday Cases in the post-*White* Era' [2008] Fam Law 873) sheds further light on this.
[82] *Mesher v Mesher and Hall* (1973) [1980] 1 All ER 126, CA.

easier? Some principled and practical work on the relationship between rules, discretion and litigation behaviour would be very valuable.

Finally, there is the emotional side of ancillary relief. So far I have said nothing about hearts and minds, or about trauma and its effects. But economic analysis, and the analysis of litigation behaviour, are incomplete unless research also addresses how people's emotional state affects the resolution of their disputes, and conversely how the ancillary relief system affects those emotions. No longer, thank heavens, is there a 'day in court' to try the divorce itself. But the need for such a day then spills over into children disputes and into ancillary relief. That does not make it a good idea for people to litigate their property disputes. But the need for confrontation and catharsis cannot be ignored, and will re-surface if simply squashed. A full investigation of the law and procedure of ancillary relief needs to address the ways there might be of helping people to deal with the emotions that are inevitably involved in the process.

CHAPTER 10

CARING FOR OUR FUTURE GENERATIONS

Judith Masson

INTRODUCTION

It appears from past practice that major Children Acts last about 40 years[1] – one to two generations – so, in 2008 it seems that the Children Act 1989 will have to serve another 20 years. This chapter does not try to predict what will follow in 2028, but sets out to discuss the changes in families, in society, and in state systems that are currently straining the 1989 code. It examines the responses required if the 1989 Act is to continue to meet the demands and expectations placed on it and to provide relevant structures for organising relationships and workable systems for resolving disputes between children, parents and carers.

TWENTY-FIRST CENTURY FAMILIES

Families in our diverse community are increasingly heterogeneous.[2] Fluid relationships between adults in families mean that children are more likely to experience changes in their family involving transitions between carers, and care by people who are not their parents. The family is not dead, but it is changing shape and losing some of the stability and cohesion it had in former times. Even in the 1980s only 25% of births were outside marriage: now the proportion is rising towards equilibrium.[3] Relationships between parents are increasingly likely to be informal, to break down whilst children are young and to be followed by re-partnering.[4] As adult partnerships form, children may develop significant relationships with adult carers who are not their parents; when partnerships fail they may

---

[1] Children Act 1908, Children Act 1948 (revised and consolidated in the Child Care Act 1980) and the Children Act 1989. There have been other Acts, notably the Children and Young Persons Acts 1932, 1933, 1963 and 1969 and the Children Acts 1975 and 2004. Although child protection powers were incorporated in the 1989 Act, parts of the 1933 Act relating to offences relating to abuse and neglect of children remain in force. The 1989 Act has been the subject of substantial amendment, but its key principles and structures are largely intact.

[2] S Smallwood and B Wilson (eds) *Focus on Families 2007* (Palgrave Macmillan, 2007); ESRC *Changing social norms, changing family law? Rights and responsibilities for partners, friends and carers* (University of Bradford, 2006).

[3] ONS *Social Trends 38* (Palgrave Macmillan, 2008), Table 2.17.

[4] Ibid, Table 2.14; K Kiernan and K Smith 'Unmarried parenthood: New insights from the Millennium cohort' (2003) 114 *Population Trends* 26–33.

lose relationships with such carers or remain with them or their kin rather than a parent. *Family* for children increasingly involves absent and re-partnered parents.[5] Children are more likely to spend part of their childhood in an informal step-family[6], a common arrangement but one which is scarcely recognised by law. Care may not be by parents at all, but by kin. 'Family and friends care' is seen by local authorities as the placement of choice for children who cannot be looked after by a parent.[7] For families at risk of care proceedings, it has the potential for preventing state intervention. Indeed, the Children and Young Persons Act 2008 gives such foster placements priority over care by strangers.[8]

The abandonment of legally recognised family forms, albeit done without a full understanding of the consequences in terms of enforceable rights and duties, raises questions about the future role of law. How should these changes be accommodated? What processes and means can be used so that informal relationships important to children can be recognised? In particular, what is the role of the courts in the recognition of relationships? The current emphasis on legal mechanisms reflects the dominance of lawyers in the processes which led to the Children Act 1989, beliefs that courts and lawyers can solve family problems (which appears live and well, at least in the Family Division of the High Court)[9] and the formalised approach to family relationships of the mid-twentieth century when marriage rates were at their highest, birth rates outside marriage were low and a high proportion of non-marital births resulted in adoption.[10] However, as Dewar[11] has noted, the law's position is no longer secure. The social acceptability of non-marital arrangements has meant that the advantages of marriage to dependent partners are ignored. The use of informal structures partly reflects a loss of respect for the authority of law. Legal orders from the courts are also less available. The reduction

---

[5] One in four children lives in a lone parent family and at least one in ten families with dependent children is a step-family; see ONS *Social Trends 38* (Palgrave Macmillan, 2008), pp 19–22 and Table 2.11; S Smallwood and B Wilson (eds) *Focus on Families 2007* (Palgrave Macmillan, 2007), Tables 1.3 and 1.4.

[6] The Office for National Statistics uses the term 'cohabiting step-family' as opposed to 'married step-family'.

[7] DfES *Care Matters: Time for change*, Cm 7137 (2007), paras 2.34–2.41; HM Government *Drugs: protecting families and communities* (2008), p 24. Care within the wider family secures the child's rights to respect for family life under ECHR, Art 8. In 2002 the Department of Health noted ambivalence about its use in *The Choice Protects Review, Friends and family care paper* (Department of Health, 2002).

[8] Section 8 adding Children Act 1989, s 22C(5), (6)(a) and (7)(a).

[9] For example, in the approach to 'intractable' contact disputes, eg *Re S (Unco-operative Mother)* [2004] EWCA Civ 597, [2004] 2 FLR 710, CA; *Re O (Contact: Withdrawal of Application)* [2003] EWHC 3031 (Fam), [2004] 1 FLR 1258, FD; *Re M (Contact: Long-term Best Interests)* [2005] EWCA Civ 1090, [2006] 1 FLR 627, CA.

[10] C Gibson 'Changing family patterns in England and Wales over the last fifty years' in S Katz, J Eekelaar and M Maclean (eds) *Cross-Currents* (Oxford UP, 2000), pp 31–55. Approximately one in five births outside marriage resulted in adoption by non-parents: R Leete 'Adoption Trends and illegitimate births 1951–1977' (1978) 14 *Population Trends* 9–16.

[11] J Dewar 'The normal chaos of family law' (1998) 61 *Modern Law Review* 467–485.

in resources for legal aid, with the consequent loss of affordable legal services, restricts access to the courts. The complex structures available in the Children Act 1989 to formalise relationships between carers and children (residence orders and special guardianship) will effectively be used only by the rich and those who have taken over caring for the state, not other informal carers. Increasingly family obligations will have to be negotiated without the possibility of recourse to the courts. It is therefore even more important that rules, procedures and entitlements are clear and readily understood.

Conceptions about what *family* means and *who is family* are also challenged by developments in genetic science. Many aspects of health are now clearly linked to genetic inheritance. DNA profiling makes it possible to identify parents with certainty, and to establish ancestry.[12] The importance of knowledge of origins has been recognised in changes to adoption law and practice,[13] and is reflected in rights to know the identity of their genetic parents for those now conceived through assisted reproductive technology (ART).[14] So, at a time when children are more likely to be cared for by people other than parents, the parental contribution to identity is in the spotlight and, as a consequence, social parenting may be seen as of less importance. Indeed, this distinction between social and legal parents has been blurred by the extension of the definition of *parent* in the Human Fertilisation and Embryology Act 1990 (and even more substantially by the Human Fertilisation and Embryology Act 2008).[15] The partner of a parent who consents to her receiving ART with donor gametes is now the child's parent regardless of their gender or any legally recognised relationship. Distinctions made between the legal parents of children conceived through ART are likely to highlight the existence or otherwise of a genetic link to their children. In this way the law can (and will) reinforce the superiority of genetic parents.[16]

---

[12] M Richards 'Genes, genealogies and paternity: making babies in the Twenty-first Century' in J Spencer and A Du Bois Pedain (eds) *Freedom and responsibility in reproductive choice* (Hart, 2006), pp 53–72.

[13] Rights of access to birth records (Children Act 1975, s 26), increased openness with post adoption contact from the 1990s and the provision of far more detailed information by Adoption Agencies: see eg Adoption Agencies Regulations 2005, reg 16 and Sch 1.

[14] These rights only apply to those conceived under the new regime (ie from April 2005) and those conceived earlier whose 'donor' has provided information for this: Human Fertilisation and Embryology Authority (Disclosure of Donor Information) Regulations 2004 and HFEA 1990, s 31 (as amended).

[15] Under the HFEA 1990, s 28 the husband or partner of a mother who conceived with donor sperm is the child's father. The 2008 Act will extend these provisions by making the mother's same-sex partner a second parent: ss 35, 36, 42 and 43. Also, the partner's name will be able to be included on the birth certificate if they had consented to the mother's ART but died before the child was conceived: ss 40 and 46.

[16] In *Re G (Children) (Residence: Same Sex Partner)* [2006] UKHL 43, [2006] 1 WLR 2305, the House of Lords decided a dispute between lesbian co-parents in favour of the genetic mother 'which must count for something in the vast majority of cases' per Baroness Hale. In *Re A (a child) (Joint Residence: Parental Responsibility)* [2008] EWCA Civ 867, [2008] 2 FLR 1593, where the (unmarried) step-father was referred to by the judges as the 'father' or 'husband' and granted joint residence rather than contact

A consideration of the adjustments to law and policy required as a consequence of changes in the nature of the family and the identity of carers first necessitates an examination of the principles on which the Children Act 1989 was based and the extent to which they have been maintained since the Act was implemented. The chapter identifies both major departures from the original principles and the development of aspects of these, giving a new emphasis to the contrasting ideas of formal rights and private ordering. The final section reviews how changes in state support for families mesh with changes in the family, particularly which families are supported, and in what ways.

FAMILY LIFE UNDER THE CHILDREN ACT 1989

The Law Commission's scheme for family relationships was based on three key concepts – parental responsibility, private ordering and family integrity.[17] The main focus was the married family; mothers and married fathers would have parental responsibility automatically. Other people would acquire it if they became the child's guardian or were granted a residence order. 'Parental responsibility' connoted the bundle of rights and obligations legal parents have at common law or by statute. It was intended to reflect the 'everyday reality of being a parent and emphasise the responsibilities of everyone in that position.'[18] Each parent would be able to act independently and would retain their powers and obligations if they divorced. This continuation of their legal status vis à vis the child avoided the need for court orders. Parents would be free to agree arrangements for children after separation; the divorce court would still need to be informed about these, but its powers to intervene would be restricted. In addition, unmarried parents would be able to agree that the father had parental responsibility, avoiding the need for a court order to achieve this. Although parents would be able to bring any dispute about their children to the courts for resolution, access by others – spouses (step-parents), relatives, strangers and particularly foster carers would be restricted. The law would thus preserve family integrity whilst ensuring that those who had a genuine interest in a child's well-being could call upon the assistance of the courts in appropriate cases. In addition, the reform of public law protected the family from state intervention unless a child was suffering (or at risk of) significant harm.[19]

---

so that he had parental responsibility. Cf *Re P (Residence Appeal)* [2007] EWCA Civ 1053, [2008] 1 FLR 198, where statutory provisions which precluded a legal status for the genetic father were ignored and he and his partner were awarded residence.

[17] Law Commission *Review of Child Law: Guardianship and Custody*, Law Com No 172 (HMSO, 1988).
[18] Ibid, para 2.4.
[19] Ibid, paras 4.41, 5.1 and 5.6.

WHO IS FAMILY?

Family law notions of relatedness remain narrowly based on formal relationships (marriage or civil partnership) or blood. The Children Act 1989 defines 'relative' as 'grandparent, brother sister, uncle or aunt ... or step-parent.'[20] It excludes people who may now be regarded as 'family', including all informal partners and everyone (except grandparents) more than a generation removed from the child. This definition determines access to the courts without a long qualifying period[21] and whether a carer is subject to regulation and surveillance, for example by being required to register as a childminder or private foster carer.[22] Local authorities are also permitted to place children with relatives for short periods without the checks which are required for placement with other foster carers.[23] The definition thus confers advantages on parents, relative carers and local authorities. However, it brings disadvantages, particularly to children. 'Relatives' defined in this way are not necessarily known to, or by, the child, and those who are known are not necessarily 'relatives'.[24] Also, substitute care presents risks, even when it is provided by relatives.[25] Surveillance not only provides protection for the child, it provides opportunities to support and advise carers. Whilst family privacy might suggest that families should be able to make arrangements without state interference, few would agree that those who become carers through arrangements made within families should have more limited access to state support when they have similar needs.[26] If family law is to accommodate the more informal structures of future families, more attention will need to be given to defining children's family relationships, identifying the circumstances in which such relationships should give rise to different treatment, and determining what that should be.

Far wider notions of relatedness are recognised in the new social family rights – paternity and parental leave, tax credits etc. There is, as yet, no common approach, but this may develop with recognition of the

---

[20] Children Act 1989, s 105(1).
[21] Children Act 1989, s 9(3)(b). A relative foster carer can seek leave for a residence order without the local authority's consent after 6 months, not a year. The Children and Young Persons Act 2008, s 36 adds s 10(5B), which will allow relatives who have cared for a child for one year to apply without leave of the court.
[22] Children Act 1989, ss 66(1)(a)(iii) and 79A(3)(a).
[23] Fostering Services Regulations 2002, SI 2002/57, reg 38; Fostering Services (Wales) Regulations 2003, SI 2003/237, reg 38. The 6-week time limit for assessments means that local authorities which cannot meet this timescale either have to remove the child or continue a placement which is ultra vires.
[24] The provision relating to foster placements (reg 38) extends to 'friends'.
[25] The view of relative foster carers in *Every Child Matters*, Cm 5860 (2003), may be too positive in the light of the research evidence: see J Hunt, S Waterhouse and E Lutman *Keeping them in the Family* (BAAF, 2008) and E Farmer and S Moyers *Kinship Care: Fostering Effective Family and Friends Placements* (Jessica Kingsley, 2008).
[26] There might be issues about discouraging placement with relatives to gain benefits, but this does not justify refusing to allow childcare tax credit to be claimed when children are looked after by their grandmother.

importance of support for working carers. When the question is whether a person has a right to paternity leave, it is sufficient that the claimant is the mother's partner (of either sex) and expects to have 'the main responsibility (apart from any responsibility of the mother)' for the upbringing of the child.[27] No proof is required of the person's relationship to the child, to the mother, or of their intentions in relation to the child's upbringing, but an employer can require a declaration by the employee in relation to these matters.[28] Parental leave is currently restricted to people with parental responsibility.[29] The enlarged definition of parent in the Human Fertilisation and Embryology Act 2008 will enable a non-genetic parent to claim,[30] but a step-parent who married the parent before the child's birth would not normally be able to do so.[31] The right to request flexible working can be claimed by a wider range of people who have, or expect to have, responsibility for the upbringing of the child under the age of 6 years, including parents, guardians and special guardians, carers with a residence order, local authority or private foster carers, and a person who is married to or is the civil partner or partner of such a person.[32] An even wider range of people can claim this right if they care for an adult, but in the case of care for children, relatives are excluded unless they have a residence order. The broadest definition applies to child tax credit – which can be claimed by anyone 'who is responsible for a child'.[33] However, only one claim can be made for any child. Carers must decide amongst themselves who will claim; if they fail to do so, the claim is determined according to who has 'the main responsibility.'[34] Rather than identify in detail who qualifies, the legislation provides a mechanism for resolving disputes between claimants, making it easier to ensure claims can be made but increasing the cost of administration. If support is to be made available for carers, wide definitions which place emphasis on the day to day contribution a person makes to the child's life will be required, but a process which needs substantial information to determine eligibility and provision for appeal will be too unwieldy and too off-putting for most purposes.

---

[27] Paternity and Adoption Leave Regulations 2002, SI 2002/2788, reg 4(2).
[28] Ibid, reg 6(2). Knowingly giving a false declaration could amount to an offence of deception.
[29] The Maternity and Parental Leave etc Regulations 1999, SI 1999/3312, reg 13(2).
[30] For example, the civil partner or partner who satisfies the agreed parentage conditions in relation to a woman who receives ART.
[31] If the step-parent obtained parental responsibility, either under s 4A or by a residence order, he could do so. A parent who was not married or civil partnered to the mother and did not jointly register the birth would also not be entitled to parental leave.
[32] The qualification conditions are set out in regulations: Flexible Working (Eligibility, Complaints and Remedies) Regulations 2002, SI 2002/3236, reg 3, as amended by SI 2006/3314, SI 2007/1184 and SI 2007/2286. The number of amendments indicates how difficult the Department of Work and Pensions found it to identify who should be able to claim what is only a very limited right. The Regulatory Impact Assessment for SI 2006/3314 explains some of the thinking behind the lines drawn.
[33] The Child Tax Credit Regulations 2002, SI 2002/2007, reg 3.
[34] Ibid, reg 2.

Definitions for one purpose may not be appropriate for another. In terms of finding care for a child whose parents cannot provide it, a broader approach is more likely to identify a person with the capacity and commitment to provide good care than a restrictive one. Definitions will not avoid the need for individual assessments, nor the need for choices between carers who are capable but have different qualities. Definitions exclude as well as include. Although there may be a case for privileging 'relatives' it is more difficult to see why the former (unmarried) partner of a parent caring for the parent's child should be regarded as less deserving than a married step-parent. Yet this is what the existing definition of 'relative' achieves. Marriage no longer provides a litmus test of the quality of relationships. Yet in relation to access to the courts for a residence order, the married step-parent can apply at any time, and a relative after caring for the child for a year,[35] but carers whose family membership was never marked by marriage to the parent can only apply after 3 years, unless they have leave of the court or consent. It is the person's care for the child, not the status of a previous relationship with a parent, that justifies their formal recognition. Informal relationships need to be assimilated with formal ones for this purpose, for example by widening the definition of relative to include partners, those whose family membership derives from a committed relationship, not blood or marriage.

REFORM OF THE CHILDREN ACT 1989

There have been substantial reforms to the Children Act 1989, particularly in the Adoption and Children Act 2002, which challenge the operation of some of the Act's key concepts, particularly family integrity. These reforms have emphasised formality in relationships by facilitating the acquisition of parental responsibility by unmarried fathers, step-parents and carers.[36] This extension of formal recognition also serves to highlight the weak position of those who cannot benefit from them, ie carers who are neither parents nor spouses, and those who are unable (for whatever reason) to access the courts.

Parental responsibility is now held by most fathers, not just married fathers and the small minority of other fathers who made a formal agreement with the mother or obtained a court order. This is not a result of the provision in the Children Act 1989 for formal parental responsibility agreements; that form of private ordering was used by only a small minority of parents. Requiring a separate formal claim proved to be an ineffective means of allocating largely intangible rights. Parents were unaware of the need for action or never got round to taking that

---

[35] Children Act 1989, s 10(5), (5A) and (5B) added by Children and Young Persons Act 2008 reduces the period for relatives to one year.

[36] Children Act 1989, s 4(1A): parental responsibility by joint registration of birth; s 4A: parental responsibility for step-parents by agreement or court order; and ss 14A–14G: special guardianship.

step. Now joint registration of a child's birth, which is generally required for the father's name to appear on the birth certificate, provides the main way for unmarried fathers to obtain parental responsibility.[37] This change was made in response to the increase in parenting without marriage and concerns that fathers who lived with the child's mother were unaware that they had a lesser status vis à vis their children than married fathers.[38] Although not limited to fathers who are involved in their child's life, the thinking behind the change was the formal recognition of responsible fathers, not encouraging responsibility through recognition.[39] Linking birth registration with parental responsibility has the double advantage of providing evidence of a father's status and avoiding the need for further action (either by the parents or the state). However, this approach conflates the issue of recognition/identity with that of acquisition of parental responsibility. Whether this matters depends on the consequences of having parental responsibility.

Whereas agreeing to registration is a responsible act on the part of the father, which saves the mother and child from the shame of unacknowledged paternity, it does not amount to an agreement with the mother about the child's upbringing, nor to acceptance of obligations owed to the child. Concern that mothers would be undermined in their caring role had previously led the Law Commission to reject reforms which would have given fathers rights without regard to their relationship with the mother.[40] The notion that two people, who might never have lived together or agreed about their child's care, could live separately and parent co-operatively reflects far more optimism about the good sense of adults than the Law Commission had held. The Children Act 1989 generally endorsed a system of separate parenting by separated parents, so each could act independently.[41] However, the courts have emphasised the importance of co-operative parenting, increasingly favoured shared residence and identified issues where consultation is required. Parental responsibility has thus become a more important status in law than the Children Act 1989 itself would suggest.[42]

Proposals originating in Sir David Henshaw's report on reform of the child support system[43] appear likely to result in parents with little or no

---

[37] Children Act 1989, s 4(1A).
[38] Lord Chancellor's Department *The procedures for the determination of paternity and on the law on parental responsibility for unmarried fathers* (1998), para 53; R Pickford *Fathers, marriage and the law* (1999).
[39] As an alternative to recognition through joint registration the Lord Chancellor's Department consulted on whether cohabitation with the mother at the time of birth should give father's parental responsibility.
[40] Law Commission *Illegitimacy*, Law Com No 118 (HMSO, 1982), paras 4.26 and 4.46.
[41] For example, there is no duty on parents to consult and very few decisions (name change, relocation, or acquisition of parental responsibility/adoption by third parties) require the consent of all those with parental responsibility.
[42] Eekelaar has argued that it is an unnecessary and confusing label: J Eekelaar 'Rethinking Parental Responsibility' [2001] Fam Law 426.
[43] DWP *Recovering child support: routes to responsibility*, Cm 6894 (2006), paras 107–109.

relationship sharing parental responsibility. Policy makers no longer view joint birth registration as evidence that unmarried parents are parenting as a couple but as providing an opportunity for the father to show his *intention* to be involved. The aim is to make fathers *take* responsibility and change men's attitudes to unplanned births. 'Making joint birth registration the default position will help to embed a cultural norm that fathers should reach the birth of their child with an expectation that they have clear responsibility for their child.'[44] This is portrayed as a matter of fathers' rights, children's rights and child welfare on the basis that joint registration will provide the foundations for the father's commitment, encourage the payment of child support and provide the child with a father positively involved in his or her life.[45] At the same time legal powers to enforce child support are being relaxed.[46] Moreover, it is suggested that these benefits can be achieved 'regardless of the type of relationship [the father] has with the mother'.[47] Following on from this, the government has announced its intention to legislate to require joint registration of birth unless it is 'impossible, impracticable or unreasonable for the father to be identified in the birth register'.[48] Procedures are to be put in place to establish proof of paternity where the mother wants the identity of the father recorded but the father denies it. Although the protection of vulnerable mothers is to be a key consideration in future legislation, only 'significant evidence', such as conviction for rape, will be sufficient to justify refusal of registration.[49] In effect, parental responsibility is to be extended to all identified fathers on the basis of their genetic contribution in the hope that the small minority of men who do not currently have it will, as a result, make a positive contribution to their children's lives.[50] It appears that no account has been taken of any negative consequences of increasing the numbers of fathers who have a formal status but no established relationship with the child's mother and therefore no basis for co-operative parenting. One possible consequence is more conflicted parenting as fathers assert their rights and mothers resist. The courts may be faced with more cases where court orders are sought to build rather than maintain relationships with children and where resolution amounts to a lull in hostilities, not the establishment of an accord.[51]

---

[44] DWP *Joint birth registration: promoting parental responsibility*, Cm 7160 (2007), para 19.
[45] Ibid, paras 16–18. This argument was supported by evidence from a study in the USA (where joint registrations are substantially lower than in England and Wales currently), see I Garfinkel et al 'In-hospital paternity establishment and father involvement in fragile families' (2005) 67(3) *Journal of Marriage and the Family* 611–626.
[46] The Child Maintenance and other Payments Act 2008, s 15 repeals Child Support Act 1990, ss 6 and 46, removing the duty on parents with care who are benefit claimants to co-operate with the Secretary of State over the recovery of child support from the non-resident parent.
[47] DWP *Joint birth registration: recording responsibility* (2008 Cm 7293), para 16.
[48] Ibid, para 27. See now Welfare Reform Bill 2009 (Bill 8).
[49] Ibid, para 29.
[50] Approximately 45,000 births in England and Wales (7% of the total) are not jointly registered. Almost half of these fathers are 'still in regular contact' with their children: DWP *Joint birth registration: recording responsibility* (2008 Cm 7293), paras 3 and 7.
[51] Poor parents with very young children appear to be over-represented amongst those who

The Adoption and Children Act 2002 made new provision for step-parents to acquire parental responsibility by agreement with the parent. The scope of this provision, and the pre-condition for its use, mean that very few step-parents are likely to obtain a formally recognised relationship with their step-children. It is limited to married step-parents,[52] and where both parents have parental responsibility they must both agree to the step-parent acquiring the status. Given the extension of parental responsibility to fathers, there will be few step-families where the father's consent is not required. Although only a formal agreement is required, as noted above, a similar process for unmarried fathers failed to result in substantial numbers gaining parental responsibility. Despite the growth in the numbers of step-families and their recognition in social law, family law remains unsure whether and how to recognise them. The current structure appears to make this a matter for private ordering, but by requiring agreement from *both* parents undermines the step-parent's partner's capacity to make the decision, necessitating use of the courts by all but the most co-operative families. That this creates real barriers is largely ignored – reflecting uncertainty about whether parental responsibility for step-parents really matters at all.

The Act also created a new status for carers as special guardians.[53] Special guardianship was conceived as an alternative means of securing care where adoption was not appropriate. It is intended to provide security for children who do not want to cut all ties with their birth family and for carers who do not wish to replace the birth parents. Where care is provided by a relative, it has long been considered inappropriate to end the parent-child relationship by adoption. A special guardianship order gives the child's carers parental responsibility, which was already available through a residence order, but with added security against interference and greater powers, including the power to appoint a guardian. Granting a special guardianship order effectively hollows out the parents' parental responsibility, leaving an almost empty shell. Special guardians' legal responsibilities to the child's parents are limited to trying to inform them should the child die;[54] their position cannot be challenged without the court's permission, which will be given only exceptionally.[55] Making these

---

dispute contact in court: L Trinder et al *A profile of applicants and respondents in contact cases in Essex* DCA Research Series 1/05 (2005), pp 9–10. Trinder and colleagues also found that agreements brokered through court proceedings did not lead to better communication between parents and that disputes were frequently re-litigated: L Trinder and J Kellett *The longer term outcomes of in-court conciliation* MoJ Research Series 15/07 (2007), pp 23–24.

[52] Unmarried step-parents can acquire parental responsibility through adoption, although this use of adoption has been discouraged since the 1970s: J Masson et al *Mine, yours or ours?* (HMSO, 1983). The number of such orders made by county courts is now around 400 per year: ONS *Marriage, divorce and adoption statistics FM2* (2005), table 6.3. In contrast, step-parent adoption is widely used in other parts of Europe, notably Germany.

[53] Children Act 1989, ss 14A–14G.

[54] Children Act 1989, s 14C(5).

[55] Children Act 1989, s 14D(1), (3) and (5). Parents require leave to apply for variation or

orders is subject to additional scrutiny by the court. However, although it is largely intended to secure care for children who are looked after by a local authority, it is a private law order and made on the basis of a simple welfare test.[56] Indeed, local authorities can avoid committing substantial resources to care proceedings[57] by encouraging foster carers (particularly those who are relatives) to apply for this order. Consequently, special guardianship blurs the distinction between public and private law and privatises child protection.[58]

The 2002 Act also addressed the disparity between foster carers' rights of access to the court to seek adoption and for residence orders by relaxing the restrictions on them under the Children Act 1989. Rather than being subject to a more restrictive regime than other carers, which precluded them from even seeking leave for a s 8 application order until they had cared for a child for 3 years,[59] local authority foster carers are now in a privileged position. They can apply for residence after caring for a child for only one year, whereas other (non-relative) carers who do not have the consent of the parents can still only do so if they have cared for the child for 3 years or have the leave of the court.[60] Although relatives are more likely to be caring as local authority foster carers than was once the case,[61] a far larger (but unknown) number of children live with relatives outside the care system. These children's (and their carers') need for security is no less than where the local authority is involved. The differential rights of application suggest that the government has been more concerned to enable foster carers to slip the shackles of the local authority (or local authorities to discharge children from care) than to secure legal recognition for carers. However, an amendment in the Children and Young Persons Act 2008[62] will, when implemented, reduce the period to

---

discharge, and leave can only be granted if there has been a significant change in circumstances since the granting of the order.

[56] Children Act 1989, s 1(1) and (3). The applicant must give 3 months' notice to the local authority, and the court must consider the local authority's report: s 14A(7), (8) and (11).

[57] For example, the court fee of up to £4,825, the substantial time of legal and social work staff in preparing documents and attending court and the cost of any additional assessments required by the court.

[58] Indeed, the introduction of the Public Law Outline (PLO) and the new fees appear to be directed at diverting cases from court: '[G]uidance places a strong emphasis on close communications with families and on exploring options for children to be supported and cared for by their wider families while making clear that timely action should always be taken through the courts to safeguard children when necessary' (Kevin Brennan, Minister for Children, at launch of the PLO, 1 April 2008).

[59] Children Act 1989, s 9(3)(c) (original wording). Leave was not required for a residence or contact application where the applicant had cared for the child for 3 years: s 10(5)(b).

[60] Children Act 1989, s 10(2)(b), (5)(b) and (5A).

[61] J Hunt, S Waterhouse and E Lutman *Keeping them in the Family* (BAAF, 2008). Approximately 18% of fostered children are placed with relatives or friends.

[62] Section 36, adding Children Act 1989, s 10(5B).

one year for relatives, putting them on an equal footing with foster carers, at least in relation to applications for residence orders and the acquisition of parental responsibility.[63]

The practice of delivering family justice through the courts has largely become a process of achieving settlement, not adjudication.[64] However, the courts have maintained their monopoly over granting parental responsibility to non-parents and strengthened their position by acquiring increased powers in contact disputes.

At a time when policy makers appear to want to encourage more private ordering, costs of legal proceedings are increasing and access to legal aid is reducing, the courts are nevertheless faced with growing caseloads. Moreover, the government appears keen to give courts more powers and to legislate more complex processes. The Children and Adoption Act 2006 is a good example.[65] Although much of this Act merely expands on the court's power to impose conditions in orders, the addition of 16 new sections suggests a new and strengthened role for the courts in contact disputes. Limitations on resources mean that this is unlikely to materialise. Contact activities, particularly programmes designed for perpetrators of domestic violence will not be widely available, nor has Cafcass been given the additional resources which would enable it to monitor contact orders or service more, longer family assistance orders. Expectations of what the family courts can and should do will be raised and dashed, adding to their already negative image.

CRITIQUE OF THE PROVISIONS RELATING TO PARENTAL RESPONSIBILITY

The Children Act 1989 adopted the term 'parental responsibility' for the bundle of rights, powers and liabilities parents had in respect of children. It did not seek to define these rights, even in general terms, leaving this to the morass of case law, although it did set specific limitations on the power of those with residence orders, and of parents with parental responsibility but no residence order. These provisions relating to parental responsibility have been the subject of two main criticisms. First, John Eekelaar has argued very persuasively that the concept is unnecessary and confusing. There are many decisions about children for which holding

---

[63] In *R (M) v Birmingham City Council* [2008] EWHC 1863 (Admin) a local authority's policy of not paying residence order allowances to relatives unless the local authority had looked after the child for 3 months or there were exceptional circumstances was upheld.

[64] R Bailey-Harris et al 'Settlement culture and the use of the 'no order' principle' [1999] *Child and Family Law Quarterly* 53; J Hunt and A Macleod *Outcomes of applications to court for contact orders after parental separation or divorce* (Ministry of Justice, 2008).

[65] As is the interaction of the court's and the local authority's powers in considering plans for a child's adoption within care proceedings.

parental responsibility is either irrelevant or insufficient.[66] So parents must maintain their children even though they do not have parental responsibility, whilst others with parental responsibility have no such obligation. Conversely, non-parents with parental responsibility cannot appoint guardians or consent to a child's adoption – these powers are restricted to parents with parental responsibility.[67] And all decisions about a child's upbringing can be overridden by the court on welfare grounds. Parental responsibility does not clearly identify what those who have it can do, or what those who do not have it cannot do. In many respects being a parent is more important. Most carers get by without parental responsibility, but this is largely because it is ignored as the basis for capacity to make decisions about children. Those who have to act on decisions – such as teachers and doctors – rely on the practical responsibility of the adult who is looking after the child, not sight of a birth certificate or court order. Joint registration of birth, more informal care by people without parental responsibility and DNA testing will lead to parental responsibility having less prominence as a legal concept. Fathers named on the birth certificate are real people who have to be considered when decisions are made. Other fathers will be unknown and disregarded unless they are obviously involved in the child's care.[68] And those who are not named and not carers are likely to be given consideration only if they have established their paternity.

Secondly, there has been criticism of the lack of clarity in the definition of parental responsibility. The Law Commission concluded in Report No 172 that it was not possible to have a contents list setting out what was included within parental responsibility. It was practically impossible to do so because parental power needed to reflect current circumstances and the maturity of the child.[69] The resulting definition in the Act is so general as to convey no clear meaning. Taking this approach also meant legislation could not be a means of guidance to parents and carers about what was expected of them. This approach contrasts with the way the Children Act 1989 included a 'checklist' to develop understandings of welfare. Whilst a more specific definition of parental responsibility could have looked like 'state nannying', it would also have provided a stronger foundation for agreed arrangements about care. The Scottish Law Commission took a different approach and set out a definition which, although lacking detail, highlighted the key rights and obligations of

---

[66] J Eekelaar 'Rethinking Parental Responsibility' (2001) 31 Fam Law 426.
[67] Children Act 1989, s 5(3) and (4) (a special guardian can appoint a guardian) and Adoption and Children Act 2002, s 51(2).
[68] Although fathers without parental responsibility should be consulted by the local authority and notified of care proceedings, this can only be done where their identity and location are known.
[69] Law Com No 172, para 2.6.

parents.[70] The Scots provision also identifies the particular obligations of parents who are separated from their children.[71]

Further attention has been given to the issue of defining parental responsibility. In 2005, the Commission on Families and the Wellbeing of Children, an independent body established by the National Family and Parenting Institute (NFPI) and NCH with the support of the Joseph Rowntree Foundation, proposed that there should be a review of all the legal and quasi-legal sources of expectations about parenting with a view to producing clear information about responsibilities and standards of care.[72] It was not intended that this should be enshrined in legislation but disseminated in ways that parents, carers and children would find useful and acceptable. This proposal has not yet been taken up. The new version of the *Children Act 1989 Guidance and Regulations, Volume 1*,[73] makes no new attempt to define parental responsibility. An attempt to add to the definition of parental responsibility in an amendment to the Children and Young Person's Bill 2008 during Committee Stage in the Lords was unsuccessful.[74]

Any statement of parents' or carers' responsibilities would not be just a codification of current law: it would also reflect values. If values are to be accepted, it is important that they have legitimacy, which will not necessarily exist in a document produced outside democratic processes, for example by civil servants or judges. Merely ensuring consultation about the form of the statement, as the Commission on Families suggested, is unlikely to be sufficient. Whilst a code can be written in more accessible language than legislation, open debate and endorsement through Parliament are important for achieving authoritative status, wide acceptance and publicity. Such a code should provide a holistic definition; parents (and others) would not be entitled to select which responsibilities they were willing to accept. Just as the judiciary have finally recognised that a violent partner cannot be 'a good parent' merely because he has not physically harmed his children,[75] so parental responsibility could come to be seen as requiring the provision of tangible support by looking after and/or financially supporting children, not merely maintaining contact with them.[76]

---

[70] Children (Scotland) Act 1995, ss 1(1) and 2(1) following Scottish Law Com No 135, paras 2.2 and 2.26.

[71] Children (Scotland) Act 1995, s 1(1)(c).

[72] Commission on Families and the Wellbeing of Children *Families and the State: Two way support and responsibilities* (Policy Press, 2005).

[73] DCSF *Children Act Guidance and Regulations, Volume 1, Court Orders* (TSO, 2008).

[74] *Hansard*, HL, vol 697, col 622 (Grand Committee), Amendment 102 proposed by Lord Northbourne, but withdrawn.

[75] *Re L; Re V; Re M; Re H (Contact: Domestic Violence)* [2000] 2 FLR 334. But in *Re F (Indirect Contact)* [2006] EWCA Civ 1426, [2007] 1 FLR 1015, CA an extremely violent father who had terrorised the mother was described as loving and affectionate to the child and allowed indirect contact.

[76] Links between contact and child support have repeatedly been rejected by the courts: see *Re B (Contact: Child Support)* [2006] EWCA Civ 1574, [2007] 1 FLR 1949, CA.

PRIVATE ORDERING

Private ordering allows families to make arrangements for their children without the need to use the courts, maintaining the integrity of family decision-making and freeing court time for disputes. Less positively, it leaves families to struggle to resolve problems without assistance, continues power inequalities and allows major changes to be made in children's lives without ensuring that their views are considered. In practice, family arrangements have always involved elements of private ordering – orders for reasonable contact, common before the Children Act, were frequently adjusted without return to court, care was arranged informally and some arrangements became de facto adoptions. What was different about the private ordering in the 1989 Act was that, as between parents, informal arrangements about children's care could generally have the same effect as if made by the courts, because the court dealt in the practicalities of residence and contact, not in status or rights.[77]

The Law Commission scheme for recognising private arrangements for children was narrowly conceived. It focused on removing the need for the court to rubber stamp arrangements. There were only a few circumstances where private arrangements about children would have the same legal consequences as court orders. The law had long allowed parents to appoint a guardian in the event of their death without requiring court proceedings; the Children Act 1989 allowed a parent to agree to *the other parent* having parental responsibility.[78] This has been extended to agreements between parents and step-parents and the appointment of *guardians* by special guardians, but in no other circumstances can a parent or special guardian grant someone parental responsibility. Thus, private ordering can take place only within the narrow confines of relationships between parents, between parents and their married partners, or to allow special guardians to make provision in the event of their death. Moreover, the Act specifically precluded parents making agreements which did more than permit another person to act on their behalf.[79] Allowing parents to transfer or dispose of their parental responsibility would clearly conflict with established protections for the child against exploitation, but this does not explain why parents should not be able to give carers *parental responsibility* whilst retaining their own obligations to their children.

Even this narrow scheme was unsuccessful in convincing parents of the value of agreements. Parental responsibility agreements were not widely used; court orders were frequently made even though the issue of parental responsibility was not contested.[80] These two problems are symptomatic

---

[77] Agreements, unlike orders, are not enforceable. Although the courts may threaten enforcement powers to obtain co-operation, they have very limited ability to achieve compliance through enforcement.
[78] Children Act 1989, s 4.
[79] Children Act 1989, s 2(9).
[80] I Butler et al 'The Children Act and the unmarried father' (1993) JCL 157.

of the difficulties in dealing with relationships through law. First, family relationships are based on mutual trust, whereas taking legal action is associated with things going wrong, an absence of trust. People do not want to think about matters such as relationship breakdown or death, or to suggest that they lack trust in their partner by seeking to clarify family matters in law.[81] Secondly, where a relationship has broken down to such an extent that recourse is had to the courts, it can only be re-established over time. The pressure to complete cases prevents this, so orders are required. The courts' acceptance of this, which itself may promote agreements, operates to undermine the idea that orders are not necessary if agreements have been reached.[82] The 'no order' principle has become irrelevant, except perhaps as a test that the arrangement to be approved in the order appears to be workable.[83]

Despite the continued reliance on orders, the idea that arrangements should not need to be made by courts is now well established. In the sphere of private law, the government has sought to promote parental agreements about children in a number of ways. Public funding has been provided for mediation with the aim of achieving settlements without recourse to lawyers. Indeed, in many cases legal aid for proceedings is not available unless a party has shown a willingness to mediate.[84] The Green Paper on Parental Separation stressed parents' higher levels of satisfaction with agreed arrangements compared with those imposed by the courts.[85] Parenting Plans[86] have been published with guidance to assist parents negotiating arrangements for children. Where court applications have been made, procedures have been developed to produce agreement and avoid court hearings.[87] In public law, a new pre-court procedure introduced as part of the Public Law Outline[88] requires local authorities to take active steps to avoid care proceedings before applying to the court, in all but emergency cases.[89] Avoiding care proceedings might involve an agreement with parents for children to stay with relatives or be looked after by the local authority. In theory, parents will retain all their responsibilities but, in practice, an attempt to end the arrangement which

---

[81] R Panades et al *Informing unmarried parents about their legal rights at birth registration* (One Plus One, 2007), p 31.

[82] R Bailey-Harris et al 'Settlement culture and the use of the 'no order' principle' [1999] *Child and Family Law Quarterly* 53–62.

[83] Ofsted has been highly critical of the failure of Cafcass reporters to address the 'no order' principle: *Ofsted's inspection of Cafcass East Midlands* (Ofsted, 2008), p 19. However, this practice was presumably acceptable to the courts, which had ceased to operate a strict construction of s 1(5).

[84] LSC *Funding Code* (2007), para 20.12.7.

[85] DCA et al *Parental Separation: Children's Needs and Parents' Responsibilities*, Cm 6273 (2004), para 23.

[86] Available from http://www.cafcass.gov.uk/publications/leaflets_for_adults.aspx.

[87] President of the Family Division *Private law programme* (DCA, 2004).

[88] Judiciary of England and Wales *The public law outline* (MoJ, 2008).

[89] DCSF *Children Act 1989 Guidance and Regulations, Vol 1* (TSO, 2008), paras 3.3–3.4 and 3.26–3.33.

is not accepted by the local authority is likely to result in proceedings where parental responsibility is formally curtailed.[90]

The reforms to the child support system are also placing far more emphasis on private arrangements than has been permitted since the 1980s. Under the scheme set out in the Child Maintenance and Other Payments Act 2008, all parents, including those claiming welfare benefits, will be free to choose whether they use the statutory scheme to secure child support.[91] Those who do not will be able to make their own agreements. Parents with care who claim benefits will also be able to retain more substantial sums in child support before losing any benefit.[92] Parents will be given support and advice to make their own arrangements, and those who wish to do so will be able to have payments calculated and enforced through the new agency, the Child Maintenance and Enforcement Commission (C-MEC). The courts will retain their current jurisdiction, which is largely limited to making consent orders.[93] The government considers that its new scheme will 'facilitate more consensual and stable' financial support for children, which will have a higher rate of compliance because they are consensual.[94] However, the main impetus for this reform has been the failure to make the Child Support Scheme work effectively. The Child Support Agency has been unable to handle the large number of cases, the excessively complex formulae imposed on it and the messy lives of its users. Huge amounts of time and money have been spent and produced massive levels of dissatisfaction but relatively little child support for many of the customers.[95] The government expects that reducing the number of cases to be dealt with by the formal system will avoid the substantial administrative burdens imposed by the compulsory system and make C-MEC better able to operate effectively.[96]

This new application of private ordering was welcomed by some of those who responded to the White Paper, but considerable concern was expressed by One Parent Families, Child Poverty Action Group and Refuge that parents would not be able to agree proper payments.[97] The consequence of ending the requirement for benefit claimants to use the formal system and the emphasis on agreements is likely to be a high proportion of parents with care relying on unenforceable, informal

---

[90] Almost one in six EPOs were sought in response to a request to remove a child from local authority accommodation: J Masson et al *Protecting powers* (Wiley, 2007), p 152. EPOs are likely to lead to care proceedings.

[91] Child Maintenance and other Payments Act 2008, s 15 repeals Child Support Act 1991, ss 6 and 46.

[92] DWP *A new system for child maintenance*, Cm 6979 (2006).

[93] Ibid, paras 2.31–2.39.

[94] Ibid, para 2.6.

[95] For an account of these failings see N Wikeley *Child Support Law and Policy* (Hart, 2006), pp 119–145.

[96] DWP *A new system for child maintenance*, Cm 6979 (2006), paras 2.7–2.8.

[97] DWP *A new system of child maintenance – Summary of responses to the consultation*, Cm 7061 (2007), para 2.2.

arrangements or having no agreement at all.[98] The levels of payments will be low, given that non-resident parents are unlikely to see any point in making payments over the benefit disregard.[99] Although parents with care will have the right to use the formal scheme, they are likely to be under considerable pressure not to do so. And unless the C-MEC is really able to achieve a proper level of payment quickly and effectively, there will be no advantage to the parent with care in the formal system and no real risk (or added incentive to comply) for the non-resident parent.

The barriers to parents agreeing contact arrangements – lack of communication and lack of trust[100] – are likely to make it difficult to reach agreements about finance. However, there is a possibility that the voluntary nature of both aspects of parental responsibility might sometimes work together to secure payments from those who want contact and to promote contact by those who pay. Given that payments will now depend on agreements and only be imposed where agreements cannot be reached, it would be legitimate for the courts to expect a father who is seeking contact to be providing financial support. Not to do so would amount to accepting that a person who has a child to stay for one night a week and alternate weekends contributes enough to the child's well-being by maintaining him or her for that amount of time. Moreover, a continuation of the strict separation of these two aspects of parental responsibility effectively amounts to an acceptance of the proposition that it is not in the child's interest to have access to more resources. The argument for linking payment and contact would be stronger if both were incidents of parental responsibility, but almost universal parental responsibility will only be achieved in 2021,[101] and directly enforceable obligations to maintain remain tied to the status of parent, not parental responsibility.

Private ordering will never provide the basis for all arrangements for care after separation, or by people other than parents. In a more informal world where access to the courts is limited, taking on care will continue to be something that just happens. Relatives will become indefinite carers, not as a result of negotiated arrangements, but because children need care and somebody has to do it. If such carers are to be able to 'make

---

[98] A Bell et al *An investigation of CSA maintenance direct payments: quantitative study* DWP research report 404 (2006), p 3. 96% of parents with care who were CSA clients cited at least one factor which would make it difficult for them to use the CSA maintenance direct system. Arranging payments completely without the agency is likely to be even more difficult for them.

[99] The government has announced a plan to disregard all maintenance payments for those receiving out-of-work benefits from April 2010: *No one written off: reforming welfare to reward responsibility*, Cm 7363 (2008), para 4.15.

[100] L Trinder and J Kellett *The longer term outcomes of in-court conciliation* MoJ Research Series 15/07 (2007).

[101] Following implementation of the Adoption and Children Act 2002, s 111.

confident, informed choices'[102] for the children they care for, they will need at least as much advice and support as parents.

GOVERNING THE FAMILY IN THE TWENTY-FIRST CENTURY

Supporting families is clearly recognised as a function of government, although which families should be supported, and in what ways, divides the main political parties.[103] Family support is political; what is provided, how much and in what ways may well depend on the election in 2009–2010. Over the last 10 years, the Labour Government has shown that it is prepared to do more to support families, but its main focus has been on helping families to support themselves through employment. Family policy has been an adjunct of economic policy.[104] Controlling family behaviour is also a major plank in government family policy. Court orders (parenting orders), fines and anti-social behaviour orders have been introduced[105] and withdrawal of benefits has been threatened.[106] Support through the provision of advice has also become a way to direct family behaviour, particularly in relation to post-separation parenting. Through support for the Family and Parenting Institute, the government is promoting education in positive parenting. The establishment of children's centres and extended schools[107] has the potential to provide (non-stigmatising) family support services. These make it easier to provide advice to families. Advice generated by civil servants and professionals may become a key source of messages about family values and parenting, replacing religion, community and law.

The government seeks to achieve responsible parenting by confident parents who engage with services and ensure their children use opportunities provided. These developments are encapsulated in *Every parent matters*: 'Families bring up children. The role of the government is to ensure that all parents ... make confident informed choices which they

---

[102] *Every Child Matters*, Cm 5860 (2003), para 2.6.
[103] The Conservative Party favours support for marriage and tax allowances which encourage one parent to care for children full-time over tax credits and benefits which encourage parental employment: see Social Justice Policy Group *Breakthrough Britain, Vol 1, Family breakdown* (2007).
[104] HM Treasury *Tackling poverty and extending opportunity* (1999); HM Treasury *Child poverty review* (2004); HM Treasury et al *Choice for parents, the best start for children: a ten year strategy for childcare* (2004); DWP *A new deal for welfare: empowering people to work*, Cm 6730 (2006).
[105] Crime and Disorder Act 1998, s 1; Anti-social Behaviour Act 2003. For a table of various orders to control behaviour and promote responsible parenting, see Home Affairs Committee *Anti-social behaviour orders, Fifth Report of 2004–05* (2004–5 HC 80), p 15.
[106] Provision has been made to withdraw housing benefit: Welfare Reform Act 2007, s 31 adding Social Security Contributions and Benefits Act 1992, s 130B.
[107] See *Every Child Matters*, Cm 5860 (2003).

feel are right for their family ...'[108] Services should not just be directed at mothers; fathers, even those with limited involvement with their children, are also entitled to support. 'Irrespective of the degree of involvement they have in the care of their children, fathers should be offered routinely the support and opportunities they need to play their parental role effectively.'[109] So the mother's caring role, which has been key in the upbringing of most families, in most societies, and at most times, may no longer be privileged. Support is intended to make better *parents*, so the reasoning follows that non-resident parents should have more of it.

The parents who matter appear to be natural or legal parents; carers who become social parents have a secondary role. Agencies working with adults are being urged to 'think family' and 'to consider the parental roles and responsibilities of their clients.'[110] But where the family is failing, the state is beginning to stress the need to support kin carers, who as 'foster carers' should have access to the sources of parenting support available to other parents.'[111] Other family carers – grandparents looking after children where the children's social care department have not been involved, and those minding grandchildren when parents are at work – are regarded as just doing what can be expected in families, so they need not be supported. Their contribution to the family is a matter of private arrangement, and not something with which the state should become involved.

The changes in the family have implications for government support for families. It is easiest, politically, for the state to support intact families[112] and leave issues about how support is used to be decided within the family. Such an approach may not meet the diverse needs of future families. Where parents and carers are not the same people, there may be difficult questions about balancing support between them. If the focus of policy is on being even-handed between *parents*, as suggested above, the contribution of caring and carers may be overshadowed. Rather than supporting the ethic of care, it may undermine it by reasserting the status or genetic link of parents or relatives. Also, resources for support are limited and have to be rationed; targeting is necessary if support is to be effective. The creation of support services will not deliver support for families who need it unless sufficient attention is given to the design and promotion of services, including outreach. This is not just an issue of eligibility: the types of services and the ways they are provided will make services more or less accessible and acceptable to young parents, non-resident fathers or older carers. Providing contact centres largely supports non-resident fathers, whereas parent and toddler groups are used

---

[108] DfES *Every parent matters* (2007), para 2.6.
[109] Ibid, para 3.11.
[110] Cabinet Office *Think family: Improving the life chances of families at risk* (2008), para 1.14.
[111] DfES *Every parent matters* (2007), para 6.25.
[112] Ibid, para 6.16: 'when necessary families should be given extra support to help keep them together.'

mainly by the mothers of young children. Similarly, if services for resolving disputes are primarily delivered through the courts, for example Cafcass conciliation services or contact activities,[113] those who cannot or do not access the courts will be excluded. Providing welfare benefits is far simpler than delivering appropriate support services, yet benefit take-up is acknowledged to be low. Even universal services which are envisioned in *Every Child Matters* and *Every Parent Matters* cannot mean uniform provision, because one type of service will not fit all parents and carers.

ADVISING AND SUPPORTING FAMILIES

The Department of Work and Pensions has acknowledged that the changes to the Child Support System will necessitate much more advice for parents. Parents will need help to decide whether to use the C-MEC and in what ways, and if they choose not to, many will need help to negotiate agreements. Uncoupling child support from the benefits system shifts advice provision away from Jobcentres onto advice agencies. Despite a likely reduction in the numbers of family lawyers who provide legal aid, the Legal Services Commission is likely to remain a major provider of advice on family and welfare benefits issues through its telephone advice line. Children's Centres and extended schools will also provide advice for families. If these advice services are to meet the needs of parents they will have to deal with the common concerns of many families when relationships fail – money and debt, relationships, child care and children's behaviour, preferably without chains of referral.

In *Every Parent Matters* the government recognises that parents need and want more advice. Indeed, it sees advice as a key way of providing support by helping parents to identify how they can help themselves:

> 'Any package of services must have at its heart parents continuing to look first to their private contacts and networks. And it must also consider the role of the private sector, notably the print and broadcast media in this field. This is not about nationalising parenting.'[114]

Advice is not neutral; it may be intended to help parents and carers identify choices and make decisions, but it will necessarily carry messages about what they *should* do, even if this is only because this is 'what works'. Although the government may be anxious to avoid being thought to control parenting, it does have some very clear messages which it wants to get across. For example, where parents separate, children should continue to be able 'to have a meaningful relationship and contact with both

---

[113] The Children and Adoption Act 2006 provides for courts to direct parents to contact activities designed to improve post-separation relationships, but similar services are unlikely to be available on a voluntary basis for others.
[114] DfES *Every parent matters* (2007), para 6.14.

parents.'[115] Non-resident parents should support their children financially by providing X% of their income etc. It will want these, not contrary messages, to be given to, and followed by parents. Moreover, the increased reliance upon telephone services and print will standardise advice and strengthen approved messages. Anyone who has ever written advice material for the government knows how carefully it considers the meanings conveyed. Whilst advice must be based on law, the open-textured nature of the law of parental responsibility and informal caring provides plenty of room for messages about how to be responsible and how to promote your child's welfare. However, advisers based in call centres will need prompts and scripts so that they can deliver advice.

Advice has limitations in enabling individuals to resolve disputes. Whereas courts (and Cafcass) have powers to coerce parties into their process, other agencies are only able to work with those who are at least willing to give it a try. The government has only repeated calls for co-operation, it has not tried other means of persuasion (carrots) or coercion (sticks). Yet, if agencies' plans are to succeed, they must secure co-operation from carers and parents without care who have continued to dispute or disengaged. This will require services which are recognised as being supportive, and able to respond to the different concerns of those looking after children, separated parents and children. The government is not proposing that parents should have rights to services but that there should be a 'minimum package of advice information and support' available to every parent through the Children's Centre.[116] This is a long way from ensuring that specialist support is available to all families who want help after relationship breakdown.

CONCLUSION

The family landscape is far less clear than it was when the Children Act 1989 was drafted. Informality, serial partnership and increasing rates of family breakdown have added complexity to family life, while amendments to the Act have reduced its clarity. Government attitudes to the role of law appear confused. On the one hand, the government is increasing emphasis on formal rights through the extension of parental responsibility to almost all fathers and new powers for the courts; on the other, it is encouraging families to make agreements without the courts or state agencies or the possibility of enforcement. Similarly, it appears uncertain about how to respond to families without legally recognised structures, so individuals' rights as carers are uncoordinated and unclear.

The state is increasingly relying on families to secure the care of future generations when parents have failed or withdraw. The privatisation of the

---

[115] DCA et al *Parental Separation: Children's Needs and Parents' Responsibilities*, Cm 6273 (2004), para 2.
[116] DfES *Every parent matters* (2007), para 7.9.

family, discussed at the time the Children Act 1989 was enacted, is far more obvious in the current policy and practice. Whilst the government wants to support families, it seems uncertain how to do this. It does not want to prefer mothers or relatives with care over non-resident parents, nor to navigate the conflicted relationships real families frequently present. It is willing to provide advice, but it does not want to take on financial responsibility, except by continuing to provide a safety net for those unable to work. It wants to promote good parenting, but without having to take an active role that incurs responsibility or expense.

There are no simple solutions to ensuring children have a good upbringing, but the government has put its faith in alerting carers to children's needs and helping them to meet them through providing information and support in terms of advice. Carers (and non-resident parents) have choices and responsibility to exercise them well. So care for our future generations is firmly a matter for parents; failing them, family or friends; and if all else fails, the state. So will advice improve care for our future generations? We will first have to learn to act on it.

CHAPTER 11

THE FUTURE OF WELFARE LAW FOR CHILDREN

Richard White

INTRODUCTION

I am pleased to have the opportunity to explore a topic which has been of personal interest for nearly 40 years. For a large part of that time I have been something of an academic, having done research, taught law and written books and articles and, until this government made it too difficult to do so, run a legal aid practice. Now I am no longer responsible for a practice, I can spend more time examining some of the basic requirements of the child protection part of the family justice system. Although I will only consider care proceedings, much of what I have to say has parallels in the private law field.

This has been a difficult paper to write for several reasons. First, there is a risk of looking back over 40 years and thinking that things 'ain't what they used to be'. And there can be no doubt that things are actually a lot better than when I started in the 70s and into the 80s. But then came the Children Act 1989 and, in my view, through the 90s progress was made both in child law jurisprudence and, crucially, in knowledge about the needs of children. It is in this decade that political mismanagement has failed us and it is galling, having practised within an excellent structure, to see it wilfully demolished and inhibited from meeting the needs of children and families. Secondly, we are dealing with a complex political situation. There are real questions to be asked about how policy is being developed and decided upon and by whom. Additionally, subsequent to the conference at which this paper was delivered and after disclosure of the tragic death of Baby P,[1] there has been intense media pressure for further regulation of the child protection system.

What I seek to do is explore the political context, the motives admitted and hidden, and the tools undermining the existing family justice system,

---

[1] The case of Baby P came to public attention in November 2008 at the conclusion of the criminal trial of the persons responsible for his death. The child died as a result of non-accidental injuries, despite 60 contacts with health or social workers over the 8 months preceding his death. The trial caused a media storm, the dismissal of the local authority Director of Children's Services and an upsurge in the number of care proceedings. See *The Times*, 12 November 2008 and see further below.

through legal aid, court fees, court services and support services. I then consider the essentials of the system and the prospects and options for the future.

THE POLITICAL CONTEXT

The Ministry of Justice Board is responsible for implementing policy in relation to family law – subject only of course to the dead hand of the Treasury. My theory is that they have decided, whether intentionally or by default, and not by transparent methods, that they should bring about a major long-term social reform of the family justice system. Gone or going is the concept of the separation of powers; under threat is the concept of a professionally supported family justice system providing an independent service for the community.

This process can be difficult to discern, especially when it is different from the published agenda and when the government controls and manages statistics. I suggest change is being deliberately managed at a pace which will not excite public disapproval. Furthermore, undermining the existing system enables the government to say 'the system does not work, we have to change the structure'. I believe the ultimate purpose is to put in place a largely administrative family justice system which will reduce judicial involvement and thereby become easier to control financially and politically.

THE LEGAL HISTORY

A cornerstone of our current law is the Children Act 1989. As has been well documented,[2] the process leading to this legislation took 5 years, an exceptionally gifted, knowledgeable and well organised team, extensive consultation with practitioners and a well-intentioned political drive. A process which had started with the Report into the care and supervision provided in relation to Maria Colwell,[3] who had died after being sent home from care, and later included *Children Who Wait*;[4] the debates on the Children Bill 1974 (which led to the Children Act 1975), the Review of Child Care Law,[5] and the Report of the Inquiry into Child Abuse in Cleveland,[6] all led to the Children Act 1989. During that time I co-directed a research project on the administrative powers of local authorities.[7] There then existed a process by which authorities could

---

[2] Peter G Harris 'The Making of the Children Act: A Private History' [2006] Fam Law 1054.
[3] (HMSO, 1974).
[4] J Rowe and L Lambert (BAAF, 1975).
[5] (DHSS, 1985).
[6] Butler-Sloss (1987).
[7] M Adcock, R White and O Rowlands *The Administrative Parent: a study of the assumption of parental rights and duties* (BAAF, 1982). See further, M Hayes, Chapter 4 above.

acquire what were then parental rights and duties (now parental responsibility) without resort to court. We recommended that those provisions should be repealed as unfair in modern society, which of course they later were.

I recount these sources, albeit briefly, because they have been influential on my thinking. They also provide a sage reminder of that to which we should not return. The Children Act 1989 provided a balanced structure which was established after long and careful debate. We now have an attempt to reorganise a central plank of that legislation through an agenda originally established by a small group of civil servants, some seconded from fields in which they had no experience of either law or children, who were determined to ignore advice from practitioners, unless it fitted with the politically driven cost demands of the Treasury.

THE CURRENT POLITICAL CONTEXT

One of the odd aspects of current government policy is that over the past few years they have spent extensive resources developing strategies for vulnerable children. Yet when it comes to consideration of the legal aspects, the focus is on cost and not on the interests of children.

Why is that? In the minds of politicians and civil servants it might be that they think too great a part of the budget is spent on too few children. It can be seen from recent publications[8] that the major concern of the government is the broad swathe of children in the community or those who are in care, because they achieve less than their peers who are not in care. In my view this rather misses the point that if you get the planning for these children right at the early stages, authorities ought to be diminishing the level of these problems.

The Every Child Matters agenda is dictated by the Department for Children, Schools and Families, yet it makes no mention of children coming into care. The Department has also been responsible for updating Volume 1 of the Guidance to the Children Act 1989 on Court Orders,[9] but that part of the agenda has primarily been left to the Ministry of Justice (MoJ). Although there is talk about cross-government consultation, priorities within Ministries are different. The MoJ have been under the Treasury cosh and operate at minimum standards and lowest cost, with impact statements in legislation devoted to whether they have an economic or financial effect. In a reversal of the aims and ideals of the Children Act 1989, legal proceedings involving children have been a victim of this drive. Treasury civil servants, who have no understanding of the standards or operation of the family justice system, set financial

---

[8] Neither *Every Child Matters: Time for Change* (DfES, 2007) nor the *Children's Plan* (DCSF, December 2007 and reviewed December 2008) make any mention of care proceedings or those children who suffer or are at risk of serious harm.
[9] HMSO (1991).

criteria as a response to broad brush political targets. The MoJ then appoint project managers with no experience or understanding of the family justice system to drive that agenda forward, and they and the Legal Services Commission implement policy to keep within the budget, uninterested in the practical effects of what they do. Any objective analysis of publications in the family justice field in the last few years as they affect children could not avoid this conclusion. The effect is that children who should be being protected within the family justice system have no natural advocate in government, at least until such time as there is a tragedy. Is it surprising that local child welfare agencies lose sight of the harm some children suffer?

THE UNDERMINING PROCESS

So how did this come about? It started in 2001 when reorganisation of the court welfare services led to serious underfunding of the newly constructed Cafcass. Then in July 2005 the government published 'A Fairer Deal for Legal Aid'.[10] It would be difficult to think of a more inapt title. It was nothing less than a start of the process to dismantle the public funding of the family justice system.

Part 7 of the paper contained the government decision to review care proceedings. The basis for this was that although in child contact and residence cases overall spending had declined in real terms by 16% between 1999–2000 and 2004–05,[11] the volume of child care and related proceedings was said to have increased by 37% since 1999–2000, while expenditure had increased, in real terms, by 77%.[12] It was admitted, even on the government's own analysis, that there were a number of cost drivers causing the latter increase, including the proliferation of parties and greater use of experts, especially expensive residential assessments paid from the legal aid fund. More work for solicitors arising from the lack of children's guardians at the start of proceedings also added to legal aid expenditure, and that happened because of the failure to fund Cafcass adequately. Delays in the court system, which frequently add to the complexity of a case, were also a fundamental cause of increased costs. None of the cost was placed at the door of poor practice, nor was it suggested that cases were not complex.

The stated terms of reference for a 'Review of the Family Justice System in the area of child care proceedings'[13] were:

> '2. A Fairer Deal for Legal Aid puts forward the case for a cross-Government, end-to-end review of the child care proceedings system. This Review will aim to ensure that the system is as effective as possible in

---

[10] DCA 'A Fairer Deal for Legal Aid', Cm 6993 (2005).
[11] Ibid, para 2.36.
[12] Para 2.37.
[13] DCA *Review of the Child Care Proceedings System in England and Wales* (2006).

delivering the Government's overarching vision for children, as set out in the Green Paper *Every Child Matters*.[14] It states that every child should benefit from:
- Being healthy
- Staying safe
- Enjoying and achieving
- Making a positive contribution
- Experiencing economic well being.

3. The Review will be taken forward to improve the cross-Government delivery of the core welfare, minimum intervention and minimum delay principles set out in the Children Act 1989. It will:
- Examine the extent to which the current system for deciding care cases in the courts ensures all resources (including children's services) are used in the most effective, efficient, proportionate and timely way to deliver the best outcomes for the children and families concerned.
- Explore the variation in routes taken to bring children into care, both in terms of the rate at which this takes place, and the way in which children enter care through the court process or on a voluntary basis. Identify good/innovative practice which enables children to be diverted away from court proceedings and, instead, to be supported in their families where this is possible.
- Examine the extent to which the core principles of the Children Act 1989 are best met by the current, over represented approach within the courts, and examine whether these principles could be better met by using a more inquisitorial system. Options to consider include:
  – Investigating the possibility of early low-level judicial interventions to encourage parents to resolve problems themselves, thus avoiding the need for full court proceedings wherever possible and appropriate; and
  – Examining whether the two stages of the court process in child protection cases (establishing the facts and determining the care plan) could be more formally separated with different attendees, procedures and levels of legal representation, and precisely where, and in what way, lawyers should be involved.
- Explore examples of best practice from other jurisdictions and assess the extent to which they may be applied in England and Wales.'

The *Review* itself produced a rather more measured report, although as Masson observes:[15]

'a review undertaken in such a short space of time by a team who, for the most part, were not well-grounded in the system was unable to identify novel, but workable solutions. Moreover, lacking data on how the current system was working, it was in a poor position to identify good practice or target practices which could make a difference'.

---

[14] *Every Child Matters: Time for Change* (DfES, 2007).
[15] 'Reforming care proceeding – time for a review' [2007] CFLQ 411 at 425.

She also makes the telling point that the Department for Constitutional Affairs presided over three separate reviews with different aims, incompatible timescales and competing priorities.

Having had input from others involved in operating the system, the so-called 'stakeholders', there were some unexceptional proposals:

'5. Reflecting the areas for improvement described above (paragraph 4.1), the recommendations aim to:
- ensure that families and children understand proceedings and are, wherever possible, able to engage with them;
- ensure that s 31 applications are only made after all safe and appropriate alternatives to court proceedings have been explored;
- improve the consistency and quality of s 31 applications to court;
- improve case management during proceedings; and
- encourage closer professional relationships.'

The problem is that the government is determined to reduce the number and length of care proceedings. It is only that which will eventually achieve their determined aim of reducing cost. My thesis is that, having been headed off on one front, because it would have been just too unpopular to say they were making changes which would have had obvious repercussions for the safety and welfare of children, they embarked on another tack. The tools with which they are now dismantling the family justice system are destruction of legal aid, inadequate provision of court services and, as part of a wider discouragement of local authorities from taking proceedings, a massive increase in court fees.

LEGAL AID

The Carter Review[16] in 2006 proposed changes to the costs system with the introduction of graduated fees across the board for both private law and care work. This was, of course, done with minimal investigation by the Carter team of what they were recommending in respect of civil legal aid. Their report had been primarily focused on criminal legal aid, with proposals for civil legal aid something of an afterthought.

Yet they felt able to make a recommendation fundamental to the future of the family justice system that a graduated fee scheme for solicitors in child care cases should replace the current system of payment at hourly rates in court. With breathtaking arrogance, in a report published simultaneously, the Legal Services Commission came up with its own scheme[17] and introduced fixed fees, clearly under pressure from the Ministry of Justice.

---

[16] Lord Carter *Legal Aid – A market-based approach to reform* (Lord Carter's Review of Legal Aid Procurement, 2006).
[17] See the Care Proceedings Graduated Fee Scheme at www.legalservices.gov.uk, which was brought into force with effect from 1 October 2007.

Alistair MacDonald said at the Annual Meeting of the Association of Lawyers for Children in November 2007:[18]

> 'We have sought to make clear to the MoJ that the new Public Law Outline and the revised Children Act Guidance are designed to be implemented and operated by specialist legal practitioners; that those twin reforms can only be effective in reducing delay and improving outcomes for children if a sufficient and sustainable supplier base of such specialist legal practitioners is maintained. We have repeatedly highlighted, as the Constitutional Affairs Committee has recognised,[19] having heard evidence from all interested stakeholders from the senior judiciary to children's charities, that the proposed reforms to legal aid constitute a "breathtaking risk".'

The MoJ and the Legal Services Commission have been alone in defending the funding changes which they introduced on 1 October 2007. And they have, of course, continued to do so, even following a decision by the Court of Appeal[20] in November 2007 that the contractual changes were unlawful. I am driven to the conclusion that this is no mere accident; nor mere foolhardiness. It is a deliberate and calculated policy to achieve an agenda beyond that which they have stated in the public domain. In spite of frequently voiced statements of support, government policy demonstrates a determination to drive lawyers and courts out of this field. The only feasible interpretation of current policy is that they are perceived as expensive and unnecessary to the outcomes which government seeks to achieve for child welfare. For the most part they are perceived as complicating what the government regards as simple. They achieve that aim by limiting lawyers' costs to fixed fees and making that area of law unprofitable and unattractive to new recruits and reducing the budget of Her Majesty's Court Service.

The legal aid system is gradually disintegrating, not just of course in relation to family law, but also in other essential areas such as mental health, housing and immigration. This disintegration is being managed in such a way that the government will no doubt say that it is the lawyers who are to blame. As the Constitutional Affairs Committee noted,[21] the relationship between the Legal Services Commission (LSC) and practice was poor. The LSC has gone out of its way to cause further deterioration in that relationship both by its provocative behaviour in conducting the court proceedings in relation to the Civil Contract, which was held to be unlawful, but also in its management of individual cases. If they can avoid, complicate or delay payment, they will do so. Guidance on the obscure aspects of the contract has been minimal,[22] and any continuing

---

[18] Association of Lawyers for Children Newsletter, April 2008, p 16.
[19] The Constitutional Affairs Committee Report, *Implementation of the Carter Review of Legal Aid*, HC 223-1 (2007).
[20] *R (on the application of the Law Society) v The Legal Services Commission* [2007] EWCA Civ 1264, [2008] QB 737.
[21] *Implementation of the Carter Review of Legal Aid*, HC 223-1.
[22] See www.legalservices.gov.uk/civil.

negotiations have one sole aim in mind: minimise expenditure. They believe they have a captive group of practitioners for the time being, so they can downsize gradually. But we have already suffered a serious loss of experienced family and child care lawyers, thereby reducing the protection which they can provide children and parents in their dealings with the state. And by these means government can ultimately control what issues are justiciable. Starving the legal aid fund is an effective way of controlling policy.

The inevitable outcome of a policy which discourages lawyers will be less well conducted cases, when the stated aims of the new procedures are to provide parents with early advice and to establish the issues at an early stage. In due course there will be neither experienced judiciary capable of managing complex cases, nor experienced lawyers to advise parties on the case. Indeed, we are already seeing as a consequence of fixed fees a deterioration in the quality of early advice on cases. This simply means they become more complex later on.

COURT SERVICES

The government has starved the courts of resources. In 2005 there were cuts in Court Service funding of 8–12%, which made the operation of the courts more difficult. Since then we have been told of further cuts.[23] There is pressure to deal with more care proceedings in the magistrates' court. That might work if they appointed more district judges, but that of course is not their plan. They want cases to be heard before lay magistrates, who are regarded as the cheapest option.

There are increasing delays in getting hearings because of a lack of judges, lack of court staff and lack of court rooms. The facilities in many courts are abysmal. The Queen's Building at the Royal Courts of Justice in which the Family Division has conducted its business for many years has been closed since September 2007, so that Family Division judges are scattered to the winds. The relationship between the judiciary and the Civil Service is, in my experience, at an all-time low.

In November 2007 Mervyn Murch noted[24] the importance of judicial continuity and questioned whether it can be achieved with a domestic bench of magistrates. One might add that in many higher courts in many areas the concept is a complete myth. Listing operates wholly at the convenience of the court system, unless a judge makes a determined effort to retain a particular case. Judicial expertise in complex cases is vital, but with the loss of lawyers with expertise in the field through the restrictions on legal aid the expertise will dissipate.

---

[23] The Ministry of Justice is in talks over a planned £1bn budget cut over the next 3 years, and wants civil courts to increasingly fund themselves: news sources generally, 18 November 2008.

[24] See Chapter 5 above.

COURT FEES

Following MoJ proposals,[25] court fees for the issue of care proceedings were increased from £150 to £4,800 in April 2008 with the rationale that the cost naturally lies with local authorities. A more blatant disincentive to issue proceedings it is difficult to imagine. Yet in the consultation paper 'Public Law Family Fees' published on 19 December 2007 it was stated:[26]

> 'It would be unlawful for [a local authority] to avoid taking court proceedings for financial reasons where they considered that to be the appropriate step. Nor, given that the local authority spending settlement reflects the additional pressure, is there any reason to think they would do so.'

If the MoJ really believed that the level of change of fee proposed would make no difference to the exercise of local authority discretion about whether to issue proceedings, they are living in a different world to mine. It is a matter of creating an ethos which is adverse to care proceedings, as much as the specific cost disincentive. It is clearly all part of the MoJ cost-cutting campaign to take matters out of the court, which will act to the substantial detriment of the interests of vulnerable children and their families. Indeed, it was widely felt that they were going through the motions in publishing a consultation paper on fees. In response to a challenge on this, Bridget Prentice, the Secretary of State, wrote to the *Law Society Gazette* on 30 January 2008 stating that it was an open and fair consultation. Yet in the same letter she stated that funds had already been transferred from the MoJ budget to local authorities. Local authorities were not able to trace these funds. (Birmingham were said to have estimated that it could cost them £1m, money they had not budgeted for.) Clearly these plans were in place from earlier in 2007, yet they were not even referred to at conferences on the future of care proceedings during the year. Furthermore, we know from unpublished papers within the Ministry in November 2007, it was already a foregone conclusion. Even if the funds were available, what does it say about the duty to protect children, that such a substantial fee is placed on it?

THE PUBLIC LAW OUTLINE

The Public Law Outline[27] (PLO) came into effect on 1 April 2008. It could be seen as having twin aims of diverting cases from the courts and, when issued, of managing court proceedings more effectively and more

---

[25] See the Magistrates' Courts Fees Order 2008, SI 2008/1052. In the supporting Explanatory Memorandum it was stated that the increase was designed (inter alia) to support the objective of discouraging unnecessary or premature use of care proceedings, when there was no evidence to that effect.
[26] Ministry of Justice, 19 December 2007.
[27] Ministry of Justice *The Public Law Outline: Guide to Case Management in Public Law Proceedings* (April 2008).

expeditiously. I have no quarrel with the PLO. As with any new provisions there must be concerns about how it will be implemented, but I do have the following observations on what I believe to be essential to its effective implementation.

A primary objective is for local authorities to carry out assessments and engage with families without taking proceedings. Pressure to do that is increased by the massive increase in court fees. If only it were that simple. The fact is that all too frequently it is not possible to achieve that until proceedings are issued, and frequently not before later stages of proceedings.

Local authorities are to be encouraged to prepare cases better before issuing proceedings. That is a laudable aim and all to the good if it is achieved – but if it means pressing parents to be involved in assessments or to allow their children to be assessed, it could become just another recipe for delay – outside the court system rather than in it. What do the current architects think the architects of 20 years ago had in mind with child assessment orders – the one significant jurisdictional failure of the Children Act?[28] While again it is laudable to seek to press parents to recognise their parenting problems and the implications of them for the welfare of the child, they are not always in a state to do so. We have to remember that care proceedings cover a wide range of circumstances and it cannot be one size fits all.

What we do know is that, although it is patchy, there has been a massive drop in the number of applications issued.[29] The number of applications will continue to be reduced – and for the wrong reasons of political pressure and finance. Then, when there is a tragedy which attracts public and media attention such as the Baby P case,[30] there is a sudden policy reversal again for the wrong reasons – political pressure and finance.

It would be wrong to suggest that authorities will not take proceedings when children have been seriously harmed or are at risk of serious harm purely for financial or political reasons, but policy does create a disincentive. The cumulative effect of policies is that local authorities will decline to take care proceedings where they should do so, or they will delay in doing so. Children will not be protected when they should be, or they will enter care when older and more damaged. The serious tragedy

---

[28] Child assessment orders are provided for by s 43. Although official statistics are no longer maintained regarding their use (sed quaere?) they seem rarely applied for and their use has never been publicly promoted. – see eg R Lavery 'The Child Assessment Order – A Re-Assessment' [1996] CFLQ 41.

[29] Cafcass records showed that nationally between 10 and 20 November 2006 there were 330 care applications; in the same period in 2007 there were 292; and in the same period in 2008 there were 369. In the Inner London and City Family Proceedings Court in the period from September 2006 to June 2007 there were 760 applications; in the comparable period 12 months later there were 528.

[30] See n 1 above.

like Baby P will be rare, but the consequences will be particularly serious in neglect and emotional abuse cases.

As Masson has aptly observed:[31]

> 'A focus on keeping cases out of the courts suggests that those setting up the Review were unaware that these proceedings have long been regarded as "a last resort" and that concerns have regularly been expressed about delays in bringing care cases. It also suggests assumptions that voluntary arrangements can achieve what might otherwise be sought through proceedings, and that the same long-term arrangements can be achieved by agreement as can be achieved through a court order. These fail to recognise that lack of parental co-operation with child protection services is a key factor in the initiation of care proceedings, and that planning for children without court orders requires good co-operation with their parents.'

Over the last few years there has been a move to place children in what authorities call kinship care. That can often mean placing children with relatives, not necessarily assessed as to their competence as well as they might be. Proposals for Family Group Conferences prior to proceedings[32] will enhance this approach. It is likely to be a cheaper option than foster care. And the fees regime will certainly encourage authorities to press relatives into service without going through legal proceedings as has historically been the case. If they can persuade (or delude) relatives into caring without the child entering the care system, they might even avoid the payment of allowances entirely.

Local authorities are likely to seek to persuade parents to agree to children being voluntarily accommodated under s 20 of the Children Act 1989. Neither the authority nor the people with whom the child is living will have parental responsibility. Previous experience shows that this will exacerbate the drift of children in care which we have fought so hard to deal with in the last 25 years, because planning for the child's future is frequently poorly administered. One only has to recall the need to introduce amending provisions[33] to require local authorities to produce care plans for proceedings to know the importance of this.

---

[31] 'Reforming care proceeding – time for a review' [2007] CFLQ 411 at 420. Masson's research findings are consistent with the previous research of Julia Brophy – see *Research Review: Child Care Proceedings under the Children Act 1989* (DCA, 2006).

[32] See the PLO (p 38) which recommends Family Group Conferences at the stage of the initial assessment. While this may be appropriate in some cases, if effected across the board there is a risk it will leave decisions to the family when intervention is necessary to protect the child.

[33] Children Act 1989, s 31A, inserted by the Adoption and Children Act 2002, s 121(2). This provision was introduced because of concern that local authorities were not carrying out the care plans they had put before the court and there was no means of enforcing them: see *Re S (Minors) (Care Order: Implementation of Care Plan); Re W (Minors) (Care Order: Adequacy of Care Plan)* [2002] UKHL 10, [2002] 1 FLR 815.

A further short term benefit to the Exchequer of a reduction in proceedings is that Cafcass will not be involved. The child would have no independent representation. Neither would the parents have any independent or legal advice. One would like to think that this structure would not be compliant with ECHR, Arts 6 or 8, because there would be an interference in family life and there would be no fair trial to decide on what would become a de facto determination of civil rights.

What might be the future agency responsible for the conduct of child welfare cases? Currently, it is the local authority, though the authority has historically taken various forms. Subsequent to the implementation of the Children Act 2004,[34] 'the authority' in England takes the form of a Children's Services Authority headed by a Director of Children's Services. It is his responsibility to obtain advice, social work, legal, medical and anything else relevant. But could this be moved into private hands like Group 4 Security or, as is presaged in the Children and Young Persons Act 2008, which makes provision to enable local authorities to delegate local authority functions in relation to looked after children,[35] to providers of social work services? We appear to be in an era where ideology trumps experience or research and, oddly, this government is attracted to the concept of privatisation in the social services. If this was the route for child protection, one would be concerned about the profit element, but it may be a future battle to be considered.

On the assumption that some cases at least do still require independent judgment, what is the likely forum? Will it be a court? What are the options – a legally trained decision-maker, a combination of legally qualified chair sitting with others with relevant expertise, like the Special Educational Needs and Disability Tribunal, or a lay bench? Or would a local committee of people already employed to take decisions about children be sufficient? In my opinion, it would be most unsatisfactory if the combined outcome of proposed changes were to be that such decisions were effectively removed from the court system. But a Tribunal properly composed might not necessarily be a bad thing, provided it satisfied the essential requirements I consider below. Frankly I cannot see it happening under the present regime, because the cost would be considerable – if it were properly done.

CONCLUSIONS – THE FUTURE

Given that we must now look at minimum standards, what are the basic requirements of a family justice system? And what future options are there to make the best possible provision? The central principles are contained in Arts 6 and 8 of the European Convention on Human Rights.

---

[34] Section 18.
[35] Section 1.

The right to a fair trial and the right to respect for family life are fundamental, but they are only a start.

The future well-being of children is one of those fundamentals that society and its legal system has to protect. Is it not a truism, almost a cliché, that unless we promote the well-being of children, we cannot progress as a society? Taken to its extreme, if we had a society where all children were in feral gangs roaming our inner cities, how long would we survive? It follows that there should be a duty, enshrined as a primary rule of law, to ensure that all laws promote the physical and mental well-being of children. The Children and Young Persons Act 2008 requires the Secretary of State to promote the well-being of children, but this does not cross departmental boundaries.

The next principle surely has to be that those who created the child have fundamental rights and corresponding responsibilities in respect of the child. If there is to be an interference with those rights and responsibilities, it should only be through an independent procedure which avoids unnecessary damage to family life and which provides those whose interests are affected with opportunity and sufficient means to challenge the intervention.

The need to protect abused and neglected children, which at its extremes leads to their removal, permanent or otherwise, ought to be one of the principles. That is for their benefit and for the protection of society to reduce the risks of later offending. The importance of early development and recognition of the attachment needs of children and recognition of the child as an individual with his or her own rights has led to more concerted action to plan for children, which might well be contrary to the rights, wishes and well-being of the parents. This principle I believe to be under threat.

Considering these principles in the context of current policy, where are we heading? I have to say that I think the future in the short term is bleak, because politicians and civil servants have too much investment in their current positions and too little influence with the Treasury to change from their tunnel vision plans. In the longer term we know what a good system looks like, but for how long will we have the expertise and structures to drive it?

It must not be forgotten that intervention in families is like conducting a complex surgical operation. If a child is in danger of losing a leg, a medical system involving a skilled team would swing into action, reflecting the importance of our thinking that saving that leg was vital to the child's long-term welfare. One might think that saving the child's mental or emotional well-being was as, if not more, important to the long term welfare of the child, but also indeed to the welfare of society. Regrettably, we are very far from appreciating that fundamental concept.

What are the future prospects within the current context? It appears to me we have these options. The government sticks to tight financial controls and its negative attitude to the judicial system. On a positive analysis within this context we would continue to have a court system operating under the present Public Law Outline, where local authorities issue proceedings on a timely basis, having where possible conducted pre-court assessments, and courts manage cases within a timetable which reflects the interests of children. At best we can only really believe that we shall see a repetition of problems set out in the reports on delay over the past 12 years.[36]

On a negative analysis there will be limited court intervention with many more powers vested in local authorities, less review of their work and discouragement of their intervention in families. This is strangely at odds with other aspects of government policy as set out in the *Every Child Matters* documents,[37] but one cannot assume that there is consistency between government departments.

If we were to embark on a less doctrinaire approach to the family justice system, I could see a number of ways of improving things. In particular, if public funding were to be restored to comparable 1995 levels, and an approach which respected the welfare and needs of children and families encouraged, all would not yet be lost.

The use of experts is a key factor in the family justice system. Regrettably, their use has become almost routine, which is one of the most significant costs drivers. But to decrease their use we would need to improve the skills of the social work force. In addition, it has to be recognised that some cases are complex and need forensic and tertiary skills.

The PLO should improve judicial control of cases. I have always been in favour of that and to my mind s 1 of the Children Act 1989 makes that requirement quite clear. Equally, I have no difficulty with one of the stated aims of identifying the issues of a case at an earlier stage of the case – preferably when an application is issued. Solicitors for parents have to take that on board as well. Parents must have an opportunity to put their case, but do they really need 'their day in court'? Is a court the best venue for them to come to terms with the loss of their child, if that is the reality?

I have never understood why some cases take so long for a final hearing. The PLO and the Issues Resolution Hearing within it should improve that. I have never been in a case which has taken more than 7 days. After 10 days I tend to think that someone has failed to manage or present the

---

[36] See Dame Margaret Booth 'Avoiding Delay in Care Proceedings' (DCA, 1996) and the Lord Chancellor's Department *Scoping Study on Delay in Children Act Cases* (March 2002).
[37] DfES *Every Child Matters: Time for Change* (June 2007).

case properly. But this really is nothing new. It happens in some courts and I fear it may be the direction from the judiciary and local authority legal advisers which is as much to blame for the lack of progress in that area as anything else.

It has been rumoured that if the PLO does not succeed in reducing costs in care proceedings, the government will take even more radical action. That would certainly be consistent with the direction they have been moving in hitherto. As Masson observes:[38]

> 'Where well-qualified professionals – social workers, lawyers, legal advisers or children's guardians – are required, these must be available or the proposed changes will fail.'

But these are not messages which the government wants to hear – just as they have ignored all the reports on delay in care proceedings for the last 12 years.

I can envisage three possible scenarios for the future of child welfare proceedings.

First, would be a well-oiled child and family friendly system to which we aspired in the Children Act 1989 and were near to achieving in some of its parts. Those of us working within the system know what it looks like, but after 20 years of search we are further away from achieving that holistic ideal than we were 10 years ago.

The characteristics would be:

(1) early intervention with support for troubled families;

(2) good early independent advice for children and families, where their right to respect for family life is being threatened;

(3) targeted expertise from the skill base appropriate to the specific problem as and when necessary;

(4) a social work force skilled in identifying and responding to the needs of children and families;

(5) an experienced independent legal work force available to those affected by any intervention;

(6) court intervention where that is more likely to achieve desired outcomes;

---

[38] 'Reforming care proceedings – time for a review' [2007] CFLQ 411.

(7) a family court providing expeditious hearings by experienced judiciary who are able to provide continuity in oversight and judgment on cases.

A second scenario is that the government machine will provide a minimalist family justice system, which offers no more than an immediate protection in the most serious cases which would otherwise attract public criticism. This will not provide satisfactory protection for children or families in the longer term. The characteristics would be that few and only extreme cases go to court. The vast majority of cases would be controlled by a local authority or similar child welfare agency. In the longer term this may be the most likely scenario and one which the government is looking to achieve by attrition in the core services on which the family justice system is dependent.

The third scenario and in the short term the most likely is that the government continues to respond to demands on a limited and piecemeal basis where under pressure to do so. The reaction to the Baby P tragedy reinforces that perception. This is not progress. It will not achieve the government-stated rhetorical goal of reducing poverty in the general child population. It will diminish the protection due to the most vulnerable. It is not what we expected when the Children Act was being considered 20 years ago. The brutal conclusion is that we are reversing that excellent legislation by stealth and without adequate consideration of the consequences.

I take the view that the only way in which we can hope to stop this policy is to get it into the open and have a proper debate on whether it is what this society wants for its vulnerable children and families.

CHAPTER 12

WHERE IN THE WORLD IS INTERNATIONAL FAMILY LAW GOING NEXT?

Nigel Lowe

INTRODUCTION

The subject of this contribution is the possible future direction of international family law. By 'international family law' is meant both the laws governing families with a foreign element and those internationally inspired laws governing domestic family law. The former issue is of course by no means new, though the phenomenon of what may be called 'cross-border families' and the frequency of consequential litigation has undoubtedly dramatically increased. Nevertheless, it is pertinent to recall that in *A Century of Family Law* an entire chapter[1] was devoted to issues involving a foreign element, as was part of the concluding chapter which focused on the 1956 Report of the Royal Commission on Marriage and Divorce (the Morton Commission).[2] But these contributions were written from a private international law or conflicts of law point of view and were confined to 'English' solutions, though, interestingly, Bland (the author of the conflicts chapter) observed that after 'the First World War the impact of foreign ideas could not be resisted, and certainly today [ie 1957] English law cannot afford an extreme chauvinism'.[3] Earlier, he noted[4] that as a result of the courts' progressive attitude in moving away from an exclusive concern with matters of jurisdiction, towards a recognition of the problem of choice of law, foreign polygamous marriages were recognised in England except for certain well defined purposes; children could be legitimate, although not born in lawful wedlock; a wife could get a divorce decree from an English court although her husband was domiciled elsewhere, and dissolution of marriage by unilateral act, valid by the religious law of the parties, would be recognised in England.

While these issues are no less relevant today, what has changed is that, increasingly, internationally agreed solutions now tend to govern these and many other types of cross-border family disputes. However, whether we can yet say we have an 'international family justice system' comparable

---

[1] See A Bland 'The Family and the Conflict of Laws' in R H Graveson and F R Crane (eds) *A Century of Family Law 1857–1957* (Sweet & Maxwell, 1957), ch 15.
[2] R H Graveson 'The Future of Family' in Graveson and Crane, op cit, at pp 433–441.
[3] At p 409.
[4] At p 379.

to our own domestic 'family justice system'[5] is perhaps doubtful given the absence of a general international family law court, although of course the European Court of Justice and the European Court of Human Rights are the final international arbiters on, respectively, the Brussels Regulations and the European Convention on Human Rights.

Whilst family law disputes involving a foreign element are not new, internationally inspired laws governing domestic family law are a post-1957 development, particularly those made either following a breach or in anticipation of being found in breach of the European Convention on Human Rights (good examples include the contact in care provisions in the Children Act 1989;[6] the amendment of the Family Law Reform Act 1969 to empower the court to override a parent's refusal to allow their child to be DNA tested in paternity proceedings[7] and the changes introduced by the Gender Recognition Act 2004 to recognise gender reassignment for the purposes of marriage[8]).

In short, UK family law has increasingly become subject to international pressure both to conform to global or European norms and to co-operate in transnational ventures to control world-wide problems. Furthermore, increasing familiarity with different legal systems (particularly continental European jurisdictions) has given new opportunities to rethink domestic family law. All of these developments may be characterised as the 'internationalisation of family law' and are one of the significant developments of the subject over the last 25 years.

THE DEVELOPING INTERNATIONALISATION OF ENGLISH FAMILY LAW

To adopt a good family law maxim, the internationalisation of UK family law has not been a one-off event but a process over time and one that is continuing. The seeds for this development were sown relatively early by, for example, the ratification in 1951 of the European Convention on

---

[5] A phrase coined by M Murch and D Hooper; see their book *The Family Justice System* (Family Law, 2002).
[6] That is, those contained in s 34, which took into account cases such as *R v United Kingdom* [1988] 2 FLR 445, ECHR; *O v United Kingdom; H v United Kingdom* (1987) Series A, No 120, ECHR; and *W v United Kingdom; B v United Kingdom* (1987) Series A, No 121, ECHR. Indeed, according to A Bainham (see *Children – the new law* (Family Law, 1990) para 1.12) many of the reforms relating to care procedures were 'inspired, if not positively mandated' by the UK's obligations under the Convention.
[7] See s 21(3)(b) added by the Child Support, Pensions and Social Security Act 2000, s 82, following Wall J's comment in *Re O (A Minor) (Blood Test: Constraint)* [2000] Fam 139 that the former right of veto was not human rights compliant. See further N Lowe and G Douglas *Bromley's Family Law* (Oxford UP, 10th edn, 2007) at pp 329 and 331.
[8] Following the ECtHR rulings in *Goodwin v United Kingdom* [2002] 2 FLR 487 and *I v United Kingdom* [2002] 2 FLR 518 and the HL decision in *Bellinger v Bellinger* [2003] UKHL 21, [2003] 2 AC 467.

Human Rights[9] and perhaps even more significantly in 1966 by permitting individuals to take their complaints about possible violation of their rights to the European Court of Human Rights in Strasbourg, and by the UK's entry into what was then the Common Market in 1973,[10] as well as by the more obvious moves such as the UK's ratification of various Hague and European family law conventions in the 1960s through to the 1980s. But such 'internationalisation' only began to have a significant impact in the late 1980s/early 1990s. At any rate, that is when it first really began to be noticed by policy makers, the judiciary and the academic community, a key marker being the Children Act 1989.

The drafting of this Act was influenced by the European Convention on Human Rights, particularly with regard to the contact in care provisions and the unmarried father's position where his child is in care. The Council of Europe's 1984 Recommendation on Parental Responsibilities[11] was also influential, both with respect to the parental responsibility provisions and guardianship (for example, by limiting the parental power to appoint a guardian during the lifetime of the other parent).

Coincidentally, at the same time that the 1989 Act was being debated, the final touches to the United Nations Convention on the Rights of the Child 1989 (sometimes referred to as the 'New York Convention') were also being made and it is inconceivable that the drafters of our domestic Act would not have had the UN provisions in mind. The UK ratified the UN Convention in 1991 (again in the confident expectation that, particularly in view of the 1989 Act, it would be fully compliant) and while not directly applicable,[12] this has been quietly influential in the development of our law, not least in the establishment of Children's Commissioners, first in Wales, followed by Northern Ireland, Scotland and, finally, England.[13]

---

[9] Though both the drafters and politicians would have been astonished that any action would have been brought against the UK – still less that the Convention would have an important influence on the re-shaping of our domestic law.

[10] Again, no one at that stage would have imagined that such an entry would have impacted upon the UK's nor indeed any Member State's domestic family law.

[11] R(84)4.

[12] Though, as Baroness Hale said in *Smith v Secretary of State for Work and Pensions* [2006] UKHL 35, [2006] 1 WLR 2024 at [78], 'Even if an international treaty has not been incorporated into domestic law, our domestic legislation has to be construed as far as possible so as to comply with the international obligations which we have undertaken. When two interpretations ... are possible, the interpretation chosen should be that which better complies with the commitment to the welfare of children which this country has made in ratifying the United Nations Convention on the Rights of the Child.'

[13] See, respectively, the Children's Commissioner for Wales Act 2001; the Commissioner for Children and Young People (Northern Ireland) Order 2003, SI 2003/439 (NI 11); the Commissioner for Children and Young People (Scotland) Act 2003 and the Children Act 2004, Part 1.

By the early 1990s the Hague Convention on the Civil Aspects of International Child Abduction 1980, which the UK had ratified in 1986,[14] was, in Thorpe LJ's words, 'invoked with increasing frequency as the number of participating Member States expanded'. Thorpe LJ made this comment in an interesting reflective paper[15] in which he explained that in the light of the growing number of Hague abduction cases, together with increasing frequency of cases having an international component, he had prevailed upon the then President of the Family Division (Sir Stephen Brown) to establish an International Family Law Committee to 'bring together judges, practitioners, academics and government officials with a special interest in international family law'. That Committee first met in October 1993 and, as Thorpe LJ said at the inaugural meeting, it derived from 'the need to address the ever increasing international perspective of family work'. That Committee has proved a useful body both as a means of collecting and disseminating information and as a mechanism through which collaborative initiatives have been promoted.

By the mid-1990s, academic interest in the growing internationalisation of family law had also begun to blossom (though perhaps, on reflection, it had taken a little longer than might have been expected).[16] In 1988, for example, Douglas published an article[17] in which she considered the European Human Rights Convention jurisprudence on family law. From then on that issue was included in Family Law textbooks. Of course, the UN Convention on the Rights of the Child spawned a number of important works, particularly by Freeman[18] and Van Bueren,[19] while others concentrated on the issue of international child abduction, the inclusion of which was one of the innovations of the 7th edition of *Bromley* published in 1986.[20] A further fillip to academic interest in these international aspects of family law was given by the International Society

---

[14] See the Child Abduction and Custody Act 1985, by which the UK also implemented the 1980 European Convention on Recognition and Enforcement of Decisions Concerning Custody of Children.
[15] 'Interdisciplinarity and Internationality in Modern Family Justice Systems' [2007] IFL 165 at 166.
[16] Note the striking comment by P Senaeve in 'Parentage and Human Rights' in *Legal problems Relating to Parentage* (Council of Europe, 1999) that 'none of the authors of the textbooks in family law which appeared in the various Member States of the Council of Europe before 1980 made any reference to the provisions of the European Convention [on Human Rights].'
[17] G Douglas 'The Family and the State under the European Convention on Human Rights' (1988) 2 Int J Law and Fam 76.
[18] See eg M Freeman *The Moral Status of Children* (Martinus Nijhof, 1997) and 'The End of the Century of the Child' (2000) 53 Current Legal Problems 503.
[19] For example, G Van Bueren *The International law of the Rights of the Child* (Martinus Nijhoff, 1995). See also D Fottrell *Revisiting Children's Rights: 10 Years of the UNROC* (Kluwer Law International, 2000).
[20] See P Bromley and N Lowe *Bromley's Family Law* (Butterworths, 7th edn), pp 338–345.

of Family Law's 8th World Conference, 'Families Across Frontiers', held in Cardiff in July 1994 (and which incidentally coincided with the UN's 'international year of the family').[21]

In summary, by the early to mid-1990s, seeds of internationalisation that in some cases had been sown decades before were beginning to take root, with policy makers, the judiciary and the academic community all being increasingly influenced by these developments. But what may have been a trickle at the beginning of the decade was fast developing into a torrent by the turn of the century, if not, to extend the metaphor, into a flood by the middle of the present decade. To highlight some of the principal developments: the 1980 Hague Abduction Convention continued to generate considerable litigation; further, international judicial conferences to consider its international operation,[22] and the general extension of the Special Commissions to review the operation of the Hague Abduction Convention to include the judiciary from 2001 onwards meant that UK judges were increasingly involved in international discussion about the working of the Convention. In so doing, judges from various jurisdictions have become more familiar with each other and each other's systems and, through the heroic efforts of Thorpe LJ, there has developed a global network of liaison judges through which some difficulties can be solved. International judicial conferences are now common and by no means confined to issues arising under the Hague Abduction Convention.[23] In the UK context, mention may be made of the ongoing Anglophone-Germanophone judicial conferences (as they are now called) which have regularly been held since the Dartington conference in 1997, and the Francophone counterpart which again was inaugurated by a Dartington conference in 2001 and which has been held regularly since. Both these conferences have proved useful outlets for discussing matters of common concern, including in particular the Brussels II and Brussels II Revised Regulations, the proposed Rome III and the 1996 Hague Protection of Children Convention.[24]

A second profoundly significant event was the passing of the Human Rights Act 1998, which was brought into force in October 2000. At a stroke this concentrated both academic and practitioners' minds on the application of human rights in family law (as well as other areas, of

---

[21] See N Lowe and G Douglas (eds) *Families Across Frontiers* (Martinus Nijhoff, 1996).

[22] Pioneered by the Anglo-German judicial conference held at Dartington in 1997 and quickly followed by the De Ruwenberg conferences organised by the Permanent Bureau of the Hague Conference in 1998, 2000 and 2001, the Common Law Conference held in Washington DC in 2000. See the reference to these conferences by Thorpe LJ in 'Interdisciplinarity and Internationality in Modern Family Justice Systems' [2007] IFL 165 at 166, n 13, and for details of the conferences' resolutions, see N Lowe, M Everall and M Nicholls *International Movement of Children – Law, Practice and Procedure* (Family Law, 2004) at pp 734–742.

[23] Details of conferences are regularly published in *International Family Law* and in *The Judge's Newsletter* (published twice a year by the Hague Conference on Private International Law).

[24] Each of these instruments is discussed further below.

course) and though it has not (as yet, at any rate) had as great an impact as some had predicted,[25] it has had and will continue to have an effect. Not least of the effects has been the need for everyone involved in litigation to have regard to the decisions of the European Court of Human Rights.[26] In other words, judges and practitioners alike now have to look outside our own system to determine how to apply domestic law. Whether the Convention will lead to more profound changes in the future is hard to say, but it still has the potential for doing so, if only because its 'rights' construct lies at odds with the essentially remedial character of the English common law system.[27]

Alongside these developments an increasing number of international instruments have been produced. First, there are those of the Hague Conference, namely, the 1993 Hague Convention on Intercountry Adoption, which the UK ratified in June 2003; the 1996 Hague Protection of Children Convention (see below); the 2000 Hague Convention on the International Protection of Adults, which the UK ratified on behalf of Scotland in November 2003 (and which is expected to be extended to England and Wales in the near future); and the 2007 Hague Convention on the International Recovery of Child Support and Other Forms of Family Maintenance. Secondly, there are Conventions of the Council of Europe, namely, the 1996 European Convention on the Exercise of Children's Rights; the 2003 European Convention on Contact Concerning Children; the 2007 European Convention on the Protection of Children Against Sexual Exploitation and Sexual Abuse; and the 2008 European Convention on the Adoption of Children (Revised),[28] as well as a number of Recommendations.[29]

As if all this was not enough, what is now the European Union (EU) began to impact upon family law. Although the EU had long had some potential to so impact, until March 2001 it did so only peripherally as, for example, through the provisions governing free movement rights and the then 1968 Brussels Convention on Jurisdiction and Enforcement of

---

[25] There was, for example, widespread speculation as to the compatibility of the principle of the paramountcy of the child's welfare; the status of unmarried fathers; the lawfulness of secure accommodation orders and about the inability of the courts to oversee local authority care plans, all of which survived human rights challenges (although in fact in some respects the law has been changed); see respectively *Re L (A Child) (Contact: Domestic Violence)* [2001] Fam 260; *B v United Kingdom* [2000] 1 FLR 1; *Re K (A Child) (Secure Accommodation Order: Right To Liberty)* [2001] Fam 377; and *Re S (Minors) (Care Order: Implementation of Care Plan; Re W (Minors) (Care Order: Adequacy of Care Plan)* [2002] UKHL 10, [2002] 2 AC 291.

[26] Section 2 of the Human Rights Act 1998 obliges domestic courts to take convention case law into account when deciding a question relating to a convention right.

[27] Query, for example, whether the paramountcy principle is truly compatible with Convention rights? See J Herring 'The Human Rights Act and the welfare principle in family law – conflicting or complementary?' [1999] CFLQ 223 and J Fortin 'The HRA's impact on litigation involving children and their families' [1999] CFLQ 237.

[28] Finally concluded on 7 May 2008 and opened for signature in November 2008.

[29] See further below.

Judgments in Civil and Commercial Matters, which had been incorporated into UK domestic law by the Civil Jurisdiction and Judgments Act 1982.[30] In fact, the Brussels Convention (which subsequently became a Regulation)[31] only impacted upon maintenance and indeed expressly excluded matters of status and rights of property arising from marriage because, according to the Jenard Report (the Explanatory Report on the Convention),[32] it was considered too difficult to unify the applicable jurisdiction rules of even the then six Member States![33] But this hands-off family law approach radically changed with the conclusion of Council Regulation (EC) No 1347/2000 of 29 May 2000 on jurisdiction and the recognition and enforcement of civil and commercial judgments in matrimonial matters and matters of parental responsibility for children of both spouses – the so-called 'Brussels II', which came into force on 1 March 2001. This instrument also began life as a Convention – in fact building upon the earlier Civil and Commercial Matters Convention – which is why it became known as 'Brussels II'. As the Borras Report (the Explanatory Report on the Convention) explains,[34] the Brussels II Convention was made possible by the Treaty of Maastricht. However, while it remained a Convention, it attracted scant attention, at least in the family law world.[35] All that changed when it was transformed into a Regulation, which it did with remarkable speed, being concluded in May 2000 and brought into force the following March. This transformation had been made possible by the Treaty of Amsterdam, which brought judicial co-operation in civil matters squarely into the community framework.[36] That this meant dealing with family matters was clearly signalled in the programme outlined by the Justice and Home Affairs Council at its meeting in Vienna in December 1998[37] and by a European Council meeting held in Tampere in October 1999.[38]

---

[30] See, for example, the discussion in C Hamilton and K Standley *Family Law in Europe* (Butterworths, 1st edn, 1995), pp 580–597.

[31] Viz Council Regulation (EC) No 44/2201 of 22 December 2000 on Jurisdiction and the Recognition and Enforcement of Judgments in Civil and Commercial Matters. Although this is commonly known as 'Brussels I', it in fact came into force one year *after* 'Brussels II'.

[32] [1979] OJ C59, p 10.

[33] The Report specifically singled out divorce as 'a problem which is complicated by the extreme divergences between the various systems of law'.

[34] [1998] OJ C221/27, para 2.

[35] But see G Shannon with T Kennedy 'Jurisdiction and Enforcement Issues in Proceedings Concerning Parental Responsibility under the Brussels II Convention' [2000] IFL 111.

[36] It was through this Treaty that Arts K1 and K3 (which were formerly part of the Third Pillar (viz Justice and Home Affairs) of the EU under the TEU, were removed to form a Community Pillar. For the significance of this from a family law perspective, see H Stalford 'Regulating family life in post-Amsterdam Europe' (2003) 28 Eur L Rev 39.

[37] Namely, Action Plan of the Council and Commission On How Best To Implement The Provisions of the Treaty of Amsterdam on an Area of Freedom, Security and Justice [1999] OJ C19 of 13 January.

[38] At which the European Council set out the so-called 'Tampere Milestones' endorsing the principle of mutual recognition as the 'cornerstone of judicial co-operation in civil ... matters within the Union' and asking the Council and Commission to adopt by the

Being a Regulation meant that the measure was directly applicable in all participating Member States. The UK and Ireland, having negotiated general opt-outs at Maastricht, decided to opt into Brussels II.[39] Denmark, on the other hand, having negotiated a different form of opt-out at Maastricht, did not opt into Brussels II.

Even before most practitioners had caught up with its existence, let alone its application, negotiations were afoot to revise the Regulation.[40] These negotiations were hard fought, controversial at times, particularly over child abduction, and protracted. But eventually, aided by a compromise over abduction, brokered ironically by Denmark, a revised Regulation was finally concluded on 27 November 2003 and came into force on 1 March 2005.[41] That Regulation is now in force in all Member States, save Denmark, ie in 26 nations, it being a condition of entry to implement it for all new acceding states. The revised Regulation ('BIIR') substantially improved the parental responsibility provisions, justifying perhaps the UK's opt-in, but it left untouched the divorce provisions which are deeply unsatisfactory (not least because of the non-hierarchal multiple choice of jurisdiction rules leading to the 'solution' of vesting jurisdiction in the court first seised and thus encouraging jurisdiction races).[42]

---

end of 2000 a programme of measures to implement this principle: see Bulletin, EU 10-1999. Subsequently a programme was drafted; see 'Draft programme of measures for implementation of the principle of mutual recognition of decisions in civil and commercial matters [2001] OJ C12 (15 January). For further discussion of these developments and of the provenance of Brussels II see eg J Basedow 'The Communitarisation of the Conflict of Laws Under the Treaty of Amsterdam' (2000) 37 CMLR 687; K Boele-Woelki and R Van Ooik 'The Communitarization of Private International Law' in *Yearbook of Private International Law* (2002), Vol 4, p 1 (Amsterdam); P McEleavy 'The Brussels II Regulation: How the European Community has moved into Family Law' (2002) 51 ICLQ 883; C McGlynn 'The Europeanisation of family law' [2001] CFLQ 36; and H Stalford 'Regulating family life in post-Amsterdam Europe' (2003) 28 Eur L Rev 39. For discussion of the pros and cons of EU involvement see N Lowe 'The Growing Influence of the European Union on International Family Law – A View from the Boundary' (2003) 56 Current Legal Problems 439 at 451–456.

[39] In the UK's case the decision to opt in was taken with little or no consultation.

[40] Prompted initially by a French proposal to adopt a Council Regulation on the mutual enforcement of judgments on rights of access to children – see [2000] OJ C234/7. Since this would have amended the Brussels II Regulation, it became known as 'Brussels IIA' or 'II Bis', which epithet continued to be applied to the Council's own proposals made in 2001 and 2002 (see respectively OJ No C332 of 27.11.2001, 269 and Brussels 3.5.2002 Com (2002) 222 Final) and to the eventual revised Regulation, notwithstanding that it repealed the original Regulation.

[41] Viz Council Regulation (EC) No 2201/2003 of 27 November 2003 concerning jurisdiction and the recognition and enforcement of judgments in matrimonial matters and in matters of parental responsibility, repealing Regulation (EC) No 1347/2000. For discussion of the negotiations leading to this Regulation see N Lowe 'The Growing Influence of the European Union on International Family Law – A View from the Boundary' (2003) 56 Current Legal Problems 439 at 470–474.

[42] See the critique by Lowe, ibid, at 462–464.

BIIR has begun to generate considerable case law,[43] and the EU dimension has become a common feature of international family law work, at any rate in London. The final arbiter on the application of BIIR is the European Court of Justice in Luxembourg ('ECJ'). Indeed, some see[44] this as one of the advantages of EU legislation, since the ECJ, uniquely for international family law instruments, can provide uniform interpretation across the Union. However, as against this, three matters of concern have been raised in connection with the ECJ's role. The first was that references (that is, referrals by national courts to the ECJ for a ruling on the application of the Regulation) would take too long and would therefore be particularly ill-suited to the resolution of disputes over children. This has been addressed with the introduction in March 2008 of the 'urgent preliminary ruling procedure'[45] under which the reference process has been both streamlined[46] and considerably speeded up. Although not designed specifically for BIIR cases, the procedure is likely to be appropriate in cases involving children, particularly abduction cases since, as the ECJ recognised in Case C–195/08 PPU: *Re Rinau*,[47] there is an obvious need for speed, lest the damage done to the relationship between the child and the left-behind-parent becomes irreparable. One would have thought that courts referring questions concerning children under BIIR will now routinely seek to invoke the urgent procedure. In *Re Rinau* itself the reference was received on 14 May 2008 and the judgment delivered on 14 July 2008.[48]

A second concern is the reference procedure itself, since, being governed by Art 68 (EC), a reference can only be made by a 'final' domestic court.[49] Notwithstanding this restriction, however, there have already been a surprising number of references.[50]

---

[43] See N Lowe 'The Current Experiences and Difficulties of Applying Brussels II Revised' [2007] IFL 183.

[44] See P Beaumont and G Moir 'Brussels Convention II: A New Private International Law Instrument for the European Union or the European Community' (1995) 20 Eur L Rev 268 at 275 et seq.

[45] See Council Decision of 20 December 2007, amending the Protocol on the Statute of the Court of Justice and the amendment to the Rules of Procedure of the Court of Justice on 15 January 2008 (OJEU L24), p 29.

[46] For example, by restricting those who can participate in the written stage of the process.

[47] [2008] 2 FLR 1495.

[48] Even before the introduction of this new procedure, BIIR references had been dealt with quite quickly; see, for example, in Case C-68/07: *Sunderlind Lopez v Lopez Lizaro* [2008] Fam 21, in which the reference was determined within 9 months.

[49] For a discussion of the Art 68 reference system see N Lowe 'The Growing Influence of the European Union on International Family Law – A View from the Boundary' (2003) 56 Current Legal Problems 439 at 460–462 and for a critique see 478.

[50] At the time of writing there have been five references concerning BIIR, namely, *Re Rinau* [2008] 2 FLR 1495; *Sunderlind Lopez v Lopez Lizaro* [2008] Fam 21; Case C-435/06: *Proceedings brought by C* [2008] Fam 27; Case C-523/07: *(A)*; and Case C-168/08: *(Hadadi)*. References can be found at http://curia.europa.eu/jurisp/cgi-bin/form.pl?

A third concern is the lack of family law experience of the ECJ judiciary. Given the importance of the court's role in interpreting the Regulation, particularly as its rulings may also have implications for the application of both the 1980 Hague Abduction and the 1996 Child Protection Conventions, this is an issue that surely needs to be addressed.[51]

At one stage it seemed that there was to be a third version of Brussels II, namely to accommodate what was known as Rome III.[52] This proposal would have meant inter alia that courts of one Member State would have to apply the divorce law of another Member State if both parties came from that state. This was not attractive to the common law states,[53] nor it seems to the Nordic states, Sweden in particular, which at a relatively late stage of the negotiations formally vetoed its progress.[54] However, notwithstanding this 'block', nine Member States have been seeking to invoke what is known as the 'enhanced co-operation procedure' (this procedure has not previously been invoked) to go ahead with the applicable law proposals contained in Rome III.[55] Although, on this particular issue, the UK, Ireland and no doubt the Nordic countries would not be unhappy with this development, in broader terms one might have some concerns, since it does strike a blow against the hitherto uniform approach of Member States (albeit that Denmark, Ireland and UK have individual opt-outs). Indeed, critics of the procedure say it will lead to a 'two–speed Europe'. Time will tell whether this will prove detrimental to the development of 'European Family Law'.

One important consequence of EU involvement in family matters is the consequential lack of individual state competence, in the sense that each time the Union exercises its internal competence by adopting provisions laying down common rules, it acquires *exclusive* external competence to undertake obligations with third countries that affect those rules or alter their scope.[56] In other words, individual Member States lose their

---

[51] The author has long advocated the creation of a specialist Family Panel to hear Art 68 references under BIIR – see N Lowe 'The Growing Influence of the European Union on International Family Law – A View from the Boundary' (2003) 56 Current Legal Problems 439 at 478–479.

[52] The Proposal for a Council Regulation amending Regulation (EC) No 2201/2003 as regards jurisdiction and introducing rules concerning applicable law in matrimonial matters.

[53] The UK and Ireland had already indicated that they would not opt in to the re-revised Regulation.

[54] See the EU Council Factsheet Decisions in Civil Law Matters – Justice and Home Affairs Council, Luxembourg, 6 June 2008. For an excellent critique of the Proposal, see T M de Boer 'The Second Revision of the Brussels II Regulation: Jurisdiction and Applicable Law' in K Boele-Woelki and T Sverdrup (eds) *European Challenges in Contemporary Family Law* (Intersentia, 2008), p 321.

[55] Under Art 43 of the EU Treaty, the procedure requires a minimum of eight Member States to present their demand for enhanced co-operation to the Commission, which must then be accepted by the Commission and approved by a qualified majority of the 27 Member States.

[56] This is the result of the so-called ERTA case law – see Case 22/70: *Commission v Council (Re European Road Transport Agreement)* [1971] ECR 263, para 17; Opinion 2/91 'ILO

independent competence to ratify or accede to or amend other international instruments, be they Hague, European or UN Conventions, in the areas dealt with by the Regulation. This has had the twofold consequence of delaying EU Member States' ratification both of the 1996 Hague Protection of Children Convention and the 2003 European Convention on Contact Concerning Children,[57] and also of limiting individual Member States voting at, for example, the Special Meetings to review the operation of the various Hague Abduction Conventions. In this latter regard, not only are individual Member States prevented from pursuing their national interests but another effect, at any rate at Hague meetings, is quickly to polarise discussions if, for example, the EU and USA take opposing views.

Where is internationalisation heading?

Examining the internationalisation process to date, the following five elements may be identified: the expansion of international family disputes; the commitment to Human Rights and arguably to a lesser extent children's rights; the entry into the EU coupled with the Union's expansion of interest into the family law field; the commitment to increasing numbers of international family law instruments, principally emanating from the Hague Conference and the Council of Europe; and, finally, the growing awareness of developments across the globe, accompanied by a consequential readiness to look at foreign solutions when considering domestic law reform and motivated perhaps by not so much a desire to conform but by a reluctance to be too far out of line. A good example is the Civil Partnership Act 2004, which was passed (surely an unimaginable development from a 1957 perspective) in the wake of a globally growing legal recognition in one form or another of same sex relationships. But one wonders, notwithstanding the express provisions of the 2004 Act and the decision in *Wilkinson v Kitzinger*,[58] for how long the English legislature/courts will be able to resist the pressure at least to recognise same sex marriages legally contracted abroad, assuming, as seems likely, a growing number of states permit such marriages. Another example might be pre-nuptial agreements. To quote from the postscript to Sir Mark Potter P's judgment in *Charman v Charman*:[59]

> 'The difficulty of harmonising our law concerning the property consequences of marriages and divorce and the law of civilian member

---

Convention No 170 Concerning Safety in the Use of Chemicals at Work' [1993] ECR 1-1061, para 26; Opinion 1/94, 'WTO' [1994] ECR 1-5267, para 77, and Opinion 2/92, 'Third Revised Decision of the OECD on National Treatment' [1995] ECR 1-521, para 31. See also C Kotuby 'External Competence of the European Community in the Hague Conference on Private International Law: Community Harmonization of Worldwide Unification' (2001) XLVIII *Netherlands International Law Review* 1–30.

[57] EU-wide ratification had been delayed because of the UK-Spanish dispute over Gibraltar; see 'The Hague Family Law Conventions' [2005] IFL 105 at 106.
[58] *Wilkinson v Kitzinger (No 2)* [2006] EWHC 2022 (Fam), [2007] 1 FLR 295.
[59] *Charman v Charman (No 4)* [2007] EWCA Civ 503, 1 FLR 1246 at [124].

states is exacerbated by the fact that our law has so far given little status to prenuptial contracts. If, unlike the rest of Europe, the property consequences of divorce are to be regulated by the principles of needs, compensation and sharing, should not the parties to the marriage, or the projected marriage, have at least the opportunity to order their own affairs otherwise by a nuptial contract?'

For the foreseeable future all five elements seem likely to continue to exert influence. Population movements across international borders show no signs of slowing, although the pattern of movement is changing. The UK, for example, especially England, has experienced since 2004 a vast influx of immigrants from Eastern Europe, particularly Poland, and this has already been reflected in abduction statistics, inasmuch as there has been a significant increase in Anglo-Polish abductions.[60] While this particular wave of immigration has subsequently settled down, it will in part be replaced by immigration from other newly acceding EU States, including Bulgaria and Romania, and conceivably from Croatia, Turkey and the Ukraine in the future. There will surely continue to be steady immigration from the Indian sub-continent and by asylum seekers and economic immigrants from developing countries. This in turn will pose problems for domestic law, not least of which is how, if at all, to accommodate Shariah law.[61]

The continuing impact of human rights

Assuming that the UK remains a state party to the European Human Rights Convention,[62] then there will continue to be both domestic and Strasbourg Court rulings which will cause the UK to change or modify its domestic law. Quite where the weak points are in substantive family law is hard to say – corporal punishment of children, perhaps; the need for grandparents to seek court leave to apply for a s 8 order (albeit that under the Children and Young Persons Act 2008, s 36 those looking after the child for a year do not require leave); the inability of a non-marital child to succeed to a title of honour and the inability of the civil partner of an entitled person to take an appropriate title; and the non-recognition of same sex marriages are some possible examples that spring to mind. But,

---

[60] In 2007, for example, 18 applications were made to the English Central Authority, which was second only to the USA, which made 23 applications, and more than from any other EU Member State. In contrast, Poland made only one application in 2003.

[61] Obviously a raw nerve for the nation, as the furore that followed the Archbishop of Canterbury's lecture 'Civil and Religious Law in England: A Religious Perspective' (Royal Courts of Justice, 7 February 2008) graphically illustrated.

[62] It seems unlikely that political threats to abandon human rights will lead the UK formally to denounce the Convention, though there might be some tinkering with the 1998 Act. Note: the Government's Green Paper *The Governance of Britain* Cm 7170 (2007) rejected the idea of repealing the Human Rights Act 1998, and added (see para 208) that incorporating the Convention rights and freedoms into UK law was only the first step in a journey which might lead to a Bill of Rights and Duties.

as already indicated,[63] there is still the potential for human rights to have more radical effects, not least because of its 'rights' construct.

The application of human rights is also problematic in the EU context, not least because of the Charter of Fundamental Rights of the European Union (approved by the Treaty of Nice),[64] which contains a number of Articles of direct relevance to family law: Art 7, which provides for the right to respect for private and family life; Art 9, the right to marry and found a family; and Art 24, which deals with the rights of the child, by—

(1) giving children the right to such protection and care as is necessary for their well-being and to express their views freely (such views to be taken into account on matters which concern them in accordance with their age and maturity);

(2) providing that in all actions the child's best interests must be a primary consideration; and

(3) giving children the right to maintain on a regular basis a personal relationship and direct contact with both parents unless it is contrary to their interests.

The precise status of the Charter has been a matter of debate since it has not (yet)[65] been incorporated into any treaty. The collective view is that it had declaratory force only.[66] Indeed, Art 51(2) of the Charter expressly states that it 'does not establish any new power or task for the Community or the Union, or modify powers and tasks defined by the Treaties'. Nevertheless, this did not prevent the Commission from relying upon the Charter to include the child's right of continued contact and the right to

---

[63] See n 27 above.
[64] [2007] OJ C303/01.
[65] The Charter was to have been incorporated into the EU Treaty by the (currently abandoned) Lisbon Treaty (see Art 6(1) and the Protocol thereto).
[66] See inter alia 'Communication From the Commission on the Legal Nature of the Charter of Fundamental Rights of the European Union' Com (2000) 644 Final (11 October 2000) and the memorandum presented to the Select Committee on the European Union by the Foreign and Commonwealth Office – included in their 8th Report, Session 1999–2000. In *R (Howard League For Penal Reform) v Secretary of State for the Home Office* [2002] EWHC 2497 (Admin), [2003] 1 FLR 484 at [45]–[52], [66]–[68], and *R (A et al) v East Sussex County Council (No 2)* [2003] EWHC 167 (Admin) at [68]–[74], [80], [93], [103], [106], Munby J referred to the Charter which he considered as 'not at present legally binding in our domestic law and is therefore not a source of law in the strict sense. But it can, in my judgment, properly be consulted insofar as it produces, reaffirms or elucidates the content of those human rights that are generally recognised throughout the European family of nations, in particular the nature and scope of those fundamental rights that are guaranteed by the Convention'. See also A Arnul *The European Union and its Court of Justice* (Oxford UP, 2nd edn, 2006), pp 375–385.

be heard when proposing revisions to the original Brussels II, and the revised Regulation itself cites the Charter (and in particular Art 24) in para 33 of the Recitals.[67]

The continuing impact of the Hague Conference[68]

The likely continuing impact of the work done by the Hague Conference, at least in the immediate future, is a bit easier to predict. The most important immediate event was the 'solving' of the Gibraltar dispute between the UK and Spain, thus clearing the way for EU-wide ratification of the 1996 Hague Convention on the Protection of Children.[69] The timing and mechanism for doing this was settled by an EU Council meeting held in June 2008, at which authorisation was given to Member States that had not already done so to ratify or accede to the Convention. The projected implementation date is June 2010.[70] The UK's expectation is that ratification will not require primary legislation but only subordinate legislation pursuant to the European Communities Act 1972. Once Member States ratify and/or accede, this will more than double the number of Contracting States, thereby transforming this Convention into a major working international instrument.[71]

The 1996 Hague Convention on the Protection of Children[72]

Given that the 1996 Convention is likely to be the next major international instrument with which international family lawyers will have to contend, it seems appropriate to say something about its application.[73] In broad terms the Convention provides for common jurisdictional rules

---

[67] It is perhaps an interesting point whether such reliance would have been possible had the Treaty of Lisbon been implemented, given its proposed limited application (see Arts 1 and 2 of the proposed Protocol) to Poland and the UK.

[68] I am indebted to William Duncan, Deputy Secretary General of the Hague Conference, for advising me about the Conference's work.

[69] Agreement was reached in December 2007, with a formal exchange of letters between the permanent representations on 19 December.

[70] See Council Decision of 5 June 2008 (2008/431/EC OJ L 151/6), by which the relevant Member States (ie excluding Denmark and those States (see n 66) that have already either ratified or acceded) are required simultaneously to deposit their instruments of ratification or accession *if possible* before 5 June 2010 (Art 3(1)) and to exchange information with the Commission within the Council before 5 December 2009 'on the prospective date of completion of the parliamentary procedures for ratification or accession. On this basis, the date and modalities of simultaneous deposit shall be determined' (Art 3(2)).

[71] At the time of writing there are 15 Contracting States, including the following EU Member States: Bulgaria, the Czech Republic, Estonia, Hungary, Latvia, Lithuania, Slovakia and Slovenia. It is understood that Canada, New Zealand and the USA are actively considering ratifying the Convention.

[72] Convention of 19 October 1996 on Jurisdiction, Applicable Law, Recognition, Enforcement and Co-operation in Respect of Parental Responsibility and Measures for the Protection of Children.

[73] For a more detailed discussion see N Lowe, M Everall and M Nicholls *International Movement of Children, Law Practice and Procedure* (Family Law, 2004), ch 24.

and for a consequent scheme of recognition and enforcement of judgments concerned with child protection. 'Protection' for these purposes is a wide term referring to both private and public law measures taken by judicial and administrative bodies to protect children.[74] In particular, it governs the attribution, exercise and termination of parental responsibility,[75] including the provision[76] that where parental responsibility exists under the law of the child's habitual residence, it will continue to exist notwithstanding a change of residence to another state and, conversely, where the law of the state of the child's new habitual residence automatically confers responsibility, it will do so on those who do not already have it. This incidentally gives potentially global significance to the provisions in the Human Fertilisation and Embryology Act 2008 conferring parenthood and thereby parental responsibility on the non-biological female partner who is registered as the parent.[77] The 1996 Convention also applies to rights of custody and access, guardianship, curatorship and analogous institutions, the designation and functions of any person or body having charge of the child's person or property, representing or assisting the child; placing the child in foster or institutional care or the provision of care by *Kafala* or an analogous institution; public authority supervision of the care of a child and the administration, conservation or disposal of the child's property.[78] The Convention specifically[79] does not apply to establishing or contesting a child-parent relationship, adoption, names, emancipation, maintenance, trusts, succession, social security, general public measures on health or education, measures taken as a result of penal offences committed by children, nor to the right of asylum and immigration decisions.

Notwithstanding these exemptions, note should be taken of the wide application of the 1996 Convention, in particular its application to *Kafala* (which is important to Islamic states) and foster care, which plugs a gap in the 1993 Hague Intercountry Adoption Convention, and more generally to public law issues, which distinguishes it from the revised Brussels II Regulation. In addition to these provisions, Chapter V contains important provisions concerning co-operation between Contracting States, inter alia to discover the child's whereabouts, providing information about the child's history, family background and current situation to another body seeking to make private or public law orders protecting the child, providing information about a state's law and available services to protect children and to facilitate agreed solutions. It also contains some particularly useful provisions for safeguarding rights of access.[80] Most, if

---

[74] See Art 3.
[75] By Art 3a.
[76] See Art 16.
[77] See ss 42–43 and Sch 6, paras 26 and 27 amending the Children Act 1989.
[78] See Art 3(b)–(g).
[79] By Art 4.
[80] See in particular Art 35.

not all, of these duties will be performed by the now tried and tested mechanism of Central Authorities, which must be set up under the Convention.[81]

The 1996 Convention has many advantages, not least of which is providing for a *global* system, and one which might be attractive to and appropriate for the Islamic world, of recognition and enforcement of custody, access and guardianship orders as well as of public law orders, which is further backed up by useful co-operative duties. Moreover, its access provisions might go some way to alleviate the generally acknowledged failings of the 1980 Hague Abduction Convention in that regard, while Art 11, which confers temporary jurisdiction to make protective orders with extra-territorial effect in cases of urgency, offers a neat solution to the problem posed by the 1980 Convention of how to safeguard and protect abducted children ordered to be returned. But the Convention is not problem-free. It is complex in itself: witness the length of the above 'brief' explanation. There are some provisions the application of which requires careful thought, as, for example, Arts 23 and 26, under which recognition and enforcement might be refused, and Art 13, which preserves jurisdiction over pending cases.[82] There must be doubts too as to how effective enforcement will be. But perhaps the greatest problem is the 1996 Convention's interrelationship with the other existing international instruments, particularly the 1980 Hague Abduction Convention,[83] and even the revised Brussels II Regulation (though it will be noted that the latter takes precedence).[84]

The 1993 Hague Intercountry Adoption Convention and the 1980 Hague Abduction Convention

From the Hague Conference's point of view the 1996 Convention completes an important trilogy of child protection instruments, the other two being the 1993 Hague Convention on Intercountry Adoption and the 1980 Hague Abduction Convention. The 1993 Convention now has almost as many Contracting States as the 1980 Convention, 76 at the time of writing. The UK ratified it in June 2003. It provides important international regulation of intercountry adoption[85] with a view to (a) ensuring such adoptions only take place after the best interests of the child have been properly assessed and in circumstances that protect his or her fundamental rights; (b) establishing a system of co-operation amongst

---

[81] See Art 29.
[82] See eg the discussion in N Lowe, M Everall and M Nicholls *International Movement of Children, Law Practice and Procedure* (Family Law, 2004) at 24.39–24.44 and 24.21–24.22 respectively.
[83] See eg L Silberman 'The 1996 Hague Convention on the Protection of Children: Should the United States Join?' (2000) 34 Family Law Quarterly 239 at 250–254 and Lowe, Everall and Nicholls, op cit, at 24.61–24.67.
[84] See Art 60(e) of the revised Regulation.
[85] For a discussion of the Convention see Lowe and Douglas *Bromley's Family Law* (Oxford UP, 10th edn, 2007), p 873ff and the authorities there cited.

Contracting States to ensure that these safeguards are protected and, finally, (c) ensuring recognition in Contracting States of adoptions made in accordance with the Convention.

So far, at any rate, few cases under the Convention have come to court[86] and perhaps for that reason it is probably less familiar to practitioners. The Permanent Bureau is currently concentrating on ensuring that the Convention works in countries of origin and are drafting a Guide to Good Practice on Implementation which will include guidance on accredited bodies and, interestingly, on post-adoption services.

Good Practice Guides were first pioneered under the 1980 Hague Abduction Convention.[87] There are currently four: on Central Authority Practice, Implementing Measures, Preventive Measures and Transfrontier Contact Concerning Children.[88] A fifth guide on Enforcement is planned. The 1980 Abduction Convention is widely regarded as a great success and certainly in terms of Contracting States it is second only to the UN Convention on the Rights of the Child, with currently 81 such states. In the near future, accessions by India and Singapore seem imminent and there is every prospect of mainland China also acceding. The challenge is whether and, if so, how to accommodate Islamic states. Nevertheless, it can be anticipated, particularly with a still expanding membership, that this Convention, both in its own right and as it operates under BIIR, will continue to generate litigation and to figure prominently on policy makers' agendas.[89]

In this latter respect it is interesting to speculate whether the time has come to add Protocols to the Convention. Switzerland in particular has made a determined effort, making formal proposals both at the April 2006 and the April 2008 meetings of the Hague Conference's Council on General Affairs for a Protocol to cover mediation and securing the child's safe return.[90] In the event these attempts failed, but in time it seems inevitable that some Protocols will be added. Indeed, the Fifth Special Commission to review the Convention held in October/November 2006 concluded:

'The Special Commission recognises the strength of arguments in favour of a Protocol to the 1980 Convention which might in particular clarify the

---

[86] Although the Convention was cited in 10 cases reported in *Family Law Reports* between 1995 and 2008, it was directly in issue in only one domestic case, namely *Greenwich London Borough Council v S* [2007] EWHC 820 (Fam), [2007] 2 FLR 154.
[87] In part inspired by the work of ICMEC; see N Lowe and S Armstrong *Good Practice Report in Handling Hague Abduction Return Applications* (NCMEC, 2002).
[88] Each Guide was drafted by the Permanent Bureau and is available on the Hague web site. The Guides are also published by Family Law.
[89] It will certainly be a key part of the agenda at the London Common Law Conference being planned for August 2009.
[90] See A Bucher 'The New Swiss Federal Act on International Child Abduction' (2008) 4 Journal of Private International Law 139 at 144–145.

obligations of States Parties under Article 21, and make clear the distinction between "rights of custody" and "access rights".'

But, nevertheless, added:

'However, it is agreed that priority should at this time be given to efforts in relation to the implementation of the 1996 Convention [on the Protection of Children].'

No doubt, too, the publication of the Good Practice Guide on Transfrontier Contact Concerning Children will also help to mute immediate calls for a Protocol on Access, while widespread ratification of the 1996 Convention will also be an answer to the Swiss call to add a Protocol on the safe return of children. But, depending on how well these developments work, they may only delay the call for such amendments. One problem with adding a Protocol is that it potentially opens the way to challenge the whole basis of the Convention, as no doubt some would wish[91] to do, given the findings that the majority of abductors (68% according to the 2003 survey)[92] are by mothers, most of whom are primary carers. Nevertheless, it is submitted that the Convention's fundamental premise, namely, that abductions are in principle wrongful, still holds good.[93]

The 2007 Hague Maintenance Convention and the 2000 Hague Convention on the Protection of Adults and possible future developments

The child Conventions are not the only Hague instruments that affect family law. One Convention, concluded on 23 November 2007, is the Child Support and Maintenance Convention, which also includes two Protocols.[94] The Convention was agreed upon by 70 states and, unusually, the USA has already formally signed it. This is another Convention that for EU Member States will require EU-wide sanction. In fact, the Hague Conference worked in close co-operation with the EU in preparing the Convention, and the Union is now thinking of how best to involve EU Member States. The EU has itself been working on a Regulation on jurisdiction, applicable law, recognition and enforcement of decisions and co-operation in matters relating to maintenance obligations, aimed at

---

[91] See eg M Freeman 'In the Best Interests of Internationally Abducted Children?' [2002] IFL 77; C Bruch 'Sound Research or Wishful Thinking in Child Custody Cases? Lessons form Relocation Law' (2006) 39 Fam LQ 281 and A Bucher, op cit, n 90 above.

[92] See N Lowe 'A Statistical Analysis of Applications Made in 2003 under the 1980 Hague Convention on the Civil Aspects of International Child Abduction', Prel Doc No 3, available on the Hague web site: http://www.hcch.e.vision.nl/upload/wop/abd_pa03e1_2007.pdf.

[93] See eg the defence by N Lowe with K Horosova 'The operation of the 1980 Hague Abduction Convention – A Global View' (2007) 41 Fam LQ 59 at 70.

[94] On which, see W Duncan 'The New Hague Convention on the International Recovery of Child Support and Other Forms of Family Maintenance' [2008] IFL 13 and D Eames 'The New Hague Maintenance Convention' [2008] Fam Law 347.

replacing Brussels I in respect of maintenance. One ambition of the proposed Regulation is to eliminate all obstacles which prevent the recovery of maintenance within the Union, in particular the requirement of the exequatur procedure (that is, enforcement procedure).[95] Time will tell whether the UK will opt into the Regulation, but it seems likely that it will at least ratify the Hague Convention. So far as the latter instrument is concerned, the Permanent Bureau is preparing two Good Practice Guides, one on implementation, which will be directed primarily at case workers, and the other effectively a handbook on the practical application. It is also planned to hold the first Special Commission to review the implementation of the Convention some time in 2009. One hope of the Convention is that it might lead to simplified and cheap national procedures. The Permanent Bureau itself is developing a technological and case support system, to be known as 'I Support'.

One further Convention worth mentioning is the 2000 Hague Convention on the International Protection of Adults. This Convention is concerned to provide for the protection in international situations of adults who, by reason of impairment or insufficiency of their personal faculties, are not in a position to protect their own interests. In furtherance of this aim it determines inter alia which state has jurisdiction and which law is applicable to take measures directed to the protection of the person or property of the adult and which law is applicable to representation of adults and for the consequential recognition and enforcement of such measures. Given the generally ageing population in the developed world, this Convention seems likely to assume a growing importance. At the time of writing, only the UK has ratified it, and only on behalf of Scotland. However, French and German ratifications are imminent, upon which the Convention will come into force. Switzerland is due to ratify in July 2009 and the expectation is that, following the implementation of the Mental Capacity Act 2005, the UK's ratification will be extended to England and Wales in the near future.

So far as future developments are concerned the Permanent Bureau is currently preparing a feasibility study on Transfrontier Mediation. Other possible future topics include cohabitation outside marriage, registered partnerships, and succession.

As will be apparent from the above discussion, the Hague Conference will remain a major player in the development of international family law for the foreseeable future. Furthermore, unlike the bodies that will now be examined, namely the Council of Europe and the EU, it alone has a *global* reach. Nevertheless, from a UK perspective these other bodies will continue to have an important role in the development of international family law.

---

[95] See EU Factsheet, Decisions in Civil Law Matters, Justice and Home Affairs Council, Luxembourg, 6 June 2008.

The continuing impact of the Council of Europe[96]

Outside its obviously important human rights remit, the Council of Europe seems to have become the forgotten player in international family law, being overshadowed particularly over the last couple of decades by the Hague Conference and, more recently, by the EU.[97] Yet, it has been and will continue to be engaged in a full family law programme. Moreover, it should not be overlooked that, unlike the EU, the Council comprises currently 47 states drawn from the whole continent of Europe and uniquely has a mandate to harmonise domestic laws. One curiosity of the Council's work is the production of Recommendations as well as Conventions. While the former clearly have less standing than the latter, being neither formally signed nor ratified by Member States, they are nevertheless addressed to *all* Member States, who are expected (if they do not already do so) to take steps as soon as possible (for example, when adopting new legislation) to comply with the standards contained in the particular Recommendation. In short, they should not be overlooked when considering the development of internationally agreed family law norms. Among the many such instruments, mention may be made of the 1984 Recommendation on Parental Responsibilities and the Recommendations on Family Mediation (1998), Children's Participation in Family and Social Life (1998) and on Policy to Support Positive Parenting (2006) and on Policy to Support Positive Parenting (2006). Others include the 1985 Recommendation on Violence in the Family, which entreats Member States to review their legislation on corporal punishment of children, the 1989 Recommendation on Contributions Following Divorce, according to which the post-divorce aim should be wherever possible to ensure that each party be economically independent and self-supporting, and Setting up a European Ombudsman for Children (2000).

At one time the UK seemed ready to ratify all Council of Europe family law conventions, but since ratifying the 1980 European Custody Convention in 1986 it has ceased to do so. In particular, it has neither signed nor ratified the 1996 European Convention on the Exercise of Children's Rights, nor the 2003 Convention on Contact Concerning Children, and it seems unlikely, given that it would be a requirement to obtain the consent of a child aged 13 and above,[98] that the UK will ratify

---

[96] I am indebted to Margaret Killerby, Director of Law Reform, and Regina Jensdottir, Head of the Public and Private Law Unit at the Council of Europe for their advice on the work of the Council. For an evaluation of the Council's family law programme, see generally N Lowe 'An Evaluation of the Council of Europe's Legal Instruments in the Field of Family' (a formal review of the programme commissioned by Council (CJ–FA (2006) 1 Rev) posted both on the Council's web site, http://www.coe.int/T/E/legal, and on Cardiff Law School's Research Papers website (Paper No 2)), http://www.law.cf.ac.uk/researchpapers/papers/2.pdf.

[97] See also N Lowe 'Does the Council of Europe's Family Law Programme Matter?' [2008] IFL 75.

[98] See Arts 5 and 6. Requiring the child's consent was expressly rejected in the reforms resulting in the Adoption and Children Act 2002.

(at any rate on behalf of England and Wales)[99] the 2008 European Convention on Adoption (Revised). In fact, the UK has in the past indicated a willingness to ratify the 2003 Convention, but this is another Convention that EU Member States can only ratify under EU auspices,[100] although in this case the EU itself has power (since it is a party to the Convention in its own right) to ratify. It may be, therefore, that the UK will eventually be bound by it. This may be no bad thing, since the Convention usefully sets out (in Chapter II)[101] general principles which domestic courts should observe when dealing with contact issues and contains (in Chapter III) helpful provisions concerning the recognition and enforcement of transfrontier contact, including the novel provision of providing a procedure for advance recognition and enforcement of contact orders, as well as providing for the prompt return of children at the end of transfrontier contact. On the other hand, the undoubted drawback of the 2003 Convention is that it will add yet another instrument to an already crowded field and in this context in particular there is a real danger that the proliferation of international instruments will in itself defeat the very object of improving the law regulating the cross-border movement of children.[102]

Whether the UK should ratify the 1996 Exercise of Children's Rights Convention can be debated. Some impetus for doing so may be given by the French ratification in January 2008 and the Council's own resolution to take serious steps to promote the Convention. It also has to be said that there is growing recognition within the UK of the importance of giving the child a real voice in legal proceedings.[103] But one drawback of the Convention is that it requires[104] Contracting States to specify at least three categories of family cases to which the Convention should apply, and there is a real danger that even among Contracting States there may be no uniformity on which areas are covered by the Convention.[105]

What, then, of the future so far as the Council is concerned? Following a meeting in Stockholm in September 2007 it was agreed that family law,

---

[99] Contrast Scotland, in which the need for consent of a child (aged 12 or over) has long been recognised: see now the Adoption and Children (Scotland) Act 2007, s 32. Although Scotland does not (yet) have devolved powers to ratify international treaties, the UK can ratify a Convention solely on its behalf, as it did in the case of the 2000 Hague Convention on the International Protection of Adults (discussed above).

[100] Indeed, the opening of the 2003 Convention for signature was delayed to resolve a dispute over EU Member States' competence to sign and ratify it.

[101] For a detailed discussion of the Convention see Lowe, Everall and Nicholls *International Movement of Children, Law Practice and Procedure* (Family Law, 2004) at 25.83–25.111.

[102] A fear long expressed by this author; see eg N Lowe 'International Conventions Affecting the Law Relating to Children – A Cause for Concern?' [2001] 171 at 178–179.

[103] See the review by N Lowe and M Murch 'Children's participation in the family justice system – translating principles into practice' [2001] CFLQ 137 and see, for example, *Mabon v Mabon* [2005] EWCA Civ 634, [2005] Fam 366 and *Re W (Leave to Remove)* [2008] EWCA Civ 538, [2008] 2 FLR 1170 at [33] per Thorpe LJ.

[104] By Art 1(4).

[105] See the criticisms, inter alia by Lowe, in the works referred to above at n 92 and n 93.

particularly child law, remains a top priority of the Council in general and of the European Committee on Legal Co-operation (CDCJ) in particular.[106] This has been further underscored by the Committee of Experts on Family Law (CJ-FA)'s revised terms of reference for 2008–2009,[107] by which it is instructed, inter alia, to draw up recommendations on missing persons and the presumption of death and on incapable adults and self-determination. In addition, it is instructed to 'prepare a feasibility study concerning the preparation of a recommendation on the rights and legal status of children being brought up in various forms of marital or non marital partnership and cohabitation and to make proposals concerning the possible follow-up to be given to the study'. This agenda will provide the opportunity to revise the 1975 European Convention on the Legal Status of Children Born Out of Wedlock and to revisit the White Paper *On Principles Concerning the Establishment and Legal Consequences of Parentage*[108] and thus to produce a modern instrument on parental responsibility.

The continuing impact of the EU

The current major preoccupation of the UK courts is with the application of BIIR with respect to its provisions on, principally, divorce and on parental responsibility. Not all the experiences have been happy ones in the sense that it cannot be said with confidence that the Regulation is being properly and consistently applied across Member States. Moreover, there is a question mark against the practicality of having to dispose of Hague Abduction Conventions within 6 weeks as laid down by Art 11(3) of the Regulation and against the justification for having to listen to the child in *all* return applications under the Hague Convention, as laid down by Art 11(2) of the Regulation.[109] There is also continuing debate about the wisdom of having, in the case of divorce etc, multiple but non-hierarchal bases of jurisdiction and the consequential reliance upon the principle that the first court to be properly seised has priority jurisdiction. This is a crude way of resolving conflicts of jurisdiction and, by thus providing for a jurisdictional race, is not in keeping with modern family thinking to encourage mediation. In short, there is a need for a review of the operation of BIIR, but this is not provided for until 2012.[110] In the meantime, however, one welcome development is that work is under way to revise and update the useful *Practice Guide for the Application of the New Brussels II Regulation*, produced by the Commission.

---

[106] Viz the 'Building a Europe for and with children' programme, which was also the theme for a conference, again in Stockholm, in September 2008.
[107] See CJ-FA (2008) 1.
[108] CJ-FA (2001) 16 Rev.
[109] See N Lowe 'The Current Experiences and Difficulties of Applying Brussels II Revised' [2007] IFL 183.
[110] See Art 65.

At one time, particularly during negotiations to revise Brussels II, there was a fear that there would be an avalanche of Brussels Regulations affecting family law. So far that has not happened, though, as has been said, work has been ongoing on a Maintenance Regulation and on the so-called Rome III on jurisdiction and applicable law in matrimonial matters which, though now halted, will not, it seems, prevent a minority of Member States going ahead with their own scheme on applicable law.[111] There are other issues clearly on the EU agenda, namely, mediation, rights of property arising out of a marital relationship and separation of unmarried couples and on wills and succession.[112] In other words, more Brussels Regulations affecting family law can be expected. In this respect the plea must be that steps are taken to ensure that they are family law-friendly.

One important limitation on the EU's ability to legislate on family matters is that because Art 65(EC) limits competence to cross-border issues affecting the proper functioning of the internal market there is no competence *per se* to reform matters of domestic substantive family law.[113] Although it had been planned (through the Treaty of Lisbon) to replace Art 65 by Art 81 of the Treaty of the Functioning of the European Union, this would have made no change to the scope of EU competence in relation to family matters.[114] Of course, it may be that in time this competence will be extended (either by stealth or by a deliberately negotiated policy), but as the law stands the EU has no competence to embark upon a wholesale programme of harmonisation.

The overall impact of these continuing developments

Drawing this section together, it can be seen that the Hague Conference, the Council of Europe and the EU will each continue to draft more international family law instruments. Although it is evident that they do not work in isolation, each institution nevertheless has its own agenda. But whether the production of new instruments can continue ad infinitum must surely be questioned, for quite apart from the difficulty of keeping abreast of these developments, there must be a concern that international regulation is becoming hopelessly complex. However, one answer to the

---

[111] See above.
[112] See 'Programme of mutual measures for the implementation of the principle of mutual recognition of decisions in civil and commercial matters' OJ C12 of 15 January 2001 – highlighted inter alia by M Tenreiro and M Ekström 'Unification of Private International law in Family Law matters Within the European Community' in K Boele-Woelki (ed) *Perspectives for the Unification and Harmonisation of Family Law in Europe*, CEFL Series No 4 (Intersentia, 2003), pp 187–188.
[113] See e g M Jänterä-Jareborg 'Unification of international family law in Europe – a critical perspective' in ibid above at 194 and Lowe 'The Growing Influence of the European Union on International Family Law – A View from the Boundary' (2003) 56 Current Legal Problems 439 at 447–450.
[114] The Lisbon Treaty would have usefully given Denmark more flexible opt-out powers which would have allowed it to opt in to individual instruments such as BIIR.

question, 'Where is international family law going next?' is that it will continue to emanate from Brussels, the Hague and Strasbourg. But this paper's final enquiry is whether there might be a fundamental change of direction and a new source of international family law, namely, a move to harmonisation.

BRINGING NATIONAL LAWS CLOSER TOGETHER

The idea that there should be some international uniformity of approach, at least in certain areas of family law, is not new. A so-called limping marriage, for example (that is, one that is valid in one jurisdiction but not in another) is as abhorrent to private international lawyers as it is to family lawyers. The traditional domestic conflict of laws approach, at least to minimise the problem, was to develop rules of recognition accepting, for example, that formalities are governed by the lex loci celebrationis[115] and, in general terms, capacity governed by the law of the ante-nuptial domicile. Sometimes, as in the case of polygamous marriages, recognition was developed both by case law and statute.[116] (Query whether recognition of same-sex marriages might follow a similar route?) The next stage of seeking an *international* solution is to have internationally agreed rules on recognition such as that provided by the 1970 Hague Convention on Recognition of Divorces and Legal Separation, implemented in the UK initially by the Recognition of Divorces and Legal Separations Act 1971. It was, incidentally, dissatisfaction with this Convention that led Germany to make a proposal that eventually led to Brussels II,[117] which contains rules of jurisdiction and consequential recognition and enforcement provisions on divorce, nullity and legal separation.

Another method of solving international differences is to develop rules of applicable law – a 'solution' favoured by civil law jurisdictions, but generally eschewed by common law jurisdictions and by England and Wales in particular. As Thorpe LJ put it extra-judicially,[118] 'Ours is not a jurisdiction that searches for and then applies the foreign law with which the parties have the closest connection'. It was an attempt to impose a common regime of applicable law that lay at the heart of Rome III and the proposal has some superficial attraction, as, for example, where two

---

[115] Not that it is always easy to determine the place of celebration, see eg *Westminster City Council v IC (by the Official Solicitor)* [2008] EWCA Civ 198, [2008] 2 FLR 267, in which the purported marriage ceremony was conducted by a telephone call between England and Bangladesh.

[116] See eg *Baindail v Baindail* [1946] P 122 and the Matrimonial Causes Act 1973, s 47, discussed inter alia in P North and J Fawcett *Cheshire and North's Private International Law* (Butterworths, 13th edn, 1999), p 755ff.

[117] See eg the historical account by P McEleavy, 'The Brussels II Regulation: How the European Community has moved into Family Law' (2002) 51 ICLQ 883 at 891 et seq.

[118] 'Interdisciplinarity and Internationality in Modern Family Justice Systems' [2007] IFL 165 at 166.

Belgians come to England to work and then seek divorce and ancillary relief. Surely, the argument goes, it is only right that Belgian law should apply. But there are formidable objections too, not least of which is, in the English context, the cost, given that foreign law has to be proved as a matter of fact. But could there be confidence that an English court could apply foreign law accurately? Then there is a question of how real a connection with the foreign state the litigants should have and finally what law should be applied where the spouses are of different nationalities or have different domiciles. At least the lex fori approach avoids all these problems. One other issue that the applicable law approach raises is whether parties should be governed by their personal religious law. Should English law, as some jurisdictions such as Israel and Malaysia do, have parallel systems of law, at least in the family context?

A third possibility is to expand jurisdictions, at least for certain purposes. For example, rather than have an elaborate (and not altogether successful) system for the recognition and enforcement of orders relating to children (technically Part 1 orders for the purpose of the Family Law Act 1986)[119] within the UK, should there not simply be a British matrimonial enforcement jurisdiction?[120] One could make a similar argument for the EU. Indeed, the fast track enforcement of access orders and 'Article 11(8) return orders' under BIIR[121] comes pretty close to that idea. In the UK context, however, the political reality is against such an idea. Indeed, the trend is the opposite way. Devolution is having a growing significance not so much, in the context of family law, in Scotland since there has always been a separate system, but in Wales where devolved competence to pass primary legislation, particularly in Field 15 – Social Welfare – is expanding.[122] So in the UK context 'international' family law is beginning to include the four constituent territories of the UK. No doubt similar developments are occurring in Spain, in which there are numerous autonomous regions.

Can or should family laws be harmonised?

The fourth method of eliminating international differences is, to use a neutral expression, to seek to make domestic laws the same or similar. As

---

[119] For a critical discussion of the enforcement process under the 1986 Act, see Lowe, Everall and Nicholls *International Movement of Children, Law Practice and Procedure* (Family Law, 2004), ch 11.
[120] A plea the author first articulated in 'The Family Law Act 1986 – A Critique' [2002] Fam Law 39.
[121] As provided for respectively by Arts 41 and 42 of the Regulation, for discussion of which see N Lowe, M Everall and M Nicholls *The New Brussels II Regulation* (Family Law, 2005), para 7.24ff.
[122] That is, Government of Wales Act 2006, Sch 5, Field 15, on which see O Rees 'Devolution and the development of family law in Wales' [2008] CFLQ 45.

Meulders-Klein has rightly said,[123] terminology in this context is important. In her view, 'harmonisation' implies a concern to reconcile the preoccupations and interests of the various systems so as to avoid conflicts and clashes and involves neither coercion nor constraint. 'Unification', by contrast, means the voluntary or imposed move to the uniformity of different systems and thus postulates greater sacrifices. At the extreme end is codification as, for example, by a European Civil Code leading to a Ius Commune. While it is probable that scholars are not always debating precisely the same issue, for convenience I will refer to the whole as the 'harmonisation debate'.

Arguments about harmonisation are not new. Pintens, himself a leading advocate for family law harmonisation, at least within Europe, for example, refers[124] to the work of two famous French legal comparatists, Saleilles and Lambert, who at the end of the nineteenth century sought to discover a 'droit commun législatif'.[125] But what is new is that there is serious argument for *family law* harmonisation. Previously, and in the not so distant past, this notion would be, and was, dismissed out of hand. Writing in 1978, for example, Kahn-Freund judged the attempt to construct a European family law 'a hopeless quest' and anyway thought it unnecessary for the political, economic and cultural future of Europe.[126] More recently Legrand, writing in 1999, claimed the current diversity of law in Europe is an emanation of the irredeemable dissimilarity of national cultures from which he postulated the impossibility of deliberate harmonisation.[127] Yet, notwithstanding these observations, there is now, particularly among continental European family law scholars, passionate debate over family law harmonisation. The principal harmonisation advocates are Pintens and Vanwinckelen, Boele-Woelki, Antokolskaia, Dethloff, Martiny and Schwenza. An increasingly passionate opponent is Meulders-Klein and in the UK the harmonisation sceptics are McGlynn and Bradley.[128] The debate has undoubtedly been sharpened by the creation in 2001 of the Commission on European Family Law ('CEFL') a body of scholars, including the author, whose self-appointed mission is

---

[123] M-T Meulders-Klein 'Towards a European Civil Code on Family Law?' in K Boele-Woelki (ed) *Perspectives for the Unification and Harmonisation of Family Law in Europe* (Intersentia, 2003), pp 105–106.

[124] W Pintens 'Europeanisation of Family Law' in K Boele-Woelki (ed) *Perspectives for the Unification and Harmonisation of Family Law in Europe* (Intersentia, 2003), p 3.

[125] See eg R Saleilles 'Le droit commercial comparé. Contribution á l'étude des méthodes jurisdiques. A propos d'un livre de Ma A Strafa', *Annales de droit commercial* (1891).

[126] O Kahn-Freund 'Common Law and Civil law – Imaginary and Real Obstacles to Assimilation' in M Cappelletti (ed) *New Perspectives for a Common Law of Europe* (Sijthoff, Leyden, 1978), p 141.

[127] P Legrand *Fragments on Law-as-Culture* (Tjeenk Willink, Devente, 1999). See also by the same author 'European Legal Systems Are Not Converging' (1996) 45 ICLQ 53 and 'Against a European Civil Code' (1997) 60 MLR 44.

[128] For an excellent introduction to the harmonisation debate, see K Boele-Woelki (ed) *Perspectives for the Unification and Harmonisation of Family Law in Europe* (Intersentia, 2003) and C McGlynn *Families and the European Union – Law, Politics and Pluralism* (Cambridge UP, 2006), ch 8.

the creation of Principles of European Family Law that are thought to be the most suitable for the harmonisation of family law in Europe.

The harmonisation debate

One of the keen debates over harmonisation in general and family law in particular is whether, because laws are culturally specific, harmonisation would lead to a loss of an important aspect of one's culture. Indeed, Legrand considers[129] unification to be a form of cultural imperialism. Meulders-Klein argues that:[130]

> 'of all branches of law, family law is as a rule the most autonomous and the most specific, being as it is so deeply "embedded" in history and a cornerstone of their future development, but also linked with the development of each individual. The values with which it is charged, its role in the attribution of legal personality, bonds of kinship, the identity and the personal status of the individual and the way families are structured, all these place family law at the very crux of society in every country. This being so, it should come as no surprise that every nation has an interest in keeping a close eye on its law regarding the status of the individual and the family which, being a *matter of public policy*, is off-limits, – *d'ordre public et indisponible* –, and mostly placed under the protection of national constitutions.'

Advocates for harmonisation dismiss this argument. As Pintens, for example, points out,[131] national laws are not fixed and not resistant to the reception of foreign family law. He instances the case of Belgians not suffering a culture shock when, in 1987, Belgium extended the *mater semper certa est* principle for establishing maternity to children born out of wedlock. As he forcibly argues, 'Cultural embeddedment does not mean that we are embedded in a culture to such an extent that we give up our identity when culture changes occur'. More recently, Scherpe has said much the same thing, commenting[132] that 'Nothing has ever prevented a national legislator from breaking away from tradition if there were good, sometimes even compelling reasons for it'. He instanced the battles over divorce, gender equality, gender change and civil partnerships. Others, such as Dethloff, argue[133] that in any event, in the family context the often differing political values and morals are on the decline such that, in most European countries, the law, rather than being shaped predominantly by

---

[129] P Legrand 'Sens et non-sens d'un code civil européen' (1996) RIDC 811.
[130] M-T Meulders-Klein 'Towards a Uniform European Family Law? A Political Approach' in M Antokolskaia (ed) *Convergence and Divergence of Family Law in Europe* (Intersentia, 2007), pp 272–273.
[131] W Pintens 'Europeanisation of Family Law' in K Boele-Woelki (ed) *Perspectives for the Unification and Harmonisation of Family Law in Europe* (Intersentia, 2003), p 8.
[132] J Scherpe 'The Gametes of a European Family Law' [2008] IFL 98.
[133] N Dethloff 'Arguments for the Unification and Harmonisation of Family Law in Europe' in K Boele-Woelki (ed) *Perspectives for the Unification and Harmonisation of Family Law in Europe* (Intersentia, 2003), p 61.

certain basic convictions, increasingly takes social realities into consideration, with the result that it is now primarily concerned with solving comparable social problems.

Another debate centres on whether or not European family laws are converging. Advocates for harmonisation argue that they are. Pintens, for example, points[134] to the spontaneous developments whereby case law and legal doctrine have played an important part aided by the Council of Europe. Others[135] point to the Nordic experience of harmonisation of family laws. But many (for example, Bradley)[136] hotly contest this, even in the Nordic context. As Antokolskaia has commented:[137]

> 'The question whether family law in Europe has been converging in the past and is converging at present remains controversial. One may find it puzzling that while the idea of convergence has been supported in the last decennia by a number of eminent scholars, the existence of convergence has at the same time been persistently denied by equally renowned opponents.'

One suspects that most of the differences lie in the viewpoint of the commentator – there is convergence if there is a desire to find it or divergence if that is what is being sought. All the author can say is that from his perspective he was surprised to find so much common ground in the fields of divorce and even parental responsibilities.

Another argument for harmonisation is perhaps best expressed by Dethloff, who maintains[138] that European families need a harmonised European family law. She argues that free movement in Europe is hampered by the substantial differences in substantive law and these are therefore contrary to EU objectives. She points first to the sheer complexity and consequent high legal costs involved in determining which legal regime applies, let alone determining how it applies, to cross-border families. Secondly she points to the fact that the different regimes can lead to the creation of 'limping family law relationships such as limping marriages, limping registered partnerships and even limping fatherhood and that this in turn can be of relevance with regard to laws relating to

---

[134] W Pintens 'Europeanisation of Family Law' in K Boele-Woelki (ed) *Perspectives for the Unification and Harmonisation of Family Law in Europe* (Intersentia, 2003), p 16.

[135] For example, W Pintens and K Vanwinckelen *Casebook: European Family Law* (Leuven UP, 2001), p 16ff.

[136] D Bradley 'A Family law for Europe? Sovereignty, Political Economy and Legitimation' in K Boele-Woelki (ed) *Perspectives for the Unification and Harmonisation of Family Law in Europe* (Intersentia, 2003), pp 80–89; cf P Lødrup 'The Harmonisation of Nordic Family Law' in K Boele-Woelki and T Sverdrup (eds) *European Challenges in Contemporary Family Law* (Intersentia, 2008), p 17.

[137] M Antokolskaia 'Introduction' to *Convergence and Divergence of Family Law in Europe* (Intersentia, 2007), p 1. See also by the same author 'Convergence and divergence of divorce laws in Europe [2006] CFLQ 307 and, for a comprehensive survey, *Harmonisation of Family Law in Europe: A Historical Perspective – A Tale of Two Millennia* (Intersentia, 2006).

[138] K Boele-Woelki (ed) *Perspectives for the Unification and Harmonisation of Family Law in Europe* (Intersentia, 2003), p 39ff.

residence permits, nationality and citizenship, social security and tax. With regard to economic consequences she cites the example of prenuptial agreements, commenting that 'if a couple move [their] place of residence to the United Kingdom, they must face the possibility that in case of divorce a substantially different distribution of marital property will be the consequence than the one envisaged under the original matrimonial property regime'. There may also be dramatic differences in entitlements to spousal maintenance after divorce and obligations to maintain children.

In the same vein, Dethloff points out,[139] the very entitlement to divorce may vary dramatically, so that a couple marrying in a state where divorce can only be obtained after a lengthy period of separation, as in Ireland, will lose their protection if they move to a state such as Sweden or Finland, where divorce can be granted either immediately or after a short period, even against the will of one of the spouses. Of course, the converse is also true, so that a couple moving to Ireland will be unable to obtain a divorce quickly even if they both consent.

Opponents of harmonisation raise still other arguments such as the fear that it is a political tool, for example, to further the goal of European citizenship, particularly if it is seen to be imposed 'top down'.[140] McGlynn argues[141] that it would stifle progressive developments in family law that accommodate diversity, since of necessity harmonisation tends towards the lowest common denominator. While this seems a fair point, ultimately it depends how far harmonisation goes.

The work of the CEFL[142]

Whatever one's views of this debate, the gauntlet has been thrown down by the creation of the previously mentioned CEFL, set up in 2001 in Utrecht under the driving force of Boele-Woelki, herself at Utrecht. The Commission comprises an Organising Committee consisting of seven members, including the author as the sole common law representative,

---

[139] N Dethloff 'Arguments for the Unification and Harmonisation of Family Law in Europe' in K Boele-Woelki (ed) *Perspectives for the Unification and Harmonisation of Family Law in Europe* (Intersentia, 2003), p 49.

[140] See M-T Meudlers-Klein 'Towards a Uniform European Family Law? A Political Approach' in M Antokolskaia (ed) *Convergence and Divergence of Family Law in Europe* (Intersentia, 2007), p 277.

[141] C McGlynn, *Families and the European Union – Law, Politics and Pluralism* (Cambridge UP, 2006), pp 110, 151 and 191.

[142] See K Boele-Woelki 'The Working method of the Commission on European Family Law' in K Boele-Woelki (ed) *Common Core and Better Law in European Family Law* (Intersentia, 2005), p 15; 'Building on Convergence and Coping with Divergence in the CEFL Principles of European Family Law' in M Antokolskaia (ed) *Convergence and Divergence of Family Law in Europe* (Intersentia, 2007), p 253ff and 'The CEFL Principles Regarding Parental Responsibilities: Predominance of the Common Core' in K Boele-Woelki and T Sverdrup (eds) *European Challenges in Contemporary Family Law* (Intersentia, 2008), p 63.

and a wider group of experts representing some 22 different European jurisdictions. Although initially funded by the European Framework Programme, the CEFL is entirely independent but by the same token has no mandate to produce binding principles. It is therefore an academic endeavour. The CEFL sees itself as the family law counterpart to the Lando Commission in the field of European Contract Law. Indeed, that is why the term 'Commission' was chosen.

The CEFL has developed three sets of Principles, on Divorce, Maintenance Between Former Spouses and on Parental Responsibilities.[143] Its fourth field of work is Matrimonial Property. The CEFL's tried and tested working methodology is to commission experts to write a national report based on answers to a detailed questionnaire devised by the Organising Committee. These reports are then analysed and the Principles distilled by the Organising Committee. These Principles are then defended against the wider Group of Experts before being finalised for publication.

In the first instance the CEFL seeks to propose principles that are functionally common to a significant majority of the legal systems analysed, though also mindful of directional trends so as to be a source of inspiration for a family law that can last at least for the foreseeable future. But this so-called 'common core' approach cannot solve all the problems, and where there is no commonality, choices as to an evaluation have to be made. The latter process has sometimes been labelled[144] (surely unfortunately) the so-called *better law method*. This of course is dangerous territory – for while it leaves room for creative drafting, it invokes the troublesome problem of justifying the choices.[145]

Another issue is McGlynn's common denominator problem,[146] for harmonisation has inevitably to squeeze out the extremes. For example, had it been included in the jurisdictions analysed (as it is for matrimonial property) it would have been impossible to harmonise Malta's law since, alone of European jurisdictions, it does nor permit divorce. Equally, there is no way that the Irish law of divorce under which the parties must be separated for at least four of the previous five years can be harmonised with Finnish law, which has no grounds for divorce but is based on the

---

[143] See respectively, K Boele-Wooelki, F Ferrand, C Gońzalez Beilfuss, M Jänterä-Jareborg, N Lowe, D Martiny and W Pintens *Principles of European Family Law Regarding Divorce and Maintenance between Former Spouses* (Intersentia, 2002) and, by the same authors, *Principles of European Family Law Regarding Parental Responsibilities* (Intersentia, 2007).

[144] See eg M Antokolskaia 'The Better Law Approach and the Harmonisation of Family Law' in K Boele-Woelki (ed) *Perspectives for the Unification and Harmonisation of Family Law in Europe*, CEFL Series No 4 (Intersentia, 2003), p 159ff.

[145] See the well directed criticism inter alia by M-T Meulders-Klein 'Towards a Uniform European Family Law? A Political Approach' in M Antokolskaia (ed) *Convergence and Divergence of Family Law in Europe* (Intersentia, 2007), pp 279–280.

[146] Discussed above.

principle of divorce on demand – that is, one or both spouses may apply for a divorce and after a mandatory period of 6 months' reflection, the divorce must be granted upon a renewed application.

For all its imperfections, what the CEFL has surely done is to demonstrate that harmonisation of at least some family law principles is possible. But the existence of these Principles raises the question of what, if anything, should be done with them. The author's personal view is that the drawing up of Principles is essentially an academic exercise which may be of use to legislators when they are considering reform.[147] He certainly does not advocate that, even if it could, the CEFL's Principles should be foisted on European states. In any event, by what vehicle could it be done? The EU currently has no competence (although this could in time change) and it is also outside the Hague Conference's remit. However, one can see the Council of Europe as a possible vehicle for promoting the CEFL's Principles. This would allow states to mull over them and subsequently choose whether or not to ratify any consequent Convention or Recommendation. Furthermore, as it happens, there is an ideal testing ground for this in the field of parental responsibilities which, as has been said, is on the Council's current agenda of work.

Another idea altogether is currently being worked on by Dethloff at the Institute for German, European and International Family Law, at the University of Bonn, namely to take a European Model of Family Law – say of marriage and divorce, into which transnational partners would opt.[148] While this may have some attraction, it makes for complication but it also adds to the current debate.

Although McGlynn thinks[149] that the CEFL's Principles make harmonisation more likely, such a development is certainly not inevitable. Indeed, the decision of the nine Member States referred to above to invoke the enhanced co-operation procedure to opt for the 'applicable law' route might arguably make harmonisation less likely. Nevertheless, the CEFL's work undoubtedly provides further fuel for future debate and it may be that the answer to the question 'Where in the world is family law going next?' will be Utrecht!

---

[147] As indeed has already been the case most spectacularly in Portugal, where Law 61/2008 was heavily influenced inter alia by the Divorce Principles (see G de Oliveira 'Changes going on in Portuguese Family Law' [2008] Fam RZ 1712).
[148] N Dethloff 'European marriage – An Optional Model or Transnational Partnerships', unpublished paper given at an International Society of Family Law seminar, Girona, April 2007.
[149] *Families and the European Union – Law, Politics and Pluralism* (Cambridge UP, 2006), pp 182–183.

INDEX

References are to page numbers.

Abduction *see* Child abduction
Abse, Leo
  legislation   52
  troublemakers   52
Abuse *see also* Child abuse
  elderly   157
Access
  care, children in   99
Adoption
  1957, in   167
  alternatives   35
  broadening the concept   33
  case study   107
  changing nature of law and practice   29
  consent   36, 107
  decline in babies available   31
  Europe   36
  European Convention on Adoption
    ratification of   281
  future   36
  Hague Convention on Intercountry Adoption   276
  Houghton Committee   53
  illegitimacy   29
  inter-country   36
  opposition   35
  permanency planning   31
  private law   30
  public law   31
  reform   53
  special guardianship orders   35
  support   34
  trace birth parents, right to   33
  welfare principle   34
Adultery
  divorce   71
Advice
  families   241
  standardisation   242
Age of criminal responsibility   168
Allen, Marjory
  child protection   51
  troublemakers   50
Alternative dispute resolution
  advantages   142
  encouragement of   139

Ancillary relief *see also* Ancillary relief in Europe
  big money cases   23
  capital compensatory payment   207
  choice of law   218
  civil partnerships   200
  community of property   203, 207
  context   203
  contributions, types of   198
  discretion   206
  economic analysis   219
  emotional side   220
  equal shares   24
  equitable distribution   206
  Europeanisation of   203, 216, 218
  fairness   191
  future of   218
  gender equality   190, 198, 219
  litigation   219
  non-matrimonial property, concept of   208
  pre-nuptial agreements   199, 209
  reasonable requirements   191, 198
  reform   218
Ancillary relief in EC law
  conflict of laws   216, 218
  discretion   203
  European Commission green paper   203
  maintenance, definition of   217
Ancillary relief in Europe
  accrual systems   205
  community of property   205
  default options   205
  immediate community regime   205
  marital property agreements   209
  non-matrimonial property, concept of   208
  separate property regimes   205
Appeals
  care orders   93
Applicable law
  development of rules on   284
Armed forces
  cohabitation reform   75
Assisted reproductive technology
  parents   223
Assumption of parental rights
  grounds   95

Assumption of parental rights—*continued*	
lapse of time	96
objections	98
parental rights resolutions	97
practice and procedure	97
removal from voluntary care	97
safeguards	98
Attachment theory	120
Australia	
Family Relationship Centres	178
Autonomy	
marriage	155
Barristers	
support from	181
Behavioural science	
family justice system	119
Besant, Annie	64
Best interests of the child	
culture	14
Big money cases	
ancillary relief	23
Bigamy	
cohabitation	62
Birth rate	8
Birth registration	
parental responsibility	228
Births, marriages and deaths	
collection of data on	2
Bloomsbury Group	65
Bohemians	
cohabitation	65
Brussels Convention 1968	
incorporation	267
Brussels II Regulation	
contents	268
divorce	282
EC law	267
European Court of Justice	269
parental responsibility	282
urgent preliminary ruling procedure	269
Bureaucratisation of family life	2
Cafcass	
care proceedings	
non-involvement in	256
passage agent role	143
risk assessments	134
under-funding	248
Care *see* Fostering, *see* Local authority care, *see* Non-parental carers	
Care orders	
appeals	93
Care proceedings	
assessments	254
Cafcass	256
child as party	91
costs, increase in	248
court fees	253

Care proceedings—*continued*	
culture	89
Director of Children's Services	256
Every Child Matters	247
fit persons orders	87
fixed fees	250
future	257
government's policy to reduce	250
graduated fees	250
grounds	87
heard, right to be	107
juvenile courts	93
kinship care	255
moral danger condition	89
parents' right to participate	91
practice and procedure	90
proper development is being avoidably prevented, meaning of	88
Public Law Outline	258
reform	
terms of reference	248
representation, lack of	256
Carter Review of Legal Aid	
costs	250
criticisms	140
implementation	139
Charter of Fundamental Rights of the EU	
status of	273
Child abduction	
Hague Convention on Child Abduction	264, 265
immigration	272
Child abuse	
Children Act 1908	49
corporal punishment	165
'discovery' of	164
parental rights	163
Poor Law	50
risk assessments	134
Child and Family Reporter	
child protection	181
Child maintenance	
contact, linked with	238
Hague Maintenance Convention	278
private arrangements	237
privatisation	23
Child Maintenance and Enforcement Commission (C-MEC)	
consent orders	237
Child protection *see also* Care proceedings, *see also* Removal of children from families	
Allen, Marjory	51
best interests of the child	14
Child and Family Reporter	181
communities	181
Curtis Committee	51
failures in system	245
guardians ad litem	91

Child protection —*continued*
   Hague Convention on the
      Protection of Children 274
   harm, meaning of 133
   interventionist approach 11
   political context 247
   public expenditure 133
   resources 247
   risk aversion 131, 133
   voluntary organisations 117
   welfare principle 20
   wishes and feelings of child 181
Child support
   non-parental carers 242
Child tax credit
   non-parental carers 226
Children *see also* Adoption, *see also*
      Care proceedings, *see also*
      Child abduction, *see also*
      Child maintenance, *see*
      Fostering
   absent and re-partnered
      parents 222
   birth rate 8
   cohabitation 6
   divorce or separation
      effect on 17, 131
   elderly parents
      duty to maintain 25
   evacuation during World War II 50
   family justice system 131
   heard, right to be 143
   informal relationships 222
   parents
      defined in terms of parents'
         relationship, children
         as 154
   postmodern attitudes to 130
   private law 86
   psychoanalysis
      child development 120
   wishes and feelings of 132
Children Act 1989
   background 246
   current policy and practice 243
   European Convention on
      Human Rights 263
   fostering 231
   future 221
   importance of 109
   parental responsibility 228, 232
   private ordering 235
   reform 227
   separated parents 228
   special guardianship 230
   UN Convention on the Rights of
      the Child 263
Children's rights
   50 years ago 148
   age of criminal responsibility 168
   circumcision 14

Children's rights—*continued*
   Exercise of Children's Rights
      Convention, ratification
      of 281
   Gillick competency 169
   UN Convention on the Rights of
      the Child 263
Choice of law
   ancillary relief 218
Christianity
   divorce 13
   fathers 13
   marriage 13
   polygamy 13
   values 12
Circumcision
   children's rights 14
   religion 14
Civil marriages
   increase in 4
Civil partnerships
   ancillary relief 200
   cohabitation reform 82
   internationalisation of family
      law 271
   introduction of 9
   marriage 159
   statistics 10
Class
   social intervention 23
Co-ownership
   family home 44
Cohabitation *see also* Cohabitation
      reform
   attitudes 57, 62, 83
   bigamy preferred to 62
   Bloomsbury Group 65
   Bohemians 65
   children 6
   common law marriage 58
   couples, attitude of 194
   deed, promises of support made
      by 68
   demographics 5
   desertion 70
   divorce
      unreasonable delay in
         petitioning 71
   divorce reform 69, 74
   duration 6
   extent and nature 59
   feminism 64
   fictional heroines 64
   history 57, 59
   illegitimacy 60
   increase in 193
   legal rights, lack of advice on 197
   legal treatment 66
   lone parents 77
   outcasts from society 63
   pledging credit 67
   pre-nuptial agreements 213

Cohabitation —*continued*			**Conflict of laws**—*continued*	
rise in	5		rules of recognition	284
separation allowances	75		uniformity of law	284
state pensions	61		**Contact**	
statistics	5		child maintenance	238
stepfamilies	9		non-resident parents	21
trial marriage, as	196		**Context, family law in**	2
trusts	68		**Continuity of family law**	11
unemployment benefits	75		**Contributions**	
war	75		ancillary relief	198
widow's pension	76		**Corporal punishment**	
wills	67		abolition	149, 165
Cohabitation reform			child abuse	165
armed forces	74		schools	165
civil partnerships	82		**Costs**	
domestic violence	78		Carter Review of Legal Aid	250
family home	79		**Council of Europe**	
family provision	78		conventions	
illegitimacy	74, 81		ratification of	280
landmark dates	58		future	281
Law Commission	83, 219		impact of	280
pensions	81		recommendations	280
piecemeal reform	80		**County courts**	
social security benefits	77		family justice system	139
state pensions	75		**Courts** *see also* Family justice	
Colwell, Maria, death of	92, 164, 246		system	
Commission on European Family			delays	252
Law (CEFL)			fees	253
harmonisation of family law	286, 289		care proceedings	253
			increase in litigation	232
principles	290		Public Law Outline	253
work of	289		services, reduction in	252
Common law marriage			**Cross-border disputes** *see*	
extent of	58		International family law	
myth of	197		**Cultural change**	
Communities			definition	114
child protection	181		families	129
ethnic minorities	178		family justice system	114
force or coercion	174, 184		late modernity, in	118
institutions to protect			social control	115
individuals	177		**Culture** *see also* Cultural change	
law and responsibility	184		best interests of the child	14
mediation	182		care proceedings	89
Muslim women, divorce of	178		Christianity	12
power	174		moral danger condition in care	
religious groups	178		proceedings	90
rights, role of	174		religion	12
silencing voices	176		**Curtis Committee**	
truth	176		child protection	51
Community *see also* Communities				
individualism	173		**Darwin, Charles, anniversary of**	
law centres	177		birth of	1
new communities, growth of	173		**Demographics**	
protection against the	174, 176, 185		changes in	3
Community care			cohabitation	6
family law	157		divorce	6
power	175		elderly	9
women	157		lone parents	8
Comparative law			marriage	3, 4
reform, influence on	3		remarriage	4
Conflict of laws	3		stepfamilies	8
ancillary relief	216			
ancillary relief in EC law	218			

Index

Desertion
  cohabitation   70
Deviance
  families   121
Devolution
  international family law   285
Director of Children's Services
  care proceedings   256
Discrimination see Gender equality
Disqualification orders
  parental rights   92
Diversity
  ethnic minorities   10
  same sex partnerships   9
Divorce see also Ancillary relief, see also Matrimonial property reform
  adultery   71
  Brussels II Regulation   282
  children
    effect on   17, 131
  Christianity   13
  cohabitation
    unreasonable delay in petitioning   71
  condonation   70
  connivance   69
  delay in petition, unreasonable   71
  demographics   6
  EC law   214
  factors causing   7
  harmonisation of family law   289
  harmonisation of laws   214
  Jewish people   15
  matrimonial offence   118
  misconduct   71
  Muslim Law Shariah Council (MLSC)   179
  Muslim women   178
  probation service   125
  rise in   7
  statistics   6
Divorce courts
  magistrates' courts, closer association with   127
Divorce reform
  cohabitation   69, 74
  Divorce Reform Act 1969   53
  Divorce Reform Bill
    'Casanova's charter'   44
  gender equality
    troublemakers   40
  irretrievable breakdown
    sole ground   45
  Matrimonial Proceedings and Property Act 1970   47
  matrimonial property reform,
    priority over   40, 45
  petitions, lack of   40
  priority of   40, 45
  ridicule   46
  Royal Commission on Marriage   42

Divorce reform—*continued*
  Society for Promoting Reforms in Marriage and Divorce   46
  special procedure   129
  troublemakers   40
Doli incapax   168
Domestic violence
  cohabitation reform   78
  criminal law, inadequacy of   27
  definition   134
  emotional, financial, physical, psychological or sexual abuse   134
  non-molestation orders
    breach   28
  occupation orders   27
  ouster orders   27
  re-discovery of   26
  risk assessments   134
  stalking   28

EC law see also Ancillary relief in EC law
  Brussels Convention 1968   266
  Brussels II Regulation   267, 282
  Charter of Fundamental Rights of the EU   273
  child maintenance   278
  divorce   214
  Hague Maintenance Convention   278
  harmonisation   214
  harmonisation of family law   288
  impact of   282
  member state competence   270
Ecclesiastical courts
  family justice system   118
Economic change
  results of   116
Economics
  marriage   22
Elderly
  abuse   157
  demographics   9
  family law   157
  Hague Convention on the International Protection of Adults   279
  maintain parents, duty of children to   25
  neglect   24
  women   9
  women, care by   157
Enforcement
  family justice system   136
Equal parental rights
  emancipation of women   192
  Guardianship Act 1973   49
  primacy of fathers   48
  reform   48
  unmarried fathers   20

Ethnic minorities
- communities — 178
- diversity — 10
- family models — 10

Europe see also Ancillary relief in Europe
- adoption — 36
- forced heirship — 205

European Commission
- ancillary relief — 204
- green paper on ancillary relief — 204

European Convention on Human Rights
- Children Act 1989 — 263
- impact of — 272

European Court of Justice
- Brussels II Regulation — 269
- urgent preliminary ruling procedure — 269

European Model of Family Law
- proposal for — 291

European Union see Ancillary relief in EC law

Every Child Matters
- care proceedings — 247

Experts
- family justice system — 258

Families
- 21st century, in — 221
- advice — 241
- advice, seekimg — 176
- behaviour, controlling — 239
- cultural change — 129
- definition — 225
- deviance — 121
- diversity of — 221
- family law, image of family in — 153
- formalisation — 222
- genetics — 223
- government support — 239, 241
- homeostatis — 120
- integrity — 224
- legal issues — 176
- postmodernity — 129
- probation service — 125
- relatedness, concept of — 225
- relatives, definition of — 225
- resources — 240
- sexual tie — 154
- socio-political context — 121
- sociology — 121
- state intervention — 239

Families in Britain
- an evidence paper — 11

Family Division
- proposal for — 126

Family home
- co-ownership — 44
- cohabitation reform — 79

Family justice system
- administrative system, government policy to achieve — 246
- behavioural science — 119
- boundaries — 114
- characteristics of family friendly system — 259
- children — 131
- civil and criminal system, blurring between — 136
- county courts — 139
- courts, development — 16
- criminality, stigma of — 113, 127
- cultural change — 114
- delays — 259
- ecclesiastical courts — 118
- enforcement powers — 136
- experts — 258
- features — 112
- Finer Committee — 127
- government's strategy, emergent nature of — 138, 141
- interdisciplinary approach — 112
- late modernity, in — 118
- legal aid — 248, 258
- magistrates' courts removal from jurisdiction of — 127
- mental health — 117
- minimalist system, move towards a — 260
- minimum standards — 256
- piecemeal response — 260
- Poor Law — 116
- positive support measures — 142
- post-modern age — 129
- privacy — 113
- psycho-social approaches — 145
- psychological aspects — 120
- public hearings, proposal for — 18
- resources — 232
- roots of system — 115
- social policy — 112
- social sciences — 119
- socio-legal consumer studies, influence — 128
- unified courts, proposal for — 126, 137

Family justice systems
- social support, as system of — 121

Family law see also Harmonisation of family law, see also International family law
- community care — 157
- discipline of — 150
- discrete subject, as — 153
- elderly — 157
- gender dysphoria — 159
- harmonisation — 285
- image of the family — 153
- individualism — 173
- Ministry of Justice — 246
- neglect of family issues — 157

Index

Family law —*continued*
   patriarchy   153
   public/private dichotomy   160
   social control   155
   text books   187
Family proceedings court
   'cascading down'   138
   encouragement of use of   137
   experienced magistrates, lack of   138
   magistrates' courts   137
   transfer of cases   137
Family provision
   cohabitation reform   78
Family Relationship Centres (FRC)
   Australia   178
Fathers *see also* Unmarried fathers
   Christianity   13
   equal parental rights
      primacy of father   48
   parental responsibility   227
   parental rights   13
   social policy   21
Fees *see* Court fees
Feminism
   cohabitation   64
Financial provision on divorce
   1957, in   160
   gender equality   161
Finer Committee
   family justice system   127
Fit persons orders
   care proceedings   87
Fixed fees
   care proceedings   250
Flexible working requests
   non-parental carers   226
Force or coercion
   communities   174, 184
Forced heirship
   Europe   205
Fostering
   Children Act 1989   231
   local authorities   231
   residence orders   231
   wardship   103

Gender dysphoria
   family law   159
Gender equality *see also* Equal parental rights
   ancillary relief   190, 198, 219
   financial provision on divorce   161
   marriage   190, 192, 201
   opting out   201
   religion   201
Genetics
   families   223
Gillick competency
   children's rights   169
Gorell Commission   126

Graduated fees
   care proceedings   250
Guardians
   wishes and feelings of child   182
Guardians ad litem
   child protection   91
   parental rights   92

Habitual residence
   parental responsibility   275
Hague Conference
   impact of   274
Hague Convention on Child Abduction
   accessions   277
   good practice guidelines   276
   protocols   277
Hague Convention on Intercountry Adoption
   ratification   276
Hague Convention on the International Protection of Adults
   mental capacity   279
Hague Convention on the Protection of Children
   application   274
   Hague Conference   274
   interrelationship with other instruments   276
   Muslims, application to   276
Hague Maintenance Convention
   EC law   278
Harm
   child protection
      definition of harm   133
Harmonisation of family law
   Commission on European Family Law (CEFL)   286, 289
   common denominator problem   290
   convergence   288
   cultural imperialism   287
   debates on   286
   divorce   289
   EC law   288
   political tool, as   289
Haynes, Edmund Sydney Pollock   46
Heard, right to be
   care proceedings   107
   children   143
Herbert, A P   46
High Court *see* Wardship
Homelessness
   Cathy Come Home   94
   reception into care   94
Homeostatis   120
Homosexuals *see* Same sex partnerships
Houghton Committee
   adoption   53

Hubback, Eva
  equal parental rights   48
  troublemakers   48
Human Rights Act 1998
  impact of   265
  parental rights   19

Illegitimacy   8
  adoption   29
  cohabitation   60
  cohabitation reform   74, 81
  extent   60
Illegitimate children
  stigma   20
Immigration
  child abduction   272
Individualism
  community, compared with the
    virtues of the   173
  family law   173
Industrial Revolution
  social reform movements   117
Institutions
  community   177
Interdisciplinary approach
  family justice system   112
  National Family Justice
    Council   143
International family law *see also*
  Internationalisation of family
  law
  continuing developments   283
  definition   261
  devolution   285
  future of   261
  International Family Law
    Committee, establishment
    of   264
  international instruments   266
  International Society of Family
    Law's 8th World
    Conference   265
International law
  reform, influence on   3
Internationalisation of family law
  characterisation of   262
  civil partnerships   271
  future   271
  pre-nuptial agreements   271
  text books   264
Intervention *see* State intervention
Irretrievable breakdown
  sole ground for divorce   46

Jewish people
  divorce   15
Journals
  articles in   151
Judges
  continuity principle   142, 252

Judges—*continued*
  removal of children from
    families   86
Judicial review
  wardship   105
Jurisdictions
  expansion of   285
Juvenile courts
  care proceedings   93
  probation service, role of   125
  removal of children from
    families   94

Kinship care
  care proceedings   255

Law centres
  community   177
Law Commission
  cohabitation   219
  cohabitation reform   83
  international influences   3
  married women's property
    reform   43
Law Quarterly Review
  articles in   151
Law reform *see* Reform
Law reports
  1957, examples of cases from   152
Legal aid *see* Carter Review of
  Legal Aid
  Carter Review   250
  disintegration of system   251
  family justice system   248, 258
  fixed fees   251
  graduated fees   250
  mediation   183
  solicitors doing legal aid work,
    decline in   180
Legislation
  Abse, Leo   52
  troublemakers   52
Legitimacy *see* Illegitimacy
Local authorities *see also* Local
  authority care
  fostering   231
  social services   124
Local authority care *see also* Care
  proceedings
  access to children in   99
  assumption of parental rights   95
  code of practice   100
  post-war policy   122
  Public Law Outline   253
  scandals   19
  voluntary care   255
  wardship   101
Lone parents
  cohabitation   77
  demographics   8
  increase in   193

Index

Lone parents—*continued*
   statistics   8

Magistrates' courts
   divorce courts, closer association with   127
   family jurisdiction, removal of   127
   family proceedings court, encouragement to use   137
   lay magistrates   94
   removal of children from families   94

Maintenance *see also* Child maintenance
   ancillary relief in EC law   217
   elderly   25

Managerialism
   social services   124

Marital property agreements *see* Pre-nuptial agreements

Marriage *see also* Married women's property reform
   age   4
   autonomy   155
   Christianity   13
   civil ceremonies, increase in   4
   civil partnerships   159
   cohabitation
      trial marriages   196
   criticism   64
   decline in number of marriages   3
   decrease in   192
   definition   13
   demographics   3, 4
   discourses on marriage   155
   dynastic needs of rich and powerful, for   188
   economic rights   22
   economic vulnerability of women   195
   Europe, decline in   4
   future   201
   gender equality   190, 192
      opting out   201
   illegitimacy   8
   individuals, for   187
   life-long union, purpose of   188
   multiculturalism   159
   patriarchy   189, 194
   preference for family form of   10
   privileging the status of   189
   purpose of legal institution   187
   remarriage   4
   social control   155
   state, interests of the   187
   statistics   3, 59
   succession   188
   traditional influences, reduction in   158
   trial marriage, cohabitation as   196

Married Women's Association   42

Married women's property reform
   Law Commission   43
   Married Women's Association   42
   Matrimonial Homes Act 1967   43
   Matrimonial Property Bill   44
   Royal Commission on Marriage   42
   Summerskill, Edith   41, 43, 44
   troublemakers   41

Matrimonial Causes Act 1857
   impact of   1

Matrimonial home *see* Family home

Matrimonial Homes Act 1967
   married women's property reform   43

Matrimonial offence
   divorce   118

Matrimonial property *see* Ancillary relief

Matrimonial property reform *see also* Married women's property reform
   divorce reform, priority of   40
   lack of knowledge   45
   petition for   40
   priority   40
   priority, lack of   47

Mayhew, Henry   63

Mediation
   communities   182
   legal aid   183

Mental capacity
   Hague Convention on the International Protection of Adults   279

Mental health
   family justice system   117

Ministry of Justice
   family law   246

Misconduct
   divorce   71

Modern Law Review
   articles in   151

Modernity, family law and   1

Moral danger
   care proceedings   89
   culture   90

Morton Commission   126, 128, 151

Multiculturalism
   marriage   159

Muslim Law Shariah Council (MLSC)
   divorce   178

Muslim women
   communities   178
   divorce   178

National Family Justice Council
   creation of   143
   interdisciplinary approach   143
   regional councils, network of   143

Neglect
  elderly 24
Non-molestation orders
  breach 28
Non-parental carers
  child support 242
  child tax credit 226
  flexible working requests 226
  identity of carers 224
  informal arrangements 223
  parental leave 226
  privacy 225
  social family rights 225
  surveillance 225
  transitions 221
Non-resident parents
  contact 21

Occupation orders
  domestic violence 27
Older people see Elderly
Ouster orders 27

Parental leave
  non-parental carers 226
Parental responsibility
  agreements 235
  birth registration 228
  Brussels II Regulation 282
  bundle of rights 232
  Children Act 1989 228, 232
  code 234
  consent to step-parents having 230
  Council of Europe's
      Recommendation 263
  definition
    lack of clarity in 233
  disposal or transfer 235
  fathers 227
  habitual residence 275
  re-definition 163
  scope of 224
  statement of responsibilities,
      proposal for 234
  step-parents 230
  unmarried fathers 49, 227
Parental rights see also Equal
      parental rights
  assumption by local authority of 95
  care proceedings
      participation in 91
  child abuse 163
  disqualification orders 92
  gender equality 162
  guardians ad litem 92
  Human Rights Act 1998 19
  non-resident parents 21
  place of safety orders 90
  smacking 166
  unmarried fathers 196
  wardship 102

Parents see also Fathers, see also
      Non-parental carers, see also
      Parental responsibility
  assisted reproductive
      technology 223
  children
    defined in terms of
      relationship between
      parents 154
  education 239
Patriarchy
  family law 153
  marriage 189, 194
  state intervention 15
Pensions see also State pensions
  cohabitation reform 81
Perry, Erskine 40
Place of safety orders
  parental rights 90
Polygamy
  Christianity 13
Poor Law
  child abuse 49
  Reports of the Royal
      Commission on the Poor
      Law 49
Population growth 2
Postmodernity
  children 130
  commitment and stability, need
      for 144
  families 129
  family justice system 129
Power
  communities 174
  community care 175
  rights 174
Pre-nuptial agreements
  ancillary relief 199, 209
  cohabitation 213
  enforcement 212
  internationalisation of family
      law 271
  legal advice 211
  marital property agreements 209
Prerogative jurisdiction see
      Wardship
Privacy
  family justice system 113
  non-parental carers 225
Private arrangements about children
  maintenance 237
  recognition 235
Private law proceedings
  tandem model 143
Probation service
  divorce courts 125
  family casework 125
  juvenile courts, role in 125
  post-war civil work 125
  social work 125

Property see Ancillary relief, see Matrimonial property reform
Proportionality
  welfare principle — 20
Psychoanalysis
  attachment theory — 119
  child development — 120
  influence of — 119
Psychology
  family justice systems — 120
Public hearings
  family courts — 18
Public Law Outline
  assessments — 254
  care proceedings — 258
  courts — 253
  implementation — 254
  local authority care — 253
Public/private dichotomy
  family law — 160

Reception into care
  compulsory arrangement, turned into — 95
  homelessness — 94
  removal of children from families — 94
  voluntary arrangements, as — 94
Reform see also Cohabitation reform, see also Divorce reform
  adoption — 53
  ancillary relief — 218
  care proceedings — 248
  Children Act 1989 — 227
  equal parental rights — 48
  priorities — 40
  reformers, zeal of — 11
Relatives
  definition of — 225
Religion
  Christian values — 12
  communities — 178
  culture — 12
  freedom of religion — 14
  gender equality — 201
  Jewish people, divorce of — 15
  Muslims, divorce and — 178
  opting out from courts and ordinary law — 201
Remarriage
  decline in — 4
Removal of children from families
  see also Care proceedings
  consent — 86
  judges — 86
  juvenile courts — 94
  lay magistrates, decisions taken by — 94
  reception into care — 94
  scrutiny — 86

Residence orders
  fostering — 231
Resources
  family justice system — 232
Rights
  communities, role of rights in — 174
  power — 174
Risk assessments
  Cafcass — 134
  child abuse — 135
  domestic violence — 134
Risk aversion
  child protection — 131, 133
  consequences of — 135
  surveillance — 135
Royal Commission on Marriage
  divorce reform — 42
Russell, John Francis Stanley — 46

Same sex partnerships see also Civil partnerships
  statistics — 9
Scandals
  local authorities — 18
Schools
  corporal punishment — 165
Schuster, Claud — 48
Seebohm Committee
  social services, reorganisation of — 124
  social work training — 122
Separation
  children
    effect on — 17
Separation allowances
  cohabitation — 75
Settlement
  encouraging — 139
Sex discrimination see Gender equality
Sexual tie
  families — 154
Silence
  communities — 176
Single parents see Lone parents
Smacking
  debates over — 165
  parental rights — 166
Social change
  cultural change — 115
Social class see Class
Social control — 16
  family law — 155
  marriage — 155
  support — 17
Social policy
  family justice system — 112
  fathers — 21
Social reform movements
  Victorian era — 117

Social sciences	
family justice system	119
Social security benefits	
cohabitation reform	77
Social services *see also* Social workers	
managerialism, culture of	124
morale and recruitment, damage to	125
reorganisation of	124
Seebohm Committee	124
Social stability	
community-based services, development of	116
Social workers	
casework training	122
lack of	124
sociology, training in	122
universities	122
Socio-legal approach to family law	2
Socio-legal consumer studies	
family justice system, influence on	128
Sociology	
families	121
social work training	122
Solicitors	
emotional support	180
legal aid work, decline in	180
recourse to	180
Special guardianship	
adoption	35
Children Act 1989	230
Stalking	
domestic violence	28
State intervention	
authoritarianism	123
child protection	11
class	23
families	239
patriarchy	15
State pensions *see also* Widow's pensions	
cohabitation	61, 75
Step-parents	
parental responsibility	230
Stepfamilies	
cohabitation	8
demographics	8
Succession	
marriage	188
Summerskill, Edith	
married women's property reform	42, 44
troublemakers	41, 42
Support	
adoption	34
social control	17
Surveillance	
non-parental carers	225
risk aversion	135

Taylor, AJP	39
Text books	
family law	187
internationalisation of family law	264
Troublemakers	
Abse, Leo	52
Allen, Marjory	50
divorce, gender equality in	40
Haynes, Edmund Sydney Pollock	47
Hubback, Eva	48
influence of	55
legislation	51
married women's property reform	41
profile of	39
role of	39
Summerskill, Edith	41
Vickers, Joan	49
Weldon, Georgina	40
Trusts	
cohabitation	68
Truth	
communities	176
UN Convention on the Rights of the Child	
Children Act 1989	263
Unemployment benefits	
cohabitation	75
Unified family courts, proposal for	126, 137
Universities	
social work training	122
Unmarried fathers	
equal parental rights	20
legal status	49
parental responsibility	49, 227
parental rights	196
Vickers, Joan	
troublemakers	49
Victorian era	
social reform movements	117
Voluntary organisations	
child protection	117
War	
cohabitation rule	75
Wardship	
case study	86, 106
fostering	103
judicial review	105
local authorities	101
parents and others interested in welfare of child	
unavailability to	102
welfare principle	101
Weldon, Georgina	
troublemakers	39

Welfare principle
  adoption   34
  proportionality   20
  wardship   101
Widow's pension
  cohabitation   76
Wills
  cohabitation   67

Wishes and feelings of child
  child protection   181
  guardians, appointment of   182
  weight   132
Women
  community care   157
  elderly   9
  elderly, care of   157
  Muslims   178